TELLING TO LIVE

Latina Feminist *Testimonios*

The Latina Feminist Group

Luz del Alba Acevedo ⁊ Norma Alarcón

Celia Alvarez ⁊ Ruth Behar ⁊ Rina Benmayor

Norma E. Cantú ⁊ Daisy Cocco De Filippis

Gloria Holguín Cuádraz

Liza Fiol-Matta ⁊ Yvette Gisele Flores-Ortiz

Inés Hernández-Avila ⁊ Aurora Levins Morales

Clara Lomas ⁊ Iris Ofelia López

Mirtha N. Quintanales ⁊ Eliana Rivero

Caridad Souza ⁊ Patricia Zavella

D1008913

Duke University Press *Durham and London 2001*

© 2001 Duke University Press
All rights reserved
Printed in the United States of America on acid-free paper ∞
Typeset in Carter and Cone Galliard by Keystone Typesetting, Inc.
Library of Congress Cataloging-in-Publication Data
appear on the last printed page of this book.
Cover art, *Circle of Ancestors*, by Amalia Mesa-Bains.
5th printing, 2007

Contents

About the Series

LATIN AMERICA OTHERWISE: *Languages, Empires, Nations* is a critical series. It aims to explore the emergence and consequences of concepts used to define "Latin America" while at the same time exploring the broad interplay of political, economic, and cultural practices that have shaped Latin American worlds. Latin America, at the crossroads of competing imperial designs and local responses, has been construed as a geocultural and geopolitical entity since the nineteenth century. This series provides a starting point to redefine Latin America as a configuration of political, linguistic, cultural, and economic intersections that demands a continuous reappraisal of the role of the Americas in history, and of the ongoing process of globalization and the relocation of people and cultures that have characterized Latin America's experience. *Latin America Otherwise: Languages, Empires, Nations* is a forum that confronts established geocultural constructions, that rethinks area studies and disciplinary boundaries, that assesses convictions of the academy and of public policy, and that, correspondingly, demands that the practices through which we produce knowledge and understanding about and from Latin America be subject to rigorous and critical scrutiny.

Telling to Live is a bold articulation of what Cherríe Moraga has called "theory in the flesh." This book continues the tradition of *This Bridge Called My Back*, and offers *testimonios* that attest to the urgency with which U.S. women of color struggle for autonomy and survival in their journey through the formidable class system in U.S. institutions. Their stories tell secrets of how a traditional, phallocentric Latino family structure serves as one more wall that these women must scale. At the same time, the stories show how knowledge of and from their everyday lives is the basis for theorizing and constructing an evolving political praxis to address the material conditions in which they live. *Telling to Live* is, in this regard, a manifesto of the color and gender of epistemology and on the plurality of "reason" and "rationality." The flesh and blood theory many of the narratives deploy marks the Latina feminist subject in process as a new type of intellectual whose knowledge of the political economy of cultural constructions serves to decenter what counts as theory and who can engage in theorizing. These *testimonios* offer the language of Latina intellectuals as an alternative site of knowledge. Written in English and Spanish and often a mixture of both, the texts stress the multiplicity of U.S. Latina experience. The authors of Mexican, Puerto Rican, Dominican, Cuban, and Hispanic origins locate themselves at the borderlands of a reconfigured Latin(a) America.

Acknowledgments

THE NATURE OF A COLLECTIVE and collaborative undertaking such as ours involves much more than compiling and editing individual writings to form a volume. We began through a collective process and have sustained that commitment and collaboration throughout. When we think about the work we have accomplished, we envision not only the product but the human connection among us, the *cariño, respeto,* and commitment to each other. At the same time, as Latinas, feminists, and academics, we know and want to recognize the importance of individual contributions to our work as a group.

Producing *Telling to Live: Latina Feminist Testimonios* has involved an elaborate collaboration and division of labor among eighteen women of diverse Latina backgrounds, across seven states in the Northeast, Midwest, Southwest, and Western regions of the country. We acknowledge and appreciate the painstaking work of the following group members in envisioning and producing this book: Iris López planted the seed of our collaboration. Patricia Zavella and Rina Benmayor served as general editors as we approached publication, including compiling final versions of the manuscript and rewriting the collectively drafted Introduction. Liza Fiol-Matta, Mirtha Quintanales, Celia Alvarez, Caridad Souza, and Gloria Cuádraz participated significantly in revising the Introduction. Daisy Cocco de Filippis, Clara Lomas, and Luz del Alba Acevedo provided *tertulia* inspirations and important theoretical perspectives. Aurora Levins-Morales helped envision the creative structure of the book. Introductions to the four sections were authored by Caridad Souza (Genealogies of Empowerment), Inés Hernández-Avila (Alchemies of Erasure), Yvette Flores-Ortiz (The Body Re/Members), and Eliana Rivero (Passions, Desires, and Celebrations). Rina Benmayor and Norma Cantú undertook Spanish copyediting. Clara Lomas, Caridad Souza, and Rina Benmayor wrote early grant proposals. Norma Alarcón, Caridad Souza, and Patricia Zavella wrote our book prospectus. Yvette Flores-Ortiz and Gloria Cuádraz compiled the first manuscript drafts sent out for consideration. Gloria Cuádraz, Ruth Behar, and Patricia Zavella made initial contacts with publishers. Patricia Zavella served as our chief liaison with Duke University Press.

We acknowledge other Latinas who participated in various ways and at the different stages in our evolution as a group: Antonia Castañeda, Doris Correa Capello, Teresa Córdova, Julia Curry Rodríguez, Elena Flores, Alicia Gaspar de Alba, Deena González, Mary Pardo, Yolanda Prieto, Alvina Quintana, Yvonne Yarbro-Bejarano. We thank the audiences who enthusiastically received our work at conference sessions of Mujeres Activas en Letras y Cambio Social (MALCS), the Puerto Rican Studies Association (PRSA), the National Association of Chicana and Chicano Studies (NACCS), and the Society for Applied Anthropology.

We are *muy agradecidas* to Reynolds Smith, Executive Editor, and Sharon Torian, Senior Editorial Assistant, at Duke University Press. They believed in the significance of this book, went to bat for it, and gave us steady support throughout the publication process. Amalia Mesa-Bains, renowned Chicana artist, MacArthur Fellow, and Director of the Institute for Visual and Public Art at California State University, Monterey Bay, very generously offered the cover image. Her amazing installation piece, titled *Circle of Ancestors,* visually captures and narrates our testimonial process. Aída Hurtado and Norma Klahn gave very helpful constructive criticism of an early draft of the manuscript. *Hermanas, gracias.* Three anonymous reviewers gave us golden words of appreciation even as they recommended important revisions. Thanks to Lynn Walterick, whose copyediting was very insightful and precise, and to Rebecca Johns-Danes, assistant managing editor, for shepherding our manuscript through production. The Document Publishing and Editing Center at University of California, Santa Cruz, provided expert assistance with word processing and formatting the final manuscript. Alexandra Mendoza was a very helpful research assistant. Special thanks to Don Harris of Photographic Services at UCSC, whose magic restored our photographs.

Many institutions supported us over our seven-year collaboration. A substantial seed grant from the Inter-University Program for Latino Research enabled us to come together in 1993 and 1994 to envision and develop this project. We especially thank then–Executive Director Dr. Frank Bonilla and the other IUP Center directors for their support. Dr. María Chacón, then IUP Program Coordinator, and Ana LoBiondo, Program Assistant, believed in and facilitated our project. Dr. Tomás Ybarra-Frausto, Associate Director of Humanities and Arts of the Rockefeller Foundation, gave us a matching grant that took us to Colorado. Our various universities, departments, and centers also provided funding for meetings, administrative support, meeting space, and material resources: The Centro de Estudios Puertorriqueños at Hunter College (CUNY); the Chicano Latino Research Center at the University of California, Santa Cruz; the Institute for Human Communication at California State University Monterey Bay; the Department of Women's Studies and the College of Arts and Sciences at Arizona State University West; the Hispanic Research Center at Arizona State University Tempe; the Southwest Institute for Research on Women at the University of Arizona, Tucson; and the Chicano Studies Program at the University of California, Berkeley.

Since 1995 the Hulbert Center for Southwest Studies at Colorado College has served as the repository of our archives of audiotapes, transcripts, and other materials documenting each stage of our project. The Center continues to act as the fiscal representative for our collective. We are indebted to Jean Lyle, who helped us establish our archives, served as administrative assistant to the project, and planned our first summer institute at Baca.

Clara Lomas deserves special recognition. She made our "summer camps" a reality, inviting us all to the Colorado College Baca Conference Center in the summers of 1995 and 1996. She also secured her university's long-term administrative support for our project. We also honor her mother, María Luisa Lomas, who has been a great source of inspiration to us. She was our first audience at Baca, and in sharing her own experiences with writing she gave us the title of our Introduction, *"Papelitos guardados."*

In keeping with our testimonial process, we would like to name, thank, and dedicate this work to those who have empowered us in special ways:

LUZ DEL ALBA ACEVEDO: To Emilio Pantojas and Maritza Pantojas for their love and support throughout my struggles; to Alejandrina Pizarro (Alejita) for her faith and prayers; and to God, the source of my strength.

NORMA ALARCÓN: I want to deeply thank my *colegas* of Latina Feminist Group for their engaging friendship. *Sí se puede hacer familia* from scratch!

CELIA ALVAREZ: To mami and papi, for believing in me and Titi Alicia, for being my inspiration—thank you for always being there. To *mis queridas hermanas* in the Latina Feminist Group, thank you for sharing from the heart and creating a safe space for me to be. To Cathy, for awakening me to my truth and your unconditional love and support.

RUTH BEHAR: To all the women of our Latina Feminist Group for their encouragement, friendship, and inspiration. Several of my pieces included in this book were written during time we spent together and I am grateful for the dialogues that made the writing possible. From all of you I have learned that without *cariño* there are no ideas, there is no art. *Gracias!*

RINA BENMAYOR: To my mother, Stella, for her unconditional trust and support throughout my life; in memory of my grandmother, Nona, who empowered me with her example, and my father, Leon, who always opted for the different road. To the many *amigas y amigos del alma,* my extended family across the continents; to my *compañeras y comadres de los papelitos* for making *cariño, confianza,* and *solidaridad* prevail throughout; and to my students, who as they tell their stories hold the promise of alliances to come.

NORMA E. CANTÚ: To *las mujeres* in my life — my mother, grandmothers, *tías, hermanas, sobrinas, amigas,* students, *colegas.* A special thank you to Elvia Niebla and to my *colegas* in the Latina Feminist Group who offered a space in their lives and hearts for my *papelitos.*

DAISY COCCO DE FILIPPIS: *A las Gabrielas en mi vida, mi abuela y mi madre, por la fuerza y bondad que me legaron.* For Nunzio, Nicky and David, Nunzi and Christie, Allison and Jimmy, my constant and generous family . . . *con agradecimiento.*

GLORIA HOLGUÍN CUÁDRAZ: To my mother, Nellie, who has infected my life with her spirit of generosity. If you only knew how much your *luz* guides every moment of my life, especially the teaching ones! To my father, Miguel, whose courage to face the unknown allowed me to pursue this journey. Your example has carried me. My six sisters and one brother have been and remain great sources of love and strength. I thank you all for enriching our lives. To all the *mujeres* and *hombres* whose lives are committed to greater well-being, I stand in awe. To Judith, for your love, friendship, and charm. *Mil gracias.*

LIZA FIOL-MATTA: To my mother, Emma Matta Méndez, and my father, Juan Fiol Bigas, for the example of their lives. To my sisters — Liana, Lynn, Lía, and Licia — and my brothers — Juan, Antonio, and Carlos — for their love and constant support. To Mildred Borrás for her longtime friendship. And, above all, to Louise Murray, *mi adorada compañera,* for challenging me with her insight and for the laughter that fills our home.

YVETTE GISELE FLORES-ORTIZ: *A mi madre, por inspirar y apoyar las y los escritores de la familia; a mis abuelas por luchar siempre contra las injusticias;* to my daughter, Xóchitl, and my son, Alejandro, my students, *comadres,* and friends for their unending support and faith in me, especially Maria Cristina Carrillo, Vilma Wilcoxen and Tiana Arruda. To the men who have inspired and fueled my warrior spirit, my father Claudio Flores and my husband, Arturo Ortiz. Above all, to my psychotherapy clients who have been my teachers, guides, and sources of inspiration, and to two very special women in my life, Dr. Michelle Ritterman and Noreen DiMaggio, RN. *Por ustedes, continúo la lucha.*

INÉS HERNÁNDEZ AVILA: To all the *mujeres y hombres constantes en mi vida,* the ones I see often, and the ones I may go long periods without seeing, and yet when we meet again, it is as if it was yesterday that we saw each other — *por ese espíritu de amor, aprecio, y respeto profundo con que nos tratamos.* To my *esposo,* Juanishi Avila, and my brother, George Longfish, for their wise knowledge of Spirit. *Gracias.*

AURORA LEVINS-MORALES: To my mother, Rosario Morales. We struggled into voice together, each empowering the other and continue to read each other's first drafts. To my father, Richard Levins, who told me stories out of history. To both of them for their respect, their political passions, and for teaching me to think of myself as a radical intellectual. To my brothers, Ricardo and Alejandro, for unending comradeship, concrete help and silliness. To my daughter, Alicia Raquel, for her enthusiastic and shining presence in my life. *Gracias a las mujeres* for love, brilliance, honesty, and laughter and for becoming a "place" I come home to.

CLARA LOMAS: I am indebted to the Latina Feminist Group for seeing this project through to the end, for their undying support, and the million laughs. My deep appreciation to my parents for the family stories, to my children, Clara Cecilia and Luis Alberto Rodriguez, for the inspiration, and to Alma Maldonado Parker, in loving memory.

IRIS LÓPEZ: To an awesome group of women, whose love and vision has made this book possible. To my *compañero,* David Forbes, whose love is a constant source of strength, joy, and inspiration. To my mother and father, my sisters, Jeanette, Francesca, and Madelene, and my brother, Elliot, I love you very much. A special thanks to my sister Jeanette, who has accompanied and supported me especially through my early career. To my nieces and nephews, I wrote this for you. To my friends Sean Krebs, a very special person in my life; Ana María Morales, Gloria Gómez, and Lorraine Lein — thank you for your love and support. To my students and mentors, Leith Mullings, Elliot Skinner, Jim Blake, and Joyce Brawn.

MIRTHA QUINTANALES: My deepest gratitude for the love and wisdom I have received from my parents and my extended family; from all my teachers and friends — in all the forms in which they have appeared along my path; from the awakened inner divinity that constantly showers me with blessings. Because of them, my life is sweet and full of grace.

ELIANA RIVERO: To my mother, María Antonia Rivero, from whom I learned to appreciate beauty and the sound of singing voices, for all the love she gave me, now reflected in my *papelitos;* to Claudia Aburto Guzmán, for reading my texts, offering good ideas and encouragement; to Melissa A. Fitch, for her detailed reading, continued support, and wonderful suggestions; and to María Teresa Marrero, who gave me wise performance pointers.

CARIDAD SOUZA: To this wonderful group of Latina Feminists who simply overwhelm me in ways I cannot yet speak. A special shout out to the three most important women in my life who continually inspire me with their courage to live, making my life brighter with their presence: my sister, Mayda Noemi Torres; her daughter, Yvette Ramos; and her daughter, Nyshai Noemi Thompson. To Elsa Pérez, a lifelong friend whose love sustains me. To Ralph R. Watkins, whose gentle love and quiet, unconditional support have taught me something about humanness, and who keeps me laughing. And to those special friends who have taught me most about loving perception, especially Marian Barragán, Sarah J. Cervenak, Karina Céspedes, Andrea Straub, and Monica Tate Meléndez.

PATRICIA ZAVELLA: To my grandmother, Eufracia Archuleta, who taught me to stand up for myself and speak my mind. To Jim Jatczynski, for his love, emotional support, and technical assistance in producing the final manuscript. To Laura and Anthony, for teaching me new things about life, and to *las mujeres de este grupo,* for your love and incredible wisdom.

Telling to Live

Latina Feminist *Testimonios*

Introduction. *Papelitos Guardados:*
Theorizing *Latinidades* Through *Testimonio*

papel. *nm.* 1. paper; 2. piece or sheet of paper; 3. document(s),
identification paper(s); 4. paper money; 5. receipt; 6. bag; 7. part, role.

-ito. *suf. for n or adj.* 1. diminutive; 2.
emotive; 3. superlative.

guardado. *adj.* 1. guarded, hidden away; 2. watched over, taken care
of, kept safe or secret, protected, including by a deity or saint;
3. maintained, preserved; 4. retained, conserved, stored.
Harper Collins Spanish-English Dictionary

OUR VISION FOR THIS BOOK has been to illustrate how Latina feminists come together to engage our differences, face-to-face, and work to find common ground. Our Latina Feminist Group began to meet in 1993 to discuss our concerns as Latina feminists in higher education and to consider possibilities for doing collaborative work. We came from the Southwest, East, and Midwest, Latinas of multiple national and ethnic origins. As we introduced ourselves to each other, described the work we do and why we are compelled to do it, we spontaneously began to weave *testimonios,* stories of our lives, to reveal our own complex identities as Latinas. This book of *papelitos* grew out of these stories, told over the course of seven years.

Papelitos guardados has hybrid meanings for us: protected documents, guarded roles, stored papers, conserved roles, safe papers, secret roles, hidden papers, safe roles, preserved documents, protected roles. The phrase was offered by María Luisa Lomas, the mother of Clara Lomas. During one of our sessions, as we read our writings to each other, she revealed that she, too, had her *papelitos guardados,* writings tucked away, hidden from inquiring eyes. As she shared how she sought expression in writing, we realized that she had captured the essence of our project. *Papelitos guardados* evokes the process by which we contemplate thoughts and feelings, often in isolation and through difficult times. We keep them in our memory, write them down, and store them in safe places waiting for the appropriate moment when we can return to them for review and analysis, or speak out and share them with others. Sharing can begin a process of empowerment. Stepping out of the roles expected of Latina women in the academy and in our communities, we bring to life our *papeles* and render our *testimonios* through autobiographical narratives, short stories, poems, and dialogues.

Initially, we came together in a smaller group, intending to undertake collaborative, comparative feminist research on Latina issues.[1] Very quickly, we found ourselves limited by traditional academic approaches, which, in the move toward comparison, tend to simplify, aggregate, and reduce experience to variables. We wanted to engage in *testimonio* to reveal the complexity of Latina identities in the United States. As Caridad Souza made clear, "We have to figure out how to talk across *latinidades* rather than through disciplinary studies, you know what I'm saying?"

Many of us, in one way or another, are professional *testimoniadoras* (producers of *testimonios*), whether as oral historians, literary scholars, ethnographers, creative writers, or psychologists.[2] From our different personal, political, ethnic, and academic trajectories, we arrived at the importance of *testimonio* as a crucial means of bearing witness and inscribing into history those lived realities that would otherwise succumb to the alchemy of erasure. However, we discovered that to move forward and develop theory as a group, we first needed to explore the complexities of *latinidad* — Latina/o identity — and compare how each of us had made the journey to become credentialed, creative thinkers, teachers, and writers. We were all proficient oral historians, ethnographers, and *testimoniadoras,* but we had never explored our diversity. We all professed in the classroom about the connection between life experience and new knowledge construction, but we had never made our own life trajectories a source of inquiry. In addition, while we were all accustomed to engaging other Latinas and/or Latin American women in giving testimony, many of us had not yet participated in public renderings of our own life stories. We had not yet experienced being on both sides of the process, sharing and generating our own *testimonios* with each other as Latina scholars. None of us was prepared for the intensity, despair, poetry, and clarifying power of our own *testimonios.* Meeting as a group over the course of seven years, we have become convinced that the emotional force and intellectual depth of *testimonio* is a springboard for theorizing about *latinidades* in the academy, in our communities, and in our lives.

Latina Feminisms: Creating Our Own Spaces

Creating spaces for Latina feminisms — *latinidades feministas* — means confronting established and contested terms, identities, frameworks, and coalitions that have emerged in particular historical contexts.[3] In charting our own course through these contested terrains as Latina feminists, we have attempted to expand traditional notions of ethnicity and nationalism, question Eurocentric feminist frameworks, and situate ourselves in relation to the activism and writings by women of color. At the same time, as Latina feminists we have felt the need to create our own social and discursive spaces.

Latina feminists come from a long line of workers, activists, theorists, and writers within their respective Latino communities. They have participated in various movements that denounce social injustice, including civil rights, anti-war, labor, human rights, progressive Cuban American politics, Puerto Rican Independence, Chicano political autonomy, Native American sovereignty, Central American solidarity. They have been central to the formation of Chicano, Puerto Rican or Ethnic Studies. They have taken part not only in the political but also in the literary and artistic activity around these movements — *teatro* and *floricanto* (street theater, poetry and music festivals) — which provide a language to celebrate cultural identity.

Along with participation in social movements, Latinas have also engaged in developing methods of political praxis. Inspired by Paolo Freire's practice of *concientización,* where communities construct self-reflective political consciousness, Latinas have contributed to empowerment efforts through literacy and giving voice, documenting silenced histories.[4] *Testimonio* has been critical in movements for liberation in Latin America, offering an artistic form and methodology to create politicized understandings of identity and community. Similarly, many Latinas participated in the important political praxis of feminist consciousness-raising. The "second wave" feminist movement honored women's stories and showed how personal experience contains larger political meaning. Other feminists have developed self-reflexive research methods and social practices, creating oral histories and feminist ethnographies that capture the everyday lives and stories of women.[5] Drawing from these various experiences, *testimonio* can be a powerful method for feminist research praxis.

Latina feminists, however, have contested the exclusion of questions of gender and sexuality in ethnic studies curricula or political agendas. Cultural nationalism has defined some of these programs or projects, insisting on idealized notions of ethnicity, *familia,* and community. Cultural nationalists often repress women's voices by reaffirming heterosexist utopic visions of colonized peoples. At their most extreme, they discredit Latina feminists as separatist and divisive, and even bait them as "traitors to the race."[6]

In the same vein, Latinas have felt frustrated with marginalizations of difference and token nods in the direction of diversity in feminist political organizations or women's studies programs. The feminist movement often ignores the tremendous internal differences among women of color, including Latinas. The movement also fails to recognize distinctive standpoints of women of color and women of mixed race. In the effort to name and theorize these complexities, Latinas are increasingly finding themselves working with women within their respective national-ethnic communities, or with other Latinas who embrace feminist ideals, even when there is a reluctance to embrace the term "feminism."[7]

Latina activist traditions resonate with those of black and other feminists of color, and form the basis for bridging different histories and origins, building cross-cultural coalitions and personal relationships. From this crucial political work, women of color theory recognizes the complex intersections of ethnicity, nationality, race, class, gender, sexuality, age, and other markers of diverse identities and commitments. Latina feminists propose that difference is not a mask that can be put on or taken off; it forms the basis of who they are in the world, in their scholarship, and in their political practice.[8] It is crucial, at this stage, to move beyond essentialism, which assumes a common Latina experience. Latinas must be placed in their varied histories, illustrating their positions within intersecting systems of power.[9]

Black, Asian American, Native American, and other feminists of color have shown how important it is to write about one's own experiences. Beginning in the 1970s, Toni Morrison, Audre Lorde, Alice Walker, Maxine Hong Kingston, Leslie Marmon Silko, and many others inspired us and legitimized subject matters and modes of writing that were previously ignored or deemed unacceptable. They brought to print oral traditions, dialects, and characters that conveyed experiences which, with rare exceptions, had not been documented before. The work of women of color inspired many academics of color to expand the "ethnic" and feminist canons. Anthologies such as *Life Notes, Double Stitch, Making Waves,* and *All-American Women* brought the voices of women of color narrating their daily experiences into our purview.[10] These texts and many more, along with the alternative publishing houses that produced them — Kitchen Table, Aunt Lute, Third Woman, Firebrand, South End — modeled possibilities of combining reading, writing, and social activism. They illustrated the possibilities of collaborative visions, creation, and production that bridged community and academy. The paths established by women of color also helped construct coalitions to negotiate differences among themselves as they moved toward significant moments of solidarity.

Chicana feminists centered in the Southwest also created theories and spaces of their own, exploring the complexities of identity and culture. As the largest group among Latinas, and able to gain access to institutions of higher learning, Chicanas served as a focal point for Latina feminisms. Moving beyond the black-white framework of racial discourse, Chicanas shed light on other facets of racialization, on those that form a continuum of color, phenotype, and privilege. Theorizing the intersection of racism, sexism, and heterosexism, Chicana writings contributed a new vocabulary of *mestizaje,* hybridity, oppositional consciousness, and the critical metaphor of "borderlands." These concepts helped mark a consciousness of resistance to the repression of language, culture, and race, and a recognition of the in-between spaces formed by those with complex identities. Chicana feminist theorists, both heterosexual and lesbian, also illuminated women-centered family life, a complicated refuge and site of male authority and privilege where women negotiate autonomy and support. Contesting their marginalization, Chicana lesbian writers took greater risks and opened up the exploration and celebration of women-centered sexuality, spirituality, and passion, attempting, as Cherríe Moraga put it, to "feed women in all of their hungers." In these ways, Chicanas, in collaboration with other Latinas, contributed to rethinking feminism, women's studies, Latino studies, and cultural studies in general.[11]

In forging political connections with feminists of color, Puerto Rican, Cuban, and other Latina writers facilitated a process of theorizing through social activism and autobiographical writing. *This Bridge Called My Back* broke the cultural nationalist paradigm by centering Latinas among women of color and by bringing lesbian identity to the fore in Latina writing. The spate of pan-Latina anthologies that followed *This Bridge*, namely, *Cuentos; Bearing Witness/Sobreviviendo; In Other Words; Woman of Her Word; Nosotras: Latina Literature Today; Latina; Compañera: Latina Lesbians; Infinite Divisions;* the special issue of *Third Woman* on The Sexuality of Latinas; and *Making Face, Making Soul: Haciendo Caras,* has charted new directions for Latina feminist scholarship and theory. More recently, the organization of activist-scholars *Mujeres Activas en Letras y Cambio Social* (MALCS) has moved from a Chicana space to one that welcomes lesbians, centroamericanas, indigenous women, and other Latinas, including those of mixed race and from Latin America. Along with *This Bridge,* these works are precursors to our book.[12]

It hasn't always been easy to negotiate a space where Latinas can collaborate to build scholarship and community. The process of creating oppositional discourses, social spaces, anthologies, or collaborative projects does not usually emerge from long-term group interaction among contributors. In the preface to the second edition of *This Bridge Called My Back,* for example, Cherríe Moraga noted, "The idea of Third World feminism has proved to be much easier between the covers of a book than between real live women."[13] We acknowledge that we must walk the fine line of contestation and complicity, ever mindful that new hierarchies may develop even within Latina feminist projects, and we must constantly negotiate difference among ourselves.

Where and How We Enter

Our use of "Latina" recognizes these tensions, even as it builds on pan-Latina/o solidarity, however fragile. We seek those spaces within and across borders where women share parallel emotional and psychic terrain along with intersecting political agendas as a means of theorizing about our experiences. Familiar with the difficulties of solidarity with other women, we self-consciously use "Latinas" as a coalitional term. We are not homogenizing and leveling our differences into an idealized, unified national/ethnic heritage, into what Eliana Rivero calls "the neutral soup of *Latinismo.*"[14] All of us emerge from various mixed inheritances, whether through ethnicity, race, sexuality, regional culture, religious-spiritual formation, class, generation, political orientation, or linguistic heritage and practice. Included in our social identities are the various places we have inhabited and traversed, and the spaces in which we have worked. Our inherited historical and political formations — maps of our crisscrossing trajectories across borders — affected our professional, intellectual, and personal development. Our testimonials continually disrupt the essentialized, homogenized understanding of Latina as we present our respective genealogical and historical inheritances. As a coalitional term, "Latina" is neither exhaustive of the many ways that Latina women may self-identify, nor reflective of all the distinctive national-ethnic groups from "Latina América" and beyond who live in the United States. Our use of the term "Latina" builds on its emergence in coalitional politics in the United States and signifies our connections through praxis to the rest of the Americas and other multiple geographies of origin.

We come to theorizing *latinidades* at the turn of the century from histories of racial-ethnic and feminist struggles. At the risk of actually losing jobs in "studies programs," putting careers in danger, or losing important personal or political relationships, we realize that some of those struggles have not necessarily sustained us. As Celia Alvarez noted, "After all this time, why are our stories still invisible in the academy? What is happening to those spaces we fought so hard to create and where does this leave us? What will motivate us to engage and reposition ourselves?" Consequently, to theorize and write about our experiences, we must create our own social spaces.

Situating ourselves in relation to our foresisters and brothers, we acknowledge their enormous contributions, including the published works, histories of struggle yet to be fully documented, and theorizing which continues. However, we also offer the prospect of a new relational process. Through our collaboration, we have been able to negotiate the geographical, political, and emotional challenges of coalitional work. We have created a collaboration that contributes to new ways of theorizing. *Telling to Live: Latina Feminist Testimonios* differs from its precursors in that it is the result of a conscious relational politics and of collaborative *testimonio,* face-to-face theorizing and production.

Who We Are

Our backgrounds are as diverse as the continent. We reflect Latina experiences in the United States: some of us are of Native American heritage while others are marked by histories of European colonization and U.S. imperialism, by multiple migrations and diasporas, economic, religious, or political. For us, *latinidad* acknowledges national origins, and at the same time explores the nuances of difference. Our identities include our heritages, cultures, lived experiences, and political commitments.

We are the daughters of field, domestic, factory, and service workers, secretaries, military officers, technicians, artists, and professionals. Our participation in various social movements fundamentally contributed to our political development. Regarding our religious influences, our group includes "Catholic girls," Protestants, Mormons, Jews, women who grew up in the tradition of *santería,* indigenous spiritualists, and women now reclaiming spirituality that transcends institutional religions. We embody the expression of diverse sexual identities — heterosexual, bisexual, lesbian, celibate, single, and those who move between sexual categories. We come from and have created a variety of "families," including single-parent, nuclear, extended biological, and chosen families that may or may not include children. While some of us do not have birth-children, we are all involved in a variety of nurturing or care-giving relationships with our own children, stepchildren, parents, nieces, nephews, friends, students, colleagues, even pets. Our bodies display a range of physical beauty and voluptuousness. We might be described within our cultures by our skin color as *"las cafecitas, indias, negritas, trigueñas, güeras y blanquitas"* (brown, Indian, black, olive, light or white) — problematic terms of endearment that evoke racist connotations.[15]

We are intergenerational, ranging in age from early thirties to late fifties. Although not the case when our group began, when some of us were graduate students, we now all hold doctorates from U.S. universities. Our academic trajectories include community colleges, liberal arts institutions, public and private research universities, alternative colleges, and "the ivies." We are disciplinary and transdisciplinary — crossing through fields of American Studies, Anthropology, Chicana/o Studies, Community Studies, Creative Writing, Cultural Studies, English, Latin American and Latino Studies, Puerto Rican Studies, Ethnic Studies, Linguistics, Oral History, Political Science, Psychology, Romance Languages and Literatures, Sociology, and Women's Studies. All of us are professors although some of us do not teach full time. We have worked in traditional academic departments as well as interdisciplinary research centers, programs, and community sites. We are chairs of departments, deans, directors of research centers, pioneers of feminist research in women of color sites, and accomplished writers and scholars.

We have professional privilege, relatively speaking, even though some of us are not tenured, some of us write and do research without institutional support, and some do not have full-time jobs. Our professional privilege comes from our locations in institutions of higher education, with good salaries and benefits, the luxury of pursuing our passions through our work, and, for some of us, tenure and sabbaticals. However, because of our professional choices — to research, think, and write about Latinas in ways that take the subject seriously — we become marginalized by institutional cultures that reproduce hegemonic relations of power. With so few Latinas in higher education and with intensifying faculty workloads, we are caught between multiple constituencies, needs, and institutional demands. So, despite our relative privilege compared to most Latinas, we are often overworked, exhausted, emotionally burnt out, and not appropriately validated for our contributions. In reaction to institutional violence or in response to our own talents and callings, many of us have created cultural, political, and professional worlds outside academia. Among us are published poets and creative writers, grassroots organizers, cultural workers, musicians, storytellers, healers, and visual artists. Whatever the medium, we yearn for creativity that provides balance in our lives and sustains our sense of wholeness.

The languages we speak come from our colonial and diasporic conditions. Some of us are Spanish dominant, others bilingual; some easily code-switch between English and Spanish; others struggle to learn Spanish or indigenous languages. A few of us negotiate multicultural situations where Black English and regional Spanish, or where different national and class dialects of Spanish, contribute to a complicated polyglot mixture. In writing this book, we made a conscious decision not to privilege standard English or Castillian Spanish, so as to honor our localized uses of Spanish, bilingual code-switching, and variety of dialects. As such, the languages of this text express the lived experiences of Latinas.

Theorizing Through Process

Our purpose in describing our process of coming together and collaborating over seven years is to illustrate how we came to theorize feminist *latinidades* through *testimonio.* While our writings may stand on their own, our collaborative process, which used the method of *testimonio,* ultimately was framed by common political views about how to create knowledge and theory through our experiences. In this way, product and process became inseparable.

By the 1990s Latina feminist thinkers and writers had been reading one another; however, geographical divides kept us enclaved. With Chicanas and Centroamericanas in the West and Southwest, and Puertorriqueñas, Dominicanas, and Cubanas in the North and Southeast, we each had our own feminist groups, but we did not necessarily know each other.[16] Returning to New York after teaching in California, Iris López proposed: "It would be a great idea to get funding to bring Latinas from the East and West coasts together, and maybe do collaborative work." As distinct communities of Latina academics, writers, and cultural workers, we focused our theoretical development and production on the specificities of women in each ethnic group, which entailed a parallel process of constructing a women-centered space in *opposition* to masculinist or white feminist frameworks. Nevertheless, we all were inspired by reading Chicana feminist writings, which were more visible and accessible and spoke to us all, even if our particular histories and issues differed. In addition, our professional lives in academia led many of us to move out of regions where our respective cultural groups reside. We began to crisscross the continent from East to West, West to East, South to North, across oceans and national boundaries to and from islands and countries south of the Río Grande, studying, working, and living in other Latina/o contexts. Our migrations mirrored larger global movements of cultures, capital, and peoples, transnationally and within the borders of the U.S. nation-state. Our geographic migrations enabled us to create a network. They also gave us insights and lived experiences on which to reconceptualize *latinidad,* as we could relate to the struggles of women in other Latino contexts. To write and theorize about a range of Latina experiences, however, required being in *sustained dialogue* with one another. Hence, we were motivated to convene physically in one place and begin this process.

Our process evolved from a small study group to several national and many regional meetings. At one of the meetings, Liza Fiol-Matta and others pressed for a new type of encounter: "What we need is a place so we can hang out, really get to know one another and see what happens." From that proposal came the two "summer camps," as we fondly came to call our institutes in the mountains of Colorado. Gradually and carefully, the composition of our group changed from a predominance of Chicanas and Puertorriqueñas to the broader group evidenced in this book (Chicanas, Puertorriqueñas, Dominicanas, Cubanas, Centroamericanas, Sefarditas, Native American, and mixed-heritage women). With careful nurturing and reflection, our process evolved into *un engranaje de deseo, respeto, confianza, y colaboración* — a meshing of desire, respect, trust, and collaboration. Over the course of these seven years, we have come to cherish the way we interact and work with one another, the atmosphere of mutual support and consultation we have built, and the liberating space of dialogue, debate, and disclosure that we have achieved. This project has been like no other intellectual endeavor we have experienced. The rewards have far exceeded the difficulties.

At the beginning, we were challenged by traditional research models, funding priorities, and different expectations regarding the scope and focus of a pan-Latina project. The expectations of our funding and conventional academic practice threatened to lock us into traditional models of comparative research that would predetermine the outcome of our labor. We wrote a proposal to the Inter-University Program for Latino Research to bring together Latinas of different origins, geographic areas, and disciplines to share work around established topics and analytical categories. We assumed that a comparative agenda would emerge through individual research contributions, but we found ourselves moving away from these more traditional frameworks.

Initially, we mistakenly assumed that we knew each other simply because we were Latina academics and writers. We had to work through different assumptions and expectations about the purpose of the group, its composition and politics, the direction it should take, and the power of representation—who would speak for the group and how they would frame what we were doing. We struggled against privileging certain aspects of Latina identity so as not to limit full participation by everyone. We learned to be more mindful of the complexities of negotiating collaboration among Latinas, and realized that a pan-Latina project entailed creating a new paradigm. Luz del Alba Acevedo explained the intent to move away from oppositional discourse to a more relational consciousness and practice *among* Latinas: "How we structure the ways we come together and tell our stories affects *how* we tell our stories. We can become more compassionate women, better feminists. And eventually new generations of Latinas will displace us, but instead of doing it in a fighting mode, they will build on our respect for one another." Implicitly this was a key theoretical and political move away from a project that works within a "hierarchy of oppressions" to one in which all racial-ethnic groups and identity markers—sexuality, race, gender, age, ethnicity, national origins, class, etc.— carry equal force.[17]

In this new pan-Latina framework, we saw all sources of oppression as crucial in structuring the subordinate social location of Latinas. In the middle of a difficult discussion about this viewpoint, Luz del Alba further explained the motivation for pan-Latina collaboration: "We come to this meeting out of a deep sense of love. We want to learn from one another." We realized that it was imperative to step back and learn more about our internal diversity and trajectories as historical groups and as women. Further, we wanted to situate ourselves in relation to our work, our communities, and our academic lives— while not privileging certain identity markers in a profoundly political project. Our goal became to move toward a different comparative research model that would seek mutually validating perspectives among Latinas, mindful of the complexities of our individual experiences.

In expanding participation to achieve greater Latina diversity, we sought to integrate women who represented other national-ethnic groups and whose work focused on Latinas in the United States. Rina Benmayor raised the difficulty of negotiating "belonging," by saying, "I hope we can think of *latinidades* not just in terms of nationality or ethnicity, but also in terms of lived cultural experience and political commitments." The national-ethnic identity categories did not encompass the actual diversity of Latinas, as they ignored difference in class backgrounds, religious traditions, sexual preferences, races, ages, cultural experiences, regional variations, and women of mixed or Native American heritage. Implicitly, we were challenging ideas about Latina identities based on nationality-ethnicity, as our group configuration attempted to reflect the complexity and the multiple material realities represented in our communities.

It was also necessary to create a space where disclosure about ourselves was comfortable, given our new-found awareness that this project would not be easy. Early in the process, Pat Zavella bravely voiced her apprehensions: "It would be so much easier if we could just write out our life stories. That would be familiar to me. Telling them publicly is very difficult, frightening, 'cause I don't know you all very well. Can we talk about this?" Other women voiced their fears of public story telling, which, in hindsight, given the stories we had kept private, was understandable. By discussing our feelings of vulnerability and mistrust openly, we began to build a space where we learned to listen, evaluate, and question each other in nonjudgmental ways. We learned how to construct a safer space that was not assumed a priori to be safe based simply on gender and national/ethnic affiliations. *Testimonio* was critical for breaking down essentialist categories, since it was through telling life stories and reflecting upon them that we gained nuanced understandings of differences and connections among us. These revelations established respect and deeper understanding for each of us as individuals and as Latinas. Through *testimonio* we learned to translate ourselves for each other.

We also decided that decisions would be made collectively, through consensus. Through the give-and-take needed for collective work, we repeatedly analyzed our group dynamics, noting misperceptions and incorporating debates about our differences into our work agenda constructively. Over time it became easier to say, "That doesn't include me," "My experience was different," or "I disagree, and here's why," knowing that disagreement would not generate great tension and that the group would think through expressions of difference or disagreement and incorporate various viewpoints. When the framework does not rest on a hierarchy of oppression, then every form of systemic violence and human agency must be taken into consideration. In sum, we learned to negotiate political and theoretical disagreements among ourselves by adhering to the premises of collective decision making, making a conscious commitment to nonjudgmental listening, building trust, and constructing an alternative, inclusive framework.

What solidified the group and the project, despite tentative beginnings, were the compelling stories about our personal and professional lives; some deep, longstanding friendships and collegial collaborations as well as a new web of developing friendships; our commitment to *testimonio;* and the common cause of trying to define and work within a relational theoretical framework. For when we narrated our life stories within this framework, we found an emerging pattern of systemic violence and cultural ideologies that continually repositioned us at the margins, despite relative privilege; we saw incredible journeys of achievement despite expectations of failure. Because our stories so powerfully illustrated how these politicized experiences came to shape our lives' work and illustrated connections among Latinas, we abandoned the idea of comparing our academic research on Latinas and decided to become subjects of our own reflection. *Testimonio* would be the primary methodology used in whatever project we pursued. *Testimonio* would be a means to bring together our creative and research backgrounds, a more organic way of collecting and generating knowledge, and a method that would move us toward an understanding of *latinidades.* And *testimonio* was a process that felt comfortable, the familiar story telling that harkened back to our mothers' and other relatives' kitchens.

In the various national and regional meetings that followed, *testimoniando* — telling our stories — generated renewed energy and deeper trust. Initially, we addressed the following key questions: How do we bear witness to our own becoming? How do we define who we are? How have we made *testimonio* the core of our work? What are some important turning points of consciousness? What is our relationship to political identities and intellectual work? What is our relationship to building new paradigms or models? What are we transgressing? .

Another area of implicit theorizing brought in dimensions of spirituality, creativity, and conscious caring for the body. We learned to acknowledge and tell how our bodies are maps of oppression, of institutional violence and stress, of exclusion, objectification, and abuse. Since our bodies hold the stress and tensions of our daily lives, we also shared stories of body breakdowns, of how we take care of ourselves, or how we do not. We discussed how our bodies express creative and carnal experiences, and compared our many styles of dancing, our appreciation of good food, relaxation, and laughter.

In 1995 we held our first Latina Feminist Summer Institute at the Baca Conference Center of The Colorado College in southern Colorado. Baca is literally on the Central Divide, in the middle of the country. Meeting at Baca was fortuitous, a real turning point for us as a group. Surrounded by the Sangre de Cristo Mountains and intersected by rivers, Baca is located in the highest valley in North America. Part of the magic of Baca is that historically it is a site of spiritual meaning, a sacred space for Native Americans where there have never been wars between indigenous peoples. The Sangre de Cristo Mountains are the mythical place of emergence for the Navajo, who were displaced by the violent incursions of Spanish and Anglo settlers. Today Baca is home to a diverse group of spiritual traditions, including a Christian monastery, a Buddhist temple, a Zen meditation center, and a Hindu ashram.[18] For us, Baca became a site that inspired narration.

Reconstructing *Testimonio*

Testimonio is often seen as a form of expression that comes out of intense repression or struggle, where the person bearing witness tells the story to someone else, who then transcribes, edits, translates, and publishes the text elsewhere. Thus, scholars often see *testimonios* as dependent products, an effort by the disenfranchised to assert themselves as political subjects through others, often outsiders, and in the process to emphasize particular aspects of their collective identity.[19] *Testimonios* with women in Latin America have focused much of the critical attention to the genre in the last two decades.[20] These texts are seen as disclosures not of personal lives but rather of the political violence inflicted on whole communities. Here, the *testimoniantes* (subjects of the texts) admit that they withhold secrets about the culture or details of their personal lives that, for political reasons, are not revealed in the stories narrated.

At Baca we created our own *testimonio* process, in which the personal and private became profoundly political. "Summer camp" gave us the time and space, free from the pulls of our busy public and private lives, to engage more deeply in knowing one another's experiences. In response to previous discussions about fear of disclosure, we carefully framed the first round of *testimonios*. We broke into small groups, each with diverse ethnic, national, or geographic membership, and addressed the following questions: Why did we pursue higher education? What did we think we were doing? What was the enticement? What did we get out of it?

These *testimonios* were critical because we began to see common themes and parallel experiences despite differences of national, ethnic, or regional background. The small groups traced what Aurora Levins-Morales called "genealogies of empowerment": "How did our ancestors, parents and especially the women in our lives validate our right to think and trust ourselves?" We named the first section of our book after these *testimonios*. We discovered that our own passions for reading and learning, for stories, and for knowing more about our heritages and communities had led us to become researchers and writers. Yet despite our success in the academy and in our creative endeavors, we all could point to moments and events that were deeply painful.

In the next round — in a large-group setting — we began to explore these difficult experiences. This time the questions were more probing: Where did the points of "breakdown" happen? How did collectivity and isolation figure in our lives? What was the process of resistance and recovery? During these sessions many of us told stories we had never shared with anyone. They were about institutional as well as personal abuses that we, the achievers — *las perfectas, las nenas buenas* — had endured through our lives. Breaking the silence, we uncovered the shame that came from abuse. Some of these *testimonios* eventually became the anonymous pieces in this book — *Latinas anónimas* — since they were about experiences that can and do happen to any Latina. Clearly, we needed to share the experiences that we had kept locked away and begin the healing process through spirited reconfiguration. For racialized ethnic women of subjugated peoples, achievement is always a double-edged sword. In becoming women of accomplishment, we have had to construct and perform academic personas that require "professionalism," "objectivity," and "respectability" in ways that often negate our humanity. Acknowledging pain helped to unveil the workings of power in institutional cultures, its human costs, and the ways individuals can and do overcome the ravages of power dynamics and abuses. Thus, honoring Clara Lomas's phrase "the alchemy of erasure," we named a section of our collective stories "Alchemies of Erasure." The section "The Body Re/members" came into being through stories about how the alchemies had disfigured our bodies; and yet, somehow we had found moments or processes of resistance, memory, and recovery. Naming pain and using collective support to begin the process of empowerment became integral to our survival as individuals and as a group. In Gloria Cuádraz's words, "I've been waiting for ten years to feel comfortable enough to say this publicly. I may never say it again, so I am grateful that we have created this opportunity." Her sentiment was echoed by Clara Lomas, "I shared something that I never shared with anyone else. What a relief to finally let go!"

In our collective debriefing after the *testimonios,* we realized that our experiences reflected oppositions of systemic violence and nurturance, injustice and empowerment. Grandparents, parents, and others noticed and nurtured us, provided guidance and encouragement, and believed in our capacity to succeed in our education. Our writings honor them, with *respeto,* love, and appreciation. On the other hand, in our homes, professions, and communities we struggle with racism, precarious economic circumstances, the consequences of being born female, and resistance to our presence in academia. A critical point in our process of theorizing was recognizing that we needed to acknowledge both dimensions of our experiences. Consequently, our writings represent an effort to name and understand the resources we were given as well as the pain that oppression produces for us. Reclaiming both memory and human agency is critical in a process of change. As the Puertorriqueñas said jokingly: *Nosotras estamos jodidas, pero también somos jodonas.*

Our collective process created other benefits. *Testimonio* engaged us at a deeper level than we had found in other feminist and womanist circles and in our own respective national communities. Our intense conversations, shared laughter, and emotional solidarity and bonding ultimately built trust, *confianza*. Despite being positioned at different points in the hierarchies of our professional lives, we worked together as equals. Invoking the Chicana criticism of people with attitude, Yvette Flores-Ortiz joked, *Aquí no hay chingonas*. In addition, bringing together the mind, spirit, and body, we shared meals and rooms, walked in the hills, went on field trips to the hot springs, the sand dunes, and nearby temples. We read our poetry and shared our writings in a night of *tertulia* we called "Café Baca." We danced together and explored really important questions such as "What is the difference between Puerto Rican and Chicana styles of dancing salsa?" And "Will you teach me?" We did all of this with the aid of untranslatable jokes and hilarious bilingual one-liners that helped ease the weariness from our intense work sessions that often lasted well into the night.

Baca became our self-declared artists' colony. We returned in the summer of 1996 to write our *papelitos,* conceptualize the structure of this book, and draft its introduction. We listened to the recorded narratives and read the transcripts from the long hours of *testimonio* and dialogue. We then sat down to write our own pieces, based on our *testimonios*. We shared them with one another, gave extensive feedback, and thus provided the support and courage to continue our writing. Ruth Behar told us that her Cuban *colegas* found that the best method for producing text was simply to put *culo a la silla* — butts to the chair! For most of us, testimonial writing was a new form, which, contrary to our academic voices, allowed us to speak with humor, beauty, spirituality, and sensuality. Many of these pieces form the section titled "Passions, Desires, and Celebrations." After debate over whether these would reify stereotypes about Latinas as passionate rather than intellectual, Eliana Rivero reminded us: "*Mujeres,* we survived all this stuff and we're still here, thriving, thank you very much. How can we ignore something so central to our existence?" Throughout, we were creating *comadreo,* the Latin American / Latina tradition of kinship, reciprocity, and commitment.

As we read our individual pieces to each other, the structure of this book began to take shape. For the introduction, we pursued a collective writing process where the whole group theorized the sections. Then, in smaller groups, we debated ideas, composed text, and brought drafts back to the whole, where we did line editing. Having eighteen women in a room, collectively writing and editing a manuscript, is a sight to behold! Of course, later, the introduction to this book was subjected to an intense process of recasting, expanding, deleting, clarifying, tightening, and polishing. A "virtual institute" created through e-mail allowed the designated subgroups and *jodonas* who took

Latina Feminist Group in Baca, Colorado, 1995
(l–r, front): Clara Lomas, María Luisa Lomas, Rina Benmayor,
Luz del Alba Acevedo, Pat Zavella; (l–r, back) Gloria Cuádraz,
Aurora Levins Morales, Celia Alvarez, Liza Fiol-Matta,
Caridad Souza

Latina Feminist Group in Baca, Colorado, 1995 (l–r):
Inés Hernández Avila, Caridad Souza, Daisy Cocco De Filippis,
Mirtha Quintanales, Aurora Levins Morales, Norma Cantú

Testimoniando in Baca, Colorado, 1995 (l–r): Caridad Souza,
Mirtha Quintanales, Daisy Cocco De Filippis, Inés Hernández Avila,
Eliana Rivero, Liza Fiol-Matta

responsibility for particular tasks to "nag" online. Smaller teams from two to eight participants have variously produced and edited drafts. We fondly designated these as the *culonas* of the group.

From our debates emerged a consensus that *testimonio* is a complex genre that has multiple antecedents and uses. From our various disciplinary backgrounds, we had each worked with a range of testimonial texts. These included oral traditions, such as those documented by nineteenth-century *folkloristas mexicanos* who gathered life stories to preserve their heritage in the face of conquest, Judeo-Spanish ballads preserved through five hundred years in diaspora, indigenous storytelling, and African slave narratives. We had also worked with witness narratives by Holocaust survivors and by Central and South American indigenous peoples and *campesinos*. Others had explored Inquisition "transcripts," confessional narratives, and even the ethnographic work of the friars who came with the Conquistadores. In social science, we had extensive experience generating life histories about Latina workers, migrations, and family lives. On the literary side, we had worked with various forms of autobiographical writing and life hi/story with antecedents in the Latin American and Caribbean *novela-testimonio*. From this multidisciplinary legacy, we found that our muses are as diverse as Sojourner Truth, Jovita Idar, Anne Frank, Mercé Rodoreda, Rosario Castellanos, Julia de Burgos, Rigoberta Menchú, Adrienne Rich, Elena Poniatowska, Cherríe Moraga, Rosario Morales, Audre Lorde, Lorna Dee Cervantes, Isabel Allende, Toni Cade Bambara, Gioconda Belli, Ntozake Shange, Sara Estela Ramírez, Leslie Marmon Silko, Joy Harjo, Luci Tapahonso, Sandra Cisneros, and Gloria Anzaldúa.

Seeking to contest and transform the very disciplines that taught us the

Working with *testimonios,* Baca, Colorado, 1995
(l–r): Gloria Cuádraz and Iris López

Theorizing *Latinidades,* Baca, Colorado, 1995
(l–r): Norma Alarcón and Norma Cantú

Informal get-together, Baca, Colorado, 1995 (l–r): Yvette Flores Ortiz,
Liza Fiol-Matta, Clara Lomas, Caridad Souza (in back),
Ruth Behar, Ceci Lomas (from behind)

skills to recover our subjugated knowledges, we reclaimed *testimonio* as a tool
for Latinas to theorize oppression, resistance, and subjectivity. Despite its
complicated history, *testimonio* captures Latinas' complex, layered lives. In
formulating a testimonial process, we engage the following questions in this
book: How can a feminist critical imaginary transform the societies in which
Latinas live, love, and labor? How can *testimonio,* as self-construction and
contestation of power, help us build the theory of our practice, and the practice of our theory? As a collective, we have come to agreement that our use of
testimonio takes place within a relational framework. Our group histories and
lived experiences are intertwined with global legacies of resistance to colonialism, imperialism, racism, antisemitism, religious fundamentalism, sexism, and
heterosexism. When theorizing about feminist *latinidades,* we reveal the inter-
relationships among these systems of power. Trained as critical thinkers, we
are forced to acknowledge that occasionally institutions or discourses about
which we are critical, such as religion or the family, produce contradictory
effects on us, serving as sources of disempowerment and autonomy, repression and privilege. For example, several of us are critical of organized religion,
yet religious traditions, practices, or schools developed our sense of confidence, discipline, and academic training. Our *papelitos* illustrate how we grapple with these contradictions individually.

The reader may well wonder why we call our own pieces *testimonios,* since
they are written and published by us, relatively privileged women who are

writers, scholars, and activists. Indeed, some of us have already written and published autobiographical texts in varied genres (poetry, short stories, chapbooks, *teatro,* music, essays, and self-reflexive scholarship), exploring issues similar to those presented here. Although mediated by our privileges, the pieces in this book are closer to the genre of *testimonio* for several reasons. Formally, these writings are the products of narratives lodged in memory, shared out loud and recorded. As such, they follow a common process of generating *testimonio.* In a parallel manner to the way that Rigoberta or Domitila's narratives speak not for the individual but for the experience of a community,[21] we see our stories as expressing the lives of many Latinas in and out of the academy. We hope our collective bearing witness conveys our outrage at multiple forms of violence toward women. Finally, we identify with *testimoniantes* because our collectivity nurtures utopian visions of social formations — families, work teams, social networks, communities, sexual relationships, political groups, social movements — that are formed on the basis of equality, respect, and open negotiation of difference. Like the polyphonic *testimonios,* constructed by accounts from different participants in the same event, this book illuminates the lives of Latinas, making our histories visible.

As feminists, however, we want to go beyond the limitations of *testimonio* and reveal the institutional violence and personal assaults that we have experienced as Latinas. This is not always possible, since many of us feel like "outsiders within," marginal to the academy, mainstream views, political groups, or even our own families. And despite the feminist mantra that "the personal is political," as Latina professionals we feel restricted in acknowledging painful personal experiences. Particularly within political projects that include multiracial groups, or men and women, or are situated within academia, we are often reminded that our needs as feminists are secondary to the "real struggle," and some of us feel vulnerable to professional or political consequences for personal disclosures.

Our book expands the construction of *testimonio* in our feminist desire to make visible and audible our *papelitos guardados* — the stories often held from public view — and to express the full complexity of our identities, from the alchemies of erasure and silencing to our passions, joys, and celebrations. In dialogue with other hybrid autobiographical modes (ethnoautobiography, "native" or feminist ethnography, autobiographical fiction), we have infused traditional literary genres of poetry and short story with the spirit of testimonial disclosure. At the same time, our *testimonios* express multiple subjectivities of individual lives, marked by uniqueness as well as shared history and context. Departing from the heroic autobiographical tradition, we are not speaking from the voice of the singular "I."[22] Rather, we are exploring the ways in which our individual identities express the complexities of our communities as a whole. As Latinas who now have experienced being on both sides of the microphone, we view *testimonios* as a practice that seeks to mediate the power relations between ourselves and our subjects. In this way, our book represents a unique praxis within *testimonio* traditions, as we have made ourselves the subjects and objects of our own inquiry and voice.

Papelitos Guardados

"Genealogies of Empowerment" begins this book, affirming that we all carry within us the memory of homelands, communities, families, and cultural traditions that situate us in our life trajectories as writers and teachers. Not merely celebratory or nostalgic, these "stories" also capture the ironies and difficulties of becoming successful, accomplished women. "Alchemies of Erasure" speaks eloquently to the many ways in which our identities have been compartmentalized and made invisible, particularly within academia. "The Body Re/Members" inscribes the corporal memory of pain and recoveries, while "Passions, Desires, and Celebrations" gives voice to moments, symbols, and relationships of sustenance and creativity. Some of the writings in this book retain the flavor of oral speech, others are more stylized. Poetry, fictionalized personal account, interior monologue, dramatic dialogue, novelistic writing, and other forms evolved from the creative process of how best to represent the range of our life experiences. In capturing our experiences, however, we relied more on what we had to say than on producing highly crafted text. We sought to preserve the raw edge of *testimonio,* and to use the voice most accessible to each of us.

Throughout the long effort to make this book a reality, we broke the enclaves, sustained meaningful dialogue, crossed the borders between disciplines and academic practices, and proposed a framework for theorizing feminist *latinidades.* In the process, we ventured into new writing modes, and built a sustaining practice of community where we remain committed to continued dialogue, collaboration, and contact, as a whole and in smaller groups. We affirmed a relational ethic of care and support for each other and for the group. In our experience this is Latina feminism at its most nurturing and creative. We think of this book as a gift to other Latinas, particularly young women, to inspire them to create their own expressions of feminist Latina identities — *latinidades.* We encourage you to carry forward, *testimoniando.*

Notes

1. The original agenda included these six topics for research: Political Economy of Latina Lives; The Mapping of Toxicities: Environmental Racism; Violence and Human Rights:

Health, Sterilization, and Addiction; Geographies of Resistance; Cultural Citizenship and Community Development; and Production and Political Use of Knowledge.

2. For references to contributors' scholarship, see Bibliography.

3. Like any term of identity, "Latina" is open to multiple interpretations. In the 1970s, when the term "Latino" (the generic masculine) gained popular currency, it reflected an anti-assimilationist political consciousness arising from community-based organizing. The aim was to be more inclusive of the multiple national compositions of our working-class communities, especially as they became more complex with new migrations from Latin America. During the 1980s, a variety of Latino research centers and programs were established throughout the country for the purpose of studying and comparing distinct national histories and experiences. In the 1990s, we witnessed the term "Latino" used in the academy as a means of reflecting common interests and transnational experiences by Latinos and Latinoamericanos living in the United States. A more recent development is the reconfiguring of Latino and Latin American Studies programs into "area studies." However, when Latinos and Latinoamericanos are seen as one category, important differences such as class, experiences of colonialism or racialization, and moments and conditions of insertion into U.S. society, are erased. Further, even though it emerged in opposition to the homogenized "Hispanic," the term "Latino" is not immune from being co-opted and reconceptualized. "Latino" can easily become a "hip" term used by the mainstream to promote corporate and political interests and agendas.

4. Paulo Freire, *Pedagogy of the Oppressed,* trans. Myra Bergman Ramos (New York: Continuum, 1973); Paulo Freire, *Pedagogy of Hope: Reliving Pedagogy of the Oppressed,* notes by Ana Maria Araújo Freire, trans. Robert R. Barr (New York: Continuum, 1997); Myles Horton and Paulo Freire, *We Make the Road by Walking: Conversations on Education and Social Change,* ed. Brenda Bell et al. (Philadelphia: Temple University Press, 1990).

5. The Bibliography includes substantial sections on "Native" and/or Feminist Ethnography and Oral History/Life History/*Testimonio.*

6. Cherríe Moraga, *Loving in the War Years: lo que nunca pasó por sus labios* (Boston: South End Press, 1983).

7. A full history of Chicana/Latina activism, creative writings, and manifestos published in alternative journals, small presses, or social-issue magazines, particularly prior to the 1960s, has yet to be written. However, for important texts that begin this project, see Celia Alvarez, *Intersecting Lives: Puerto Rican Women as Community Intellectuals* (Temple University Press, forthcoming); Katherine Angueira, "To Make the Personal Political: The Use of Testimony as a Consciousness-Raising Tool Against Sexual Aggression in Puerto Rico," *Oral History Review* 16/2 (fall 1988), pp. 65–94; Rina Benmayor, Ana Juarbe, Blanca Vazquez Erazo, Celia Alvarez, "Stories to Live By: Continuity and Change in Three Generations of Puerto Rican Women," *Oral History Review* 16/2 (fall 1988), pp. 1–46; Rina Benmayor, Rosa M. Torruellas, Ana L. Juarbe, "Claiming Cultural Citizenship in East Harlem: "*Si Esto Puede Ayudar a la Comunidad Mía* . . . " in *Latino Cultural Citizenship: Claiming Identity, Space, and Rights,* ed. William V. Flores and Rina Benmayor (Boston: Beacon Press, 1997); Alma M. García, ed., *Chicana Feminist Thought: The Basic Historical Writings* (New York: Routledge, 1997); Carol Hardy-Fanta, *Latina Politics, Latino Politics: Gender, Culture, and Political Participation in Boston* (Philadelphia: Temple University Press, 1993); Mary S. Pardo, *Mexican American Women Activists: Identity and Resistance in Two Los Angeles Communities* (Philadelphia: Temple University Press, 1998); Rosa M. Torruellas, Rina Benmayor, Anneris Goris, and Ana Juarbe, "Affirming Cultural Citizenship in the Puerto Rican Community: Critical Literacy and the El Barrio Popular

Education Program, in *Literacy as Praxis: Culture, Language, and Pedagogy*, ed. Catherine E. Walsh (Norwood, N.J.: Ablex Publishing Corporation, 1991). See also Section VII, Latina Feminisms and Latina Studies, in the Bibliography.

8. Gloria Anzaldúa, *Making Face, Making Soul: Haciendo Caras* (San Francisco: Aunt Lute Foundation, 1990).

9. For key texts that theorize the intersection of race, class, gender, etc., see Section VI, Women of Color, in the Bibliography.

10. See Patricia Bell-Scott, *Life Notes: Personal Writings by Contemporary Black Women* (New York: Norton, 1994), and *Double Stitch: Black Women Write about Mothers and Daughters* (New York: Harper and Row, 1991); Asian Women United of California, *Making Waves: An Anthology of Writings by and about Asian American Women* (Boston: Beacon Press, 1989); Johnnetta B. Cole, *All American Women: Lines That Divide, Ties That Bind* (New York: Macmillan, 1986). See also Gloria T. Hull, Patricia Bell Scott, and Barbara Smith, *All the Women Are White, All the Blacks Are Men, But Some of Us Are Brave: Black Women's Studies* (New York: Feminist Press, 1982).

11. For references to key works in Chicana and Latina feminist theory, see Section VII, Latina Feminisms and Latina Studies, in the Bibliography.

12. See Alma Gómez, Cherríe Moraga, and Mariana Romo-Carmona, *Cuentos: Stories by Latinas* (New York: Kitchen Table: Women of Color Press, 1983); Evangelina Vigil, ed., *Woman of Her Word: Hispanic Women Write, Revista Chicano-Riqueña*, 2d ed. (Houston: Arte Público Press, 1987; first published in 1983); "Bearing Witness / *Sobreviviendo* — An Anthology of Writing and Art by Native American / Latina Women," *Calyx* (A Journal of Art and Literature by Women), vol. 8, no. 2 (spring 1984); Roberta Fernández, ed., *In Other Words* (Houston: Arte Público Press, 1994); Maria del Carmen Boza, Beverly Silva, and Carmen Valle, eds., *Nosotras: Latina Literature Today* (Binghamton: Bilingual Review Press, 1986); Lillian Castillo Speed, ed., *Latina* (New York: Simon and Schuster, 1995); Juanita Ramos, ed. *Compañera: Latina Lesbians (An Anthology)* (New York: Latina Lesbian History Project, 1987); Tey Diana Rebolledo and Eliana S. Rivero, *Infinite Divisions: An Anthology of Chicana Literature* (Tucson: University of Arizona Press, 1993); Norma Alarcón, Ana Castillo, and Cherríe Moraga, eds. "The Sexuality of Latinas," Special Issue of *Third Woman* (vol. 4, 1989); Gloria Anzaldúa, ed., *Making Face, Making Soul: Haciendo Caras* (San Francisco: Aunt Lute Foundation, 1990).

13. Cherríe Moraga, "Refugees of a World on Fire: Forward to the Second Edition." *This Bridge Called My Back: Writings by Radical Women of Color* (New York: Kitchen Table: Women of Color Press, 1983).

14. Eliana Rivero, "*Fronterisleña*, Border Islander." *Michigan Quarterly Review*, Special Issue, *Bridges to Cuba/Puentes a Cuba*, ed. Ruth Behar, vol. 33 (fall 1994): 672.

15. It's only the darker hues that are used in "endearing" ways. One rarely hears anyone say, "*Oye, blanquita, mi amor . . . !*" (hey little white one, my love). It is always "*morena*" (dark one or mulatta) or "*negrita*" (little black one) that convey the sense of "we love you even if you are dark." While "*güerita*" or "*colorá*" (light skinned, blond or redhead) are used in some instances, their use connotes a positive process of whitening: "You are special because you are light."

16. For references to Latina autobiographical anthologies, see Section I, Latina Mixed Genre Literary Anthologies, in the Bibliography.

17. "The Combahee River Collective, A Black Feminist Statement," in *All the Women Are White, All the Blacks Are Men, But Some of Us Are Brave*, ed. Gloria T. Hull, et al., pp. 13–22.

18. At the same time, water and land rights disputes among Native Americans, Hispanos, and

Anglos continue to erupt in social tensions. Ironically, we also remember *"una vieja loca,"* a liquor store owner who, visibly uncomfortable with a group of Latinas in her store, complained, "They're all chattering, chattering, chattering [in Spanish]." When we objected to her attitude, she became threatening and said, "You want trouble? I'll give you trouble!" and threw us out.

19. For a discussion of *testimonio* in Latin American literature, see Section III, Latina/Latin American *Testimonio*, Section IV, Oral History/Life *History/Testimonio*, and Section V, "Native" and/or Feminist Ethnography, in the Bibliography.

20. For primary texts in the genre of *testimonio*, see Section III, Latina/Latin American *Testimonio*, in the Bibliography.

21. Doris Sommer, "'Not Just a Personal Story': Women's *Testimonios* and the Plural Self," in Bella Brodzki and Celeste Schenck, eds., *Life/Lines: Theorizing Women's Autobiography* (Ithaca: Cornell University Press, 1988), pp. 107–30. The recent controversy raised by David Stoll, who applies a positivist notion to the "truth" of *testimonio*, illustrates that the genre includes partial renderings of complex experiences that extend beyond the personal. See David Stoll, *Rigoberta Menchú and the Story of All Poor Guatemalans*. Boulder: Westview Press, 1999.

22. Betty Bergland, "Postmodernism and the Autobiographical Subject: Reconstructing the 'Other,'" in Kathleen Ashley, Leigh Gilmore, and Gerald Peters, eds., *Autobiography and Postmodernism* (Amherst: University of Massachusetts Press, 1994), pp. 130–65.

1 Genealogies of Empowerment

Remedios is . . . my hunger for a story, a history,
that makes sense of everything I am and
all that I have found to love.

AURORA LEVINS MORALES

ACH OF US IN THIS BOOK has a complex story about our mestiza
inheritances that defy simplistic explanation — stories about living on
the borders of various classes, nations, regional cultures, languages,
voices, races, ethnicities, migrations, sexualities, creative abilities, academic
disciplines, and even cultures of resistance. In this section we sketch out the
genealogies that have informed our individual paths to personal achievement.
The complicated structures of inheritance and identity formation, legacies of
colonial and patriarchal subordination influence our lives as thinking women.
They have shaped our resistance and fueled our cognitive desires, the will to
knowledge and comprehension. Beneath the indelible imprint of historical
displacement lies a conflicted sense of pride in our accomplishments and hard
work despite how they reflect the strength of our cultural heritages and inner
resources. More subtle but pivotal influences come from our families, friends,
communities, and life events that have also helped us negotiate the markers of
our achievements and validate our right to pursue our goals. Our genealogies
of empowerment draw on these early lessons as the blueprints for a thriving
process of self-created and self-defined freedom and independence.

Sorting through our inherited and self-fashioned *mestizajes* allows us, as
Aurora Levins Morales writes, to listen to our "own discomforts, find out who
shares them, validate them, and exchange stories about common experiences,
find patterns and systems of explaining how and why things happen." For
some of us, bearing witness to social injustice became the catalyst for our
involvement with ideas, kindled by the women who surrounded us. Very
often it was those unconventional conventional women in our lives who, by
actively contesting the inconveniences of gender constraints, "shaped our
souls." Some of us were accorded male privileges and found that the experi-

ence seared our hearts with an insatiable desire to learn and know, to move farther despite our female gendering. For others still, our very female gendering ignited a rebelliousness rooted in the unfulfilled aspirations of our female lineage. We drew quiet lessons from the deafening silences and unshed tears around us that taught us to see the nuances in our social worlds. We learned to be grateful for such small miracles as the joy and inner strength that comes from conquering a fear, the reciprocity of an open-handed sharing of ideas, or the sweet beauty of an unconditional, platonic love. While our hunger for intellectual and social justice still propels the utopian dreams that have nourished us, only the homemade theories we create out of our shared lives really help us to make sense of everything that we are and all that we find to love.

Certified Organic Intellectual

Aurora Levins Morales

I

I HAVE BEGUN THIS ESSAY a hundred times in a hundred different ways, and each time I have struggled with the same deadly numbing of my mind. Hashing it out once again with my parents on the phone, this time we go for the food metaphors. When I was a child in rural Puerto Rico, the people around me ate produce grown on local soil, chickens that roamed the neighborhood, bananas cut from the stalk. It was unrefined, unpackaged, full of all those complex nutrients that get left out when the process is too tightly controlled. But during the last few years before we emigrated, advertising finally penetrated into our remote part of the island. Cheeze Whiz on Wonder Bread was sold to country women as a better, more sophisticated, modern, advanced, and healthy breakfast than boiled root vegetables and codfish or rice and beans.

When I call myself an organic intellectual, I mean that the ideas I carry with me were grown on soil I know, that I can tell you about the mineral balance, the weather, the labor involved in preparing them for use. In the marketplace of ideas, we are pushed toward the supermarket chains that are replacing the tiny rural *colmado;* told that storebought is better, imported is best, and sold on empty calories in shiny packaging instead of open crates and barrels of produce to which the earth still clings.

The intellectual traditions I come from create theory out of shared lives instead of sending away for it. My thinking grew directly out of listening to my own discomforts, finding out who shared them, who validated them, and in exchanging stories about common experiences, finding patterns, systems, explanations of how and why things happened. This is the central process of consciousness raising, of collective *testimonio*. This is how homemade theory happens.

I am also the child of two cultures of resistance. I grew up among *jíbaras,* a multilayered name for country people, which is used on the one hand to romanticize the imaginary "simple but honest" noble peasants or coffee workers of yesteryear and on the other is a common put-down implying stupidity and lack of sophistication, like "hick." But which originally meant, in the language of the Arawak people, "she who runs away to be free," referring to the mixed-blood settlements of escaped slaves, fugitive Indians, and European peasants who took to the mountains to escape state control. I was raised in one of the oldest of those settlements, a place called Indiera, listening to people talk. I am also the daughter of an urbanized descendant of the impoverished island elite. My mother came from small-town *hacendados* fallen on hard times and grew up in the collective working-class immigrant culture of New York City in the 1930s and 40s with an inheritance of practicality of pride in work well done, of adaptability to the shifting currents of history. She became a communist in the late forties, was a feminist before there was a movement to back her, and when any piece of politics makes her queasy, she trusts her own gut feeling over anyone else's credentials.

And I grew up as the tropical branch of a tribe of working-class Jewish thinkers who were critiquing the canons of their day from the shtetls of Eastern Europe, arguing about identity politics and coalitions, assimilation and solidarity way back into the last century. My father's great-great-grandmother, a rabbi's wife in 1860s Ukraine, challenged the patriarchal rules of Judaism by standing up in temple and calling out, "Your God is a man!" His grandmother Leah Shevelev, an immigrant to New York at the turn of the century, was an organizer of garment workers and unemployed women and worked as a birth control educator with Margaret Sanger. His father helped found the Communist Youth Movement. In the extended family over which my great-grandmother Leah ruled, my father grew up an internationalist, profeminist man and an original, creative thinker who loved intellectual work and was unimpressed by the rituals and self-importance of academic institutions.

So I grew up in a family of activists who were thinking about race and class and gender and the uses of history and literature long before there were college courses to do this in, a mother who was a feminist in the 1950s, a father who told me bedtime stories about African and Chinese history and taught biology as a liberation science. How I think and what I think about grows from my identity as a *jíbara* shtetl intellectual and organizer. I was taught to trust in these traditions, in the reliability of my own intelligence combined with that of others.

In the women's consciousness-raising groups I belonged to in the early

1970s, we shared personal and very emotional stories of what it had really been like to live as women, examining our experiences with men and with other women in our families, sexual relationships, workplaces and schools, in the health care system and in surviving the general societal contempt and violence toward us. As we told our stories we found validation that our experiences and our reactions to them were common to many of us, that our perceptions, thoughts, and feelings made sense to other women. We then used that shared experience as a source of authority. Where our lives did not match official knowledge we trusted our lives, and used the collective and mutually validated body of stories to critique those official versions of reality. This was theory born of an activist need, and the feminist literature we read, from articles like "The Politics of Housework" and "The Myth of the Vaginal Orgasm" to the poetry of Susan Griffin, Marge Piercy, Alta, rose out of the same mass phenomenon of truth telling from personal knowledge.

Of course, in the euphoria of finding validation for what was common to us, what was not soon became glaringly obvious. The powerful differences between us in the way our womanness was shaped by class, "race," sexuality, age, our cultures, had been artificially smoothed over. Almost immediately, groups of women of color, lesbians, working-class women, Jewish women, disabled women found ourselves undergoing the same process of testimony, fighting once again for our own specific truths. My discovery of a community of womanist of color writers, artists, thinkers was probably the most profound validation I've ever received of my right to exist, to know, to name my own reality.

But as academic feminism drifts further and further from its activist roots, as the elite gobbledygook of postmodernist jargon makes it less and less acceptable to speak comprehensibly, I have more and more often found my trust in myself under assault.

I watch my life and my theorizing about it become the raw materials of someone else's expertise, and I am reminded of the neem tree of India, used for millennia as an insect repellent, now being patented by a multinational pharmaceutical company. Peasant women developed the technology for extracting and preparing the oil for local use, but to multinationals, local use is a waste. The exact same process, done at much higher volume, and packaged for export, is what they have been able to patent.

My intellectual life and that of other organic intellectuals, many of them women of color, is fully sophisticated enough for use. But in order to have value in the marketplace, the entrepreneurs and multinational developers must find a way to process it, to refine the rich multiplicity of our lives and all we have come to understand about them into high theory by the simple act of removing it, abstracting it beyond recognition, taking out the fiber, boiling it down until the vitality is oxidized away and then marketing it as their own and selling it back to us for more than we can afford.

2

The local *colmado* of Barrio Rubias, which is just across the road from Barrio Indiera Baja where I was raised, used to sell two kinds of cheese. *Queso holandés,* Dutch cheese, came in great big balls covered with red wax. If it got moldy, it did so from the outside in, so the center remained good, and one could trim the green from the rind. Or you could buy something called "imitation processed cheese food product." Both began in the mammary glands of cows. But the "processed cheese food product" like its contemporary relatives, Velveeta, or the individually plastic-wrapped Kraft singles, was barely identifiable with any of the processes of their production, and what is more, when it spoiled, it did so thoroughly. All the capacity for resistance of a solid cheese with a rind had been refined away. Nevertheless, it often sold better. The packaging was colorful, mysteriously sealed, difficult to open.

We have been well trained to be consumers of glossy boxes, ziplock bags, childproof bottles, and copious amounts of plastic wrap and cellophane. We are taught to be distrustful of bulk foods and to rely on brand-name recognition. The students I work with have been taught to give books so much more authority than they give their own lives that with the best will to comply they find it extremely challenging to write autobiographical responses to the readings and lectures. What they know best how to do is arrange the published opinions of other people in a logical sequence, restating one or another school of thought on the topic at hand.

When the package is difficult to penetrate, they rarely ask why the damn thing has to be wrapped up so tight. They assume the problem is with them. When I first reentered higher education, as a middle-aged professional writer with many years of public speaking behind me, even with all the confidence these things gave me, I felt humiliated by the impenetrable language in which academic thinking comes wrapped these days. But I thought it was just a matter of overcoming my awkwardness with jargon. A problem of lack of training. Like recently decolonized countries that embrace all the shiny wonders of nuclear energy, determined to have what the empire has had all along, I thought this slick new arrangement of words just needed to be acquired.

But I no longer think this. The language in which ideas are expressed is never neutral. The language people use reveals important information about who they identify with, what their intentions are, for whom they are writing or speaking. The packaging is the product being sold and does exactly what it was designed for. Unnecessarily specialized language is used to humiliate those who are not supposed to feel entitled. It sells the illusion that only those who can wield it can think.

A frequent response to those who resist exclusive language is that they are intellectually lazy. Like other forms of gatekeeping, the whole point is that we, and not the gatekeepers, are responsible for getting ourselves in. We must stop what we are doing, forget what we came for, and devote our energies to techniques of breaking and entering. We are required to do this just to win the right to join in the argument. If we are uninterested, we are assumed to be incompetent. But my choice to read the readable has to do with a different set of priorities. Language is wedded to content, and the content I seek is theory and intellectual practice that will be of use to me in an activist scholarship whose priorities are, above all, democratizing.

3

At the time that I was first struggling to hold onto my own intellectual integrity within academia, I had little validation in my daily life for these feelings. I struggled to be "good" and do as I was supposed to, felt that I must be missing something when most of what I read seemed shallow or irrelevant to my work, felt that somehow feminist theory should be more exciting to me. Maybe, I thought, it was a lack of academic skill that was the problem. But most of what I read seemed so many levels of abstraction away from activist intentions and lived experience, from the problems I wanted to solve, that it had become an intellectual exercise, academic in that other sense of the word — disconnected from daily use. To fully understand it, to really engage and argue in that place, I would have had to abandon what I had come there for — to learn new things about the liberatory uses of history for Latinas — to devote my time and energy to studying the ideas of those I found least trustworthy or useful, instead of doing my chosen work with and about my own peoples.

Now, looking back, I remember my life in the feminist movement of the early 1980s. At conference after conference I would stand in the hall trying to choose between the workshop or caucus for women of color and the one for Jews. I remember how every doorway I tried to enter required leaving some part of myself behind. In those hallways, I began meeting other women, the complexity of whose lives defied the simplifications of identity politics. In conversation with them I found the only reflections of my full reality. Much of the feminist theory I tried to read in graduate school was written in rooms whose doors were too narrow. They required me to leave myself and my deepest intellectual passions outside.

Like my immigrant ancestors, my intellectual home is constantly being revised, refined, redecorated. But over the years it has been those same women I met in the hallways, the ones who had survived against all odds, with whom I have made rooms big enough to include all the richly complex and contradictory truths of who I am. This gathering of Latina feminist scholars has been such a room. Because the minute we found a way to gather and talk, we threw away the outside agendas and began making theory out of the stuff in our pockets, out of the stories, incidents, dreams, frustrations that were never acceptable anywhere else.

Each of us brings to the table the nourishment we know everything about, from planting and harvest to the most sophisticated techniques of preparation. It is that wealth of tribal, local, particular, and personal knowledges, individually crafted and set forth on the common table, that feeds me now. It is this process I teach: listen to your hunger, listen to the hunger of others, learn from experienced cooks, taste as you go, use fresh ingredients, know your supplier, and buy organic. ¡Buen provecho!

My Father's Hands

Yvette Gisele Flores-Ortiz

First Memories

R*ecuerdo las cortinas de encaje francés, acariciadas por la brisa, y el olor salado del Mar Caribe. Recuerdo su voz que me dice "eres mi reina," y recuerdo sus manos, las manos de mi padre.*

Strong, calloused hands, *cuarteadas por el aceite y los solventes, manos de hombre fino que debió tocar el violín, manos de mecánico, como decía mi madre, que me sacan de la cuna, manos que me alzan para que yo pueda observar el mundo.*

Nestled against his shoulder, supported by his strong, working-man's hands that could have played the violin, I can see the world, his world . . . but facing backwards. *Empecé la vida mirando para atrás.* I can only see where he has been, *su pasado, el pasado.* Nestled in his arms, *al lado del Atlántico en Panamá,* I can feel Costa Rica and his longing for the land he left behind.

Empecé la vida mirando para atrás; my future would be charted by my father's longing *y el testimonio de dolor, deseo y tristeza* embodied in my mother. *Tengo once meses y no recuerdo la cara de mi madre, pero sí sus sollozos.* My father's hands and my mother's tears provided my foundation. At the core of my being is strength and sorrow.

Migraciones/Migrations

I am the product of multiple migrations, from the French great-grandfather who left the comforts of the south of France (or so the story goes) to help build the Panama Canal in the late nineteenth century, to the Chinese immigrant enslaved in Costa Rican mines in the 1880s, to the two *mestizas, las hijas*

Claudio and Yvette Gisele Flores-Ortiz,
San José, Costa Rica, 1953

Yvette Gisele Flores-Ortiz, San José,
Costa Rica, 1957

de Anayansi,[1] who partnered these men. I am the daughter of a man who fled his father's tyranny and took his broken heart, in search of dreams and dollars, to the Panama Canal. I am the daughter of a woman whose only dowry was a broken marriage and two sons, who found in the *tico* (citizen of Costa Rica) a mirror for her sadness and *desarraigo. Soy una tica-panameña, una panameña-tica, soy la hija de dos desarraigados.*

I was their bridge, *el puente que unía sus tristezas. El puente construido de pasión y miedo en 1952. Mi madre temía a su pasado y mi padre a su futuro; yo era su presente.* I was the site of connection in their desperate lives, the site of belonging. I was expected to give meaning to their lives. I was to fulfill mother's bourgeois aspirations, I was to actualize father's working-class dreams — I was to become a *doctora,* a physician, *un médico,* gendered female but entitled as if I were a male, *por ser la única hija del primogénito de la familia Flores.*

Yo era su puente, colgante, duradero, y fuerte. Pero un puente cannot move or choose sides. It must hang suspended in-between. It must be strong, *pero debe ceder,* to hold their pain, to balance their desires. As their bridge I had to occupy dual spaces *a la vez.* I had to serve as bridge between multiple migrations: *de Panamá a Costa Rica, de Costa Rica a* South Central *Los Angeles, de lo Latino a lo gringo y a lo afro-americano. La joven de trece años,* the thirteen-year-old girl that I was, served as bridge to connect *los desarraigos. Los suyos y los míos,* theirs and mine. *Pero también fui y sigo siendo mi propio puente.* I was and continue to be my own bridge, *entre Centroamérica y Aztlán, entre Latinas y Chicanas, entre feministas latinas y feministas blancas. Puente con base en dos mundos a la vez.*

"*El dolor debilita,*" *decía mi madre entre suspiros,* swallowing her tears. "*Nos tiene que gustar Los Estados Unidos. Este es el sueño de tu padre. Lo hicimos por tí.*"

We came to the United States *para que el puente pudiera ser doctora. A pesar del desarraigo, las pérdidas, la tristeza, yo, la fuerte, la que conectaba tristezas viejas a nuevas, no tenía derecho a sentir mi dolor.* My mother who never cried taught me to be strong. I, the child of migration and pain, was not allowed to grieve or to hurt, *porque el dolor debilita y las lágrimas ahogan.* I, who did not cry in order to be strong, became a psychologist, a healer for modern times, an expert in other people's sorrow.

---

1. Anayansi is the Panamanian construction of Malinche, alleged to have been Vasco Nuñez de Balboa's mistress, and therefore considered a collaborator with her own oppression. Anayansi, raped and enslaved by Balboa, is the Panamanian symbol of female perfidy and male colonization.

"Nosotras fuimos francesas, blancas y adineradas," decía mi madre entre suspiros. *"Pero como los hombres todo lo joden, ahora somos pobres, negras y cholas* (mestiza, *indígena-*'looking')*."*

These were the lessons of my mother, as she taught me how to read. My mother, the seamstress' daughter, the battered child of an alcoholic Frenchman (*era borracho pero blanco*), embodied the legacy of migration, colonization, and miscegenation. My mother, who was refined, and gentle, embodied her father's infidelities and other *violaciones.*

"No hay que confiar en los hombres, ni depender de ellos. Mírate en este espejo," decía ella, the once-French, white, privileged woman, now relegated to housewife of a "simple" auto-mechanic. She followed her husband to Costa Rica, leaving behind her family, her career, her future, and her past. *"Pero lo hice por ti, mi nena, porque las niñas necesitan tener papá."* My mother, who grew up without a father, sacrificed to give me one.

"Tú vas a estudiar para que no seas la criada de ningún hombre, porque no se puede confiar en ellos. Mira a tus tías, todas dejadas, abusadas, o preñadas, por no tener educación." Lessons in distrust my mother taught me along with the multiplication tables. Men were not to be trusted. My father, in his absence, did not offer an alternative voice.

"Tú tienes que estudiar para que seas libre," to which the chorus of my *tías, las dejadas, abandonadas, y preñadas,* silently assented. I never had the courage to ask my mother what good her education did her.

My father did not speak to me of his past or of his sorrows. Instead, his strong mechanic's hands led me on Sunday outings . . . to the zoo, the park, and the cemetery.

"Aquí está tu abuelita, se llamaba Jesús, pero le decían la Chusa. Era una santa mi madre," decía mi padre, fighting back the tears, as he placed flowers on her grave. *"Ella siempre te cuidará; porque yo la amo, ella a ti te quiere."*

My father's hands wove the historical connection to his mother, his country, his past. He taught me to love his mother, she who died young consumed by rage and sorrow, with a broken heart. She the silent witness of her husband's infamies. She who taught her son to be noble, to become a good man. She who did not/could not for the children's good stop her husband's weekly beatings. She who spat in his food, when he came home to eat, *después de dejar la cama de la otra.* She, who by dying, freed her son to leave home. *Ella, Jesús, quien también vive en mí.* She who reaffirmed my mother's lessons of *sufrimiento, abnegación,* silent witnessing, and *subversión.*

My father's love for his mother clouded the passion he might have felt for mine. My mother's rage toward her father's violence, addiction, and betrayal obscured the love she might have felt for my father. I was to build/learn affection from their passion, hatred, distrust, and pain. I learned these lessons well.

I grew up in a home created by two people bound by obligation and unfulfilled desires. They gave me their best gifts. My mother gave me her intellect and a legacy of keeping secrets; my father gave me his love and taught me to be proud and never to ask for anything I could obtain myself. They both taught me to fight for my rights by enslaving me to their desires.

"Nadie tiene el derecho de quitarte lo tuyo, nadie tiene ese derecho." My parents' greatest gift was to instill in me the seeds of rebellion and *derecho*. No one had the right to deny me an education; no one had the right to challenge my pride. These were the lessons I learned. But neither taught me how to speak, although I knew three languages, because of the silence in their own lives.

My parents could not speak of their commonalities, blocked by a wall of pain and indifference. To speak of love was to revisit pain. Their marriage was the battleground where foreign invasions, conquests, and surrender of generations past were continuously refought. His working-class hands could not penetrate the walls of her pain and disappointment. Her unfulfilled French dreams could not accept his working-class offerings. So they lived their lives in silence.

"Hija, dile a ese hombre que ya está su comida."

"Hija, dile a esa mujer que no quiero comer."

I could not tell them that their warfare, their *reclamos y resentimientos me trituraban*. I was their bridge, silent, silenced, strong.

My father's strength and my mother's sadness were the companions of my childhood and adolescence. Their expectation of my achievement carried me through my educational experience in the United States. Failure never was an option.

"Hija, tienes que educarte, para eso vinimos a este país." We came to this country so that I could get an education, that was the only thing my parents agreed upon. High school diploma, B.A., M.S., Ph.D. were my gifts to them, repayment for sacrifices made.

Consejos No Escuchados/Advice Not Followed

"Hija, nunca seas maestra. El profesorado sería una buena profesión si no existieran escuelas o burócratas/child, never become a teacher; teaching would be a good profession if there were no schools or administrators."

My mother tried to warn me, *pero fue en vano*. I did not listen. I had seen her happy among her books; I had seen her patience and tenderness as she taught me. Her praise for my academic achievements was the kisses she could not give me, the embraces trapped in her body. I longed for her touch and fell in love with words, with learning, and with teaching.

My mother's bourgeois ideals and her secret commitment to social justice guided me, unbeknown to us both, to academia. My father's love, his faith in me, and his disappointment with my life's choice gave me the *ganas*, the will to succeed. Living in the minefield of my childhood home prepared me somewhat for the daily indignities of academic life.

"Hija, pero ¿de qué te quejas? Ganas bien, vives entre los libros, inspiras estudiantes. Hija ¿de qué te quejas? A tí no te pega tu marido."

"No mamá, pero sí me agrede esa institución." I am not battered by an alcoholic Frenchman or a *tico-chino*, but I am battered by academe.

"Hija, pero ¿de qué te quejas? En todos los trabajos hay que tragar mierda. Ignóralo y sigue p'alante."

"Sí papá, pero no puedo, porque empecé la vida mirando para atrás, mirando injusticias, no las puedo negar."

"Madre, tu tristeza nutrió mi intelecto, padre tu fuerza inspiró mi sobrevivencia."

My father's hands and my mother's swallowed tears fuel the passion that informs my teaching and helps me survive institutional violence. And the memories of home, of ocean breezes, French lace curtains, and ocean smells, finally free my voice.

Vignettes of a Working-Class Puerto Rican Girl in Brooklyn, New York

Celia Alvarez

War Booty

MANY PUERTO RICANS were soldiers in the U.S. army during the Korean War, including my father, Maximino. Privileged by his pain, my family bene-fited from the war booty he received as a veteran. This included access to the public housing near the Brooklyn Navy Yard in the early 1950s.

My mother, Celia, lived with my father and my grandparents, Cele and Pedro, in the Fort Greene Houses, until the three of us were born. A so-cial worker later suggested that my parents move to their own apartment in the Farragut Houses. Overlooking the Manhattan Bridge, our apart-ment at 111 Bridge Street was complete with running water, elevators, and no roaches. Uncle Sam, our landlord, provided residents in the projects with better-than-tenement-like-conditions and rent commensurate with their working-class salaries.

My father was fortunate to get a stable "city" job with a New York City hospital. He worked for thirty-five years in the mailroom of Cumberland Hospital, never taking a sick day. His pension made it possible for my par-ents to retire in Puerto Rico in the late eighties. They were part of the re-turn migration of those who made the sojourn with them to New York in the fifties.

Geographic and economic stability were no minor feats for Puerto Rican families then, or now. Despite the obstacles, my parents chose to stay in New York and not go back and forth to Puerto Rico like many other Puerto Rican families at the time. This was the price they paid for my access, and that of my brother and sister, to a continuous educational experience in the United States.

Throughout his years in New York, I remember my father fighting for the

The Alvarez family: (l–r) Celia, Maximino,
Celia, Max, Candida, Brooklyn, New York circa 1957

equal rights of *los Hispanos*. His struggles with discrimination at work were reminiscent of those he experienced in the armed services years earlier. Regardless of the Purple Heart he had earned in Korea, the U.S. citizenship accorded to Puerto Ricans since 1917, or his bilingual fluency in English, I was born in 1954 with the imprint of *Brown v. Board of Education* on my forehead. As my own life trajectory unfolds, history catapults me into the civil rights struggles for educational equity in the United States.

Memorable Moments of a Five-Year-Old

When I was five years old I went to Puerto Rico for the first time.
    I remember . . .

Crying hysterically on *la letrina,* terrified I was going to fall in!
Having to go outside the house to take a shower!
Letting the pigs out of the pen, and running as fast as I can!
Taking a picture with *titi Reina,* with a *pato* on her lap.
El pato se cagó y ella casi se muere!
Going back home to the Farragut projects
And telling my sister
How lucky we were to have running water and
How we didn't have to worry about falling in some bottomless
pit every time we did number one or number two.
I remember the privileges of living in NYC public housing.

Books, My Love

While I was growing up in Farragut, books were my sanctuary. I created a room of my own, as I read my way "to knowing." I took my books with me everywhere: to bed, the bathroom, and the kitchen table.

I did my homework in the kitchen, in the middle of mami cooking *arroz con gandules,* the television blasting, the fire engines blaring, and the cacophony of noise from the Brooklyn-Queens Expressway soaring from below. It was at the kitchen table I learned to focus so well. Today it is where I still do my best work.

As a young girl, I had a voracious appetite for reading. Every week *papi* would take me to the public library in Fort Greene and patiently wait while I selected another stack of books to take home. Mami may not have read me bedtime stories, but I am indebted to her for speaking Spanish at home and making me read *El Diario La Prensa* every day.

On a regular basis I would raid my older cousins' *Scholastic* magazines and bring, as my mother would say, *más papel* home. One day, papi surprised us with a set of the World Book Encyclopedia. I read each volume from cover to cover, including the entire set of children's classics — *Huckleberry Finn, Treasure Island, Robinson Crusoe* and *Robin Hood* — that accompanied it.

Books took me on many unanticipated paths outside the walls of my fourteenth-floor apartment. In the midst of the daily chaos, I found myself. I am grateful to mami and papi for entrusting me with the power of knowledge, and for teaching me the responsibility that comes with knowing.

School Daze

At the suggestion of one of our public school teachers, my mother took my brother, sister, and me out of P.S. 7 in the early sixties. She enrolled us in St.

James when I was in third grade. My first day, I was accompanied by a fellow student to the third grade class. As I walked into the classroom, I was relieved to see some familiar faces. I knew everyone in the room had been taught to write script in the second grade except me. But I hadn't been exposed to script yet, and I didn't want to be found out! I felt so small standing next to my new teacher in all her religious regalia. I stared upward to catch a glimpse of her powerful gaze. She glared down at me with her bright blue eyes. I was overwhelmed by the black veil and the habit she wore as a Sister of Saint Joseph.

Several months later, a Sister monitoring the lunchroom sent a fourth-grade classmate home. When I got home from school that day, around three o'clock, I found a crowd of people circling my building. My classmate's mother was pale with terror. Her little girl had been coerced in the elevator to the fourteenth floor, sexually abused, and thrown off the roof. This was not the first time in the projects that someone's guts had been splattered on the sidewalk — but I knew her, and her mother, and she did not deserve to die for talking too much in the lunchroom that day.

For me, it was just another school day, and I had to carry my books up fourteen flights of stairs reeking of urine.

Silence Begins at Home

Patricia Zavella

MY FAMILY LIVED WITH unspoken tensions. The major one was that my father was *Mexicano,* actually Tejano, while my mother is a Hispana. That makes me the daughter of a mixed heritage. I don't know why it took me so long to figure this out, perhaps because my coming of age occurred during the Chicano Movement, when I proudly proclaimed a Chicana identity and, like many others, looked toward Mexico for cultural affirmation. My own family history was more complicated and based in the United States. As I tried to understand my heritage through oral histories and storytelling, I found a wall of reticence on both sides of the family. And every time I hear the stories again, a new piece of information emerges, so I have changed this *papelito* many times. My process of self-discovery, then, began with archaeology where I had to unearth and piece together the family lore, well aware that there are gaps. I also dredged up my own memories of the past, and found the themes of nostalgia and loss — of my childhood, of closeness with my grandmother, of our homeland — and the importance of seeing the complexity behind people's statements.

On my mother's side, I am fourth generation born in the United States, at least as far as I can figure. My family was originally from northern New Mexico and joined the nineteenth-century migration of *Mexicano* families to southern Colorado, where they settled near Trinidad. My grandmother, Eufracia Abeyta Martínez Archuleta, was born in the valley of Trujillo Creek in southern Colorado in 1908, and my great-grandfather, Francisco Abeyta, was born near Tierra Amarilla, New Mexico, when the region was still Mexico. I think. From my attempts to piece together my grandmother's story, I learned that she was one of fourteen children, with two sets of twins. Grandma married at age fourteen to a good man, much older than she. She is the family

The Zavella children: (l–r) Pat, Day, Mary, Dede, Sally,
Tony at Grandma's house, circa 1957

chronicler, keeping old photo albums that are silent about her childhood or her parents. Grandma does not want to tell any more about her history or contribute to our efforts to find our roots. "My voice sounds funny on the tape," she complains. "It makes me feel old to talk about this," she says, closing off further discussion. "Getting old is awful." Grandma now struggles with health problems, she cannot travel like she used to, and she had to sell her house in Colorado Springs. Grandma has always been proud and self-reliant, often out of necessity.

I ask to hear the story about Grandma's heroic move to the city again and again. My grandfather, Guillermo Martínez, was a farmer, although to make ends meet he also worked as a coal miner. During the Depression all the men were out of work, so when he got paid, my grandfather would buy groceries for several families. Despite the poverty, life was filled with extended family outings and sharing resources. My mom recalls summers as a child on the farm where she, her siblings, and her cousins picked and ate so many cherries that they would get sick. My grandfather died of pneumonia in 1936, when my mother was six years old. The family was devastated. The union contract contained a clause specifying that if a miner died of pneumonia after three bouts, his widow was ineligible for insurance benefits. Thus the union paid hospital and burial expenses, but nothing to the family. Pregnant and trying to support five children by herself, in desperation my grandmother sold the farm to my great-uncle Mike and moved to Colorado Springs. She packed up their belongings in a trailer hitched to the old Model A, loaded in her mother, the five children, the dog, and a neighbor girl who could not bear to be separated from my mother, and drove herself. My great-aunt still has the original family farm.

Almost two decades after Grandma told me her version of this story, I tried to confirm it with my mother, aunts, and uncle, and each added a layer. It turns out that my great-uncle Mike, then living in Colorado Springs, had found Grandma a job and then gone to Aguilar to talk her into moving. She resisted, vehemently, but after weeks of pressure eventually relented. There wasn't much choice. Grandma cried the entire trip to Colorado Springs. My mother explained: "She knew things were really tough. Sometimes, all we had to eat was oatmeal three times a day." Grandma applied for welfare. My mother recalls with indignation how the family of six received a mere thirty-five dollars a month. Even so, they were subject to unannounced visits by the *gringa* social worker, who asked the children if they had enough food to eat and shoes to wear. "So she *had* to go," my uncle recalls. After she took the job, Grandma sent back the last welfare payment and then began the trek to the big city with her children.

Actually, Colorado Springs at that time was a small town, one where Mexican Americans were a minority, and there were occasional signs posted in local businesses that announced "No dogs or Mexicans." My aunt recalled that a group of "Spanish boys," working in the Depression program Conservation Corps, came into town one day and tore up the signs. "But the feelings remained. There were some places where they wouldn't serve you."

Grandma worked at various jobs to support her children. During World War II she worked in a factory on the graveyard shift so she could be home in the mornings to send her three daughters and two sons to school. "I spent most of my time trying to stay awake," she laughed as she recalled. When the manager heard that she had a sick mother and so many kids (tragically, her youngest had died), he allowed her to arrive late or to miss work when necessary. "It was much better then." Somehow Grandma managed to purchase her small house on the edge of town, near the railroad tracks. One of her proudest accomplishments is that all five of her children graduated from Catholic schools. With the help of occasional employment by the older children, the family never experienced the shame of welfare again.

While my grandmother will tell tidbits about overcoming adversity, she will not reveal any stories about our heritage. I vaguely recall hearing the story about my grandfather, who apparently had been raised for a while by Indians. One day, he and a friend were walking when they saw a group of Indian men, who they feared would kill them. My grandfather and his friend hid in the lake, using reeds to breathe, and avoided capture. When I asked my grandmother about this story recently, she looked away and declined any further

discussion. My historian friend Ramón Gutiérrez tells me that Tierra Amarilla, where my great-grandfather was born, is a Genízaro settlement, originally a village of displaced Indians, probably Pueblo or perhaps Navajo. I
wonder if my grandmother's silence protects us from learning about our Indian past, or if her parents protected her from such knowledge. Grandma also
does not say much about her own childhood on the farm. The family was
poor: of fourteen children, only six survived. I'm sure there were many hardships that she does not want to remember.

My mother, Isabel Aurora Martínez Zavella Schnebelen, had been the
spoiled child. Born premature in Delagua, a mining camp near Aguilar, Colorado, during the Depression, she was so small and motionless they thought she
was stillborn. My great-grandmother set her near the wood-burning stove.
The baby stirred, alive, and she was cherished thereafter. My mother was
devoted to her grandmother. After they had moved to Colorado Springs, my
great-grandmother had a stroke and needed help for walking and bathing.
Mom attended her every need, was spared the regular female chores, and never
learned to cook. Great-grandmother Feliciana Muñíz was an assertive woman,
who, even though bedridden, would demand that her grandchildren speak
Spanish in the home. My mother recalls that if they spoke English, Grandma
Feliciana would worry that they were talking about her. She wouldn't allow
them to sing songs in English either: *"Canten estas canciones en la escuela, no en
la casa,"* she would lecture them. Shy and self-effacing, my mother has a quiet
strength and occasional spunk. She tells the story of standing up for herself at
Catholic shool: "I hated the nuns. I once told one — she was a mean old lady —
'I'm not here to serve as your penance!' " Working as a salesclerk at Kress, my
mother met my father, who was stationed at the local air base. Good Catholic
that she is, my mother eventually had twelve children.

About my paternal relatives there is even more silence. My father, Antonio
Abram Zavella, was born in Laredo, Texas, a border town. His parents, from
Nuevo Laredo across the river in Mexico, died when he was a child and he was
raised by an older sister. Thus we never knew our paternal grandparents and
did not meet most of my father's relatives until his funeral, when I was an
adult. The story goes that my father was a troubled child, thrown out of a
series of schools until he was sixteen; then he lied about his age and joined the
Air Force. The white intake clerk misspelled his name, changing it from Zavala
to Zavella, informing him, "Now you're Italian." My father never returned to
his given name, for, as he explained to my brother, "Things were tough in
Texas." All of my relatives on his side are Zavalas — we are the only Zavellas.
Over time, in the course of setting up his own small television repair business,
my father would create several pseudonyms. Sevilla, with a Spanish tinge, was
his favorite, hinting at unspoken shame for being Mexican.

Because the Air Force transferred my father a lot, our family made year-long forays into other states—Florida (twice), where I was born, Maine, South Dakota (twice), and eventually southern California—punctuated by long stays with Grandma. Grandma being the matriarch of our extended family, her house was a home base for all the relatives who left the area. We all have nostalgic memories of picnics in the Garden of the Gods or Pike's Peak, snowy winters, and Grandma's old house.

Grandma's place was a wonder, resplendent. She had a small wood frame house and detached garage that she converted into a cottage where we stayed, surrounded by flowers and trees, with a vegetable garden and huge strawberry patch in the back. Grandma loved hollyhocks, morning glories, gladiolas, dahlias, succulents, and, like most Mexican women, roses. I grow these flowers now myself to honor her. She kept a small red wooden chair reserved for the youngest grandchild. A number of us claimed it as "my chair," as over the years we all were enthroned there at some point. I, too, keep a chair for the grandchildren, only I will have to wait for mine. Grandma's home was always immaculate, filled to overflowing with knickknacks, stacks of *Good Housekeeping* magazines, hanging photographs, and materials for her endless hobbies.

Grandma is a whiz at making things—crocheted doilies, embroidered linens, Christmas ornaments, wall hangings, household decorations. She made matching outfits for my sisters and me, sewn on her treadle-driven machine. Her work is always ornate and beautiful; it is amazing what her arthritic hands make out of some modest ribbons and threads. Somehow we got a television early on, with a small screen. She would never just sit and watch TV but was always busy, and, when sewing or embroidering at night, would stick out her tongue slightly in concentration. And, despite her concentration on her work, she kept a sharp eye on us, immediately noticing any infraction of decorum.

There were fascinating things to get into at Grandma's house: perfumes, makeup, bubble baths. We celebrated our femininity, creating curly hair with bobby pins or rag curlers my mother made, which prodded our long hair into ringlets. I loved watching my mother and grandmother dress up for special occasions, usually for church. In my mind's eye, I can see my mother dressed up for a special air base dance in a strapless pale blue chiffon gown. Sometimes we got to play dress up ourselves, parading around in high heels, long dresses, and beads.

When she was in an expansive mood, Grandma would show us her china cabinet—filled with exquisite crystal vases and company dishes. Whenever the women pulled out the dessert bowls, I would draw conclusions—"We're going to eat good tonight"—and the adults would chuckle. Grandma would make big batches of *atole* or bread pudding, the smell of cinnamon wafting throughout the kitchen.

"Grandma, what are you making?"

"*Puntos,*" she said as she chuckled.

"Yay, Grandma's making *puntos!*"

I would run to tell my sisters in excitement. It was some time before my mother informed me that *puntos* meant that Grandma was scoring points with her grandchildren. Her other pride and joy was the big wooden bureau that contained all the lace doilies, tablecloths, and pillowcases she had made. On top of the bureau she kept her saints—a huge statue of the Sacred Heart, to whom she had a special devotion, and The Blessed Virgin, all demure in pale blue. St. Anthony, patron saint of lost souls, was another favorite. She would sometimes turn his statue around and scold when something was missing until he helped her find it.

The Spanish language was one of the earliest conflicts between my parents. They were native Spanish-speakers as children but became fluent in English once they enrolled in school. My mother tells the story of her own language repression: "The nuns rinsed my mouth out with soap for speaking Spanish on the school grounds." Her voice still breaks when she recalls this bitter experience. My father claimed that Mom did not know how to speak proper Spanish. He teased her about the way she pronounced words and her growing inability to remember Spanish after so many years of speaking English. Being raised in Colorado Springs, she did speak differently from my father. He rolled his *r*s in an exaggerated way, and in English had a barely perceptible South Texas twang. My mother and her kin softened the *r*s, close to dropping them, and their pronunciation of Spanish almost sounded Anglicized. It was only as an adult, surrounded by Archuletas, Vigiles, and Martínezes, that I realized this was a regional difference. To halt my father's badgering, my mother stopped speaking Spanish at all, except with my grandmother and adult relatives. This lapse in Spanish was not particular to our family. All of our cousins grew up as English-speakers.

Our lack of Spanish was a sore point with my father. One day when he was in one of his drunken reveries, he made us children line up and demanded that we sing the Mexican national anthem. He began teaching us the words. After much coaching and correction of our pronunciation, we managed to finish the first stanza. We were losing interest, however, because we did not understand the words. He began to tease us—how could we be Mexicans and not know the Mexican national anthem? We glanced at one another, wondering ourselves. We had never been to Mexico. We had no relatives there; none of my aunts or uncles had ever been there, that I knew of, and no one talked about it. Like other American children raised in the fifties, I had only television stereotypes of Mexico as a far-away country, with sombrero-wearing bandidos, cactus, and a blazing sun, a place remote from my life.

Spanish was the language of adults, reserved for secrets, scandals, gossip, and the ritual of daily greetings. All the grandchildren were teased for not speaking Spanish or not pronouncing correctly what we did say. "They sound like *gringuitos*," my aunt would complain. (Later I found out that, born in Colorado, she had learned English as her first language as well.) We cousins would shrug to each other, acknowledging our generational difference from the grown-ups. How were we supposed to learn if our parents didn't teach us?

However, I learned to pay attention whenever Spanish was spoken, quietly pretending to play when the adults were talking. I recall my aunt once saying, "They wouldn't let us into the swimming pool because we were Mexican." I could hear the hurt and shame in her voice as the adults glanced my way and then began speaking in Spanish. We children were protected from such matters. There were no overt lessons about how to confront such discrimination ourselves. It would take a nationalist political movement for me to feel the power of collective anger over such outrage.

When we were away from Grandma's house, our family centered on my father, who was witty and loved telling jokes or fooling people. He was an intelligent man, an electronics technician with some college education, who liked poetry, photography, fast cars, flying, wrestling. He had a passion for music, somber Mexican mainly, Agustín Lara or Toña la Negra, or manic jazz (John Coltrane), which he played over and over again and drove us crazy. He always dressed impeccably, clean cut, in starched white shirts that had to be ironed perfectly, dark dress pants, and polished shoes, often a tie and sports jacket. He was a handsome man with shiny, curly black hair, chocolate-colored skin, a slight paunch, and strong muscles.

My father was very *Mexicano* and military. It was a volatile combination. He would not teach my mother to drive nor permit her to work outside the home, even if there had been someone to care for the children. My mother made every effort to soothe him, feed him, and take care of him. My father instilled in us a clear sense that we were supposed to show him our respect, attending immediately to any of his requests. Responsibilities—making a military bed and helping clean up—were imposed on us at a young age. As part of his regimentation, he would number us children. As the oldest, I was Number One. "Number One, bring me a glass of water. Number Two: my glasses. Number Three, where's the paper?" It was my responsibility to keep my siblings out of harm, but I found this out the hard way. When I was about five, my parents and I were sitting downstairs, watching television, when my sister started screaming. We rushed upstairs to find her in the bath with shampoo burning her eyes. But it was I who got in trouble, since I had not been watching her.

I became adept at trying to avoid trouble, especially if my father had been drinking. As soon as a child would start crying he would yell, "Shut that kid up!" So to avoid getting in trouble myself, I would jump up at the first whimpers of my siblings. (I still wince when I hear babies crying in public.) We were supposed to be quiet and disappear when he no longer needed anything. Especially when he was drinking, he would start arguments with my mother, exploding in curses in English and Spanish, shocking us. We were never allowed to use such language, and indeed we were supposed to be as still as possible. He often admonished us, "children are to be seen and not heard," and his favorite dismissal was "beat it." In the midst of his silencing, I became an observer and learned to assess situations: was he drunk, in a bad mood? How could I avoid trouble? How could I keep things under control?

Early on I was taught the importance of keeping busy. I was an energetic child, rambunctious and easily bored, and sometimes I would tease my sisters just for the diversion. My mother was always trying to keep me occupied: "Patsy, why don't you run around the house," she would suggest, and I would return in a flash. "Run around the house ten times." "I did." "Are you sure that was ten? Well, run around some more."

More often than not there were chores to keep me busy. As I got older the responsibilities grew heavier and I became like a second mother to the youngest children.

Despite the strict discipline, when we stayed with Grandma life was idyllic for us. I recall lying in bed in the mornings, half-asleep in the soft, filtered sunlight, listening to my mother and grandmother begin their day.

"*Buenos días.*"

"*Buenos días.*"

"*¿Cómo amaneció?*"

"*Bien, ¿y tú?*"

"*Pues bien, gracias a Dios.*"

The odor of freshly made tortillas, coffee, and bacon would beckon us up the stairs into Grandma's warm kitchen. Breakfast always included tearing off big chunks of tortillas and spreading on butter and homemade strawberry jam. Grandma's tortillas were famous, large and so thick you could peel them and create a pocket for fillings, delicious plain, hot off the griddle. Her pale green kitchen was the center of the house, holding interesting things like teapots on the shelf near the window, a mess of potted plants near the back porch, or the big clay *toro* bank that my uncle smashed when it filled up with pennies.

This nostalgic reminiscence is the one I want to remember about Grandma's house, not the one of being left in charge of my siblings for a short time when I was five, feeling scared and alone. I much prefer the sunlit version and so does Grandma. After reading a draft of my story about her house, she wrote to thank me. "I sure enjoyed the story. I laughed and I cried and remembered how much I enjoyed having you girls and your Mom with me even though we didn't have much money. But I guess we were happy."

As a young child I hadn't realized that we were poor, probably because we had such rich rituals. Grandma is a devout woman and the Church was a refuge from any problem. She attends Catholic mass every Sunday and Holy Day of Obligation, often goes to church to pray rosaries during Lent or to attend novenas. We prayed before meals and before going to sleep. Since I was the oldest, Grandma often took me to church with her. I knew I must wear my finest clothes, present a ladylike demeanor, and remain perfectly still during the mass. If I occasionally strayed from her etiquette, she would pinch my arm, her tongue sticking out the side of her mouth. Grandma was quite fashionable, wearing dresses she made herself, often a hat with a veil, matching earrings and beads, high heels, and white gloves. No little old lady in black for her! I learned that deportment, dignified public presentation, was important. When I got older my mother would lecture: "We might be poor, but when you go out, you wear clothes that are clean and neatly pressed."

Now whenever my partner, children, and I travel we always visit the Catholic churches. Despite being a lapsed Catholic, whenever I'm with my mother or grandmother, I attend mass without question. I savor the beauty of churches, with their soothing stained glass windows, flower arrangements that mark the seasons, long white candles, musty incense, cool holy water, majestic robes and lovely linens. I love the cadence of rosaries, the serene voices of high masses, the solitude of praying in a church, the comfort of fellowship with other parishioners. Churches remind me of Grandma.

Grandma sometimes worked as a housekeeper for white women. Some days she would come home tired and grumpy, talking about *las gringas* who were stingy and picky about her work. Since they couldn't pronounce her name, Eufracia, they called her "Flossy" or "Frances." Grandma spoke flawless English but some of her employers patronized her. Grandma mimicked their voices: "Now *Flossy*, do it this way." One Jewish woman in particular demanded that Grandma keep separate the meat and milk dishes. In silent revenge for her mistreatment, Grandma took control when the mistress was out of sight. "In the kitchen I do what I want. What does it matter if the dishes are mixed?" Grandma could rationalize her behavior since they were Jews and did not believe in Christ, and they treated her badly.

At other times she told stories about standing up to those who tried to swindle or intimidate her. At one point, a phone salesman kept calling, asking for Mr. Archuleta. Each time Grandma fibbed and said he wasn't home, because she didn't want the salesman to know she was alone. Finally she became exasperated with his harassment and put a piercing noise device on the phone. He never called again. Although Grandma is short and petite, we all knew that no one scared her and there was nothing she couldn't do. Paint the garage, lay linoleum in the living room, use a power saw to make something, speak up for her rights — these were part of her repertoire of skills. Of course I admired her.

Once enrolled in school, I came to love it. Because of our many moves, we had to pack up our belongings again and again. We were always the new kids in places where there were very few Mexicans. I recall the third grade in New Underwood, South Dakota, where, after the first spelling test, which I aced as usual, the teacher suddenly became very friendly. "You're so different from the other Mexicans." She smiled patronizingly. I looked around. The only other Mexican was an ugly boy with buckteeth and a crew cut. I looked at him with leery eyes — why would she compare me to him? I realized that she assumed that Mexicans were dumb and had not expected me to perform well. Despite her odd comment, I was pleased with her praise and resolved to show her I could perform well consistently. I heard a variant of this loaded statement many times during the first weeks at a new school. The sting never lasted long, however, and I often would become the "teacher's pet." Hand out papers, dust the blackboard, whatever little chore the teacher had, I did willingly. I was excited about school, loved to read, always wanted to learn more.

The third grade was also when I learned that being different would open us up to merciless taunting. We had just moved to New Underwood and I had one friend at school, Randy Rakes, someone I knew from the air base in Rapid City when we had lived there. Randy and I picked up our games from the past. One day I was chasing him furiously when I was surrounded by a crowd of young, freckled-faced toughs.

"Leave him alone, nigger. Leave him alone or we'll beat you up."

"Yeah, stop chasing him."

"*Nigger.*"

I stopped dead in my tracks, curious and afraid. Why were they calling me that bad word? Why didn't Randy say anything? I explained that he was my friend and we were just playing. They were not impressed. The playground became a lonely place where I cautiously stayed near my sisters, fearful of more insults or worse.

It was time for my mother to deliver her seventh child. She hoped for a boy. Five girls and one son was not enough for my father. He wanted more sons. Mom left at night for Rapid City, far away. I was in charge, nine years old, but well-prepared. I stayed home from school since we could not count on my father. We lived on Main Street, and across the street was the only bar, open even during the day. My father spent a lot of time there. While Mom was at the hospital, he rarely came home.

I knew how to cook, simple fare anyway — oatmeal, scrambled eggs — and I already did housework and watched the babies. The youngest was only a year and a half. After the kids returned from school we would play hide-and-seek among the tall weeds in the back yard or jump off the shed roof. My mother wasn't there to stop us.

One day while Mom was gone I started to fry some potatoes for lunch. I put the oil in the frying pan and then left. When I came back the oil was smoking. I ran and turned off the stove and put a lid on the skillet. Then I rounded up the kids and took them outside, like the fire drills we had learned at school. When the smoke did not turn into fire, I went inside and carefully got a pot holder and dumped the oil. I was so scared. What if I had burned down the house? What if my brother and sisters had been burned? I would have never forgiven myself. Should I send someone to get my father? The kids were so young, they didn't really understand the danger. I let them go back inside while I cleaned up. They were hungry so I had to heat the skillet once again to make their lunch. When Mom came home I told her the story. She clucked with worry. "You did good, *m'ija.*" The next week I returned to school. The nice *gringa* teacher didn't believe that I had stayed home to take care of my siblings. "But you're so young!" she exclaimed. I got embarrassed, realizing I should not have shared this family secret.

As I got older, I learned to retreat from all the responsibilities. I would get lost in books. Each week I would walk to the library and return with a stack of books that I pored through. I remember reading *Redbook Magazine,* articles about Margaret Mead in the South Seas. The attraction of traveling seemed so removed from my daily life — I was drawn to the exotic. I had become a quiet child, timid and bookish, set on the path of becoming a scholarship girl.

My accomplishments became a source of pride at home. My father noticed my good grades and teased me with the nickname "the brain." This was a decidedly mixed blessing for a girl in a family that eventually would include six sisters who were praised by my aunt for their beauty and charm. While all of us were clever, I was different, the one who got top grades. Meanwhile I envied the little white girls who wore lace and ruffles, and I desperately wanted to fit in at school.

One evening after he had been drinking, my father sat me down. He promised to give me a dollar for every A I got on my report card. Nice challenge, not too hard. Several months later I proudly handed him my report card with fifteen A's. He wasn't impressed. Why didn't I get straight A's? I was going to have to work harder. He never paid up. I realized that only perfection would be good enough, and in school, at least, I came as close to perfection as possible. A few months later my father sat me down again and said he didn't want me to get married until I was twenty-five and he wanted me to be a scientist. Since he had been drinking, I did not take his words seriously and certainly did not see myself as a scientist in the making. But to quiet him I agreed.

We were stranded in the middle of the desolate prairie in cowboy country.

Weeks passed, and we hadn't heard from my father. He had left the Air Force and had gone to California in search of work. My mother and we seven children, my youngest brother an infant, were to follow as soon as possible. We yearned for the land of sunshine and palm trees that my father painted in his letters. Mom grew more irritable as the weeks passed, and we didn't know when we were leaving. Finally she received word. We were to take the bus to Colorado Springs, where my father would meet us and drive us to California. It was the dead of winter. We packed up all of our belongings. The beautiful china that my father had brought from Korea, our toys and photo albums — these we stored with Randy's parents, our only friends in New Underwood. Our plan was to return some day and pick up our boxes of treasures. We never did. Years later we heard that the Rakes had moved to Alaska, and we never found out what happened to our stuff. My mother has very few family pictures or mementos of our childhood.

The trip was exciting. Since we children could only carry one small package apiece, we had to leave our cherished dolls. I carried a lunch pail filled with crayons and pencils, and my sister had a packet of coloring books and tablets. We all bundled up in our best coats and mittens. The novelty soon wore off as mile after mile of snow-covered expanse passed by. The bus occasionally stopped at other small towns, and we would all troop to the bathroom and maybe get a snack at one of the counters. The fellow travelers were very kind to us. "How many children do you have?" they would ask incredulously, as they helped my mother herd us back onto the bus. We were used to that; sometimes while riding in our station wagon, we kids would hold up fingers to passersby as they counted heads.

We arrived in Colorado Springs after dark, a light snow obscuring the way. Mom got the bus driver to let us off near Grandma's house instead of going all the way downtown. We had to walk only a few blocks. I had someone's hand, Mom was shooing along several others, my sister was holding the baby. She started off in the wrong direction and soon slipped on the ice. We all rushed to help. After more slipping and whining, we finally got the whole crowd turned in the right direction. We knocked on Grandma's door, our visit a surprise. She gasped and said over and over, "Why didn't you let me know? Why didn't you call me?" She immediately set to work, getting our coats off and warming up food. We were home, surrounded by family, where we were loved and nurtured. Even though we never got to stay for long, each visit at Grandma's house was a blessed respite.

You Speak Spanish Because You Are Jewish?

Rina Benmayor

Mi padre era de Grecia	My father came from Greece
mi madre de Nueva York	my mother from New York
se casaron enĝiuntos	they married each other
para que naciera yo.	and so I was born.

take-off on a fifteenth-century Judeo-Spanish ballad

WHEN PEOPLE HEAR ME speaking Spanish they often ask me, "Where are you from?" I used to hate that question because the only way I could answer was with a complicated story that seemed to leave people more confused than ever. But I love the story, so I have learned to tell it, in versions long or short.

I am one hundred percent Sephardic, a Spanish Jew *por los cuatro costados,* according to history, via Spain ("Sepharad"), the Ottoman Empire (today Northern Greece and Turkey), and, more recently, New York. I have lived my own migrations too, *mis propias vueltas por este mundo:* from New York to Mexico City, to California, back to New York, back to California, with long retours and detours through the Spanish-speaking world—Spain, Mexico, Cuba, Puerto Rico. A "wandering Jew?" Perhaps, but the epithet doesn't quite fit.

My parents' home language, and that of our *ancestors,* is Ladino, a dialect of fifteenth-century Castilian Spanish, lexically peppered with Turkish and Hebrew, with sounds that resemble Portuguese. It is a language preserved in exile and diaspora for five hundred years, understandable to any modern Spanish speaker. When they met in New York, the only common language my parents had was Ladino, "our Spanish." For my Nona (the Sephardic term for grandmother) and all the aunts and uncles of her generation, it was their mother tongue, although through cultural contact, education, and migrations, they also spoke Greek, Turkish, Bulgarian, French, Italian, and, later, English.

A language story often gets told at family gatherings. My father has a cousin who witnessed the Nazis round up and deport her entire family, right before her very eyes. She was left behind, through one of those historical accidents that frequently occurred in that part of the world, where ethnicity and nationality are not a complete match. Her husband's family held Italian citizenship,

Rina and Raymond Benmayor,
Mexico City, 1953

although they had never set foot in Italy. And so they were spared. The story recalls their journey across the Atlantic, on their way to New York in 1951, and it goes this way:

> One day, a passenger approached us. He was an English colonel, the starchy kind, and he asked:
> "Where are you coming from?"
> "We are coming from Greece," we said.
> "Oh, you are Greeks?"
> "No, we are not Greeks, we are Italians."
> "Oh, is this Italian you are speaking?"
> "No, we are speaking Spanish."
> "But how come you are speaking Spanish?"
> "Because we are Jewish!"
> "You are from Greece but you are Italians? You are speaking Spanish because you are Jewish? This is too much for me!"

A language story, a migration story, a story about cultural survival, about racism, a genealogy of empowerment.

At the age of seven and a half I began to acquire a language story of my own. I became bilingual. Somehow, my father got the opportunity to work in Mexico City, mass-producing plaster statuettes. Fed up with New York winters, he moved my mother, brother, and me to Mexico, where I attended bilingual schools. By age ten or eleven I considered myself a most proficient translator —

of Nancy Drew mysteries! Those *papelitos* are still among my secret treasures. Several years ago, at a Library of Congress forum on E. D. Hirsch's *Cultural Literacy: What Every American Needs to Know*, I spoke about the meaning of growing up bilingual in another country. I noted how different my experience was from that of Mexican and other Latino children whose families migrate to the United States. For in Mexico, my first language, English, had the value of cultural asset rather than deficit. I went to schools where Spanish was the majority language of instruction, but English was also part of the daily curriculum for everyone. Thus I was saved from the trauma of educational racism. Besides, I added, coming from the family that I do, the mere idea of English Only, of monoculturalism, runs sharply against the grain. The history of Sephardic Jews in the Ottoman Empire is, among other things, a fascinating case study in cosmopolitan cultural contact, multilingualism, and cultural retention.

When I was twelve, my mother and I left Mexico City and embarked on a long bus ride back to California, where my grandparents had since retired. Attempting to overcome a difficult marriage and the tragic accidental death of my brother, my mother became a single parent and I an only child. She worked as a secretary, the career for which many a garment worker's daughter had trained. I slowly worked back into English and regained my accent, but Spanish kept me connected to my unusual childhood. It allowed me to remember. I could have made a small fortune in high school for all the Spanish homework I did for friends.

Somewhere in college, I lost my tongue. As an undergraduate at Berkeley, I took a sociology class taught by a visiting Argentinian whose English was impossible to understand. I remember going to ask him to explain the material to me in Spanish. There I was in this man's office, paralyzed and mute. I couldn't access the language I was claiming to understand. It wasn't until graduate school, while going for my fallback teaching credential—the profession that every daughter of a secretary trains for just in case—that I regained the language of my childhood and reconnected to my family heritage. It took only one semester of Spanish grammar and literature courses for me to abandon the notion of teaching in high school and to enter, instead, the doctoral program in Spanish literature.

Graduate school was also where my political identity matured. As a Berkeley student in the sixties, I witnessed the Free Speech Movement, protested the war in Vietnam, and fought for the introduction of an Ethnic Studies major on campus. I was not Chicana, but I understood that cultural identities, allegiances, and alliances could be built on more than just blood heritage. I understood something about the deep cultural connections that can come through language; I understood something about social class; and I understood something about crossing borders. And it was graduate school as well where my cultural, intellectual, and professional identities came together. To this day, I encourage my students to make those connections for themselves. I remember the power of the moment when your past and present "click" into place. My watershed moment happened one day in the Survey of Spanish Literature class. The professor walked in with a tape recorder and began to play *romances,* medieval Spanish ballads, sung a capella by elderly Sephardic women to Middle Eastern melodies. He proceeded to explain that these songs had been recorded in the late 1950s, in Los Angeles! I knew then and there that I would go back into my community to collect these songs and that I would write my doctoral dissertation on this ancestral ballad tradition.

I gathered my own collection of Sephardic ballads in the 1970s, lugging my tape recorder from house to house of elderly Sephardim in Los Angeles and Seattle. I related my texts to a rich and well-documented Spanish ballad tradition; I examined the cultural meanings of Sephardic interpretations of medieval Spanish texts; and I straddled the fields of literary study, folklore, and ethnographic practice. But that was just the beginning of a life merging disciplines, geographies, and cultural borders. Later on in my professional career as a professor of Spanish and Portuguese, I migrated from Spanish literature and Sephardic ballads to *trovadores* of the "new song" movement in Cuba, and then from narratives in song to life-story accounts of Puerto Rican women in New York. The latest phase of my migrations has been from *testimonios* of women's empowerment in *El Barrio* (where my mother was also born and raised) to pedagogies of empowerment in my classrooms, as a professor of oral history and literature at California State University Monterey Bay.

I don't know about the "wandering Jew." Each migration seems more like a coming home, like pulling through the weft of language and culture and looping it back over the warp of this life in the making. I live and work in U.S. Latino, Latin American, Caribbean, and Hispanic cultures, so what kind of a Latina am I? My short answer goes something like this:

> Spanish speakers who meet me frequently ask, "Where are you from?" expecting me to name a nationality. They are puzzled because they can't quite place my accent. It is native, but it isn't Puerto Rican, it isn't Cuban, and after all these years of cultural contact it is no longer clearly *mexicano.*
>
> "I'm from here," I usually reply, meaning the United States.
>
> "But, where are your parents from?" they insist, perceiving difference and fishing for a country of origin.
>
> "Well, it's a long story," I laugh. "I was born in New York; I lived in Mexico for several years as a child; my family is Sephardic [I add "Spanish-Jewish" if I sense that an explanation is needed], I used to teach Spanish and have worked in Latino communities for many years."

"Oh, your parents are Mexican, then," they reply, in desperate need of a signifying national identity.

"No, my father was born and raised in Greece and my mother in Harlem, of Greek Sephardic parents, also." By this time, I have either thoroughly confused them or piqued their curiosity.

"O ¡interesante!" they reply, and I remember the starchy English colonel.

Getting There *Cuando No Hay Camino*

Norma E. Cantú

IT'S ALWAYS DIFFICULT to start at the beginning, for it is often difficult to locate a beginning. I can't truly say exactly when it was that I decided to be a professor, to be a writer, to be an administrator, to be a folklorist, to be a literacy tutor trainer and tutor, to be a poet, or to be any of the myriad of persons that I am. It's far easier to trace how I came to be a daughter, a sister, or any of the various relationships that required no choice, at least not one that I can take credit for.

Given that I did not know a single person with a Ph.D. when I graduated from high school, I find it quite remarkable that I earned one. Graduation from high school began a long process that culminated in a Ph.D. As a Chicana getting a Ph.D. in English in 1982, at a time when it was unusual enough for any of us to graduate from high school, I felt privileged. What an achievement that was for someone like me. There were no maps to follow; the path was not well trodden. No one in my family, indeed no one from my neighborhood or my barrio community, had traveled that path before; only a precious few had earned a high school diploma.

On a day in late May 1965, I graduated from Martin High School in Laredo, Texas. Graduation night. My parents and my aunt cram into the too-small Martin High School gymnasium to see me walk across the stage. That hot humid night I received a high school diploma, which they and I thought was the highest possible attainment for the oldest daughter of eleven children of a working-class family that often worked in the nearby fields when the smelter laid off laborers like my dad. I received two surprises that night: one my best friend Berta had hinted at, a gold seal on the diploma from the National Honor Society; and the other a much more important one, a college tuition scholarship. I had given up hope of receiving any scholarship money after Ms. Contreras, the senior class counselor, had indicated that I should go work for the telephone company. When I had gone to request the scholarship application forms, she had made it clear that I couldn't possibly expect to go to college, even after my college entrance examination scores had come back not half as bad as I'd feared. When I saw the commencement program, with my name listed as recipient of a tuition scholarship to Laredo Junior College (LJC), I felt tingly all over, and even forgot the one-inch-heel pumps pinching my toes. When they announced the Rotary International scholarships, I was called up to the stage to receive the document that I thought was my lifesaver. I was near tears and ruined the photo the professional photographer snapped with my *muecas*. In fact, several times during the ceremony I actually did shed tears; I surreptitiously wiped them with the edge of the robe that felt as hot as wool in that non-air-conditioned gym that May evening.

It was 1965. The Vietnam War raged on and President Lyndon Johnson had just launched the War on Poverty. Laredo became one of the main battlefields in the antipoverty war. So we had opportunities, at least those of us who were receiving government surplus commodities did. *"El queso,"* as my father called it, helped get us by. Although we always received more than just cheese — cornmeal we never used, flour, butter, beans, and canned beef and chicken that my mother fixed with a spicy sauce and even used for tamales during the Christmas season — everyone called it *el queso*. We didn't receive everything every time; usually there were surprises, dried prunes, or peanut butter, raisins or cans of corn. One of the programs designed to battle poverty, the Neighborhood Youth Corps, offered me my first full-time job as an assistant clerk at the Laredo Independent School District personnel office. My duties were to file and fill out index cards for the district's employee files. I was eighteen and anxious to start college. It was tedious work that gave me time to dream and compose poems which I memorized and later wrote down. But after barely a month I was reassigned as a teacher's aide at my old elementary school, Don Tomás Sánchez. There I was under the expert tutelage of Mrs. Adelina García. She soon became my mentor. I wanted to be a teacher, had wanted it since the summer after seventh grade, when I started my own *escuelita* in our backyard. I loved my job. In the fall I would start college and earn my degree and become a teacher. It seemed so easy.

At the time, I was also being courted by a lanky dark doe-eyed boy who waited until I got out of my job and walked me home sometimes. So I knew happiness. But that summer was over too soon and not soon enough. My "boyfriend" and I didn't go too far *con el noviazgo*. I couldn't get phone calls from boys. Besides, he was still in high school, although he was older than I. When my summer job ended and I went on to college, I could only see him in church. Predictably, things deteriorated. I remember his khaki pants, scuffed brown shoes, and the white cotton short-sleeved starched shirt he wore like a uniform whether he was going to church or to school.

The end of the summer of 1965 brought the end of my first job and my first romance. It marked the beginning of a new life. My mother and I had bought fabric to make my skirts and blouses for school. We also copied some preppie dresses from a magazine — could it have been the issue of *Seventeen* that Berta and I bought at Statler's on Matamoros Street? Statler's. The only newsstand and the closest thing to a bookstore we had in Laredo at the time. One of our favorite downtown hangouts. In the early sixties, going to *el centro* meant taking the bus to a downtown bustling with the business of a border town. Shoppers from Nuevo Laredo added to the hustle and bustle of the Laredo business community. *La gente* went *al centro* to pay utility bills, shop at J.C. Penney's and Sears. The five-and-ten stores, Kress, Neisner's, McClelland all clustered on Convent Avenue, the main thoroughfare to and from Mexico. Berta and I discovered a dusty old bookstore that sold used books and old magazines and *revistas* situated across from Richter's El Precio Fijo. It was on the same side of the street where Polly Adams sold designer clothes and Hollo-way's bakery sold cream puffs, not just *pan dulce* as did La Reynera or El Aguila bakeries. Berta and I loved to walk downtown and stop at Deliganis Cafeteria for lunch. We felt grown up on our own downtown on a Saturday morning.

Although a year younger, Berta and I were the closest of friends, bound by a love of reading and of words. All through high school we shared the secrets of our crushes and our life's dreams. We belonged to the Pan American Student Forum where we served as officers my senior year; we worked with the school paper, *The Journal*. Both of us were members of the select CSC — the Courtesy Service Club — that glorified service and allowed us to be ushers during foot-ball games, as well as PTA and open-house events.

That fall I began classes at Laredo Junior College. On the first day my friend Velma Morán picked me up with one of her older sisters who knew all about college and advised us to be *bien truchas* and register as early as possible so that classes wouldn't be closed. As we arrived to register we went in different directions because the process was alphabetically arranged. Holding onto my precious scholarship letter, first I went into the "Corral," as the student center was called. Here professors were seated behind folding tables filling in names of students, as they came up to register, in long ledgers that were class rolls. They handed you an index card — different colors for the different classes — that you would then turn in to your professor. I waited in line to register for the basic first-year courses: composition and rhetoric, political science, his-tory, algebra, and French. I had wanted to take chemistry, but the class was closed. I refused to sign up for biology like all my other friends because I had heard that you were required to collect insects, a task I knew I could never complete. The first semester went by too quickly, and although I didn't make the dean's list, I felt proud of my A's, B's and even the C I struggled to get in French—I refused to take Spanish like everyone else because I felt I already knew it and couldn't see the point—even though it would've meant an easy A. I did finally catch on that I needed to devote more time to the French class, and the next semester I improved my grade considerably.

In the second semester I applied for and was hired in some kind of work-study program. It wasn't much, but it helped me buy shoes, bus tickets, and a more substantial lunch than a Baby Ruth candy bar. My parents were unable to help with even these minimal expenses. Books were always a problem, and often I went through a whole semester borrowing and making do without a textbook. It became difficult to get rides from Velma because of my job, though. So I would walk. Mornings, I'd get off the bus at the corner of Convent and Victoria and walk along orange tree-lined Victoria Street, past the Laredo Independent School District offices, where I had worked, past the Victorian mansions, past the railroad tracks and onto the campus, the abandoned Fort McIntosh. I'd sit in old Army barracks turned classrooms—the potbellied stove in the middle of the room and the cigarette burns along the wall attested to the earlier inhabitants. I worked in the library housed in the Fort's old chapel; the musty smells of religion and books greeted and comforted me. Reading and thinking—exactly what college was supposed to be! I overlooked the racist history lessons and the condescending sexist male professors. I pretended all was right with the world even after a crying incident in speech class because I could not distinguish between "kiss" and "keys."

But too soon—in fact, the following year—I see that I must quit. The poverty at home becomes unbearable; I cannot see myself selfishly sitting in a classroom while my siblings need things—shoes, clothes, food, school bus tickets. My family's needs become greater than my own. So I get a full-time job at Central Power and Light Company, forget my dreams of getting a degree, of going out of town to finish college, of becoming a teacher. My college friends apply, get accepted, leave for universities in Denton, Houston, Austin, San Antonio, San Marcos, Kingsville, while I stay behind and cry everyday sitting at the typewriter where I must use carbon paper to make multicolored copies of the records of new electricity connections and disconnections. I'm a clerk so I also cashier at the drivethrough window. Soon I am promoted, fill in for anyone who's sick or on vacation, learning all the "desks," even the contract one where Ted O'Neil sits. My mentor who has trained me at the office, Vicente, commits suicide one Sunday night, and on Monday morning I cry to hear of it. In disbelief I sit dumbfounded all day unable to concentrate. The boss, Mr. Slaughter, comes in smoking a cigar that makes me nauseous. His secretary laughs when I begin taking night classes at the community college. "Dreams, you'll never get a degree," she sneers as she prepares for her weekly bridge club rendezvous after work. I am surrounded by a new world, the office. I know it is to be temporary, yet fear that it will become permanent, that I will become trapped like everyone says, like my coworkers who have been working for "the company" for over twenty years. I fear that I will suddenly wake up one Monday morning and find I'm ready for retirement with nothing to show for my life except a Ready Kilowatt pin. And I party with the "girls," my coworkers Aminda, Buddy—from Bore for Aurora—Ronnie, Arabella, and some who come to work and then go. In the summer it's college students, the daughters of employees, who work with us. We travel to San Antonio, Monterrey, Corpus Christi, go across to Nuevo Laredo for dinner, drive to Mirando City to Lala's Restaurant for their famous puffy tacos. I even join the bowling league. And yet I'm miserable.

Things at home are better. I can buy shoes for my siblings, Celia, Geri, Julio, give them milk money, pay for dance classes for the youngest girls, treat them all to movies, trips. I buy the Blue Lady—a Rambler station wagon—after years of taking buses everywhere, and I give the kids rides to school and pick up my coworker Emma, who is fifteen years my senior and a friend. All is well, at least until my brother quits high school, joins the Army, goes to 'Nam and is killed. It's 1968. It feels like I'll never be able to finish school and that he's abandoned me—now I must shoulder the load for both of us. I must be "*muy mujer*" to work and go to school. I can't see how I'll ever get out. I apply for a transfer to the office in Kingsville so I can attend school there; I already have over ninety hours of junior college credit. Later, when I do move to Kingsville, I realize that the racism in the office had denied me the transfer. But I don't know why I am not transferred and believe it's that I'm not good enough or smart enough. Eventually a branch of Texas A&I University opens in Laredo at the community college campus, and I feel like the mountain has come to me; I won't have to leave—at least not yet. I will get a degree in spite of the geographical isolation and the institutionalized racism of the state's higher education system. To finish all the required courses for a degree in English and political science in secondary education, I must quit the office job so I can do my student teaching. During the long years of night school, some professors understand and let me take classes independently although it isn't policy; others are hard-nosed and skeptical of my ambition, don't trust me to make the grade. But I do and prove them wrong. I read Shakespeare till 3 A.M. and write history papers during lunch hours, and I still manage to have a life. I give myself the weekend for friends, Leticia, Gloria, Ani, Elvira, Becky, most of whom have already come home after getting degrees and now take classes for the hell of it. We hang out in Nuevo Laredo, go to the movies, read Sor Juana Inés de la Cruz and Marx, register voters, join the Raza Unida Party, dream of what we'll do when we get on with our lives. Some of these same friends marry, move away; others stay home, take care of aging parents. Twenty years later they are teachers who still take a class now and then for the hell of it. I was the *atrevida* that no one doubted, everyone trusted. Parents let their daughters go on trips if I was going — to Corpus to the beach, to Guadalajara, to Monterrey.

Finally, I graduate with my bachelor's degree. But I purposely do not fill out the paperwork required to get certified to teach in Texas public schools — I didn't want to fall into the trap of teaching and becoming stagnant as had happened to some of my friends who had returned from college only to become part of the system we had planned to change. I am bridesmaid to Berta, who marries and moves to Corpus; and to Elvira who marries and stays in Laredo. As I walk down the aisle I try it on for size, and I know that it'll never be for me — that being tied to a man is as alien to me as drinking gasoline. What's good for the car is not good for me. I know that marriage will become another trap. I avoid it.

In 1973, when I apply to the master's program in English and for the teaching assistantship in Kingsville and get both, I cry with regret and with joy. Regret because I really want to go to Stanford, where I've heard all the best teachers are, where I can live in the Bay Area and see plays, films, sit in a café drinking coffee and meeting others who write — Chicanas and Chicanos whom I read about in *El Grito*. Joy because at least I won't have to begin teaching at Martin High School in the fall and eventually apply for the certificate. I am gloriously happy when I move into a cottage in Kingsville with two housemates.

I exist on the periphery of all the drinking parties, the marijuana, the dances — *Tejano* and country — I am on a mission and I focus on my graduate classes. After one semester, I move and go live in a dump, but alone. I send money home from my meager TA's salary, and I feel guilty about the things I can't provide for my youngest siblings Geri and Celia and Ricky, but we manage. I cry every Saturday evening when I walk five blocks to the Circle K to call home on the pay phone and I hear those beloved voices. Sometimes they surprise me and arrive in Papi's white Ford station wagon, with two-year-old Nono my nephew in tow. I live simply, like a nun, and love the simplicity, the solitude, the peace. I don't miss the partying in Laredo, but I do miss my friends. I toy with becoming a Buddhist, spend hours meditating; but I still attend the Newman Center masses and even lead religious retreats patterned after the SEARCH retreats that I led in Laredo from 1970 to 1972. I work with Upward Bound in the summers, and finally in 1975 I move on.

The decision to apply to Ph.D. programs came as a surprise, for I didn't realize that's what I wanted. Dr. Hildegard Schmallenbeck, an English professor in Kingsville, first put the idea in my head, and it felt comfortable but scary. One afternoon a classmate originally from Germany, Utte, an outsider like myself, and I spent hours talking about where we would go after the master's, and somehow, suddenly, I just knew I wasn't going back to teach at Laredo Junior College. When I broke the news to my family, Papi made me cry, accusing me of not wanting to come home, of having betrayed the family, of becoming too educated and being ashamed of them. Now I can understand his fears of losing a daughter to the academy, to an alien world. At the time, though, all I could do was feel guilt and hate and resentment. I was accepted by a number of schools in the Midwest — Ohio State, Kent State, Oklahoma — but not to the only school to which I had paid the application fee — Stanford. Alas, I wasn't destined to go there. At the urging of one of the VISTA workers in Laredo, I wrote to the English department at the University of Texas and received a curt letter painting a dismal picture of their graduates' futures, in effect discouraging me from applying. It was, however, Nebraska that asked me to apply. Professor Ralph Grajeda, a Chicano professor in their Department of English, called in early spring and talked to me about applying. The fact that a Chicano professor called made a difference; also, I must confess I felt flattered — they wanted me to apply. So I did. And although I got financial aid packages — mostly in the form of tuition reductions along with teaching assistantships — from other schools, Nebraska offered what I felt was the best deal: a teaching assistantship the first year, instructor level the second year, a flexible work plan so I could take courses and teach the classes I wanted. Nebraska made me what appeared, from 1200 miles away, an offer I couldn't refuse. In mid-April 1975 I announced to my father where I had chosen to go. He continued his tirade against my going anywhere. I grew suspicious, however, when within a couple of weeks he seemed calm and accepting. Soon I learned the reason for his change — the family had received a graduation announcement from a cousin living in Lincoln. I would be staying with family; it was okay to go to Nebraska.

My graduate work was arduous. Because I had not been exposed to much of what other students had and because, being the only Chicana/o in the department I felt a tremendous responsibility, I had to work much more than the other students. Yet I always felt I was just barely prepared. I also worked with the community, visited the prison, did translations, had a Spanish-language radio program, wrote poetry, and managed to keep a high grade point average. There were so many incidents in which I confronted racism that it would take a book to tell of all of them; suffice it to say that I made myself strong and thick-skinned — *hice concha* — to survive. I was still the same person, but I had grown; I had matured and had developed survival skills that served me well. No longer would I believe everything others thought or said about me and my abilities. I would fend for myself and fight only those battles worth fighting. Many stories from my years in graduate school tell of the racism, the discrimination, the mentoring, and the support that made up that part of my life. I choose not to dwell on them. Maybe someday I will revisit those times and assess how much I've grown.

In 1979, when I received a Fulbright and went to Spain, I found out who my true friends were. Some of my classmates blatantly scorned, claiming that the only reason I had received anything was because I was Chicana. Some professors also expressed amazement, which made me question my abilities. Once I interacted with my fellow Fulbrighters in Spain, the doubts fell by the wayside. I realized I could hold my own with the other graduate students from Ivy League schools as well as from the University of California at Berkeley and the University of Michigan.

My family was supportive but suspicious. Would I return? What was I doing over there? *¿Y sola?* My father could never understand. I did return; in fact I came back from Madrid to Laredo to teach at Laredo State University, although I had not finished my dissertation. In 1980 I teach alongside professors who treat me as if I am still their student. I'm the only Chicana, in fact the only female in an academic division of arts and sciences composed of seven male faculty members. I have to speak up for women constantly, point out my colleagues' sexism and their off-handed comments that insulted and harassed women students and me.

For the next two years I worked on my dissertation whenever I could. Since I am a night person, I stayed in the office typing away on the old Smith-Corona that I had inherited from my old mentor, Dr. Briggs. The summer of 1981, Mami and my sister Elsa and her two kids, Nono and Klariza, came with me to Nebraska. While I worked, they took care of all my needs, visited with family and all in all provided support, doing my laundry, cooking; my sister even helped with some research and typing. Without their help, I would not have finished. In the fall of 1981 I still had not finished, and I began my second year of late-night sessions. After teaching all day, I worked on my dissertation. In 1982 I returned to Lincoln alone and determined to finish. But had it not been for invaluable help from the Ford Foundation Dissertation Completion project at the University of Michigan, I don't think I would have. As with many events in my life, it was pure serendipity, or as we say in Laredo, *pura chiripada,* that led me to be a fellow that summer. I was in Lincoln housesitting for a professor at the University, Miguel, and his wife Chris Carranza, when I learned of the program. I was lucky to be able to spend an August in Ann Arbor working alongside others who like me lacked only finished dissertations to complete their doctorates. That was when I met Chicano and Chicana scholars including Pat Zavella, Chris Sierra, Laura Rendón, David Montejano, Emilio Zamora, and Aída Hurtado. After a grueling writing schedule, I finished — mostly because Carlos Arce talked to me about the impossibility of the manuscript ever being the perfect one I was shooting for. "Let it go," he advised, "it's ready." I did, and I went back to Lincoln to finish all the details, get the required signatures, and still make it to Laredo in time to begin the fall semester. Driving nonstop from Lincoln to Laredo, I arrived one evening in late August, to be greeted by Papi with open arms: "¿Ya acabaste m'ija?" and I burst into tears of exhaustion, relief, joy, "Sí, al fin."

Reflection and Rebirth:
The Evolving Life of a Latina Academic
Iris Ofelia López

Birth Pains/Growing Pains

ON A FRIGID DAY in January 1953, my mother arrived home at her three-room, cold-water flat from the factory where she worked, after picking up my older sister, Francesca, at the babysitter's. As she stood in front of the tenement, fishing for her house keys in her pocketbook, a huge dog appeared out of nowhere, put his paws on her shoulders, and threw her off balance. She fell backward, flat on her back, but fortunately a mound of snow broke her fall. Because she was nine months pregnant, and my one-year-old sister had landed on top of her, she could not stand up. She lay there until a man walking down the street helped her to the apartment door.

Her labor pains began that night just as a blizzard hit the city. But she refused to let her cousin take her to the hospital because she feared she would be mistreated there as she had been during her first pregnancy. It became too late to call an ambulance; the roads were impassable. I was born at home the following morning and lay attached to my mother by the umbilical cord until the ambulance arrived. Two weeks after my birth, my mother returned to work at the clothing factory because my father was ill and we needed the income.

I sometimes consider this story a metaphor for my life, containing as it does the seeds of my work and most of the elements of my lifelong interest in questions about gender, poverty, ethnicity, family ties (literally and figuratively!), community support, reproductive rights, and the limited choices open to poor women. I became an anthropologist primarily because I wanted to write about the Puerto Rican experience in New York City as I knew it, not as it had been portrayed by others. As I look back, this story resonates with a deeper meaning of birth, the bringing forth of a more integral self-awareness

Iris and Francesca López in Brooklyn
(l–r), circa 1955

and evolved social consciousness through the transcendence of family, neighborhood, gender, and ethnicity.

My mother, who is Cuban, had thirteen brothers and sisters; my father, who is Puerto Rican, is an only child. Together they had five children, four daughters and one son. Even though we grew up poor in Brooklyn, I didn't realize how poor we were because everyone around us was in a similar or worse situation. In fact, I always thought we were better off than our neighbors because my mother gave them our hand-me-down clothing, and she always stressed the importance of sharing what we had with the less fortunate.

I grew up in a bilingual home. My mother, who had emigrated from Cuba when she was twenty-one, spoke only Spanish, while my father, who had moved from Puerto Rico at the age of twelve, spoke to us predominantly in English. With each other, my siblings and I spoke English, which was our first language. My main concern with Spanish was that I learn to speak it correctly. I encouraged my mother to correct my Spanish and grew exasperated if she did not.

When I began grade school and learned to read, my mother often asked me to teach her to read English, but I couldn't because I didn't know how to teach English. I remember feeling guilty about this as a child, until through trial and error, and by reading the English newspaper, my mother slowly taught herself English. Even though she understands and speaks English today, my siblings and I still speak to her only in Spanish. I admire my mother's tenacity in teaching herself English. She was one of my main role models. Throughout her life she has successfully overcome any number of obstacles, and I came to emulate her in many ways.

Perfecta: Escape from Fear and Abandonment

Both of my parents modeled hard work, persistence, and discipline. For as long as I can remember there was always a sewing machine at home, and my mother, who is an excellent seamstress, made my sister and me many matching outfits. She also learned to be handy around the house, sewing beautiful drapes, upholstering furniture, and helping my father to paint and wallpaper our apartment. I learned to be self-disciplined, defer gratification, and acquire new skills.

My mother kept a clean house where everything was neatly arranged. She also taught us the virtue of cleanliness and attention to personal appearance. She insisted upon ironing our clothes and always looked her best whenever she left the house — these things shaped my sense of aesthetics and taught me that poverty does not prevent people from exercising agency, creating beauty, and transforming their environment in any way they can. On some level, I think they also taught me never to accept the status quo, to learn that change is possible.

Another thing that I learned from my mother was to be perfect. I remember, for example, arranging and rearranging furniture for hours until she was satisfied that it was exactly right. The positive aspects of perfectionism have served me as an academic, but I'm still unlearning the negative aspects day by day.

My father is a talented and hard-working man. He provided for us, for most of his life working as a cook. For many years he rose at two in the morning so that he could start cooking by four A.M. While we were growing up my father occasionally lived at his place of work because it was too far to commute from home to work everyday. Although he did the best he could to provide for us, he suffered from temporary memory loss, a condition technically known as *fugue,* the Latin word for flight. Whenever life became too stressful, he would leave us without warning, returning only when he had recovered his memory. When he returned home, my mother always took him back because she loved him, felt he was a victim of his illness but otherwise a good husband and father, and believed that the most important thing was to keep the family together. No one really knows what caused my father's amnesia. I suspect it is related to his having been an abused child; his stepfather, a boxer, beat him sadistically, an experience that may have been so traumatic that he developed the ability to disassociate.

I later realized that I picked up certain patterns from my mother that I came to identify as codependent. A codependent lacks good emotional boundaries, often takes on other people's feelings, and tries to fix and/or control their lives. Codependency is a common problem in our society, transcending gender, ethnicity, and class. As an educated woman, I have the advantages over my mother's generation to reflect upon these things. There are those who argue that Latinas are not codependent because their family-oriented culture motivates them to help others. I disagree. Codependency is not caused simply by caring behaviors directed toward others, although this is a predisposing factor. Rather it arises when the person helping others sacrifices his or her own needs and feelings for others, and enmeshment occurs. For example, a Latina/o can be family-oriented and not be codependent if s/he establishes good boundaries, is able to take care of herself/himself, and also appropriately care for the needs of her/his family. As the family designated caretaker, I am still learning to navigate between upholding nurturing Latino/a family values, taking care of myself, and maintaining healthy relationships with everyone who is a part of my life.

Mírate en Este Espejo/Look In This Mirror

Although my family life was rich in companionship and love, it also felt unpredictable and restricted. Having a father who came and went created considerable economic and emotional hardship for our family and induced in me a fear of abandonment. It was difficult for my mother not to be distressed, supporting five small children on the salary of a factory worker. As a codependent child myself, I tried to make up for my father's loss by becoming a surrogate parent for my younger siblings. From a young age, I also became my mother's confidante. Like other children forced to grow up before their time, I tried to be the perfect daughter, mature beyond my years, and became hypervigilant about other people's needs while ignoring my own. Since my mother did not want us to go through what she had experienced, she often reminded us how important it was to get an education and a profession so that if our husbands became ill or turned out to be *sin vergüenza*, literally a person without shame, we could leave our marriages and support ourselves. Her constant refrain, *mírate en este espejo*, "look in this mirror," was a powerful and sad message that made me resolve to live my life better.

Because my parents were also very strict when we were growing up, we were not allowed to go many places unsupervised. For that reason I spent too much of my adolescent life watching television. Television was my main escape as well as my primary means of entertainment. For me and my siblings, our daily supplement consisted of cartoons and shows such as *Dennis the Menace, Leave It To Beaver, The Donna Reed Show,* and *Father Knows Best.* For part of the day I could retreat into a make-believe world where the family was happy. On Sunday evenings our entire family watched *Bonanza* and *The Ed Sullivan Show.*

Television was a bridge to the world outside school, home, and church. It made me aware of class differences and gender roles. Because the neighborhoods in which the characters in *Dennis the Menace* and *Leave It To Beaver* grew up were so remote from my reality, until I was nine or ten I did not believe that people actually lived in such neat suburban houses. On the way to a Baptist religious camp in Pennsylvania one summer day, my jaw dropped as I stuck my head out the window and saw row after row of little white houses. At that moment I began to realize how different our lifestyle was from others.

Getting Erased: Too Dark/Not Puerto Rican Enough

When I was growing up we lived in different multiethnic neighborhoods in Brooklyn. These places helped me transcend my parochialism and enhanced my appreciation of cultural differences. The first one was Puerto Rican and Italian and was a real community. We lived in a six-story apartment building where everyone knew each other and the corridor smelled of sweet onions and sautéed garlic. To our dismay, my mother first discovered and learned to cook eggplant from two of our downstairs Italian neighbors. My siblings and I hated the strange, oblong, purple vegetable and we groaned and made faces whenever she cooked it. To this day my sister Francesca can't eat ratatouille.

Not having acquired good basic skills from a substandard childhood education eroded my self-confidence and later made my academic journey more challenging. As low-income "Spanish" kids, we went to schools that had typically overcrowded classrooms and few, if any, resources. Some of my grade-school teachers screamed at us and punished us by forcing us to put our heads down on our desks for what felt like hours. I had teachers who threw chalk and erasers in the classroom. One teacher had a reputation for slamming kids against the wall. All the kids in the school were terrified of her.

I was inquisitive and academically advanced for my age. Until the third grade I was the teacher's pet because of the maturity I displayed and my desire to please. Even so, I was not able to get the help I needed. For example, in the third grade, my teacher, Miss Augustine, told me that I was reading at a sixth-grade level and that she wished she could give me more individualized attention. However, the class was too large, and instead of assisting me she asked me to help her teach the other children how to read better. At the time I was flattered to be my teacher's assistant. Today I realize the extent to which my academic development was stunted.

As the ethnic composition of the neighborhood changed from Italian to Puerto Rican, my parents moved a few miles away to a commercial strip, which was largely populated with Italian immigrants, because they thought it was quieter and safer. I lived in this locale from the ages of twelve to fourteen. On our block were a barbershop and a dimly lit espresso café. This café was patronized by mafiosi who paraded arm in arm up and down the block on Sunday afternoons. Continuing the upwardly mobile trend, a few years later we moved to the German part of the neighborhood.

Even though we lived in harmony with our neighbors, growing up in a predominantly white neighborhood made me more color conscious because of the stigma associated with being Puerto Rican and my emerging awareness of white privilege and ethnic prejudice. My sister Francesca's first job was at a local Italian bakery. I sometimes wondered if she was hired because she is as fair skinned as any Northern Italian. However, I learned that while she may have had white privilege in one context, she became a victim of ethnic prejudice in another. Both she and I were each discriminated against because of the color of our skin. For instance, in junior high school the race issue intensified as different ethnic and racial groups from various neighborhoods came together in the same place. Junior High School 111 had a large African American student body and the various ethnic and racial groups segregated themselves into smaller groups and gangs. There was a lot of interracial tension in the school. Ironically, in this setting my dark skin protected me and made Francesca a target of some attacks because she didn't fulfill the stereotype of what a Latina looks like. The crisis intensified in high school. Because we lived on the border of Brooklyn and Queens, I was sent to a predominantly white high school in Queens, while Francesca was sent to a predominantly black high school in Brooklyn. One day a gang of black girls set her hair on fire in the school. Luckily, a teacher was passing by and put out the fire. The following day Francesca was transferred to my high school. Once she was there some of the white kids thought they were paying her a compliment when they told her she didn't look "Puerto Rican or Spanish." In contrast I was told I was "not like other Puerto Ricans." I consider both of these perspectives racist; they render us invisible since the exception proves the rule and serves to maintain the same racist stereotype. For instance, my sister and I took turns in being discriminated against because of the color of our skin. Even though there is no denying that white privilege exists when comparing the experiences of two sisters from the same family, it is a more complex issue. In certain settings, I was the target and in others she was. Although my sister Francesca was very successful in her career as a manager for AT&T, of all the people I grew up with, including my Italian friends, I was the only one who went on to higher education.

My immediate family was not particularly color conscious but my mother's white Cuban relatives were. When I was eleven or twelve my grandfather and one of my aunts in Florida warned me to stay out of the sun because my dark skin would become even darker, which they did not consider attractive. In another instance an uncle picked up my arm in front of other family members and compared it with one of my fair-skinned cousin's. His words were "like salt and pepper"—a phrase I would hear again as my high school friends compared my sister Fran and me. This was an ignorant message that objectified us both.

As well as exhibiting ethnic and class prejudice, most teachers had low expectations of students, especially the girls. No one ever suggested that I might go to college. The insidious assumption was that, regardless of race and ethnicity, it was a waste of time for girls to go to college because they grow up, get married, have children, and stay at home. My math teacher made this point clear to me when I did not immediately understand a problem he was explaining. In an exasperated tone he exclaimed, "Forget it, you won't need it anyway." Teachers like this man eroded my confidence and rendered me invisible. It frustrated me, hampered my development, and made me feel mathematically impaired.

A Search for a Personal and Cultural Self

In high school I met Charlie and Gustavo, two U.S.-born Latinos like myself. They were considered the best art students in the school. What made them unusual to me was that they had developed a deep sense of ethnic pride. It was Charlie who first talked to me about the history of Puerto Rico. I was impressed to learn that Puerto Ricans were great writers, musicians, and poets. He also talked about how good it felt to be accepted unconditionally. We were fifteen years old, and we talked about poverty, racism, violence, and other forms of social injustice. This new perspective stimulated my intellectual curiosity and helped lay the groundwork for my interest in ethnic studies. It was the beginning of my consciousness-raising as a Latina.

Like most people of their generation my parents rarely talked about their ethnic background. The only time I heard my mother adamantly state she was Puerto Rican was when she was offended by an Italian neighbor who told her she did not look Puerto Rican because of her fair skin and the elegant way she was dressed and groomed—like many other women my mother went to the beauty parlor once a week to have her hair fixed. At this point, it didn't matter to her what Spanish-origin group she belonged to. She claimed to be Puerto Rican because she was tired of this ethnic prejudice. It was not until I was in high school that I discovered my mother's father was Puerto Rican. When he was twelve years old, in the early part of the twentieth century, he immigrated to the Dominican Republic and then to Cuba with his parents. In Cuba he saved enough money to buy a coffee ranch when he was older. His upward mobility contributed to my mother's valuing of hard work, discipline, and education, which she passed on to us. Although my father was born and raised in Puerto Rico, he was told that his father, a merchant marine, was Arabic. Given the provincial tendency of many New Yorkers to pigeonhole people, my background created an identity crisis for me because my friends, some of whom were white, insisted that I choose an ethnicity, and I wasn't sure what I was — Cuban, Puerto Rican, or North American. In those days my alleged Arab heritage was too abstract to relate to.

My junior high and high school experiences were radically different from those I had in grade school because by the age of fifteen I had started to internalize the message that I wasn't special. Like other poor kids with my background, I had learned to read adults and not to expect much from them. I started out in an academic program in high school, although I still cringe to think I graduated with a general diploma because I did not pass my economics final by one point. I talked to my teacher about how important it was for me to graduate with an academic diploma after spending four years in the program, but she would not be persuaded. I can still see the disdain in her cold blue eyes when she told me she wasn't going to change my grade. I was angry because I knew that for one point she would have given her favorite white male students a chance to make it up. I felt so humiliated and ashamed that I told no one, not even my parents. I did average work in high school because I was preoccupied with my family life, felt the teachers didn't care, and found the curriculum boring.

I knew that I had not received a good education and I still desperately wanted to learn. As disappointing and discouraging as my educational experience had been, I realized that a college education was the only way out of poverty, given the limited options open to women — marriage or low-wage, dead-end jobs. My mother's words about her being a mirror for my life echoed in my mind and gave me the strength and courage to push on to college.

One day I made an appointment with my high school counselor, Mrs. Rappaport, and asked her for a college application. She refused to give me one, and along with two other teachers suggested that I become an airline stewardess because I was "tall and pretty." Even though becoming an airline stewardess did not seem like a bad prospect to a sixteen-year-old Puerto Rican/Cuban girl from Brooklyn, it infuriated me that they did not consider me smart enough to go to college. I would not be dissuaded. To me, success meant independence and being able to help my parents emotionally and economically. I knew that college was the only route to the choices and freedom I sought. After I insisted, Mrs. Rappaport reluctantly gave me a college application that — as was the case for so many other black and Latino students in the late sixties — tracked me into a community college. I do not know how I managed to stay hopeful, but I plodded on.

I was fortunate that open-enrollment policies coincided with my graduation from high school. These days I meet many professors who are against open enrollment. Once again they see me as the exception and think they are flattering me when they say, "With your ability you would have made it even without open enrollment." This comment angers me because it reveals that these people know nothing about my life and it implies that other students from my background will fail regardless of the opportunities available to them. This is wrong! If open enrollment had not existed when I graduated from high school, my grades and general high school diploma would have kept me from going to college. These opportunities make a lifetime of difference to students.

When I started at the Borough of Manhattan Community College (BMCC), I was surprised and disgusted to learn that I had been preregistered into a secretarial program. I dropped it immediately and registered in the social sciences but the message was clear: I should not be in college. At BMCC I again had little guidance. Registration was chaotic. I felt lost amidst the hundreds of frustrated students running from table to table, trying to register for classes. The lines were interminable, snaking down and around long corridors for what seemed like blocks. I had not received any notification about the freshmen orientation session, so I had no idea how many or even which classes I should be taking.

Intentionally or not, the process served to weed out anyone who could not tolerate chaos and ambiguity. In addition to a poorly organized registration, BMCC had a series of other problems. In 1970 the campus was located near what was at the time the red-light district of 42nd Street, close to Times Square. In order to get to my classes, I had to walk past marquees for triple X-rated adult films, where leering men stood around and made lewd remarks. As an overprotected seventeen-year-old woman, I did not feel safe in this hostile environment.

The physical environment at BMCC was also depressing. The main building was dismal, with dingy hallways. The elevator was often broken; even when it worked it was too small to carry the large number of students in that building, so we all walked up and down six flights of stairs numerous times a day. At that time, the BMCC campus had buildings more than a mile distant from one another. One of them was on 51st Street, the other two on 72nd Street. Sometimes classes were arbitrarily assigned to the uptown or downtown buildings. In order to change classes, I had to take a subway and pay another fare, which I could ill afford. Not only was my experience at BMCC costly, it was also frustrating and illogical. To add insult to injury, the college did not offer basic services to its students. For example, I still remember with sadness the day I asked the librarian in the main building if there was a library orientation; she said there was not. I could not believe that this was college life. A few years later, when I went to private schools, including New York University and Columbia, I was disturbed to realize how substandard the education and services were for poor CUNY students. These services cater to the affluent students, providing them with a fuller range of academic supports.

That is why the Civil Rights and Women's Rights movements were such positive and electrifying experiences for me. They gave many of us hope for positive change. Suddenly this drab college was transformed into a contested terrain where students and faculty alike felt we could make changes together. The Black Power movement was meaningful to me because I was able to learn about my own history and gender inequality, which made studying personally relevant. Courses in Ethnic Studies and Women's Studies provided me with the first forum in which I could articulate and express my ideas and listen to others put into words my experiences of erasure and social injustice. Some of the ugly truth about the world started to make more sense as I learned about capitalism, class, race, and gender oppression.

My most powerful experiences at BMCC were not limited to academic matters. I and others learned to build community and effect social change. We did this by identifying social and/or educational problems, such as the lack of library services for students, and collectively developing strategies to solve them. Building community meant finding the courage to transcend our private worlds and become part of a larger one where we worked successfully together. The camaraderie and the chance to collaborate with politically conscious students, radical professors, and counselors such as Jim Blake, Joyce Brown, Ruby Leavitt, Jim Pearlstein, José Irrizary, Rex Matei, Cathy Chamberlin, and others made the slogan "The personal is political, the political is personal" all the more meaningful to me.

In retrospect, the Civil Rights and Women's Rights movements provided me with the knowledge and helped me find the courage to continue developing my life in a significant way. Even though I participated in political students' activities, worked twenty hours a week, and took seventeen to twenty-one credits a semester, I graduated from BMCC in two years with a 4.0 average as a result of careful planning and the encouragement of some of my professors and counselors.

Before I graduated, I applied to and was accepted at New York University with a merit-based Martin Luther King Scholarship. Although I was extremely happy to have received it, I was troubled because it didn't cover my full tuition, room, board, and books. I don't recall how I heard that the Ford Foundation helped students, but I decided to pay the foundation a visit. I made an appointment to talk with whoever agreed to see me. On the day of my appointment, I summoned my courage and took my transcript with me as the best evidence of my abilities. When I arrived, the secretary ushered me into a plushly carpeted waiting room. Shortly thereafter she escorted me into an office. Behind a desk sat a large, stately, kind-looking African American man. I told him that I had been accepted to New York University and appreciated the Martin Luther King Scholarship but that the award wasn't large enough to cover room and board, and I needed a place to study because of the lack of privacy in my parents' apartment. I explained that I had to wait until everyone went to sleep late at night so that I could lock myself in the bathroom to read and write my papers. I did this by sitting on the toilet seat, balancing the typewriter on my lap, and reading and typing late into the night. I showed him my transcript and he congratulated me on my academic record. After chatting for a few more minutes he left the room and asked me to wait in his office. When he returned he announced that he had increased my scholarship so that I could live in the dorms. I was stunned and very grateful. I thanked him profusely. By the time I got downstairs I was worried about how I was going to tell my mother I was leaving home.

My mother cried when I told her I was moving into the dorms but she was proud that I had been accepted to New York University. I majored in Spanish literature and minored in Anthropology. One of the most difficult obstacles I confronted was contracting Bells Palsey in the first semester of my senior year. It was tough having facial paralysis at the age of twenty, but I was determined to overcome this handicap. I went ahead with my plans to go to Spain as an exchange student in my last semester. Six months later I was fortunate that the Bells Palsey was only mildly visible. I took my brother Elliot to Spain with me, in accord with the role I had assigned myself as a caretaker of my siblings and because I thought it would be a good experience for both of us.

Overall, Spain was a positive experience, although I felt the sting of racism and sexism there in a way I never had before. As a young Puerto Rican woman with dark skin and long flowing hair, I was treated as an exotic, and, like the other Spanish women, I was unable to read a book in the park without being sexually harassed unless I sat near the children's playground. As had happened with my sister Francesca, I once again confronted people's surprise that the fair-skinned Elliot was my brother. We were often asked to show our passports to prove that we were related.

Before I left for Spain, I had applied for a Ford Foundation fellowship to go to graduate school. I received it because I graduated NYU with a 4.0 point grade average and because at that time few Latinas/os had applied in the field of Anthropology.

Spine of Steel: Rage, Isolation, and Otherness

I entered the graduate department of Anthropology at Columbia University in 1975. Being there was an enriching experience as well as a painful, enraging, and alienating one. There were not many U.S.-born Latinas from the inner city in the department, and I was only the second Puerto Rican woman to matriculate since the 1950s. In my first year I was acutely aware of my own ethnicity and the academic advantages that many of my fellow students who had gone to private school had over me. Yet I was determined to succeed.

In my second year, I faced one of my biggest challenges. Because of my naïveté and the fact that I had not majored in anthropology as an undergraduate, I had a devastating experience with a well-known professor, Morton Fried. In my first year, I wrote a paper titled "The Social Responsibility of the Social Scientist." The gist of my paper was to remind anthropologists that they had to be more vigilant to ensure that their studies were not inadvertently used by the sponsoring governments to further exploit the people they worked with. At the time, Project Camelot, a notorious study undertaken in Latin America, was linked with Latin American intelligence bureaus. Among the studies that I examined in my paper was Julian Steward's work, *The People of Puerto Rico*. Although I did not accuse Steward of collusion with the Puerto Rican government, I surmised that this investigation could have been used by the Puerto Rican government to help implement Puerto Rico's colonial and industrialization program, Operation Bootstrap. I did not know that Steward had been Fried's mentor and even though Fried considered himself a liberal, he became so enraged by my paper that he tried to have me expelled. He put a letter in my academic file criticizing the paper and suggested that I was better suited for the political science department. If other professors in the department—Leith Mullings, Elliot Skinner, Ralph Holloway, Daisy Dwyer, and the late Eleanor Leacock—had not come to my rescue, he might have succeeded in having me removed.

I wrote this paper because at the age of twenty-two, I thought that graduate school was a place where students could openly challenge and receive ideas and knowledge. I had come from a tradition at BMCC and NYU where I was encouraged to speak my mind, and the Civil Rights movement had made me feel empowered as a student. Columbia University was the antithesis of this tradition. I was disappointed in what seemed to me at the time to be a static and socially irrelevant academic program. Even though my department had participated in the Civil Rights movement, by 1975 it appeared that it was a thing of the past for some professors and had not affected others at all. Unintentionally, I was frequently finding myself at odds with their ideas and values. For instance, once in a classroom I objected to the characterizations "barbarian" and "uncivilized" for non-Western societies that the professor and a few others still used. I had also developed as my anthropological goal to undertake socially relevant research in my own community, and I was shocked and distraught when they told me that I couldn't do this because it wasn't "objective." I had already begun to doubt that objectivity existed in the social sciences, an idea only starting to be questioned in 1975, and my experience at Columbia with some biased professors reinforced the myth of a value-free social science. I believed that the most objective we can ever be when doing research is to try to be aware of our biases.

Even though I thought I was politically astute when I entered Columbia, I did not understand the threat a young vocal woman of color posed for faculty members and students when I openly criticized the discipline of Anthropology for its colonial legacy and ethnocentrism. I became so discouraged that I wanted to change disciplines, but I did not do so for two reasons. First, an officer at the Ford Foundation whom I trusted cautioned me that if I transferred out of anthropology, I would risk losing my fellowship. I felt locked into keeping this award; I could not afford to give it up. Second, and equally important, Leith Mullings became my mentor in my second year, and from that point on I felt supported by her and Elliot Skinner, who helped me persevere in the program. They taught anthropology from a race, class, and gender approach that I found relevant and meaningful. As a professor myself today, I fully understand and appreciate the constraints and pressures they worked under, and I am grateful for their assistance and courage. Because the Ford Foundation stipend did not cover my living expenses, I taught part time at BMCC. Teaching working-class students was also a way to counter the alienation I felt in the anthropology department, and it grounded me in a more concrete and socially relevant setting.

In the process of completing my Ph.D., I realized that there were things I liked about anthropology, once its racist, classist, and sexist European paradigms are transcended or at least identified and problematized. Even though I still have reservations about certain anthropological premises, its interdisciplinary and cross-cultural perspectives make this field more exciting and less static than any other social sciences; it is still one of the few disciplines where students can create their own area of study. By choosing and developing my own anthropological paradigms, I have since done many exciting studies, including those in my own community that I had earlier envisioned.

By the time I received my doctorate from Columbia, I had decided that I did not want to make another personal sacrifice for my career. My main desire was to find an academic job in New York and reap some of the rewards for which I had worked so hard. My first full-time teaching job was in the Department of Latin American and Caribbean Studies at the City College of New York (CCNY), which is part of the City University of New York (CUNY). I chose this school because I was committed to work with working-class students.

City College has a proud history but is an exceedingly underfunded college with eight three-hour courses a year and one course off for research. Although a small cadre of committed professors and administrators are dedicated to the student body, there are many problems that have a negative impact on students and professors. They resonate with my own early educational struggles. For example, many professors have low expectations of the students in the social sciences. In fact, some of them feel that the establishment of open enrollment was the downfall of academic standards at City College. There are also double standards for professors of color based on tokenism. In order to fulfill a quota, professors of color often are assigned to do more committee work than other faculty members. In my first year, in addition to sitting on numerous committees, I was appointed by the president to serve as director of the Latin American and Caribbean Exchange Program linked with the Autonomous University of the Dominican Republic. I directed this program for five years. Although I was fortunate to have Jean Weissman as assistant director, we lacked many necessities. I did not, for example, have a computer in my office until I became director of the Women's Studies Program twelve years later. Moreover, because of the dearth of Latino/a faculty members, we generally have larger classes and a bigger student following than other professors. At times I had sixty students in one class with no additional compensation or assistance, and we were not compensated for being good teachers. Such a teaching workload made it difficult for me to keep up with my scholarship and impeded my promotion. In contrast to other professors, my colleagues and I were not promoted to associate professors until we had been at City College for thirteen or more years.

I earned tenure in my fifth year. Then I was recruited for and accepted a two-year visiting appointment at UCLA in the Anthropology department. During this time, I wrote the first draft of my book, *Sterile Choices: An Ethnography of the Medicalization of Puerto Rican Women's Reproduction*. In the two years, I also taught five courses. At UCLA I confronted racism in its most insidious form and learned more about the double-edged sword of tokenism. I had never been to the West Coast before. I met some outstanding colleagues in the Chicano/a Studies program, in Women's Studies, and the Writing Center. Some of these faculty were supportive and stimulating. But overall, my experience was one of alienation. I felt unsupported and treated as a token in the Anthropology department. Even though I had been recruited as a visiting professor, there was an understanding that at the end of the two years, I would be considered for a tenured position. This never happened because, as the only Latina professor in the department, I had to meet the unfeasible task of writing a book manuscript, finding a publisher, and obtaining a book contract by my second year if I wanted to be considered for tenure. All the while, I was adjusting to California car culture as a new driver, feeling lonely and isolated, and preparing two new courses, one of which had sixty students and no teaching assistant and the other, a graduate course I had never taught before. In my second year I taught full time. By then, it became apparent to me that I was undergoing a similar experience as my Latina predecessor, who had left angry and disillusioned the year before. We were both recruited and then given little or no support. Although the faculty member who recruited me did so in good faith because she felt that I would be an asset to the department, I ended up feeling like a token when I realized that the only other women of color in the department were one African American woman and an Asian woman who had been recruited along with me. It was an unfortunate coincidence that by the second year, everyone who had supported my appointment — the chair, the provost, and even the president — had stepped down or left. The new interim chair did not support me, and short of telling me outright, made it clear that he felt I was receiving special privileges because I was Latina and that I should not be there.

The insidious nature of tokenism is that it is a no-win situation. To be recruited as a token and given no support is to be set up for failure with the blame placed on you. If you try to rectify the situation, you are regarded as having a sour grapes attitude. I would like to see a system developed that would support well-intentioned faculty who are recruited to try and correct the underrepresentation of faculty of color in their institutions. This should be a nonpatronizing workable support system that monitors the appointment to tenure. Ironically, years later, I was rejected for a job that was a joint appointment between Women's Studies and the Chicana/o Studies program in a small private college in southern California because I was not Chicana. Once again, I experienced the same process of exclusion, only this time by Latinas.

I returned to City College in 1992 and spent a year there, and in 1994 I won a National Research Council / Ford Foundation Fellowship to do a postdoctorate at the University of Hawaii at Manoa. That was one of the best years of my life and it stimulated my interest in Pacific and Asian-Pacific Studies. The fellowship was important to me for several reasons. First and foremost, it enabled me to spend nine months writing in Hawaii. Second, it allowed me to share time with my brother Elliot, who was then living there. Third, it provided me with the opportunity to live in one of the few societies in the United States where there is a relatively high degree of tolerance and harmony among different ethnic groups. The experience was unique for me; Hawaii was the first place where I did not feel like a minority. Last, it gave me the support and inspiration I needed at the time. I am extremely grateful to Chris O'Brien and Tom Rozzell for the three years after my post-doctorate year, during which I was sponsored to attend their unique, humanitarian, and inspiring inter-disciplinary annual conference that enables a large number of students of color to come together. This is a supportive network that I maintain to this day.

Many changes have occurred at City College during the seventeen years I have taught there. In line with the national trend to downsize public educa-tion, the perception at this moment is that City College is being transformed into primarily an engineering and science school in response to a master plan envisioned by CUNY and supported by the Republican mayor, governor, and their cronies. In order to implement this plan, City College was targeted for negative media attention that began with the unscholarly publication *City On a Hill: Testing the American Dream at City College*. This book glorified City College's era of academic excellence and blames its academic downfall on open admissions. This publicity helped rationalize the demotion of all Ethnic Stud-ies departments into programs. This publicity also justified the shifting of resources from the social sciences and humanities to the professional schools and departments such as engineering, physics, architecture, and the Sophie Davis School of Medicine. As a young student who supported fledgling Eth-nic and Women's Studies programs, I never imagined I would see their demise now as a professor at CUNY. In addition, despite the faculty's efforts, remedia-tion has been denied to students at all CUNY schools. Students are now ex-pected to go to community colleges to learn basic academic skills that they should have acquired but did not in high school. Having been both a student and a professor at a community college, I feel that this policy is set up for failure; given government cutbacks, the city is not going to commit the vast amount of resources that would be required to make this program viable.

Since the establishment of the remediation requirements throughout CUNY, the number of students of color at City College has dramatically declined and resources have been cut to the bone. For example, for almost a year the North Academic Center, which houses the social sciences, did not have one function-ing photocopying machine. Today the administration is making more uni-lateral decisions for faculty and students. It has already started to implement a larger teaching load requirement that drastically limits the time faculty mem-bers have for doing research. This is a time of deep demoralization at City College. A core of faculty, administrators, and counselors has been resisting, to little avail. We are hopeful that, together with the newly elected New Caucus who will represent us in the union, we will be able to make positive changes in terms of salary, teaching load, professional life, and academic development commensurate with the research universities.

Personal Evolution

My journey from inner-city, working-class young woman to a Latina professor was and still is a rewarding challenge. I am grateful that I have been able to persevere and learn from the adversities in my life despite the odds. I am proud of my students and of the work I have been able to accomplish with them at City College. To name only a few of City College's successes: Jose Segarra is completing his doctorate at the Harvard School of Education; Sylvia Montero is earning a masters in the graduate program of Psychology at City College; and Rene Padilla is a case manager for an HIV program at the Bronx Citizens' Advice Bureau. On a professional level, I want to continue to help my students by working with them and others so that together we can improve the City University of New York. I can better fulfill these goals when I take care of my own needs, such as being able to pursue my own writing and scholarship within a supportive climate. On a personal level, I am practicing to live in the present and meet my own expectations, to appreciate myself and others more, to surround myself with more accepting and caring people, and to be able to enjoy my accomplishments and the good things that life has to offer. After much personal work and growth, I am now in a mutually healthy, supportive, and loving relationship. One of the main lessons I have learned is that to take care of one's needs is not a selfish, Anglo value of individualism. On the contrary, it enables us to better care for our families and those whom we love in a healthier way. We all need to take better care of ourselves physically, emotionally, and spiritually so that we can live a fuller, more meaningful, compassionate, conscious, and self-directed life. As a private person I have found it difficult to share personal aspects of myself here; however, I hope that those who "look in *this* mirror," which is my life, can gain some inspiration and courage to more fully realize themselves. By sharing I also hope to help "my community" and, further, to universalize the meaning of "my community" to include all like-minded people.

Mi Primera Amiguita: Carmelita

Gloria Holguín Cuádraz

Cada día venía por café.
Y cada día venía a ayudarle a mi mamá.

But now, I wonder
How did she feel going home to an empty house?
¿Cada día?

How did she feel leaving a houseful of eight kids,
a clatter of *sartenes*
and a house full of noise?

We were her family.
Yet, she was my very own.

I learned the meaning of friendship
from Carmelita
born in 1888
seventy years before
I was born.

I grew up with Carmelita
walking my childhood
next to my hunch-backed
white-haired friend
With the biggest pea-sized *verruga*
jutting out of her chin.
I loved to play with it
wondering if it could really come off.

My relationship with her
takes me back to a time when time didn't matter.

My little sister would ask me,
"How can you stand it? Taking those
slow, tiny steps all the way to the store?
. . . all the way downtown?"

Downtown we would go
down Stanley Place
up K Street
across the dusty railroad tracks
into Main Street, Brawley
home of the "cattle call" rodeo
and the "wildcats."
Over the years
the store clerks came to know us;
I was her little companion
and she was my best friend.

For everyone she would buy a little something
a *pañoleta,* a bottle of fake perfume from Rexall Drugs
a coloring book from Newberry's
And for me,
I got to pick whatever I wanted.

One day she took me to Town Shop
and bought me a whole package of undies
— one for every day of the week!
Sunday Monday Tuesday Wednesday
Thursday Friday and Saturday.
How I loved being her *favorita.*

My world with Carmelita had no time.
Unconditional love
has no clock
no minute hand
no hour hand.

She was known in the *barrio*
as "*la mujer abandonada*"
rumored to have been left by her husband
and who chose to live the rest of her life alone.

Irene Cuádraz, Carmelita, Gloria Cuádraz,
and Butchie, Brawley, California (l–r), circa 1967

But she wasn't so alone.
She had me.

And she had all my brothers and sisters.
She had the neighborhood
as she went from house to house
Collecting all the *chisme* anyone could ask for!

And she had *every* stray cat and *gatito*
lucky enough to be
dropped off in front of her house.

"Mom, I'm going to Carmelita's."
"Carmelita, Carmelita," I would shout
as I skipped all the way to her house
or run at full speed
coming to an abrupt stop
when I approached the door
then politely knock
"*Mi negrita,*" she would say,
"*Vamos a la tienda,*"
e íbamos mano en mano.

I don't know when I started loving her.
Looking back
I see her tiny, lopsided *pasitos*
for me
only meant *more time* with her.

I never really knew why she was the only woman
who lived alone in our street.
I never knew what caused her hunchback.

All I ever knew
was that I was her "negrita."

The House That Mamá Biela Built

Daisy Cocco De Filippis

A la memoria de mi abuela, Gabriela Menéndez Henríquez
Santo Domingo, 1898–1984

CIUDAD TRUJILLO, 1957–1962 and beyond

I was eight years old when I first saw the house. It was white and royal blue, and in the middle of a row of colonial homes its white and blue appeared to be heaven, looking after the earthly browns and greens of the other structures surrounding it. Although I was often kept out of adult conversations I was so eager to join in, it did not take me long to figure out that we were different. It wasn't for nothing, I told myself, that we had a white and blue house when everyone else's was either brown or green.

The house was directly across from the Palacio de Justicia, as the courthouse was known. I've often wondered why it was always bustling with people and important-looking lawyers when even I knew then that the real thing, the miscarriage of justice during Trujillo's regime, took place elsewhere, in the middle of the night, in the loneliness of highways, in the mysterious turns of vehicles down the mountains, or behind the lugubrious windows of *La cuarenta,* his most notorious torture chamber.

Nevertheless, it was apparently a very busy place. Many of our own friends and relatives often found themselves at our door, usually coming to or from el Palacio de Justicia. This made for quite a bit of entertaining conversation, especially when it came to breaking language codes. *El chivo,* the goat, for example, was Trujillo. La señora Flores was his mother, and so on. The house belonged to Mamá Biela, although she did not live in it then. Mamá Biela was Mami's mom, my favorite person in the world then and now, for a day does not pass without my knowing that she still is *mi mejor amiga.*

The house was in the middle of the block. If you left it to your right, you would soon find El Carol Morgan, the school where Americans, children of the Dominican oligarchy (born and raised in Santo Domingo but with their eyes on the prize), attended classes. I remember we were fascinated by the forbidden aspect of it. It was surrounded by high fences. In its yard, brownish pine trees had replaced the hibiscus and bougainvillea of other neighborhood homes. Certainly the majestic palm trees lining George Washington Avenue, *el Malecón,* just two blocks away, had not found their way to the proud and forbidding doors of El Carol Morgan.

We often left the house to our right, as we made our way to our favorite place in the whole wide world those days, el Parque Ramfis, known today as el Parque Hostos, after Trujillo's oldest son and the rest of *el Generalísimo*'s family were forced to vacate their tropical paradise. I realize now that its democratic element must have been its most appealing element to me. Only in the park could I forget my dainty *niña de la casa* ways and shove and push as I played the *trompo,* a gyrating contraption that could turn as fast as you pushed it. And was it ever pushed fast, usually by the *maniceros* and *paleteros,* vendor-children who spent most of their time trying to sell the ware they carried on a wooden tray, strapped around one shoulder by a leather belt.

El Parque Ramfis was a source of discovery and mystery. It was there that neighborhood adolescents went to be kissed for the first time. It was there that the *sirvientas,* experiencing a sense of temporary freedom, became children again by joining our games on the slides or swings, or turned adolescents who quietly whispered to their lovers, protected by the shelter of a tropical almond tree.

In el Parque Ramfis there was much to explore and to understand. It took me a while to realize that the "house" whose doors were closed to children and women was actually a reading library. I often asked Mamá Biela why. And she would answer, "*Mi perla,*" as she would often call me, since we both discovered the etymology of my name, "*los hombres son así.* It really does not matter. See how comfortable it is to read here, on this bench, feeling the sea breeze?" But I am moving too fast. Let me go back to the white and blue house where this tale began.

When I was eight years old, Mami was expecting her second child by her second husband. The wonderful penthouse on the fourth floor of the Edificio Menéndez (owned by Mamá Biela's brother) had become a problem. My mother, enduring a very difficult pregnancy and extreme anemia, found herself unable to continue to climb the four flights of stairs to our apartment. Mamá Biela's house on Arzobispo Portes, having been recently vacated by its tenants, was the ideal solution.

As you entered the house a big living room and dining room greeted you. The mahogany furniture had seen better days but we liked it because it was big and comfortable. At the center of the living room was a piano Mami used to play after dinner. To the right were a number of bedrooms and a bathroom.

Daisy Cocco, San Cristóbal, Dominican
Republic, 1954

Toward the back, on the left, there was a kitchen where *el fogón,* the charcoal
pit, produced day after day a number of *delicias criollas; el platanito maduro frito*
was considered food of the gods by us kids in those days.

In the middle of the house toward the back was an indoor yard. When I first
entered the house, the *guayabas* and the *cerezas* in bloom then gave me the
comfort I needed after having had to "abandon" our apartment by the sea. But
I was to find out soon enough that there was no room for *guayabas* and *cerezas*
in Mami's world now that she had to cope with the birth of her fifth child. The
guayabas and *cerezas* were pulled out, uprooted just as I had been so many
times in my young life, and replaced by cement. After a number of years, the
plants managed to break through the cement and to grow, a little, in the
cracks — the only green allowed in that sad patio.

Quiet and serene for most of the day, the house came to life in the evening
when *la colonia italiana,* comprised of a number of Dominican women who
had married Italian professionals who had come alone to set up or to build
Trujillo's houses, streets, factories, sugar-cane-processing plants or refineries.
At night there was music and the sound of a melodious, slightly foreign
language that spoke of art, music, and culinary delicacies.

I was fascinated by all of it and soon came to prize conversations with adults
only, having tired of the silly squabbles of the other neighborhood children. I

cherished my uniqueness as I began to accept my "difference" from them. I learned to speak Italian when I was quite young. I learned about music, and at the hands of Violetta and Giacobbo I received the most beautiful introduction to one of my life's passions, opera.

This childless couple, an aging Italian violinist who played in the national symphony and his wife, a young black Dominican soprano, were intrigued by my precocity and interest. I spent many an hour listening to their stories about the difficulties in casting an opera or finding the right costumes or surmounting challenges in stage design. By the ripe old age of eight, I was quite sophisticated for my neighborhood. I was so content with my circumstances I did not even mind the many *pullas* about my being *la señorita de los macarrones,* the daughter of a divorced woman, on her second husband, living in *la casa del italiano.*

Mamá Biela came to visit one evening on her way to her friend's house. It was the first time she had seen me socialize with my stepfather's circle of friends. I remember how quiet she became. She sat in the corner of the room. Her hands folded together, her fingers moving in a vertical motion, reminiscent of piano playing. Two days later she telephoned. She asked Mami to allow me to become her "chaperone" as she roamed the city, visiting old friends of her family.

This was the beginning of my introduction to another *casa,* one without roof and gates. Mamá Biela had been a teacher long before women were able to educate themselves for the classroom. For years she had taught at the Salomé Ureña school until one day, impatient with the lack of diligence of one of her pupils, Mamá Biela, four feet eleven inches and one hundred pounds, picked up the wayward pupil and literally threw her out of the class, by way of the window. Fortunately, the classroom was on the first floor. Mamá Biela, however, had come to the realization that it was time for a change.

With my "chaperoning" days began my hands-on, on-the-road introduction to Dominican culture, our people, and our literature. Mamá Biela was a practical woman. By the time I was eight years old and she was fifty-nine, she had done away with most frills. There was a dressmaker on the far end of town who made her simple cotton dresses. Mamá Biela's shirtdresses had a row of buttons in the front and two big pockets, one on each hip. These dresses and her adoption of sneakers freed her from most "female" inconveniences such as carrying handbags or wearing heels.

Armed with an umbrella, her wallet and keys in her pockets, we set out most Friday and Saturday evenings to visit not only her friends but old friends of the family's, and in particular the last remaining friends of her mother's. As we walked, she used the street names to introduce anecdotes, historical events, or literary pieces. This is how I learned about the contributions to Dominican education and literature of women like Salomé Ureña, Lea de Castro, and Ercilia Pepín. The Arzobispo Noel prompted anecdotes about a colorful man of the cloth who had political aspirations and successes. Streets named after our liberal leaders of the independence movement, Duarte, Sánchez y Mella, evoked their own unique place in her world of tales. Even Santana, the dastardly, treacherous, ambitious, lecherous leader during the first years of the independent Dominican nation, had his place in her tales and folklore.

But of all our activities, even above the conversations about those monarchs of Dominican folklore, the *ciguapas* and *galipotes*, I enjoyed with some of her old friends, I treasure those quiet moments we spent in the park reading poetry or discussing nature. I think I became a teacher because Mamá Biela's lessons shaped my soul. As I reflect on my life, I could not say as others have that I learned everything I needed to know about life and teaching in kindergarten, for I learned it in the company of my grandmother. I still remember the hours we spent together in the park as she introduced me to the study of tropical vegetation when I was very young.

As I write these lines, I recall in particular my introduction to a leaf: it was something to be touched, to be smelled, to be drawn, to be named, to be studied, to be discussed, to be praised, to be sung about, to be celebrated. As we drew and colored a leaf, Mamá Biela taught me the scientific nomenclature of its parts and we discussed its relation to the soil, the trunk, the flowers, the fruits, the air, the weather, and so on. We also read poems about nature and discussed the intricacies of recreating them in a painting. Her lessons combined theory, discussion, experience, application, and above all a sense of the interconnectedness of all living things as well as the relationship among the diverse manifestations of the human intellect and spirit.

In 1962 I left Santo Domingo to join my mother, who had moved to New York, a pattern that would be repeated throughout her life. When Mamá Biela and I parted, never to live in the same town again, I thought I would die. I believed I would not survive the uprooting. But like the leaves from the *guayabas* and *cerezas* in my mother's patio, I also managed to "sprout" even through all the cement I found in New York City. Somehow during those hard first years of separation I was able to draw strength from all Mamá Biela and I had shared.

I know now that Mamá Biela suspected the changes that life would bring me and realized early on in my life that I needed a different kind of foundation and dwelling. The house Mamá Biela built for me is one I can take with me wherever I go, for it is made of memories and an understanding of who I am. It is a dwelling supported by the confidence, pride, and belief in self Mamá Biela instilled in me. I realize now that if I am a builder today it is because in those early years I was shown how to get the materials in my imagination and the tools from my resilience and intelligence.

In 1984, having received my Ph.D. and on the eve of the publication in the Dominican Republic of my first book, I returned to Santo Domingo to find my Mamá Biela deathly ill, spending her last days at home. From her bedroom, Mamá Biela could hear the conversations with some Dominican writers and intellectuals who had come to visit me. Somehow, Mamá Biela found the strength and enthusiasm to tell all who came to see her *"que todos los escritores de la capital han venido a conocer a mi perla."*

Lightning

Mirtha N. Quintanales

WHEN I WAS SEVEN years old I suddenly became terrified of thunderstorms. My fear was undoubtedly triggered by witnessing lightning strike a royal palm tree nearby. It was an afternoon during late summer. My parents, brother, and I were having lunch at a party given by a colleague of my father who owned a big house "out in the country." The storm rolled in without any notice. Then it all took place at once: the blinding light, the deafening sound, the burning tree. On a hill, in the front lawn of a private home in rural Pinar del Río, Cuba's easternmost province, I saw what happened.

I didn't know anybody who was afraid of thunderstorms. I eventually found out about my grand-aunt Cheche's problem, but that was much later, when I had already come to terms with my own fear. Not at the moment of the frightening incident nor at any time after did I find much empathy from the adults around me.

Only Abuelo José Pedro, my mother's father, who used to be very fond of children, acknowledged the trembling that used to overtake me when the first bright outlines of lightning appeared in the Cuban sky. I sought, even if I never verbalized it, actual physical protection, preferably the broad lap or embracing soft arms of a female family member. That need was never satisfied. Yet Abuelo's attempts to be there for me gave me some consolation. I loved him and considered him to be a wise old man.

"*Mirtica,*" he told me the first time he and I found ourselves together during a thunderstorm after my fear started. "You know," he whispered almost conspiratorially, "some people say that all the light and the noise happen because God and the angels are bowling up in Heaven. But that's not the way it is. When you first see the lightning, start counting slowly until you hear the sound of the thunder. The longer the time between light and sound, the farther away the place where lightning has actually struck. It is very scientific."

He and I, my younger brother, four cousins, and any other children who happened to be around during a thunderstorm would make a game of counting. I remember, on some occasions, watching my grandmother lift her eyes from her sewing — an activity she inevitably engaged in every time it rained — and smile at my grandfather as he played with the kids. She would let her glasses slide down her nose and, peering above them, would look at my grandfather with much sweetness.

Abuelo taught me how to find distraction from my fear, but not how to make it go away. During the counting game I would observe the other children. Their laughter was loose and from the belly. Mine, when I allowed it to happen, was at best nervous and cerebral. To me it was all a very serious business, keeping my fear at bay.

All the wisdom of a seven-year-old led me to believe that being afraid of thunderstorms was a serious personal problem. This kind of weather was a regular feature of the Cuban rainy season, usually during August and early fall. Was I going to suffer from this affliction yearly for the rest of my life? The thought made me shudder.

God was not an automatically accepted presence in the life of my extended maternal family, with whom my brother and I spent much of our time. Whether God existed at all was at best a matter of conjecture and rare debate. My mother, perhaps the only person in the family to openly exhibit any religious leanings that I could discern, was by no stretch of the imagination an obvious believer or regular churchgoer. Sometimes she'd take me to Sunday morning mass; and she arranged for me to prepare for and have my first communion. She even once took me with her to visit some friends of hers who were nuns in a rural convent. But for some reason she never talked to me about religion. My father had been an altar boy in his childhood, and he was something of a Methodist when he attended a Methodist school as a youth, but as I was growing up he simply wanted nothing to do with churches or clergymen or organized religion. Indeed one of the most notable stories I heard as a child was that of my baptism.

As I was told, my father didn't want me baptized, arguing that one should choose one's religion as an adult and not have it forced upon one as a child. But my mother insisted, and he finally consented. Nevertheless, I almost didn't get baptized because the officiating Catholic priest would not accept the Russian (and surely Communist) middle name my father had selected for me. When it became clear that either the name stayed or there would be no baptism, he finally performed the rite. At some point I discovered that my grandfather had been a Christian Scientist all his adult life, and that an aunt was a devout Catholic. However, as I was growing up, the adults around me kept whatever life of faith they had mostly to themselves.

Given this background, God with a capital G seemed to be just a little

The Quintanales family: (l–r) Mirtha, Mirtha, Roberto,
Cecilio, Jiménez Studios, Havana, circa 1953

beyond my reach. Nevertheless, I somehow felt that this shadowy figure was possibly my only recourse in my earnest attempt to overcome my fear of the light and noise in the sky. Finally, after much thought, I made an appeal for grace. Every night I prayed. "God, I don't want to be afraid of thunderstorms. We have them here all the time. Please help me. Please help me not to be afraid." I addressed the Divine in a personal way, although I had absolutely no image of a personal god.

After this deeply heartfelt prayer, I would imagine myself in the midst of a thunderstorm, not only not afraid but actually enjoying it. For a year and a half I did not fail once to carry out this nightly ritual. It was accompanied by an exercise that only many years later I would recognize as a technique for entering into meditation.

Finally, one day, the fear was gone. Just like that. I tested myself, first by standing in front of a window and looking directly at the illuminated sky. Then I would actually step out into the balcony of our Havana apartment and allow myself to feel the raindrops striking against my skin, light and thunder all around me, almost a part of me, as if there were no barriers between my being and this amazing natural phenomenon. I still remember the overwhelming feeling of joy and of inner strength I felt in the face of this great miracle. God exists. I was sure of it, and with effort on my part his help had turned out to be not only effective but spectacular. I was in awe and deeply grateful.

I never told anyone about this experience. Years later, as an educated adult living in the United States, I diminished its power and beauty by dismissing the miracle as the simple consequence of high motivation and psychological conditioning or positive affirmation on my part. No big deal. Yet deep within, the feelings of wonder and gratitude remained despite all the scientific explanations or acquired academic skepticism. I now acknowledge and honor the miracle I experienced as true. So I take this opportunity to thank God for such a kind gesture in helping his small and trusting charge. I also thank my grandfather, José Pedro Font, who, although unable to remove my fear, pointed me in the right direction, simply by loving and respecting the child I was.

New York City, Winter 1988
(Rewritten Fall 1996)

My Name Is This Story

Aurora Levins Morales

MIGRATION IS A STORY that changes each time I tell it, and I've told it thousands of times. The journey from the impoverished coffee barrio of Indiera Baja de Maricao to the university-dominated community of Hyde Park in Chicago, surrounded by ghettos. The journey from *rubia* to spik. How that first long, cold winter of 1967 I became darker in the eyes of people and institutions, acquiring social color even as the sun faded from my skin. How my middle-class culture, my actual coloring, the Jewish half of my name, and the will of my white liberal friends not to see me or allow me to name myself kept my *puertorriqueñidad* bottled up, and this ability to pass left me feeling like a ghost trying to communicate with the living. How class shifted and slid. In Indiera, being the daughter of a junior professor among the children of coffee workers made me painfully privileged, cut off from people I loved by the possession of electricity and an indoor toilet. In Chicago, at triple the salary and prestige, how we scrambled to pay bills, living at the edge of the UC territory on a mixed-class street near the ghetto border. The racism that wrapped itself around me like a hurricane and eventually gave me a clear eye to look back and see the racism I had not been forced to notice as a *rubia* child. I could tell it again. It's juicy and full of things that need saying. But today I need to tell this a different way. To say that the shape of my journey, the writer's voice I carry, the places I call home are what they are because I grew up female and Red.

My parents met in New York City in 1948, in the Communist Party. My father is of Russian Jewish immigrants and longtime radicals. My mother from the fallen aristocracy of Naranjito, landed families who had lost most of their privilege by 1929 when my grandparents took the boat, and who landed into hunger and work as janitor, laundress, seamstress, stock clerk. My father grew up singing the International in Yiddish-speaking Brooklyn. My mother grew up in Harlem and the Bronx and found Marx at Hunter College. In 1950, blacklisted and facing my father's possible drafting into the Korean War, my parents came to Puerto Rico. They had been given the name and address of Jane Speed and César Andreu Iglesias as contacts. They quickly became friends and together formed a Communist Party *núcleo* in the mountains of Maricao where my parents bought the farm I was born on.

I grew up in a Marxist home at a time of international decolonization struggles, my imagination filled with Cuba and Vietnam, Angola and Guinea-Bissau, Chou En-Lai's China and the Bolivia of *El Che*. I grew up listening to groups of young men talking excitedly about strategy and theory in our living room, while women sat silent, or, if they spoke, were ignored. I grew up with a mother who was a feminist without a movement, who moved farther and farther from those meetings where her comments kept being attributed to my father. I also grew up in a barrio with very few options for women, where intelligence and curiosity were restricted to the daily struggles and the doings of one's neighbors, without room to make other choices than young and plentiful childbearing, agricultural and household labor, food stamps and a pot of *gandules*.

In the mid-1960s three factors converged on my family and pushed us out of Indiera. The most obvious and public was my father being denied tenure at Río Piedras because of his highly visible political activism on campus, his travel to Cuba, and his way of teaching biology, which was innovative and exciting and also tended to undermine hierarchy and empower students. But there were two other forces that were at least as powerful. From the time she started school, my mother always loved studying, loved education, craved it and relentlessly pursued it. It took her from 1947 to 1959 to complete her B.A., in summer school, in evening classes, however she could. And as soon as she did, she enrolled immediately in graduate courses, and kept on taking them during summers spent in Michigan while we lived in Puerto Rico. My father losing his job became an opportunity for change, and she decided to go for a doctorate in anthropology, which meant moving to the States. My father's acceptance of a job at Chicago depended on my mother getting accepted as a grad student. Her intellectual hunger propelled us.

The third factor was that I was entering puberty surrounded by girls who were getting pregnant at fourteen; attending a junior high school in Yauco where grown men hung around the gates trying to pick up seventh graders; spending my lunch hours writing love notes in English for schoolmates who asked me to tell their boyfriends things like "I want to have your baby." My mother was terrified that I would be swept away into the sexual illusions of my friends, so my parents pulled me out of school. I spent a year doing correspondence courses in English to prepare for high school in the U.S. The constricted possibilities and peer pressures surrounding young girls in Indiera, the kind of adolescence available to me there, became a powerful motivating force in our journey away.

The Chicago I landed in in 1967 was on fire with the Civil Rights and Black Power movements, antiwar activism, and the explosion of what was called the women's movement. If Neruda taught me that a poet could be passionately engaged in politics and write eloquently about it, it was white feminist women like Susan Griffin, Marge Piercy, Adrienne Rich, and Alta who taught me that writing about typing, housework, motherhood, the tangle of sex could be as powerful and gut-wrenching, as tender and exquisite as anything else in literature—that my life was worthy. At the same time, the white women around me and my mother, both of us members of the Chicago Women's Liberation Union, said things like "Mexican women don't need feminism because they are at the heart of their families and already have the power and support they need. Black women find empowerment in the fight against racism, not sexism. The movement is white because we're the only ones who need it." They could not yet envision a feminism shaped by the needs of brown women. Nevertheless, white feminism began the process of giving me voice.

It was not until 1978 that I found my first community of women of color writers. A group of us had all taken summer jobs interviewing randomly selected women in San Francisco on their experiences of sexual assault, and we were the interviewers sent into the Mission District, Chinatown, Filmore. In protesting the racism within the project, in sharing the stories we were gathering, and their weight on our hearts, we found each other. Cherríe Moraga, Kitty Tsui, Luisah Teish, Luz Guerra. Each of us led to others. Finally, I began having the conversations I hungered for most. I remember us laughing until our sides hurt, gathered around a potluck of our favorite home foods, about all the lies we had been told about ourselves and each other's people, a healing cleansing laughter that fed our poetry.

So what I want to say today is that because I was female, and because I was raised with a passion for politics in a profeminist family, my literary home, the writers with whom I live in community, whose work I need late at night for affirmation and wait for most eagerly, are defined not by ethnicity but by politics. For all the pleasure I take in the delicious craft of island writers, in the righteous rhythm and fire of the Nuyoricans, this is not the writing that I need the most. It is the writing of U.S. women of color, a handful of clear-headed white women, mostly Jewish, a few men who engage gender, mostly gay, that sustains me and gives me context.

This tribe called "women of color" is not an ethnicity. It is one of the inventions of solidarity, an alliance, a political necessity that is not the given name of every female with dark skin and a colonized tongue, but rather a choice about how to resist and with whom. This is one Puerto Rican reality: that it has been, not in nationalist self-affirmation, but in the critiques of feminist women of color of their own cultures, that I have found the space as a Puerto Rican woman to speak most truthfully about my real experiences, not the ones I was supposed to be having as a U.S. Puerto Rican. That it was here I could freely name the ambivalences and contradictions, had space to fiercely defend Puerto Rico from colonialism and still claim what I love about the United States, still critique what I find unbearable about Puerto Rico.

Feminism has nearly as long a history in Puerto Rico as in the United States, but colonialism has prevented the full-grown development of movements, cultures, and communities of resistance that have been possible for women in the United States, and neither my mother nor I is willing to ever again do without strong feminist community in our daily lives. At the same time, that same imperialism has gathered and shaped my multiethnic home, created those conversations with Filipina, Chicana, African American, Chinese, Japanese, Salvadoreña women all in one room. It is the history of the twentieth-century world full of migration, loss, and invention that has made their voices, our shared dislocations, my deeply felt internationalism so necessary to the flowering of my own Puerto Rican woman's voice.

So this is how it comes home. That not only does my sense of myself cross many national boundaries, but my sense of Puerto Rico has also opened up, multiplied, shed mythology, and become itself international. Five years ago I set out to write *Remedios,* a history of Puerto Rican women in prose poetry. But I found myself needing, for the sake of truth, to write also about women in Mali and Angola, Spain and Turkey, Peru and Mexico, Jamaica and Hawaii, New York and South Dakota, all of whom were part of our past—to expose the multiple roots and entangled branches of the Boricua tree. *Remedios* is my return migration, my journey back, with a new and differently opened eye, to share with the *isla* I left at thirteen, my hunger for a story, a history, that makes sense of everything I am and all that I have found to love.

Resisting the Alchemy of Erasure:
Journey to Labor Ideas

Clara Lomas

In the early seventies, when I had the chance to pursue a post-secondary education, I immediately knew that I could not turn down the opportunity I intuitively sensed had been the unfulfilled dream of several generations in my genealogical lines, both maternal and paternal. To this day I clearly remember the hot mid-August day one of the UC San Diego Chicano recruiters rang our front doorbell. As I opened the door, a three-feet ray of sun darted into the house, silhouetting Joe López in the mist of the steaming desert heat. Why had I not returned my Intention to Register form, he inquired. As he came into the house, I had to admit that my working-class parents could not afford to send the eldest daughter of seven to college. Although on graduating from high school I had applied to a few universities with the help of recruiters such as Joe, I feared it was just a dream to imagine that I could pursue a university education. Joe was doing a follow-up that day to remind me that students of working-class background like me now had opportunities that we should not pass up. The political struggles and student movement of the late sixties were finally materializing in unprecedented university programs. That day he brought with him the ray of hope my family had wished for quite some time. I knew then that I had to take on the responsibility — at the very least — to attempt to carry out an intellectual activity which could have an impact on social change. Hadn't most of the family stories I had heard dealt with struggles against natural and unnatural disasters overcome by sheer perseverance? When facing adversity, I had to remember that I came from a long line of survivors of these disasters: from floods and earthquakes to the Mexican Revolution, the Great Depression, and poverty. As far back as my parents could remember, our families' journeys had been spawned by intense political upheavals and marked by migrations, immigrations, and dislocations across geopolitical borders. I felt impelled to heed those stories. I had to take strength from them not only at that initial moment when I feared the new challenges ahead, but also throughout the entire educational journey to the Ph.D.

As I was growing up in the twin border towns of Caléxico/Mexicali, I would hear stories of the family members' yearly migrations from valley to valley, following the fruit and vegetable harvests in northern California during the summer months. On my mother's side of the family we would hear of *las piscas* (harvests) of carrots in Holtville, grapes in Fresno, strawberries in Santa María. On my father's side, the stories would focus mostly on my father's journeys to canneries, in an ice plant in Roseville (north of Sacramento), and in packing plants: plums in Hollister, tomatoes and peaches in Sacramento, dates in Indio. During the late fall, winter, and early spring months it was back to the Imperial Valley and Mexicali areas to harvest carrots and lettuce. For migrant children, these months were the time to attempt to keep up with their very fragmented education. Half a century would go by before this migrant pattern would be altered. Because of my parents' determination to guarantee their children a stable, continuous education, it wasn't our nuclear family that was out there migrating with our relatives. In the fall of 1952 my father and mother met in Caléxico and soon thereafter decided to marry. My parents resolved to do everything in their power to raise a "traditional family": father with a steady job; mother at home with kids; lots of children with solid educational possibilities. In other words, they wanted to offer their own nuclear family everything they had not been able to have as they were growing up. Given my parents' upbringing, it now seems amazing to me how they took agency to change the lifelines of at least two generations of migrant workers.

As far as my father could piece together, at the turn of the century his grandparents, Don Bernardino Ayala and Doña Petra Romero, had owned a bakery and various properties in Guaymas, Sonora. They had led rather sedentary lives until the wrath of the Mexican Revolution stripped them of every possibility of maintaining their source of income. With Don Bernardino's death in the early twenties, his only son, Luciano, was convinced by the *enganchadores* (recruiters) of the Colorado River Land Company (which had brought irrigation to the rich valley desert lands) to work seasonally in the wealthy cotton fields of Mexicali and the Imperial Valley. Luciano's plans, as those of so many other seasonal migrant workers, were to return home with the means to reestablish his family's business. *Como había sucedido con tantas otras personas que venían del interior de México a la frontera a juntar lana y regresar a sus respectivos pueblos, Luciano no regresa. Porque, por más que trabaja uno como burro, nunca se llega a juntar bastante lana.*[1] By the time Luciano

1. As had happened with many other people who came from the interior of Mexico to the border area to make money and go back to their respective towns, Luciano did not return. Because, although one works hard as a mule, one can never save up enough money.

arrived at the sparsely populated Mexicali/Imperial Valley basin, the hierarchical labor, social, and racial structure in the desert valley was well established. With the Newlands Reclamation Act of 1902 Anglo settlers had become land- and water-rights owners. The Chinese, Japanese, and Hindustani laborers who had been attracted to the area were now allowed to lease land from the Colorado River Land Company. The native Cucapah Indians and the Mexican laborers had been excluded from any possibility of land ownership, yet were welcomed en masse as cheap labor. *La compañía había convertido la región en una gran hacienda donde los mexicanos trabajábamos casi como esclavos.*[2]

Since Luciano could not send home enough money to maintain the rest of the household, Doña Petra and her three daughters eventually followed him to "the Egypt of the West," the richest cotton-producing area of the time. Entire families migrating to the cotton fields of the north would meet, working and socializing side by side. These would be the circumstances under which the three Ayala young women would meet their future husbands: the Fernández and Lomas cousins. *Tata* (grandfather) Vicente, who should have been a Fernández also, was by that time a Lomas. The family lore has it that after great-grandfather Fernández abandoned his family, my great-grandmother defiantly retook her maiden name—a bold statement in those times—and had all her children's last names changed accordingly. Thus the maturest son of the Fernández family, Vicente Lomas, was to court and eventually marry the eldest of the Ayala sisters, Abundia, as they continued the migration routes of the Mexicali/Caléxico valley, crossing the international borders at a time when the border patrol was virtually nonexistent. At this time, Mexican cheap labor was not only welcomed, it was critical, to the prosperity of the region.

As was typical of these border migrating families in the twenties, the birthplace of their children also became an accident of national and international economic circumstances. Consequently, *Nana* (grandmother) Abundia gave birth to her children in different towns on both sides of the international border. The eldest, Alejandro, was born in Brawley in 1927, and my father, Alberto, was born in Caléxico in 1929. After the Great Depression, when the Mexican laborers were no longer welcomed in the cotton fields, the new immigration laws were stringently enforced. As a result, the youngest in the family, Armando, was born across the border in Mexicali in 1931. In response to the dictatorship of Porfirio Díaz, which had opened the doors to foreign investment to the detriment of the majority of its own population, a revolutionary

2. The company had converted the region into a great hacienda where we, the Mexicans, worked almost like slaves.

tremor shook Mexico at the beginning of the century. The revolution unleashed a political and economic torrent that carried the family north and across the national boundary at the beginning of the twenties. Approximately a decade later, an economic downturn in the United States pushed them back across that geopolitical boundary. Ironically, the planned symbiosis, the names of the so-called twin sister cities — Mexi/cali (Mexico/California) and Cal/éxico (California/Mexico) — would be developed to privilege only a few commercial enterprises on the U.S. side. The vast majority of the borderlands peoples would have to adjust their lives to the whims of the economic demands of the expanding agribusiness transnational corporations.

Interestingly enough, the family history up to the 1930s on my maternal side was not too different from that of my paternal side. Three generations ago the cotton mecca also pulled them in the direction of Baja and Alta Californias, while the Mexican Revolution pushed them out of their more sedentary lives. Although Tata Emeterio Aguirre and Nana Edwiges Leyva had also met in the cotton fields toward the end of the twenties, their life trajectories up to that moment had been considerably different.

Tata Emeterio was born in 1909 into a quite turbulent period for his family and the entire country: his mother died the year after his birth, just as the Mexican Revolution was breaking and as his grandfather was assassinated by the Federal troops for his support of the revolutionary effort. Due to their political beliefs and his father's assassination, great-grandfather Don Candelario and his two brothers left their farms and families behind in eastern Durango to join the Zapatista army in southern Mexico. He remained in armed struggle in Chiapas and other southern regions until 1918 when internal political conflict with the Carrancistas prompted him to flee to the United States: *Porque mi familia había pertenecido a los zapatistas, nos perseguían los carrancistas, quemaban nuestras milpas de maíz. Teníamos que huir por el monte y escondernos de los del gobierno. Entonces parte papá Candelario, llevándose a una nueva esposa de catorce años, Donaciana, y a mi hermano Pancho, hacia los Estados Unidos, para salvar su pellejo. Con esta nueva "familia" se podía proteger de los del gobierno para disimular su huída. Cruza la frontera por Nogales, Arizona, y allí trabajan en el algodón en varios pueblos. Con el tiempo se compra una calecita y una mula, y de esa manera parte de Mesa, Arizona, hacia el Valle Imperial. Se vienen por el camino de madera que en ese tiempo se usaba para poder cruzar el desierto de Yuma.*[3]

3. Because my family had belonged to the Zapatista faction, we were persecuted by the Carrancistas. They would burn our corn *milpas*. We had to flee to the mountains and hide from the government soldiers. Then, father Candelario flees for his life toward the United States, taking with him a new wife, Donaciana, barely fourteen years old, and my brother Pancho. With this new "family" he could protect himself from government soldiers by disguising his escape. He

Once in the Imperial Valley, in 1920, great-grandfather Candelario sent for Tata Emeterio. He remembered his teen years migrating through California: Fullerton, Fresno, Watsonville and back to the cotton fields of the Valley, going to school only intermittently. The wages his father earned in the fields by himself were not sufficient to support the family. Only together, children and adults working in the labor camps, were they able to earn subsistence wages. Tata Eme's infrequent appearances in school were increasingly humiliating rather than positive educational experiences. He stopped attending school after third grade. Although his own education had been minimal, that was not Nana (Vicki) Edwiges's experience, owing to her rural middle-class upbringing. Her parents, Don Braulio Leyva, a Spanish marine merchant, and Doña Blandina, a Maya Indian in charge of the family financial interests, afforded their eight children the luxury of the highest education possible in the rural area, which was limited to grammar school. A captain of one of the well-established Compañía Liera's vessels, Don Braulio was able to accumulate some wealth: properties, livestock, and imported goods. While Don Braulio spent most of his time at sea, Doña Blandina was in charge of running the household and the family small businesses in the rural community of El Amole, near Los Mochis, Sinaloa. Nana Vicki would recall that with the coming of the railroad to the port and with the dire economic situation caused by the political turmoil in the country, *el transporte marítimo perdió su importancia* (the ocean transportation lost its importance), and the young men in the family began to respond to the recruitment calls by the *enganchadores* of the Colorado River Land Company to work in the cotton fields. In 1923 the rest of the family decided to join them. They traveled in one of the few Liera vessels still in business, from Los Mochis to El Mayor, Baja California. They were caught in a severe storm and lost all of their possessions. Their arrival in late November in the dry, cold desert was particularly brutal, for they were accustomed to the tropical weather of the coast. At the age of seventeen, Nana Vicki saw for the first time the borderlands that were to be her home for most of the rest of her life. *Llegamos junto al canal Wisteria. Al día siguiente de nuestra llegada, salimos todos los hijos a buscar trabajo en las piscas del algodón. Llegamos a fines de noviembre, vestidos ligeros para clima tropical, y allí ya había llegado el tiempo de las heladas por la noche. No traíamos ropa gruesa para cubrirnos del frío. Y sin embargo así tuvimos que salir a trabajar. Al final del día teníamos nuestras ropas completamente rotas y las manos sangrando por lo difícil que era piscar el algodón.*

---

crosses the border at Nogales, Arizona. They work in the cotton fields in various towns. With time, he buys a small buggy and a mule. They leave Mesa, Arizona, toward the Imperial Valley. They traveled on the wooden road used to cross the Yuma desert.

Son navajas las puntas secas del casquillo de algodón. Fue una lucha sacar las motitas — cada una de ellas — con las manos sangrando. Nosotros que siempre habíamos tenido quienes trabajaran para nosotros bajo buenas condiciones. Ahora nos encontrábamos trabajando bajo condiciones abominables. [4]

Nana Vicki and Tata Eme married in the "carrot capital of world," Holtville, in the Imperial Valley, and continued migrating throughout California. As had happened in my father's family, their children were also born on both sides of the border, the first two in Los Angeles and the last in Mexicali. In the 1930s, as a result of the Depression and the consequent repatriation of Mexicans, they became victims of the massive deportations. Nana Vicki would never let us forget the devastating and dehumanizing experience they had to endure. *A tu Tata lo habían convencido de que debería regresarse a Mexicali, pero no me daba por vencida de que yo tenía que dejar mi ciudadanía estadounidense. El maldito oficial de inmigración por fin me amenazó con quitarme a mis hijos nacidos en los Estados Unidos y mandarlos a un orfelinato. Humillada, tuve que aceptar que me echaran con los otros millares de mexicanos.* [5] My mother was one of those two U.S.-born children who would have been placed in an orphanage had Nana Vicki stuck to her guns.

These circumstances, which seem extraordinary to us now (although quite common for the border people in the first part of the twentieth century), caused both my parents to be born in the United States and raised across the border on the Mexican side of the "twin cities." Difficult economic and family circumstances made it impossible for them to continue their education beyond grammar school in Mexicali. At the age of three, my father became *huérfano de padre* (orphan without a father) when he lost his father. In 1932 Tata Vicente died after making heroic efforts to save a burning house nearby. Nana Abundia, left with the heavy responsibility of raising three boys, vowed not to remarry to avoid the risk of having her boys mistreated by a potentially abusive stepfather. She took a job as a laundry woman assisting the personal

---

4. We arrived near the Wisteria canal. The following day we all went out to look for work in the cotton fields. We had arrived at the end of November, dressed for tropical climate, and here we were in a place where it would freeze at night. We didn't have warm clothes appropriate for that weather. Nonetheless we had to go out and work under those conditions. By the end of the day, our clothes were shredded. Our hands were bleeding from picking the cotton. The dry pointed ends of the cotton boll are knives. It was a struggle to pull out the cotton balls — one by one — with bleeding hands. We, who had always had people to work for us under good conditions, found ourselves working in abominable conditions.

5. They had convinced your grandfather to return to Mexico, but I would not give up my U.S. citizenship. The vicious immigration officer finally threatened me with taking my U.S.-born children and having them placed in an orphanage. Humiliated, I was forced to accept being thrown out of the country with thousands of other Mexicans.

Resisting the Alchemy of Erasure 109

secretary of Baja California's governor, Rodolfo Sánchez Taboada. The fact that the boys had no father not only stigmatized them socially; it also affected the family economically and in terms of their educational possibilities. When Mexican president Lázaro Cárdenas expropriated foreign interests in Mexico, the lands previously owned by the Colorado River Land Company were redistributed to families who worked the lands in Mexicali. All families were entitled to fifty acres except those families which did not have a male head of household. Thus my father's family received only two acres, which did not yield the crops necessary for the family to sustain itself.

Nana Abundia took many domestic jobs to enable her to keep her boys in the Escuela Cuauhtémoc through sixth grade. It was the Yaqui Indian in her that helped her hold her head up high during those hard times, my father would say. He would also tell of their difficulties in school, despite the fact that he and his older brother were at the top of their class. *Cuando yo tenía nueve años, por ser Alejandro y yo los más adelantados de la clase, nos iban a mandar a la Ciudad de México. Ibamos a recibir la bandera de nuestro nuevo Ejido Coahuila de manos del presidente Cárdenas. Sin embargo, el Sr. Ledesma se levanta en la sesión de la escuela de padres de familia y pregunta por qué no se mandaba a hijos de algún ejidatario; que los Lomas eran sólo los hijos de la viuda. Por lo tanto nos negaron la posibilidad de representar a nuestro ejido.*[6] They did, however, have another opportunity to represent the small farmers of the area when, through the intervention of Governor Sánchez Taboada, they were selected to attend the Instituto Técnico Industrial de Aguas Calientes in Tijuana. It was my father's most triumphant and traumatic moment in his pursuit of a solid education to change his family's economic situation. He would often tell us how much he enjoyed life as an academic intern at the institute, describing his many academic successes and the final tragic incident that ended his studies there. Soon after he won a speech competition on a critical assessment of the Spanish Conquest, his right hand became infected and he almost lost it. The school administrators were not sympathetic about his medical condition and did not excuse him for the days he was hospitalized. He was not allowed to continue his studies at the institute. After he completed sixth grade in Mexicali, Nana Abundia and my father made every effort to have him enrolled in the Calexico schools, but to no avail. Years later, as a U.S.-born citizen, my father qualified to be drafted for military service, but as a young man his citizenship did not entitle him to an education in the United States.

6. I was nine years old. Because Alejandro and I were the most advanced in the class, we were selected to go to Mexico City. We were going to receive our new Ejido Cuahuila flag from the hands of President Cárdenas. Mr. Ledesma, however, gets up in the parent-teacher school meeting and questioned why the sons of a farmer were not sent instead of the Lomas boys. After all, weren't the Lomas boys only the sons of the widow? Consequently, they denied us the possibility of representing our farming community.

As fate would have it, Nana Vicki and my mother also attempted to take advantage of my mother's U.S. citizenship to enroll her in the Calexico schools after she had completed her elementary education. And they too ran up against the same roadblock: the out-of-the-country tuition was exorbitant, far more expensive than the trade and professional schools in Mexicali. At the age of approximately twelve, then, both my parents had to give up the dream of continuing their educations and begin helping to support their families. For several years they both followed the migrant routes, until they met while working at their first permanent jobs at the beginning of the 1950s at the largest and most prosperous department store of border area, S.H. Kress. After their first three daughters were born in Mexicali, they moved across the border to Caléxico in order to secure for all their children the education they had not been able to secure for themselves. Continuing in what was the tradition of the family, their other four children were born on the U.S. side of the border.

Given the stories they told about their education beyond grammar school, I think one could almost characterize my parents as *autodidactas* (self-taught persons). My father told of reading avidly under dim lighting as he traveled the California migrant routes from the age of twelve. Appalled by the horrid conditions under which migrant workers were forced to labor in the United States, he felt compelled to document them. Throughout the years his notes grew into short stories, and eventually he reworked them into a novel. His experience in having it published was another disappointment. *Envié la única copia del manuscrito a una casa editorial en la Ciudad de México y un año después recibí un ejemplar del libro en forma de pago. Lo peor de todo es que se me perdió la novela en uno de los campos laborales.*[7] He slowly taught himself to read and write in English, secured a stable job in Calexico, and took correspondence courses to attain his G.E.D. Through his example, he instilled in us a love for books and knowledge.

During my mother's childhood, it became evident that her brother's education took precedence. She had to concentrate in becoming an exemplary wife and mother. When she was faced with the challenge of helping her children with homework in another language, however, she taught herself the English required to handle the task at hand. As we, the oldest of her children, were entering junior high school, she found herself bewildered by our inquisitiveness and dismayed by her inability to answer all of our many academic inquiries. Prompted by those intriguing questions, she sought answers at the local library. She would get up early enough to get herself, my father, and her six children ready for work and school, then escape to the public library. She

7. I sent my only copy of the manuscript to a publisher in Mexico City, and a year later received a copy of the published book as payment. Unfortunately, that copy was lost in one of the labor camps.

would steal the morning hours — before going back home to have lunch ready for all of us — reading with her weathered Spanish / English dictionary next to her. She studied history, philosophy, religion, anything she could get her hands on to satisfy her own curiosity. *Cuando cumplí los 34 años me dio el campanazo. Ya llevaba casi la mitad de mi vida casada y me sentía más atrasada que cuando me había casado. Me decidí hacer todo lo que hasta ese momento no había podido hacer: tomé clases de natación, clases de inglés, impartí clases de catecismo; empecé a estudiar el curso por correspondencia del "income tax."*[8] She would only get a few hours of sleep trying to assimilate as much information as possible. At times I would catch her in the middle of the night reading or writing. Not until she attended one of the "Baca summer camps" did she finally confess: *En ese tiempo, siento una gran urgencia por expresarme a mí misma, mis inquietudes. A pesar de todo mi mundo alrededor, no tengo con quién compartirlas. Escribo y escribo; me expreso para mí misma, y guardo mis papelitos. Ya llegará el momento propicio, me decía a mí misma, para sacarlos y compartirlos con las personas adecuadas que sepan aprovecharlas.*[9] After my youngest sister started preschool, my mother began to participate in her school as a volunteer parent. As the years went by, she spent so many hours at the school that many parents mistook her for the principal. She became the PTA president, organized the parents to support bilingual programs, and confronted the school board on the need to fund better buses for student excursions and more nutritional foods in the schools. She became such a strong presence and voice in the community that the school board tried to incorporate her as one of their members. Because of what many of the city's leaders considered her "confrontational" (read subversive) activities, my father was constantly approached by them to "put your wife in her domestic place." But father defiantly retorted, "She has my full support!" Through the help and concerted effort of some four hundred parents, my mother had managed to transform her new-found knowledge into effective activism.

I have shared here only a few of the innumerable bilingual narratives that members of my genealogical line have not allowed to become subsumed in the alchemy of erasure. From my grandparents' survival skills and perseverance to

8. When I turned thirty-four years old, it hit me. I had been married half of my life and I felt so behind, more so than the way I had felt when I had married. I decided to do everything that I had not been able to do up to that moment: I took swimming lessons, English classes; I taught catechism; I took an IRS income tax preparer's correspondence course.

9. During that time, I feel a tremendous urgency to express myself, my concerns. Despite my whole world around me, I don't have any one to share them with. I write and I write. I express myself for my own good and I safekeep my written expressions. The appropriate time will come, I would tell myself, to bring them out and share them with those who will know how to take advantage of them.

my parents' determination and strategizing to make our education possible, from the political and economic migrations and dislocations to the precarious existence on the borderlands of two unequal nation states, I have been empowered by a genealogy—captured in stories through several generations—to continue the journey to "labor ideas." To their memory, I raise my glass of "labored ideas" and toast their overcoming the natural and unnatural disasters they confronted, their perseverance against all odds to fulfill a dream that my particular historical circumstances in the early seventies allowed me to carry out. I have drawn from their strength to enter uncharted territories as a first-generation university student, to bear the challenges in institutions where my linguistic and cultural experiences are considered "disadvantaged," to weather the wintry towers of tokenism, to fight against assuming excessive working loads due to my ethnic background. I carry with me their survival strategies when in political and ideological battles, when learning new languages critical to comprehending new experiences, when ambiguity is the order of the day, when pronouncing my name in Spanish is making a political statement, when my citizenship is questioned in an intellectual space, when disciplinary borders are imposed on my work in order to give birth to my expression.

That mid-August day in the borderlands desert I intuitively knew I had to overcome my fears to begin my new journey, to continue my families' journey. I have learned from them to value education—although that valuing no doubt comes as well from my terror of a life without it.

Esta Risa No Es de Loca

Caridad Souza

Esta risa no es de loco. Se están riendo de mí.
Me dicen que yo estoy loco pero se están cayendo
de un coco. Porque de mí no pueden reír . . .
— HÉCTOR LAVOE, *Vamos a Reír Un Poco*

Esta Locura Tiene Raíces.

I'M NOT EXACTLY SURE when it was that I began to feel crazy, but I think it has something to do with being Puerto Rican, and working class, from a woman-headed family, and a girl-child who has come of age in the late twentieth century. It's really quite a feat to be a Puerto Rican woman in the late twentieth century. You barely exist outside your own imagination except in the form of vicious stereotypes. The only way to bring your own self out of oblivion is to remind folks about that peculiarly colonial/postcolonial relationship the United States has with a small island in the Caribbean and its people in diaspora. The huge wall of silence that always stops a conversation among people in the United States whenever you bring up those "controversial" issues they'd rather forget speaks to the way Puerto Rican women get continually erased. It always makes me feel so crazy.

My first lessons in erasure happened during my early childhood within my extended family. I was born in the South Bronx at the tail end of the baby boom, my Puerto Ricanness always suspect to my mother's family. Although on the surface I seemed to fit all the appropriate Puerto Rican identity markers, there were wrinkles in this fabric. My father was the child of dual migrations. His mother, an orphan from Ponce, Puerto Rico, migrated to the United States as a domestic servant during the first significant wave of Puerto Rican migration in the early part of the twentieth century. My paternal grandfather migrated to the United States from the Cape Verde Islands. I was four years old when he died, so I had little contact with his relatives. My father, although New York born and bred, brought that culture alive for me through specific spiritual beliefs and practices that connected me to my African heritage through a particular cosmological world view. My mother, on the other hand, was part of the "great migration" of Puerto Ricans to the United States that began at midcentury. She passed down to her children some historically and regionally specific cultural values and practices that connect me to my *puertorriqueñidad*. But her Puerto Rico was the one of her childhood in the fifties, a Puerto Rico partly constructed through the imaginings of a migrating female colonial subject. She fed us the nostalgic narrative of island paradise interspersed with stories of poverty and hardship that made sense to me only after we moved to the island when I was eight years old. That's how I got to be a child of multiple diasporas. But the glaring contradictions in my family's narrative were what started me off feeling crazy.

Very early on, questions of race, culture, and color permeated my family's politics and my psyche. My maternal grandmother, an indomitable matriarch, always had nothing but praise for the half German-American children of one of her daughters. She let everyone know that my aunt's kids were her favorite grandchildren, pointing to their "pedigree" German background. My mother's children were part African; my maternal grandmother took absolute pride in the fact that her own parents were not. She bragged that her mother was from Venezuela and her father from Italy. This set her apart from the rest of us mere mortals except, of course, for her favorite grandchildren, with whom she shared a racial affinity based on Europeanness. No one ever talked about her dark-skinned husband, nor about how much my mother resembled her father in color and features. There was never any talk about the racial roots of my mother's family, even though many family members were dark-skinned. Only my mother, who was said to resemble her paternal grandmother, was called "*la negra*" in that derogatory way that Puerto Ricans have when they participate in their own erasure.

It was on my father's African background that all the family's anxieties about race and color were mapped. He was referred to by my mother's mother as "*ese perro*" or "*ese desgraciao.*" My mother said it was because my father was an asshole. But the way my grandmother praised the alcoholic German-American husband of my mother's older sister makes me wonder. My father's Cape Verdian background was never referred to directly by anyone. Even my father referred to his father as Portuguese, only when pressed admitting that he was from Portuguese West Africa. The fact that my father's mother was an island-born Puerto Rican woman made him somewhat acceptable. He spoke Spanish, related to Puerto Rican culture, even self-identified as Puerto Rican. But my father was always the outsider in my mother's family, and they never ceased to remind us. While his difference was never explicitly articulated in racial terms, we understood that we were somehow lesser because we were his children. We heard all about it through the family *bochinche* network from relatives and family friends who were never concerned about the impact such gossip might have on young ears. The denial and silence about race in my

Leander Souza, Jr., Rosario Souza, and
Leander Souza, Sr. (l–r), circa 1947

family confused me, made me feel like maybe there was something terribly wrong with me. But I could never quite put my finger on what. The fact that I was so light-skinned confused me even further. In contrast to my mother's family, my father's spiritual practices celebrated Africanness and singled me out as the heir to his spiritual legacy. Yet the message from my mother's family was quite clear: my father's offspring, not quite white, not entirely black, would always be suspect, always be less than. His heathen spiritual practices testified to his inferiority. I learned to accept ambivalently that other heritage, my difference. That ambivalence became the root of my craziness.

How The Craziness Sets In

My father moved us to Puerto Rico in 1972 in the midst of the global recession. There I learned that my siblings and I were different from islanders in some other ways. The local kids called us *gringos* and *los americanitos,* but we never really understood the implications of those labels. We had other reference points for identity, those we brought with us from the United States. As far as we were concerned, we were Puerto Rican, since being gringo meant being white, and we knew we weren't that. While I could tell there were some palpable differences between me and the other girls in my barrio, I always believed these differences had more to do with my mother's status. After various attempts at "making it," my father left us in Puerto Rico and returned to New York to find a job so he could send for us. To the people in the village we lived in, however, my mother appeared to be a single woman with her children. Unattached women were thought to be dangerous. My mother was branded a whore simply because she was alone, before she had the opportunity to engage in any behavior deemed inappropriate. My mother wasn't opposed to having a lover or two. But that's beside the point. She was a whore, and, by association, her four daughters were considered junior whores-in-training. What else could the daughters of an unattached woman be? It was the beginning of a racialized sexualization that would haunt me throughout the rest of my childhood and adolescence. Before I even thought of myself as a sexual being, my sexual identity was established and judged. When people started to treat me differently I felt a sense of unease but I could not put my finger on what bothered me about these interactions. There were always these knowing glances that I was supposed to understand. That type of understanding would not come until I was much older.

When my father finally sent for us we ended up in the small seaside community of Far Rockaway, Queens. Growing up in a multiethnic community that included various Latin American groups, Russian Jews, Italian-Americans, Irish-Americans, African Americans, along with various newly immigrated groups, like West Indians, Asians, and Arabs was integral to my developing sense of ethnic identity. The experience of living among so many different groups taught me about systems of hierarchy external to the United States. I was introduced to the way other countries understood themselves in relation to the United States. It also was a site of cross-cultural exchanges of music, language, dance, and values that have become part of my intellectual trajectory. This folk education gave me a more complex understanding of the society I lived in, with all its myths and contradictions, which proved useful when I later chose my life's work.

It was in Far Rockaway that I spent the rest of my formative years, and it had an important impact on my sense of *puertorriqueñidad*, and my craziness. Far Rockaway had a Latino community where Puerto Ricans made up approximately 50 percent of the population, along with Dominicanos, Chilenos, Colombianos, and Salvadoreños. I constructed my ethnic identity in relation to other Latino groups. The experience of living in a predominantly Latino area, as opposed to a predominantly Puerto Rican area, provided me with a nuanced sense of Latin American racial, national, and class dynamics. Thus I was not only aware from an early age that my own ethnic group was a despised one within the context of the dominant society; I also quickly perceived that Puerto Ricans were at the bottom of the hierarchy of Latin American groups as well. I didn't learn until I was a teenager the specific class dimensions of our racialization or how sexualized Puerto Rican women were among Latin Americans.

Shortly after my family moved to Far Rockaway, my parents permanently separated. The ending of their turbulent marriage instantly thrust me into a "female-headed household," part of the increased poverty during the eighties described as the "feminization of poverty." The change in our household composition, and our subsequent fall from the working class into the ranks of the poor, meant we were subjected to severe material deprivation. My parents' separation also meant we were emancipated from the tyranny of a despotic "male head-of-household." We often went hungry, were never adequately clad, were even transient homeless for some time, but we were free from my father's reign of terror. My class identity is grounded in my experience of living in a woman-headed household that barely subsisted on public assistance, an experience that was simultaneously constraining and liberating for my family.

To the rest of the world our status as "female-headed household on welfare" meant we were less than human. We were often treated rudely and always suspect; different kinds of people felt entitled to violate us whenever they felt like it. My mother found herself in many situations where she had to defend one or all of her children from an abusive person in authority. She said it was because she had no man around to protect us, but I think it had to do with the repulsion and suspicion we evoked because we were a woman-headed family. Once, for example, the superintendent in a tenement building we lived in yelled at me when I reported to him that a windowpane in one of the bedrooms fell out, shattering on the floor, almost cutting me. I was already a practicing smartass at age fourteen, so when he suggested that "windows just don't fall out by themselves," I responded with "So what? You think I got up on a chair and knocked it out myself?" He said, very seriously, "Yeah." I was so shocked I was speechless. I knew right then and there that no matter what I said, no matter the truth, he would believe I purposely broke that window. It was my first hint that we were thought of as less than human.

In the multiethnic context of my childhood I constantly had to negotiate the politics of being a Puerto Rican girl. This meant that whenever I visited friends, I was subjected to a certain scrutiny by wary mothers who wanted to assure themselves I wasn't *that* kind of Puerto Rican. No matter the ethnic background of any of my friends, whether Colombian, Jewish, Dominican, or Italian-American, once their mothers found out I was Puerto Rican, I could expect an interrogation at my first visit. My parents raised me to mind my elders and inculcated in me an ethic of respect that won me the approval, sometimes even the affection, of my friends' parents. But the fact that I was Puerto Rican and poor was enough to render me suspicious. Despite passing the entry exam, I was still subject to undue questioning whenever anything was lost or missing and whenever my friends got into mischief. I worked hard to please the adults, going out of my way to comport myself appropriately and to abide by any household rules. But my racialized ethnicity and class identity marked me no matter how well I behaved, no matter how respectful I was, no matter how much I followed the rules. My name was always the first that came up whenever something went wrong. I learned to anticipate this scrutiny and develop elaborate arguments in my own defense. It annoyed the hell out of the adults and didn't endear me to them, but their scrutiny ceased to affect me as much.

That *Puta* Thing that Just Doesn't Go Away

Specific gender and sexual ideologies governed my behavior as a young girl and adolescent in this community. The label *puta* (whore) was used within this Latino community for girls and young women to uphold the rigid lines of sexual propriety. Any woman who didn't conform to the prevailing gender and sexual norms was a *puta*. The word tethered us like a huge ball and chain. So great was the power of this label that none of us escaped constructing our sexual identities without, at some level, addressing the *puta* thing. For someone like me who was poor, from a woman-headed family on welfare, and Puerto Rican, the label *puta* had a particular resonance. My explicit sexualization meant that I didn't merit the respect "ladies" get by virtue of living in households with a male head. For better or worse, I did not get the kind of patriarchal protection most Latinas do. The lack of male presence at home left me open to whatever assaults and attacks men deemed appropriate for someone of my station. It didn't matter that I wasn't even interested in sex with men, that I didn't have a boyfriend, and that I was not actively pursuing a man. Junior whores-in-training like me, guilty by association, bore the brunt of the psychological and sociopolitical impact of the *puta* label. More than anything, it was this label that taught me some of my most important lessons about patriarchal domination and masculine violence.

Sexual stigma was status- and color-oriented among Puerto Ricans in this community, but it was more intensely racialized outside the Puerto Rican enclave among Latinos and other ethnic groups. I lived with the stigma of the word *puta*, carrying it around like a marker of my worth, an index of how I should be treated. Even before I had a chance to define my own sexual identity, the label preceded me like a calling card. Once a friend's older brother, who was on a home visit from the military, decided I had grown up enough to bestow his masculine virility on me. He cornered me in his sister's bedroom and tried to kiss me. I pushed him away with such force that he slammed against the wall. He seemed surprised by this and said, in all earnestness, "What? You want to go to a hotel?" Perhaps my friend's constant refrain—that the only thing Puerto Rican women were good for was to cook, dance, and fuck — should have tipped me off. Until that moment, I really didn't know that I was open season even to the boys I grew up with once they became men. It was another one of those revelatory moments.

These types of incidents taught me to anticipate whether or not knowledge about my woman-headed-household-on-public-assistance background might matter to people. I carefully selected my friends based on the position they took. This *puta* thing also meant that men assumed I was sexually available to them, especially after they learned that I was Puerto Rican. Somehow *puertorriqueña* became synonymous with *puta*. And since I was undoubtedly a *puta,* the logic went, then I must also be interested in casual sex with any man who approached me. Whenever I wasn't grateful enough to oblige a man's sexual interest in me, I was treated abusively, sometimes even violently. Since for me the sexual attention of men was always dangerous, usually painful, and always unsolicited, I avoided contact with them. I steered clear of sexual encounters with men and worked hard never to find myself in a position where I was alone with a man for fear of his expectations and their consequences. I constantly fended off unwanted sexual attention and sexual attacks, becoming an expert in dodging and evasiveness to avoid such encounters. I learned to watch for the ways people might misperceive me sexually, to read between the lines, to intuit whether double entendres meant a dangerous situation was brewing. Consequently, I was never all-consumed with finding a man to settle down with in a relationship, unlike many of the women I knew. Since my gender and sexual identity were not defined relationally by attachment to a man, I concentrated on developing relationships with women. Yet, despite my lack of engagement with men, the stigma of being a *puta* made me feel more than a little crazy.

No Great Expectations

No one expected much out of me. There are no great expectations for little Puerto Rican girls from women-headed families on welfare. I achieved in spite of this, exceeding all their expectations for someone from my background, and sometimes even my own. In many respects I've become the quintessential American achievement story. From an outsider's view, I've defied the odds. My achievements are celebrated by the very people who expected nothing from me. After struggling to get out from under the weight of my sociopolitical inheritance, after struggling against the stereotypes about me within and outside of the Latino community I lived in, after struggling to get beyond the structural constraints on my life and grappling with my low self-esteem, I've become successful by their standards. More importantly I've become successful by my own standards. But the damage is still there. Now I wage a new struggle to remind people that none of my achievements are guaranteed. And that it's all been at a cost. And while, yes, I'm better off materially, and perhaps even more in control of my life, while academia and intellectual work offer me a certain refuge, and while a lot of hard work on my part has paid off, much of it is a result of institutional support. The end result is that all of this has enhanced my ability to see contradictions and to grapple with them in ways that can benefit me.

For a long time my ability to read the cultural, social, and political contradictions in my life made me feel really crazy. They tore me apart. But the basis for my sense of craziness is really a world that compartmentalized me a priori into social categories that I still do not fit. I was born into these categories without much say, and the expectations and stereotypes about my potential really only measure the biases upon which they were based and not my social worth as a person. No matter my own values, I realized I would be judged by societal assumptions about who I ought to be, not who I actually was. These assumptions used superficial understandings of me that certainly never considered my views. My fate was sealed before I could have a say. In the world I was born into, I used to feel like I was crazy. These days I've learned that what is crazy is a world that is so structured by inequality and injustice that it doesn't nurture poor Puerto Rican girls simply because they are poor Puerto Rican girls.

Only recently have I been able to appreciate my ability to "see" beneath the surface; how these experiences have taught me to be aware of my surroundings; and what it means to be marked by race, class, gender, sexuality, and ethnicity. It has given me an edge. I've learned, for example, that political allies come in a variety of shapes and forms, and I've learned to choose them on the basis of ideological and political persuasion. I've also learned about partially situated perspectives, about the transparency of claims to objectivity, and about the importance of cross-referencing. The life situations I've narrated have taught me much about how people come to view things, about how our biases mediate our perspectives. From my family I've learned a healthy distrust for authority and for the "official story." From the way that race, class, gender, sexuality, and ethnicity have come together in my life, I've learned that people will question facts before they question their convictions, especially if those convictions support stereotypes about others that benefit them in some way. I have witnessed how the adults around me were wrong about their perceptions, how authority figures make mistakes. Much later I learned that racist ethnocentrism, misogyny, and elitism share a foundation in a very logical, rational system of domination and oppression.

One of the most important ways my life experiences have prepared me for academia has been to develop my own internal standards and to look to those standards for validation. Otherwise I would have to accept the assessment of a world that despises me. The world I live in does not validate little Puerto Rican girls. So I've developed my own measures of success, of progress, of achievement. Learning to redefine categories, to question received ones, and to create new definitions and concepts means I participate in creating alternative perspectives. Why accept definitions from others when they were not only possibly wrong but potentially harmful? I've learned to question everything. People have their own sense of meaning, and they also make meaning as they move along the trajectories of their lives. I learned that I don't have to accept their meanings, especially if those meanings were constructed to devalue me. My own meanings, perspectives, and interpretations are just as valid, just as useful.

Laughter has always been a part of my survival mechanism, one that I learned within my family. Although I'm usually serious, I find myself almost ready to explode with giggles at the most inappropriate times. Or a word sounds strange and I laugh to myself. Sometimes I will remember a silly moment and will chuckle out loud while sitting on the train or bus. That kind of laughter has always marked me as crazy. Laughter helps to heal the crazies. Lately, my laughter sounds less like the screech of a crazy woman than of someone who delights in the world I see, disorderly, contradictory, and complex as it may be. Recently, I was taking one of my students to an awards banquet. Her mother, who was in the car with us, turned to me and said, *"Cari, tú no te crees nadie."* An immigrant from Latin America, I understood her words to mean that I am not pretentious. I laughed heartily at this. It's hard to be pretentious in a world that devalues you at almost every turn. *Pero esta risa no es de loca.* I'm having the last laugh. Only this time it's the laughter of a woman grounded in who she is regardless of how she's been marked.

So I guess the last laugh is on me.

A Escondidas:
A Chicana Feminist Teacher Who Writes/
A Chicana Feminist Writer Who Teaches

Norma E. Cantú

I WANT TO EXPLORE the various selves that I am, and I decided on *a escondidas* because much of who I am has been an unfolding of who and what I was all along *a escondidas,* hidden so deep inside that not even I knew who or what I was. *A las escondidas* we called the game of hide-and-go-seek we played at dusk, before being called in to supper. Here I'll play *a las escondidas* with myself as I have over the last fifty years of finding out who I am.

In the sixties and seventies I didn't have terms like "racism" and "sexism" to name that which I experienced; it took living certain, often painful circumstances that gave me these terms. I call myself a Chicana feminist, so I want to talk about how I came to do so. Until fairly recently I thought of myself as a teacher who writes. Now, more and more I am thinking of myself as a writer who teaches, and the Chicana feminist identity is inherent in both of these, the writer and the teacher. These two identities have also been *a escondidas,* so it is time to dig and find out what they mean. I want as well to explore the roles of writer and teacher and how the writer was hidden for so long.

How I Became a Chicana

I'm in graduate school in Nebraska and the state education agency has found my name on some list and calls me to be a trainer in their in-service program for teachers. In spite of the fact that Chicanos/as have been in Nebraska since the 1890s, only now do the authorities feel that they must deal with the issue of cultural difference. The increase in Laotian and Vietnamese immigrants has prompted them to hire me to talk to teachers about cultural diversity. It is the mid-seventies—maybe 1976—and I arrive at the high school gym of a rural school district where the K–12 teachers have gathered. I am to talk for forty-five minutes, and then they will ask me questions. Before I speak, however, the administrator, who has either been coerced by the state to do it or is genuinely interested in having a staff sensitive to the cultural background of its students, introduces me. And I can't believe my ears. He is doing what many others do there in the Midwest: he introduces me as "Spanish." In my introduction to the workshop I correct him somewhat and say I'm not really Spanish, I'm from Texas, and there are a few chuckles from the group but it's obvious no one gets it. Afterward, I ask why he said I was Spanish, and, baffled by my question, he explains that he did not want to insult me by calling me Mexican. "What would you prefer I call you?" he asks. I don't hesitate a minute. "Chicana," I answer. Prior to that I would've said Mexican American, but that one incident was like a watershed after all the discrimination and the racism I had quietly experienced and often excused. I would define myself, and Chicana was exactly the term that would define me. I had read Chicana/o literature; in fact, the first poem that ever moved me to uncontrollable tears was about *las piscas* published in *El Grito*, which I had read while browsing in the stacks at the university library in Kingsville, Texas. I had attended rallies and canvassed for voter registration for José Angel Gutiérrez's Raza Unida Party; I had boycotted grapes and attended marches in Austin, but I had never come out and called myself a Chicana until that epiphanous moment. Only those who had left Laredo and had gone to universities and colleges elsewhere knew that that's what we were, although my mother's cousins would visit from Chicago and talk about *"la chicanada"* as if it meant all of us. I call myself a Chicana for many reasons: my ethnic heritage, my ideological position, and my identity. But the most important one is that I know who I am, what I feel I am: *soy Chicana.*

Gaining a Feminist *Conciencia*

I remember the VISTA workers—Robin, Sylvia, Bruce and Eric, or was it Craig?—and their enthusiasm. They were my age or younger, but they were worlds away from me with their college degrees and their privileged lives. They came to Laredo during the War on Poverty and brought their marijuana cigarettes, antiwar sentiments, and idealism. They rented a house and lived together, and I thought they were the coolest. Yet I sensed their paternalism; their obvious amazement that I knew more than they did, that I read more, thought more—or so it felt—belied their attempt to treat me fairly and not as someone who needed saving. Sylvia, of Italian background, who took the Silva Mind Control course, cooked a mean spaghetti and played classical violin. Her deep dark eyes and long silky black hair almost made her one of us except that she spoke Spanish with a heavy accent and barely at all. Denise was

Houston upper class and always gave me the impression of just slumming. She was always quick to confide in me and share the infelicities of her illicit relationships, including her liaison with a priest. I must have been shocked, but all I remember is feeling a strange sense of intrigue. The guys were around too — was it Eric or Craig who taught me and Ani to play the guitar? I made such noise — my father discovered me strumming "Guantanamera" late at night in the kitchen and proceeded to tell me that that was no way to learn to play. "*Eso se aprende lírico, no hay que leerlo en un libro,*" he scoffed. It was hopeless. Tone-deaf and without a guitar or time to practice, I would never learn to play all the Joan Baez and Canto Nuevo songs. Poor Eric (or Craig), with his laughing hazel eyes and long curly locks, never did let on. We continued with the lessons until he left. I believe he had a degree in accounting, and as his year was up, his father wanted him to go back to Iowa (or was it Idaho?) and work with him in his hardware store. But I'm getting to the point in a rather roundabout way — what I started to write about was the fact that it was Sylvia, my VISTA friend, who introduced me to the concept of feminism — she had read *Sisterhood is Powerful*.

After work at the office I often dropped by the VISTA workers' house, and one day, as I came in, she handed me the book and insisted that I read it. I did. I devoured it, in fact. As I was reading, I had a sort of epiphany as things seemed to fall into place: the sexism at school, at home, and at work. The situation at the office — Central Power and Light Company, where I worked 8 to 5 — surfaced first because the office sexism ran deep. No one questioned the sexual harassment, the sexist practices. Often I would notice that something was not right. Even though I had no name for it. I complained that it was wrong that the men told dirty jokes in the office just to see my naïve and embarrassed reaction, wrong that the male clerk earned more, because he was "head of household," than my equally qualified friend who was divorced and a single mother. After that book, there was no stopping me; I began to call it what it was, and not just at the office, but at home where my father reigned and my new-found resistance caused further rifts between us, and in my university night classes where professors would glibly make sexist remarks. The one I remember objecting to was one professor's favorite answer to the question of how long a paper should be: "Like a girl's skirt, long enough to cover the subject and short enough to be interesting." In the early seventies this was cute and tolerated; unfortunately — and confirming that we've come a long way but we're not there yet — I heard a male colleague repeat the answer in the mid-nineties.

I call myself a Chicana feminist because I continue to be woman identified and I continue to call for equality. I am but one more in a long line of feminists from Laredo. Almost a hundred years ago, La Liga Femenil did pretty much what Las Mujeres, the women's group I work with, does now: focus on women's issues, including education and justice. I didn't need the VISTA workers to discover the sexism in my life, but I found in these kindred spirits encouragement and hope. In some way, they offered an alternative I had not considered before. Their privilege opened doors for them, allowed them to come to our community where the political machine ruled and to disturb if not wholly overthrow the status quo. I saw their college degrees as a license to right wrongs. They couldn't help me with what I needed to know of Jovita Idar and Leonor Villegas de Magnón and many others, but they offered through their example a path I wanted — indeed, I needed — to follow. In fact, I didn't know about the men and women who had come before who also felt that way. Not until I read Marta Cotera's *Diosa y Hembra,* when I left for graduate school in the late seventies, did I discover the Chicana heroes who would become models to emulate. What a discovery that book was; I felt that I was not alone, that there were others who had felt and thought like me. In the early eighties I and a group of women, among them academics, labor leaders, social workers, and students, founded Las Mujeres, a feminist group that seeks to continue the work of our foremothers.

How I Became a Teacher

I was born a teacher. During the summer before the seventh grade I ran an *escuelita* at home. It just seemed the right thing to do, to ask all the neighbors to let me teach the preschoolers to count and get used to going to school. We sang rhymes in English and Spanish; I taught them the alphabet; we played games; and most important of all, they were getting used to attending school. Later, in the early seventies, I led religious retreats and taught a *doctrina* class of Catholic Christian Doctrine (CCD) at church. Through high school and much of the time when I worked at CP&L, I earned money tutoring algebra and English. So, when I chose education as my major, I was headed on the only path I could imagine. I had a knack for teaching and I knew it. So everyone was shocked when, after years of night classes and many sacrifices, I finally completed my bachelor's degree but didn't get the certificate; I sabotaged the process. I didn't apply for the certificate until, with Ph.D. in hand and a secure position at the university, I felt that taking the required exams would aid in my teaching students to prepare for the exam; that was 1984. I must have sensed back in 1973 that getting that certificate would trap me, that I would never be able to leave. I had seen my friends return from Austin, Denton, and San Antonio with teaching degrees and succumb to the expectations: teach and get married. But I was convinced that the only way to fulfill my larger destiny, that is, come back and work with the community, was to go to graduate school. With or without certification in the state of Texas, I continued to do what I had been doing since the seventh grade — teaching. I love teaching at the university because it allows me to do the things I love most — to read and to talk about what I read, to think out loud during these discussions and to think on paper as I write my papers, deliver talks, write my fiction and poetry. I can't conceive of a better life. I know now that I didn't want to teach elementary or even high school — I just didn't have any other models. I didn't know anyone who had a Ph.D. until pretty much into my college coursework. At that time, all you needed to teach at a community college was a master's degree; that's what my professors had.

There's one goal in my life that I can unquestionably say I have achieved and mastered: I am a teacher. One of my most rewarding experiences, however, was not in an academic setting. It was teaching an octogenarian how to write her name. She came to the Housing Authority's Colonia Guadalupe during a testing period for our literacy classes and whispered to me that she didn't really want to learn to read or to learn English at all. All she wanted was to learn to write her name before dying. That evening, when she could write her name on her own, after we worked laboriously for over two hours, we both hugged and cried at our success. I felt rewarded beyond words.

Yes, I am a teacher, but I also write, I always have. So for most of my almost thirty years of teaching, I have said I am a teacher who writes. Only recently have I begun to say I am a writer who teaches.

How I Became a Writer

I am a writer who teaches. But I also write. My earliest fiction pieces were written in elementary school, and I barely remember them. Then, in high school, I worked with the school newspaper and dreamt of being a Brenda Starr. Somewhere along the way I learned to hide the fact that I wrote poems and stories, and only once in a while would I let my guard down and share my writing with someone. Of course, I didn't send out things for publication, either. My first creative publications were poems in small local publications like *Metamorphosis* in Seattle and Angela DeHoyos's *Huehuetitlán* in San Antonio. I slowly braved an audience as we would gather to read poems at someone's house to commemorate Sor Juana Inés de la Cruz's birthday. When I wrote *Canícula,* in the summer of 1993, I knew that I had crossed a threshold and that there was no going back; I was a writer. The novel had been a long time coming. I'd written *Papeles de mujer* almost fifteen years earlier, and it was time for the next part of the story, but I just didn't have the time. One thing that academia does to writers and which I have not been able to shake, is its incredible demand on our time, so that there is none left for writing. Of course, if I taught at a large university, things might be different, but I chose to come back to Laredo, where I teach four classes a semester, including a graduate seminar and at least one, but often two, writing classes. The teaching load, plus all the committee work, and the scholarly work, such as writing and presenting papers at conferences, being on boards, and myriad other duties, leaves little if any time for my writing. So I try to get away at least for one summer session to write what I've been delaying all year. It's frustrating and not very productive, but that's how it's got to be, at least for now.

Dar a Luz: Birthing a Self

The role of my foremothers, both academic and familial, has been critical in shaping my face and my soul, as the Aztecs would say. Of course, there have been men who have influenced who I am — my father looms gigantic, as do professors who understood my needs and fed me intellectually what I hungered for: F. Alan Briggs at what was then Texas A&I at Laredo, Paul Olson, and Ralph Grajeda at the University of Nebraska. Unfortunately, there are also the men who influenced the person I became through anything but positive actions. The professor who took my research and published it under his name; the professor who wrote me a letter declaring his love for me after I had finished his class and in fact had already started teaching — a severe blow to my self-confidence, for he had always lauded my work and now it was all suspect. But I do not want to dwell on the men, lovers or mentors, good or bad. I want to celebrate the women. My mother, *mis abuelas, mis hermanas, mis tías, mis vecinas, mis amigas, maestras, estudiantes, y sí, por qué no,* lovers who have opened doors, shed light, *en fin* helped make the path an easier and sometimes harder one. It would take a book to tell how all these women nurtured, inspired, encouraged, nudged, and even embarrassed me to do what they all knew I could do and deep in my heart wanted to do. I'll have to limit myself and selectively, intuitively, paint the picture with broad brushstrokes. *Familia.* That's how I would define all of these women, because they cared like *familia* would. Of course, some were blood relatives, but not all.

Bueli and Mami

Bueli taught me to read in Spanish, and Mami supported my school endeavors, sewing costumes so I would participate in school programs, helping me with math up to the point in junior high when algebra baffled her and, try as she might, she couldn't help me. Both were instrumental in instilling a love of learning in me. As a four-year-old, I learned to read in Spanish, sounding out the words for *Bueli* while she ironed or did some other household task.

My mother and her mother, Bueli, sent me off to the *escuelita,* my first formal schooling. I went well-trained in the activities of school — I knew how to write and read in Spanish and I could *declamar* short poems. I was articulate and talkative like the first child usually is. But when I went to Don Tomás Sánchez Elementary School and entered Mrs. Rogelia García's first-grade classroom, things were radically different. I didn't understand anything; neither did my classmates. My mother left with tears in her eyes and with stern advice: "*Aprende todo lo que te enseñen.*" And I did, painful as it was. When I was moved to Saunders Elementary School later that year to Miss Montemayor's classroom, things did not get better, although by then I had learned that in school, as at home, being good paid off, so I should not do what I wanted but what others wanted. My Spanish helped me to learn English, and I quickly moved to the top group. I was soon teaching the other children to read from a thick reader, *With Jack and Janet.* I now ponder how it was that I was teaching instead of learning new things myself. But one thing for sure: I felt smart, and I knew I wanted to be a teacher.

Las Tías

My aunts influenced me in their own ways, too. My dad's sisters and the grandaunts as well as my mom's sister formed a culture of women that nurtured me as I grew.

Tía Licha: my mom's sister became a second mother as she didn't have daughters and often we were left in her charge when my parents traveled to visit a sick relative or attend a wedding out of town. The stories of her youth and of my maternal grandparents are her legacy to me, and perhaps a strange sense of humor that surfaces unexpectedly. She cried once when I hinted that I might want to be married. I was in high school, and I think her tears told me more than any number of sermons would have.

Tía Tuta: My dad's *cuñada* gave me the first book I ever owned. When I was fifteen she sent me the gift with Mamagrande, a book of etiquette for young women. I was disappointed that it wasn't a novel or a dictionary, but was thrilled and read and reread that little book with the picture of a young blonde woman on the cover. I lost it in one of my moves during my graduate school migration.

Tía Luz: My dad's youngest sister was a role model. Single until the age of fifty-two, she embodied the freedom that I yearned for. She traveled, ran a business, had money. But I could also see sadness in her eyes as one after another of her *pretendientes* would not pass the test and Papagrande would forbid his presence in her life. No one was ever good enough for his youngest daughter. She gave me my first bilingual dictionary, which I treasure to this day. I was in high school and studying Spanish with one of the meanest teachers in the school when I asked my father for money to buy one. Tía Luz happened to be spending Holy Week with us and overheard my request. On her next trip up from Monterrey, she brought me the precious book.

Tía Carmen and *Tía Lydia:* They were my dad's older sisters, and I didn't particularly care for them. Both were gossipy and self-centered and only deigned recognize me because I was the oldest. They treated my sisters with disdain, and one of them once spread rumors about me that really hurt — or perhaps what hurt most was that my father believed her. In retrospect the rumors were inoffensive, but I was devastated. I had taken a vacation to Oaxaca and Chiapas with two friends, one of whom was a priest in our parish. Shortly after the trip I moved to Kingsville to get my master's degree, and my friend the priest left the Church to move to Austin to study nursing. My aunt interpreted this turn of events thusly: I was pregnant with the priest's child and he had to quit the Church in disgrace; I was living in sin with him or perhaps having an abortion — which at the time was not just "immoral" but illegal and deathly risky. When my dad confronted me with this information, I was stunned. I cried, of course, and denied everything. I still can't believe my father believed her.

Las Tías Abuelas

The other *tías* were grandaunts, but they too had an influence on who I am. Tía Piedad, my grandfather's sister, wrote a book on health and beauty, and in a way planted the seed that I too wanted to be a writer. Tía Chita and Tía Toña, Mamagrande's sisters, were spinsters who knew their own minds and would argue politics with the men until late at night. I loved listening. Tía Cata was my dad's cousin; she worked her whole life on a ranch for the Anglo owners, raised her kids in an even worse climate than Laredo — in West Texas, where segregation was alive and well. She was strong and generous and compassionate to a fault, an Angel of God, people said of her. And her daughter, Tía Trine, is my aunt in Nebraska; she settled out of the migrant stream when her first husband was so jealous he drove her to leave after years of accusations of infidelity (he didn't believe cousin Lala, the youngest, was his because she was blonde and didn't look like the older children). She remarried and then divorced again, when that man was mean to his stepchildren, treating them like servants, barking orders, "Bring me water for shaving, bring me hot coffee, bring me another blanket."

Las Jovitas

And then there are the intellectual precursors — Las Jovitas, as I call them, and the *comadres* who taught me to think and to question as well as to write. I feel that I have inherited the work of these turn-of-the-century feminists and writers as well as that of the later ones whose work still remains to be studied. Jovita Idar, Jovita González, Leonor Villegas de Magnón, and many others blazed a trail with their work. Unfortunately, I didn't know about them when I was in high school and needed to know there had been others who, like me, yearned to think, to write, and to engage in philosophical discussions. I thought, and others around me confirmed it, that I was strange or rare, and I felt out of place. I remember attending a CYO (Catholic Youth Organization) party with friends and spending the whole night in the parish library and not in the hall where the others were dancing and drinking pink punch. Only one of the guys dared venture in there. We had a long conversation, while Berta and my other friends danced and flirted with the other guys.

Literary Works — Writers and Thinkers

In high school it was *The Diary of Anne Frank,* the Bröntes, George Eliot, and a host of romance novelists including Corín Tellado and Caridad Bravo Adams that intrigued me. In the sixties and seventies I read the works of Sigrid Undset, Pearl Buck, Sor Juana Inés de la Cruz, Rosario Castellanos, Elena Poniatowska, and Virginia Woolf, along with male writers like Loren Eiseley, Pablo Neruda, Federico García Lorca, and Regis Debray. I remember reading Josefina Niggli and rejoicing because she wrote about the land I knew between Monterrey and San Antonio; I read *Las Tres Marías* and memorized a Sor Juana poem, yes, *Hombres necios.* And all along I was looking for what I found in Chicana/o literature: first in journals and magazines like *El Grito* and *Caracol,* and at the *Floricanto* gatherings like the one in Corpus Christi in 1978 where I first heard Inés Hernández, Evangelina Vigil, Lorna Dee Cervantes, and Carmen Tafolla, and later in the eighties in the works of Gloria Anzaldúa, Cherríe Moraga, Sandra Cisneros, Angela de Hoyos, Ana Castillo, and Pat Mora, a literary heritage that still is forming as I read the works of women who have come before us as well as the wellspring that has sprung from Latina and other women of color writers.

My influences come from many directions, from all over the world, from the spoken word, and from literary publications. Women like Simone de Beauvoir and Simone Weil right alongside Rosario Castellanos and Julia de Burgos shaped who I am, how I think, and what and how I write. But on an equal plane are my mother, grandmothers, sisters, cousins, teachers, *comadres, vecinas* and all the women whose lives have touched mine.

Canto de Mi Madre/Canto de Mi Padre

Inés Hernández Avila

I AM MY MOTHER'S DAUGHTER and my father's daughter. I am the mother of my beloved sons and the grandmother of my precious grandchildren. I am wife to my husband, my *compañero en carne y hueso, espíritu, conciencia y corazón.* I am a becoming woman. I am earth, fire, water, and wind, and my spirit sings me to wholeness as I dance my spirit into joy. I am guided by my heart's intuition, and my heart is wise, generous, loving, and brave, even after withstanding assault upon assault. *Mi fuerza está dentro de mí, y me conecta con el corazón de la tierra y el corazón del cielo. Esa unión, del cielo y de la tierra, es eminentemente y provocativamente amorosa, justa, sensual, compasiva, sabia, y creativa.*

My mother's people are the Nimipu, the Human Beings (to distinguish ourselves in our language from our relations in the animal, plant, water, stone, and sky worlds). We are known as the Nez Perce, the name the French trappers gave us because they said they saw some of us with pierced noses. We do not say Nez Percé (Nay-pehr-say) with the French pronunciation. We say Nez Perce (Nez Perse), with anglicized accent. It doesn't matter, it is not our real name. We are Nimipu. According to our oral tradition, we are *Itsee-yii-ya-nim ma-mi-yats,* the Children of Itseyaya, Old Coyote, who created us when he washed his hands and mixed the water with the blood of the monster he slayed to bring the different tribes into being. I have other drops of blood, too — Iroquois and Flathead, on my mother's mother's side, French and Shoshone, on my mother's father's side. But my Uncle Frank says we are ninety-nine percent Nez Perce of Hinmaton Yalatkit's (Chief Joseph's) band, originally of the Wallowa Valley in Oregon, and now from Nespelem, Washington.

As a Nimipu woman, I come from people who have survived genocide and lived to tell of it in this century. Only 121 years ago, my great-grandfather

Heyum Kish Kish, Grizzly Bear Standing, was a young warrior, eighteen years old, helping in the attempted escape of our people into Canada. When I imagine what that journey must have been like, the 1700-mile forced march of about 750 people, women, children, old people, including 200 warriors, resisting under the most extreme duress the assaults of approximately 2,000 military and volunteers over the course of the four months of struggle, when I read and hear from my family the accounts of this suffering and of the collective intelligence that allowed our leaders to do the best they could for our people under the circumstances, I understand my mother's high threshold for pain, and her mother's, and my aunties' and our people's. I understand why I have always been able to get up when I have been knocked down, over and over again, in so many ways. I know why I can look people in the eye after they are sure they have defeated me, and I see their shock that I have come back, that I did not disappear off the face of the earth.

I come from women who do not give up. What is their source of strength and dignity? The certainty that we are deeply from this land, that we are a part of this hemisphere and it is a part of us in a very particular way, since the beginning of time. The bitterroot, the camas root, the chokecherries, the huckleberries, the mountains and the rivers, the eagles, grizzly bears, and coyotes know us. The land knows us because we belong to it and we come from a very specific and sacred place on this earth that is associated with us and gives us roots. The land knows me even as I fumble around doing my best to know her better. As my mother has always told me, we are the First Ones, the First Americans. As her father said, we are the red tradition of this hemisphere.

My father's people are from the Eagle Pass / Piedras Negras region of the U.S. / Mexico border (my father's father's people were originally from San Luís Potosí before migrating to Coahuila). My grandparents moved with their children from *la frontera* to Galveston, Texas, in the early 1920s, where they quickly became integrated as respected members of a vibrant *mexicano* community in which everyone knew everyone, and where people managed to build and nurture lifelong friendships in the midst of the common *pleitos,* crises, dysfunctions, and *chismeando* that goes on in any community.

A mis abuelitos, yo les decía "Mamá y Papá," because I was their first grand-child — at least my grandmother's; my Papá had been married before; his first wife died and left him with two children. I often felt like their youngest daughter. As a child, I would drop everything to go with them, and they would always assume that my parents did not really have much say, which never ceased to amaze my own mother. There was a battle for me, for my allegiance, even then. Would I go with "Mommy" or "Mamá"? *En los dos lados era consentida,* although my father insists that his parents, especially my Papá Sabas, really spoiled me. I believe my Papá favored me for many reasons,

Inés and parents, Rudy and Janice
Hernández circa 1952

not the least of which was his own Indianness that caused him to see himself proudly in my mother's eyes, and to *consentir* his granddaughter who adored his humor, his calm intelligence, his gentlemanliness, and sense of community.

My father and my twin uncles, like my Papá and his father before him, were *carpinteros maestros,* the kind who knew how to build meticulously, delicately, with integrity and grace. My father had an artist's hands and mind; his gift to me, via my Papá Sabas, is the example of an innate sense of vision, of wholeness and unifying principles, with a mathematically/relationally inspired attention to particularities, to detail. I witnessed the self-discipline that carried him through everything he undertook, the *compromiso* to do his very best; the loving way he cared for his tools, dear to him because they were his, or his father's, or his father's father's; the drive to manifest his worth through his *hechos,* through being a *persona de palabra,* a legacy from his parents, a way for his name to be remembered honorably, lovingly, and gratefully.

My father, son of his parents and very much like his brothers and sisters, was there for all his family, especially for my mom and me. He was of the old school, a man who would not drink or smoke cigarettes in front of his parents, a man who lovingly cared for his mother (with another brother and a sister) when she could not care any longer for herself, saying to me, "She did this for us when we were children." Generous heart, he would go fishing and give all the extra fish away to his family or our neighbors, and when two of our neighbors died (at different times), men who were his friends, he made sure to help their widows with house repairs, "in memory of his friendship with their husbands." When the sons of one of those widows speak of him, they still refer to him as "the Captain." *Capitán del barrio, mi papá. Hombre constante, hombre firme y fuerte.* Loyal to his family, he was of the opinion that critiques can be given internally, within family circles, but in the world outside it is important to be there for family members, standing by them. He always told me, "You're my daughter, I'm on your side. No matter what, I'll back you up. I just ask one thing of you. Don't ever lie to me, because I need to know what I'm working with." *Admiro de la sencillez y profundidad de esta enseñanza.* This is his legacy to me, and one I give my sons and grandchildren, which I hope they will pass on.

Un ejemplo concreto de quién era mi papá; at the age of about thirty I almost gave up my spirit to death. I was painfully distraught because I thought the Great Spirit of the Universe (*para darle nombre a ese Misterio*) wanted me to give up my life. My father saw me at this moment, really saw me, and said to me with incredible conviction, "Nothing is going to happen to you!" Overcome with tears, I could barely answer, "How do you know that?" He raised himself to his full height, responding, "Because I said so!" His words appeared as a lifeline, and I took them and held on, eventually coming to realize what he meant. For him, his words were an articulation of his faith, his connection to his God, a certainty that his prayers would save me from any danger that might harm me. For me, they were a reminder that I wasn't alone at the very moment when I had let myself forget everything but my fear. My father's intervention helped me fight back, and my warrior spirit took over.

One of my first gestures on my own behalf was to do ceremonial dance, *la danza Conchera,* which a group of us in the Austin/San Antonio area had begun to learn, more earnestly. I remember the date, 21 January 1979, because it was my Mamá Inés' birthday. When I went to *danza* that day, I felt a female spirit enter my body to help me dance. She was almost palpable to me. As I looked down at my feet while I was dancing, I noticed her body inside mine, giving me strength. She was a powerful woman, a grandmother I knew who had been vigilant to protect me in my struggle with death. It was fitting that she would be there with me on my own grandmother's birthday, blessing my formal declaration on behalf of my spirit and my well-being.

As I began to get well, I remembered that when I was much younger I used to think I would die when I was thirty. I did die, in a sense, because I left behind another life *que ya no me pertenecía — entré en otra etapa de vida*. It's not that I disavow who I was before — it's all me — but at this turning point I began more consciously to work on discerning what was good for me and letting go of what was not. Much of what I have learned has come through sacred dances from the North and the South, *pero son mis padres quienes originalmente me legaron el amor al baile, y mi papá quien me enseñó el poder del espíritu y de la voluntad.*

My mother raised me to know I was capable, I was intelligent, I was an artist. In my childhood, whenever I drew a picture, she would tell me how fine it was. When I would burst into song, she would say, "Oh! So beautiful! What a wonderful voice she has!" as if announcing it to the world. Whenever I achieved something good in school, she would congratulate me, at the same time treating it as a matter of course, making me feel that everything came naturally to me. "Mom, I made a 97 on the math exam!" I would say. "Well, I should hope so!" she would answer with a smile. Even now, if I embark on a new venture, as I've done with my work on relief prints, monoprints, and intaglio, her response is, "Of course, you would know how to do this! You're an artist. You can do anything!" Needless to say, all of my grandchildren are wonderful artists; that is how I see them, and that, I hope, is how they see themselves.

My Mamá Inés had a similar and frequently-articulated faith in my abilities, although, in her case, she was certain these abilities were mine because I was her granddaughter, and in many ways they were. She is the one, with my Papá Sabas, who insisted I grow up speaking Spanish, for which I am forever grateful. Had the decision been left to my parents, English would have been the only language in my life; they are unfortunately of that generation who believed their children would best be served by not "mixing languages" (English was also their common language; they did not learn each other's languages). My heart breaks that I did not learn Nimipu as a child, except for occasional words here and there; the task as an adult is that much harder. *Ni modo.* My Mamá Inés, very much like my mom, had a sense of self that was clear and certain; both of them had married fairly late for their generations, my *abuelita* at thirty-two, and my mom at twenty-five. Each of them was clearly her own woman, and each loved literature, reading, and writing. My mom gave me the love of books, and insisted I learn the nuances of English grammar; my Mamá Inés gave me the love of song and poetry, having been a *declamadora* (and a *maestra* in Mexico) herself when she was young; she insisted I learn the nuances of Spanish grammar. Mamá Inés also confirmed my mother's approval of my singing, telling me frequently, *"Tienes voz pa' cantar.*" She lived to her early nineties, and was blind for much of the last part of her life. When I was growing up, through high school, I used to visit her in the afternoons, and we would listen to Spanish-language radio together, discussing the merits of the many *mexicano* songs, styles, themes, and singers. I learned to sing *canciones mexicanas al lado de ella,* deepening my love for her and for the land that is Mexico. For all my mom emphasized to me our (hers and mine) "First Nations" standing as Native people, my Mamá Inés y Papá Sabas dedicated themselves to having me understand the honor of being Mexican. Even though my Mexican grandparents became naturalized citizens (learning to speak and write perfect English), and my Papá Sabas taught citizenship classes, it was always very clear to me that an integral part of my identity was/is my *mexicanidad.*

From my parents and my families on both sides *aprendí lo que es ser buena gente,* which is, in the end, what unites "being Indian" and "being Mexican" from the cultural standpoints by which I was raised. I learned what being "good people" is about, how to treat people, how to respect them, how to pay attention to details, to people's feelings, to situations, to personal and social dynamics. I learned discretion. I learned how to read other languages, the language of the body, the language of silence, of song, of dance, the language of collective contemplation. I learned compassion, not only for people but for the land, the waters, the ambiente, and for all the other *criaturas de la naturaleza.* I learned how to protect myself and *darme mi valor como mujer y como ser humano.*

Am I saying that all my family and family life was/is without difficulty or *tragedia? No, claro que no.* Am I saying my childhood and growing-up years were idyllic, that I went through no turmoil or *tristeza?* No. Am I saying that I never had problems communicating with my parents, or with other members of my family? No. What I am saying is that when I think of how I have been empowered, I have to go back to my family circles, and I have to go back to my parents. I am old enough now to have a sense of neutrality about what I have gone through, I can see what my parents and grandparents wanted for me, for us, and what strategies they used to achieve their goals. While I now have my own answers and strategies, I have kept and hold dear to me what is good, just, strong, and beautiful of their teachings.

I am deeply grateful that my parents found each other, loved each other, and were each other's best friend, even when they disagreed with each other. My dad was a Marine in World War II; after the war, he was stationed on Bremerton Island in Washington. My mom was working at Boeing Aircraft Factory in Seattle as a riveter, as she had done throughout the war. On one of my father's leaves, they met; he began courting her and then returned to Texas. He sent for her, and they were married in Galveston. That is how a Nimipu woman managed to end up in Texas; a mountain woman, a horse woman found herself on an island in the Gulf of Mexico, having captured the heart of a *mexicano/americano*, who saw in her his life's partner, a woman who would take his hand and match his love, his discipline, and vision. They are warriors, and this is an honoring song for them.

Daughter of Bootstrap

Luz del Alba Acevedo

I WAS BORN IN THE ERA of Operation Bootstrap, some years after its official beginning according to historians. I witnessed the rapid and dramatic transformation of Puerto Rico into an industrial and urban center. I incarnate the Puerto Rican version of the baby boomers, which we used to call the "Carnation babies' generation," after the brand of evaporated milk that led the way in modern advertisement. Carnation Evaporated Milk came to substitute powdered milk as the food of choice for a generation of children of the upwardly mobile white- and blue-collar working classes.

Operation Bootstrap (a free translation of *Operación Manos a la Obra* — Operation Hands to the Task) is the name given to the set of policies that made up Puerto Rico's industrialization and modernization program. Following the end of World War II, there was a massive and concerted political, social, economic, and human effort and investment to develop the island's infrastructure and industrial capacity. A network of roads, electricity, telecommunications, and running water, as well as dams, office buildings, and new urban settlements, sprawled rapidly around the major urban centers of the island.

As the urban middle classes expanded, the two-income household became the norm. The burgeoning middle class embraced the modernization project articulated by Operation Bootstrap. Education and mass consumption became the fulcrum of upward mobility, the tickets that guaranteed the life described in the government slogan *el progreso que se ve* (the progress that you can see). Private schools proliferated as fast as expressways. Shopping malls (big and small) emerged as the favorite sites for mass consumption by the middle class. The *supermercados* (supermarkets) replaced the corner grocery stores. Kresge, K-mart, Gem, Zayre's, and Woolworth became the general stores. These were followed by other chain stores such as Sears and JC Penney's, Tom McCann's, Kinney's, Baker's.

I did not realize that I was a daughter of Bootstrap until I looked back on my life from the perspective of a migrant. I am the youngest in a family of four. Mom, Dad, my brother, and Cuco my *sato* dog, a mongrel mixed with German Shepherd, my father proudly remarked. My early childhood unfolded in Villa Palmeras, a working-class *barrio* of Santurce, where the houses were built from a combination of wood and cement blocks with cardboard interior divisions. My parents migrated to San Juan from the western towns of Adjuntas and Mayagüez, in search of the Bootstrap dream. My father became a civil servant, while my mother remained a homemaker, although she was a seamstress and dreamt of becoming a high-fashion couturier, like Carlota Alfaro (the famous Puerto Rican fashion designer). As mine was not a two-income household, it took us about ten years to realize one of the Bootstrap dreams, buying a house in one of the new middle-class suburban developments called *urbanizaciones*. I was about to become an adolescent when we finally moved to one of these *urbanizaciones*. There were lots of them, with shiny new cement homes, all alike, all perfectly square and lined up along carefully "planned" cement streets. There were *urbanizaciones* of all kinds and for all tastes, with American names (Country Club, Hyde Park), with Spanish names (Villa Andalucía, Villa Navarra), with names of rural allure (Lomas Verdes, Sierra Linda), and even names in Spanglish (Valle Arriba Heights, Sabana Gardens). These became the living quarters of the new white- and blue-collar workers.

It was in our new suburban home that I finally realized my lifelong dream of having a Christmas tree. A six-foot pine imported from Michigan or Canada was bought in the supermarket's parking lot and decorated with lights and ornaments bought at Sears. The decorations included a white spray that simulated snow. Yes, snow. Another one of those acquired fantasies made possible by movies with Spanish subtitles and dubbed TV series, and materialized when the Mayor of San Juan, Doña Felisa Rincón de Gautier, brought snow in airplanes for children to play in at the San Juan International Airport. I missed the spectacle of snow falling in the tropics because my father would not allow me to go to such an event. This "happening," broadcast on television, became part of my generation's collective memory.

American fast food and Spanglish are also products of Bootstrap. Puerto Rican fast food, *cuchifritos* (fried pig's intestines) and other fried foods (*rellenos, alcapurrias*), was replaced by Burger King, McDonald's, Big Boy, and Tastee Freeze. *Arroz con pollo* and *fricasé de pollo* (chicken with rice and stewed chicken) were quickly replaced by Kentucky Fried Chicken, Golden Skillet, and Church's Fried Chicken. In looking back on my life, this must have prepared me for migration. Although my cravings for *cuajo* (pig's stomach) and *mofongo* (mashed fried green plantains) never ceased, I was content with a Whopper or a KFC at the end of a long day.

Party politics was very much part of the environment created by these quick transformations. The *caravanas* (car rallies) became part of the modern political campaign. Long lines of American cars (Chevrolets, Buicks, Fords) drove in caravans down expressways and rural roads, flying party banners in red, blue, or green from the windows, their horns honking frantically, and loudspeakers on the roof of the lead car broadcasting party slogans and jingles: "*Jalda arriba va cantando el popular*" ("The Popular climbs the hill, singing," the theme song of the Popular Democratic Party), or "*Esto tiene que cambiar*" ("Things must change," the slogan of the pro-statehood New Progressive Party), or "*Nuestro es el futuro . . . nuestro es el derecho a la libertad*" ("The future is ours . . . the right to liberty is ours," the jingle of the Independence Party). This scene was repeated every four years, adding social excitement with a folkloric twist to the already hip urban life. The banners showed people's affiliation to political parties as well as their stance toward the unresolved issue of Puerto Rico's political status. A red face of a *jíbaro* (peasant) painted over a white banner represented Commonwealth, a blue *palma* (a coconut palm tree) represented Statehood, and a white cross over a solid green flag, Independence. Nowadays, Puerto Rican politics still continues the campaign tradition of singing in the streets. Instead of loudspeakers on the roofs of cars, pickup trucks are equipped with amplifiers, blasting music through every community, stopping for hours at the street corners, playing the competing slogans along with popular music, especially *merengues,* the product of our most recent migration, the Dominicans.

Spanglish, as well as code switching, became commonplace in my generation. It was not uncommon for me to speak Spanglish, especially among friends, because it served as a statement of difference. Two factors reinforced this emerging language form: relatives who migrated and the radio broadcasts of *tus canciones favoritas en inglés* (the hit parade), which included songs by the Beatles and the Rolling Stones. "She Loves You Yeah, Yeah, Yeah" played alongside Ruth Fernández's "La Bomba" or Tito Rodríguez's "Tiemblas," a bolero from the hit album in Spanish *From Tito with Love*. These songs seduced the minds of the young generation that began to sing English songs with a Spanish accent or songs in Spanish translated from the English. *La Nueva Ola* was the hit matinee TV show where these hybrids came to life in the voices of teenage idols: Celines, Pepe Luis, Lucecita Benítez, Tammy, and Julio Angel.

But most significant of all was the impact of the Fania All Stars salsa music. Puerto Ricans, Cubans, and other Latinos such as Willie Colón, Ray Barreto, Héctor LaVoe, Ismael Miranda, Pete El Conde, Celia Cruz, Johnny Pacheco, and, of course, *el judío maravilloso* (the marvelous Jew), Larry Harlow, made the first Latin opera Hommy, parts of which appeared in the first hit film in Spanglish, *Our Latin Thing*/Nuestra Cosa. I remembered watching this film four times in a row. I also used to go to the live salsa concerts of the Fania All Stars at the Hiram Bithorn Stadium with my two best girlfriends in school. My girlfriends (one white and another *trigueña*) were Spanglish-speaking, New York-born Puerto Ricans who came to the island as teenagers with their returning migrant parents. There was always debate about the difference in the dancing styles and salsa music culture among Puerto Rican *salseros* in New York and on the island. But, as usual, the resolution to these discursive conflicts was to be found on the dance floor. There, the difference made no difference! We were all *salseras*.

In accordance with my parents' modern mentality, I was thoroughly schooled. I went to the best school a civil servant's salary — and his annual loans — could buy, a private Catholic school. This was an extremely expensive proposition, an economic burden shared by the entire family. My grandmother and her sister on my father's side were the ideological enforcers of the modern mentality that valued education. Based on their personal experiences working as a social worker in the rural areas and a school teacher in the public school system, they appealed to my father's sense of paternal duty and coaxed him to enroll and keep us in a private school even if it meant no food on the table. We never went without food, literally, but there were times that the only food was *arroz blanco con garbanzos* (rice and chick peas). I hated that meal! But every two weeks or so *la línea* (a car from the public transportation line from Adjuntas to San Juan) would come by our house to deliver a care package from my grandmother: one or two *racimos de guineos verdes* (bunches of green bananas), a box of *viandas* (root vegetables), and a couple of five-pound cans of butter from *la* PRERA (the federal agency that distributed surplus food in the 1940s, later on distributed by the Social Welfare Office, where my grandmother worked as a social worker). It was exciting to hear the horn of the *público* bringing the goodies from my grandmother. Green bananas with olive oil and *bacalao* (salted codfish) were a delightful alternative to rice and chickpeas with no *patitas* (pig's feet). This "in kind" contribution to our staple diet was the way my father's family subsidized the high cost of private schooling. The rewards of these economic "sacrifices" were reaped at the end of the school year and during graduation (sixth, eighth, and twelfth grades), when the glowing report cards were received and my name appeared on the honors lists. My achievements were dutifully celebrated by my grandmother, who made a trip in *la línea* to attend our graduations and other celebrations. Like other Puerto Ricans I later saw at airports in New York and Chicago, grandma came loaded with big cardboard boxes tied with rope and full of *guineos verdes*, of course, and candies and gifts for the family.

Attending private school was a difficult economic enterprise laden with social contradictions. The competition was not only academic but social. In a private Catholic school, my peers were mainly from the white upper-middle classes. They belonged to exclusive clubs such as La Casa de España (a hanging place for people from the school sorority), or La Casa Cuba (the hangout for upper-class Cuban exiles). They celebrated their "sweet fifteen" (not sweet sixteen) birthday parties in glamorous hotel ballrooms. In contrast, I was the poor *trigueña*, the dark-skinned girl who lived in a barrio and later moved to a remote working-class *urbanización*. Using her skills as a seamstress, my mother always managed to negotiate the social difference that existed between our life and that of my schoolmates. My mother was my chaperone at all school activities and dances, where she proudly bragged about the uniqueness of my clothes, carefully designed and tailored by her. Her sewing skills were indeed unmatched by the recently arrived off-the-rack boutique dresses; she was indeed the Carlota Alfaro of the working classes. In the realm of clothing and physical appearance, an important terrain for social competition among the youth, I had a distinct advantage of a mom who put into practice her finer sewing skills. In shielding me in the field of social competition, my mother also realized her dreams of "haute couture." Her dresses were celebrated by my classmates, and she made me feel like a glamour girl. Although I did not hang out in the exclusive clubs, the social differences among classmates were not my consuming obsession. Good grades were.

The color of my skin was an issue, creating a strange twist of national pride with racism. The male peers in my class called me *Taína* because my features resembled what Puerto Ricans think of as "Indian." This label defined me as an exotic and sensuous prey on the verge of extinction. Even the *piropos* I would get from men, as I walked or crossed the streets, alluded to the image of the *Taíno* Indians: "*India chula, qué buena tú estás, negra*" ("India baby, you're really hot"). These insulting, offensive, and harassing remarks, filled with racial and ethnic undertones, provoked in me mixed feelings of rage and shame. The burden of these experiences led me to retreat from the social life of my school despite my mother's willingness to mediate the social tensions. I chose to hide in my room with my books during most of my high school and university years. My reclusive behavior was accepted as long as I kept achieving in school and lived up to my mother's expectations of becoming like my father, an educated "professional." I believe that my mother never realized the meaning and implications of her desires until much later.

Ironically, in the context of the emerging modernity and middle-class consumerism, the extended family ties of my rural migrant parents facilitated the income-pooling strategy and personal frugality that enabled me to acquire an education. Education was worth the economic sacrifices. In my parents' way of thinking, education was the ticket to my future in more ways than one:

upward mobility for me and an insurance policy in case my husband *me saliera malo* (turned out to be a bum), since my destiny was to be married and have children as my parents did. But life takes many turns, and as it turned out I did not become a lawyer as they wished, my husband did not turn out to be a bum, and I did not "give" my parents a litter of grandchildren. Instead, I went on to study in England and the United States and became a political scientist, a job my parents never quite understood, except for the teaching part.

My decision to attend graduate school abroad in England was met with ambivalent opposition by my father. My parents had an unspoken fear that we would grow apart. As an undergraduate student, I lived at home and spent most of my time with books. I was seen as a model student and daughter who did not date often and went out mostly with female friends, one of whom was an older woman (ten or twelve years older), who shared with me her life experiences and took on the role of a big sister. My education ceased to be an economic burden. I got reduced tuition for making the dean's honors list, which released the economic pressure of taking out an annual loan to pay school tuition.

But my desires to pursue graduate studies in the social sciences, rather than go to law school, threatened to alter the family order. I became a disobedient and a subversive daughter affirming the modern ambition of attaining a degree, an educational project that they had instilled in me for years, but through a path that they never anticipated. Going to England was out of the question. That was something they could not imagine. My father and mother must have felt like Dr. Frankenstein. Yes, I was going to study; yes, I was opting for a career. But where? I patiently and stoically resisted my father's authoritarianism and peculiar ways of opposing my desires. I stood firm and unmovable for two long months of his silence, indifference, sarcasm, and accusations of *tú estás loca* (you are crazy). My mind was made up. They had succeeded all too well in making me an educated and independent woman. When a telegram accepting me to graduate school in the land of the Beatles came to the door of our house, four days later my parents and relatives from every point on the island took me to the airport. I was gone.

I still can hear my aunt's words of farewell (she was a school principal in Adjuntas, who got a university degree attending summer programs and Saturday classes, while my mother took care of my cousin and my uncle): "If I could turn back the clock of my life, I would do exactly the same thing you are doing today." Her words of support reflected, in a way, the promise of progress made by Operation Bootstrap to her generation. I always felt that my aunt aspired to become what she thought I was becoming, a fearless woman who would travel the world capable of challenging the gender expectations that had tied her to family tradition and rural life in spite of her professional achievements. This marked the beginning of my journey as an *extranjera y peregrina* (a foreigner and a pilgrim), a woman migrant in pursuit of the Bootstrap dream, only now outside the geographical boundaries of the island.

My studies abroad awakened me to ethnic and racial dilemmas I had never confronted. In England I was defined as an international student. This was a label that allowed me to be different racially and culturally. I spent most of the time with my Brazilian girlfriend who only spoke Portuguese. I lived for a while in the house of a Chilean exiled couple and spent hours with the Venezuelan crowd. This experience allowed me to discover my Latin American identity. And then I was discovered by first- and second-generation Indian and Pakistani migrants. My physical features resembled those of women from these countries. Yet my fully Westernized appearance and demeanor were looked upon by some with great curiosity. I felt that some Indian and Pakistani men looked at me as a kind of renegade who did not fit their cultural and gender expectations. As I strolled in the streets and wandered in the markets I was approached and addressed in a language unknown to me, and when I could not respond, I was looked upon with disbelief. I also realized then that the negative reactions of some British shop attendants were rooted on my "Eastern" appearance. I became part of the colonial "other" for the British and discovered their racist side.

Racial dilemmas intensified when I moved to the United States and traded labels. I was no longer an international student but a black Puerto Rican woman. This was the label I was given by a Polish man working as a building superintendent in Chicago. When I went to see an apartment for rent I was greeted with the phrase "No blacks are allowed here." A week into my arrival on the "mainland," race had become the strongest defining feature of my identity. I remember that during a discussion with my thesis advisors, I defined myself as a black woman and one of them wasted no time in replying, "No you are not! You are a Puerto Rican." At that moment I felt that I was required to make an impossible choice between race and ethnicity, as if they could not coalesce in a defining self. Later on, after I became a professor, this tension became an excruciating issue. For some of my colleagues and students I was a positive role model who embodied the gender, race, and ethnic trinity, while others defined me as the insubordinate other. The racial complexities and ethnic prejudices encountered in my academic and professional journey as a Puerto Rican black woman were not part of the instruction manual handed to the migrant children of Bootstrap.

My journey back to the island, in 1995, has made me realize that I am a woman whose view of the world was deeply affected by the modernity project of Operation Bootstrap. I do not see Bootstrap as a good or a bad program but as a political project that affected people's lives differently. For Puerto Rican women on both sides of the ocean, modernity implied different life options and meant radically different things. The values of modernity gave me the strength to survive a pilgrimage. I had a sense of direction despite the vagaries of life. At the same time, the racial, ethnic, sexist, academic, and professional experiences I lived empowered me to confront the vestiges of my contradictory heritage as the daughter of Bootstrap.

As a society, Puerto Rico is not what the architects of Bootstrap envisaged. It can be described as a peripheral postmodern society. The modern coexists with the postmodern. Class, race, and gender identities coexist with new identities shaped by consumption, new-age spiritualism, and lifestyles (surfers, rappers, rockers, auto club identities, etc.). Each morning we wake up listening to the never-ending news of yet another victim of domestic violence, child abuse, corruption in the high circles of government, killings, and police takeovers of public housing to control gangs. Political campaigns are not concerned with the traditional means of political persuasion but with selling carefully crafted images of a young governor whose appeal is not the "modern sense and sensibility" but the postmodern allure of living *la vida loca*, life in the fast lane. The politics of peripheral postmodernity contrast sharply with the rational pretenses of the project of modernity. The governor campaigns going from one beach to another in a highly polluting JET SKI, delivers one-line speeches while singing and dancing to Ricky Martin's worldwide pop hit song *La Copa de la Vida*. He arrives in jeans, riding a bike to the electoral college, and when the political campaign is over, the governor amuses the public by rappelling in caves at a tourist recreational site. As we are entertained by this style of political leadership, corrupt public officials and civil servants swindle money from AIDS programs to finance their personal consumption and political campaigns. Super-moms, of all types, married, divorced, single, heterosexual, and lesbian, all of them white and middle class, are coming out to put "the house in order" and rescue the country from collapse. Women have become politicians and are competing with men and other women in electoral politics for the highest positions at all levels of government.

At the personal level, I have rediscovered the love of an aging mother who has a hard time understanding what I have become, a professional woman, the very thing she wanted me to become. I am not what she envisioned in her dream of modernity. My mother, who endured my father's verbal abuses, the family hardships, and loneliness, believes that daughters, unlike sons, are supposed to take care of mothers and surround them with grandchildren. I have come home to face the contradictions of modernity and must reconcile myself to an identity forged in multiple cultural sites through experiences of difference. Almost fifty years after my mother left Mayagüez, we visited her hometown. Things had changed but they were neither better nor worse, they just were. You cannot go home again. Home is wherever you are and whatever you have become. It is not the place: it is the memories that inspire a life course that ties us down or sets us free. *Recordar es volver a vivir,* only this time remembering was an act of re-living differences within ourselves and with others. In the visit to my mother's hometown we realized that difference was the source of our strength and that what has brought us together is an act of love, not family obligation or sociocultural imposition. We finally understood that the pursuit of the Bootstrap dreams set our lives apart and contradictorily shaped our identities in ways neither of us ever imagined.

I am, indeed, a daughter of Bootstrap. My parents, willingly or not, participated in the process of producing the conditions of modernity espoused in the political project of Operation Bootstrap. I participated more as a consumer of modernity than a producer of it, and I had to endure the trials of living with new values, rules, norms, and social expectations regarding modern life. My identity reflects the contradictions brought by the process of socioeconomic and cultural transformation that shaped my life experiences and determined the opportunities that paved the way to the woman I have become. The woman I have become, in turn, represents a site of political struggle over the definition of self that synthesizes the national and transnational dimensions that determine my experience as a Puerto Rican woman regardless of the geographical spaces I occupy. I am a woman, a professor, a daughter, a wife, a Puerto Rican. Not a mother, not an American, not a migrant anymore, but a wanderer at heart. I have enjoyed the journey but I have not yet arrived. There is still more to come and this *papelito* is just at the midpoint.

Beyond Survival: A Politics/Poetics of
Puerto Rican Consciousness

Liza Fiol-Matta

dedicarse al rescate de un poeta
de las garras del bilingüismo colonial
no es cosa fácil.

es rescatar a la vez memoria, escribir historia,
inventarse imágenes que llenen las lagunas,
inventarse a uno mismo como hecho innegable,

es dejar dicho: fui, así que fuimos;
soy, así que somos; y seguiremos siendo.

es agacharse en las estaciones del subway
y documentarse, escribiendo obsesivamente en libretas,
en cualquier hoja de papel: estoy y escribo.

Rescuing a poet
from the claws of colonial bilingualism
is not an easy thing.

It means rescuing memory, writing history,
inventing images to fill in the blanks,
inventing oneself as an undeniable fact,

leave having said: I was, therefore we were;
I am, therefore we are; and we will continue being.

It means squatting in subway stations
and documenting oneself, writing obsessively in notebooks,
or on any piece of paper: I am here and I write.

IN THIS ESSAY I attempt to define the cultural space I occupy as a middle-class, college-educated, bilingual, lesbian, white Puerto Rican woman. In the process of exploring how a bilingual and bicultural writer comes to consciousness about her languages and her identity, I have discovered that, writing at the beginning of the second century of colonization by the United States, I must still struggle to reappropriate my history and take back the power to define myself.

Puerto Rican lives have been codified by a series of articles of war and legislative acts. Puerto Rican history, however, is made up by more than these. We also have the examples of resistance of the Grito de Lares uprising against the Spanish in 1868, the ceding by Spain of a short-lived but hard-fought autonomy in 1898, the internationalism of Luisa Capetillo and the early feminist and labor movements, Pedro Albízu Campos and the Nationalist Party, the brave march of Nationalists in Ponce in 1937 that ended in their massacre, the revolutionary actions of Lolita Lebrón and others in the attack on the House of Representatives in Washington in 1953, the draft resistance movement during the Vietnam War, the Young Lords Party, the continued struggle of Puerto Ricans in various independence movements, and the renewed mobilization against the U.S. Navy's presence on the island of Vieques.

So it should come as no surprise that, given the complex history of Puerto Rican colonialism, I make for an uneasy American citizen. My imposed U.S. passport erases my real nationality; my accentless American English betrays no regional affect. However, one aspect of the recovery from the indignities of colonialism is to have survived the sojourn of identity recovery and returned to tell the tale. Thus my trajectory in defining my Puerto Rican consciousness is a story of recovery of/from language, of/from dislocation and exile, of/from displacement and marginalization. It is a story of surviving disruption and invalidation, and of putting into words the possibility of wholeness despite continuous interruption. More importantly, though, it is a story that goes beyond survival.

Because I am a product of a colonial history, I find myself situated in what Homi Bhabha calls "the *in-between* spaces." Just as Puerto Rican history has not been (to use Bhabha's words) "a continuous narrative of national progress," Puerto Rican consciousness reflects a narrative fragmented by/in "the meanwhile." We are located in an in-between space created by colonialism: in-between languages, in-between geographies, in-between racial discourses.

It is never far from my mind that I have been forced by historical forces into a cycle of migration that has felt at times like an overwhelming reciprocal betrayal, a doubled geographic dislocation. Like many Puerto Ricans, I struggle to inhabit a place that can hold the contradictions of nationalism, *patria*, migration, exile, and diaspora. But there is no place for me on my island, nor am I totally comfortable in the United States. The geography of my world is as much conceptual as territorial. It is as much Northeastern United States as it is Caribbean, as much Army bases as island, as much the subway as ocean and horizon. Chicana poet Lorna Dee Cervantes' words resonate for me when she writes: "Every day I am deluged with reminders / that this is not / my land / and this is my land." But sometimes I mean both my island and this land.

Like so many immigrants, I have been engaged in a lifelong tug-of-war of language, which mimics the back-and-forth travel between the island and the misnomered "mainland." Neither Spanish nor English is my second language. When I was younger, I struggled thinking that one or the other made me more authentic. But I now accept that my bilingualism and biculturalism are my inheritance. Or, as Guillermo Gómez-Peña puts it: "The border-crosser develops two or more voices. . . . We develop different speaking selves that speak for different aspects of our identity."

The New York Puerto Rican poet Sandra María Esteves writes of this simultaneously double-voiced identity in her poem "Not Neither":

> Being Puertorriqueña Americana
> Born in the Bronx, not really *jíbara*
> Not really *hablando bien*
> But yet not *gringa* either,
> *Pero ni portorra, pero sí portorra* too
> *Pero ni que* what am I? . . .

In 1958 I was six years old and recently arrived to the United States from Puerto Rico. My father, a career Army officer, had been stationed in Fort Chaffee, Arkansas. As a member of a local Brownie troop in Fort Smith, Arkansas, I was selected to represent my troop onstage during a ceremony in which we handed over what I remember as a jar full of coins as part of a fundraising drive for the town. I did not really know English yet, but for several days I practiced saying the name and number of my troop and the amount we had collected. This was my first public performance in the United States, the first time my "public" voice was heard; maybe it was the first time I realized I had a public voice. I remember being called up to the stage and the microphone brushing my lips. My recollection is that I bowed my head and shyly mumbled the required words in this new and foreign language. I vaguely remember going back to my seat.

I have always felt a twinge of unease for the little Puerto Rican girl, who, speaking her accented English, was such a novelty in her Brownie troop in that segregated Arkansas town. On the other hand, I would not be surprised at all to learn that I probably volunteered to get on that stage and speak. Two years later, at Loretto Academy in El Paso (with my father posted at Fort Bliss), I was onstage again, this time playing the piano in the school talent show. Just as I hadn't known English two years before, I had never played the piano either. Nevertheless, I performed my spontaneously composed piece, "The Happy Clowns." I think there was already something of the survivor in that child, uprooted as she was every year and a half as her father was transferred from posting to posting. There was something in her that wouldn't be silenced, that forced others to take notice of her.

While I am wary of employing the language of recovery and abuse to name the results of systemic political and colonial oppression, I nevertheless have found it useful to think in these terms. I am not saying that individual recovery can take the place of political action, but that this recovery is an important part of political activism. The literature of Latinos/as is full of references to the ways that bilingual or "Spanish-surnamed" children are subject in the classroom and playground to the kinds of sudden disapproval that confuse the "good" children they are trying to be. This abuse begins early in the educational process of Latino/a children and continues as we take survival strategies into the workplace and the world at large. Theorizing colonialism as abuse can yield insight into why we may feel that no matter how much we modify our actions and attempt to measure up to norms imposed from outside, we do not seem to be able to develop satisfactory strategies to protect the self. No matter how well we speak English, or how light or dark our skin is, or how well we do in school and work, there is always the lingering doubt that we are not "loved for who we really are" but for the facsimile of the dominant culture that we can, with varying success, represent. Perhaps the key to the colonized child's survival can be found in Albert Memmi's assertion that "the colonized's liberation must be carried out through a recovery of self and of autonomous dignity."

Like so many children of immigrant parents, I often translated for my mother. I can remember very clearly being in Rose's (a Woolworth-type store in Columbia, South Carolina) and translating between my mother and saleslady. I say "between" because that is where I remember being placed, or perhaps placing myself. As a child I was not only linguistic go-between but also physical separator between the hostile (after all, not understanding my mother can only be a hostile act) and the nurturing (my mother who in all other ways is competent, creative, in control). The Conquest-era drawing from the Florentine Codex of Malintzín/La Malinche comes to mind— she/me standing between the conquerors/salesclerks and the Mayans/my mother. A girl child sacrificed to the act of translating, sleeping with the enemy, learning the enemy's language in the enemy's schools. In my case, this battle/conflict imagery/metaphor is especially appropriate; my father the proud U.S. Army officer, my mother his unhappy captive in the Army bases of the United States. Refusing to speak English, refusing to go to the wives' luncheons, refusing to be content separated from her homeland. Her laughter and spirit darkened, shut away. My father says that when we went to visit Charleston (I guess this was sometime in 1963) my mother cried when she saw the sea. She had not seen the sea in all the time we had lived in the U.S. I don't remember her crying. I do remember seeing Fort Sumter off in the distance.

Latina writers often explore the nuances of language and its importance in family life and identity formation. Hear Gloria Anzaldúa on language: "So, if you want to really hurt me, talk badly about my language. Ethnic identity is twin skin to linguistic identity — I am my language. Until I can take pride in my language, I cannot take pride in myself." Cherríe Moraga equates language and return to the mother/woman/*mestiza* as source: "Returning to *la mujer* scares me, re-learning Spanish scares me. . . . In returning to the love of my race, I must return to the fact that not only has the mother been taken from me, but her tongue, her mothertongue. I want the language, feel my tongue rise to the occasion of feeling at home, in common. I know this language in my bones . . . and then it escapes me. . . . 'You don't belong. *¡Quítate!*'" Rosario Morales recalls: "I cried when I heard my voice on tape for the first time. My voice showed no signs of El Barrio, of the South Bronx. I had erased them, helped my teachers erase the signs that I had been a little girl from the tenements who couldn't speak a word of English when she went to kindergarten, not even to say, 'I need to pipi, I'll wet my pants,' to say, 'I'm scared, I want to go home.'"

In a poem by Pat Mora, a Mexican mother — a woman perhaps with much in common with my own mother — struggles to learn English in order to understand her children:

> . . . I'm forty,
> embarrassed at mispronouncing words,
> embarrassed at the laughter of my children,
> the grocer, the mailman. Sometimes I take
> my English book and lock myself in the bathroom,
> say the thick words softly,
> for if I stop trying, I will be deaf
> when my children need my help.

In the towns where my father was stationed, there were no Puerto Rican neighborhoods. Our Puerto Rican lives were lived in our home and our backyard, shared with the one or two Puerto Rican families whose time there overlapped with ours. The memory of my mother's *tristeza*, what Judith Ortiz Cofer describes as "the sadness that only place induces and only place cures," hurts even now. Yes, Spanish was my mother's tongue, but my memory of the sound of her voice — reciting poetry, singing old Puerto Rican songs, laughing, scolding — is interrupted by her heart-wrenching silences. She, hostage in U.S. Army bases, made sure that Puerto Rico was alive in her home, that Spanish was alive. Her daily life was an act of subversion.

My mother's story would be incomplete, however, without its denouement. She had graduated in 1945, at seventeen, with a degree in Biology from the University of Puerto Rico. At forty-seven she went back to school, this time enrolling in Spanish literature courses. This was after my father had been reassigned to the island. After finishing a B.A. in Spanish, she earned an M.A. in linguistics, then taught Spanish at Interamerican University. Until then only my mother's private voice had seemed strong; her spirited renditions of Spanish poetry recited from memory filled the house. She had not stood in front of audiences and courtrooms and classrooms like her children were to do. But, back in Puerto Rico my mother, who had spent so many of her years in the United States publicly silent — her psyche bruised by the imposed America of her surroundings — began to talk in the language of transformational grammar and sociolinguistics. She became active in the Puerto Rican Independence Party. Her public voice emerged.

Although I left the island twenty-two years ago, it is always in my consciousness. I often think of the line in Puerto Rican poet Luz María Umpierre's "The Mar/Garita Poem" that says *"hay una isla en Edison, New Jersey"* [there is an island in Edison, New Jersey.] There is, in fact, an island/*hay una isla* in this room in this apartment on this street in Manhattan where I am writing this sentence. Just as I am/there is an island in the academic institution in which I work. The Puerto Rican body/psyche is a geographical space of its own, an island in the ocean of American "ethnicity" — unassimilated, multiaccented, defying the racial paradigms of this country. Being Puerto Rican is an enactment of a virtual reality, the incarnation of our *tierra natal* in the island of our bodies. In a world that is theorizing postcolonial national identities, we are still in an anachronistic colonial relationship with the United States, and that relationship invades both our lifelike dreams at night and our dreamlike daily lives.

As absurd as it may sound, the Caribbean is a problematic, contradictory space in which to anchor Puerto Rican-ness. With our long-standing relationship as its most willing and faithful consumers, Puerto Rico has increasingly become an extension of the United States. We live with strip-malls anchored by Dunkin' Donuts and Burger King franchises, Christmas displays of Santa and snowmen. Yet I daily define myself as a Caribbean person. My Caribbean students and colleagues — from Trinidad and Tobago, Jamaica, Barbados, Dominican Republic, Guadeloupe, Haiti, Cuba — and I sit in my windowless office in a renovated factory recalling colors, sky, light, ocean, the taste of salt in the air.

Inevitably, our nostalgia turns to pain, to the anger of Jamaica Kincaid when she says of her native Antigua:

> Sometimes the beauty of it seems unreal. . . . It is as if, then, the beauty— the beauty of the sea, the land, the air, the trees, the market, the people, the sounds they make—were a prison, and as if everything and everybody inside it were locked in and everything and everybody that is not inside it were locked out. . . .

and we awaken from our daydream remembering why we are no longer there.

Puerto Rico in my dreams is always a city landscape: my grandmother's house in the Condado and the lemon and avocado trees in her backyard, the narrow streets of Old San Juan at night, the nondescript Puerta de Tierra section that separates Old San Juan from the rest of the city, the college I attended in Santurce. But in recent dreams a new image has emerged: a panoramic highway, paid for by federal moneys set aside by the statehood party specifically for this project, rings the island. To build this highway, however, the shoreline has been sacrificed. Beaches have been allowed to erode, towns near the shore have been deliberately flooded, arable land lost. And at night there is no access to the highway or the ocean beyond. Puerto Rico has been converted into an island prison, a self-destructive shrinking body.

Despite a childhood spent on American Army bases, it was my adult choice to live in New York that recontextualized for me the reality of being Puerto Rican. For several years after settling in New York, I continued to identify myself as being "from the island," a survivalist nationalism blinding me to the greater possibilities of identifying with those who had, until my own migration, been the "other Puerto Ricans," *los de allá*. Much of my personal struggle with language, exile, and the notion of betrayal of my *madre/patria* played itself out in a narrowly conceived space between pure (i.e., heroic) nationalism and total (i.e., traitorous) assimilation. But, almost unnoticed by me, the conversion happened; they, and I, became *de aquí*. I have become *una puertorriqueña de nueva york*.

Today I share my life with a Dutch-American woman who also owns two languages and cultures. Daily the sounds of Spanish and Dutch and English fill the house in rapid succession. One son calls from the Hague, my father from San Juan; my sisters drop in for dinner, another son and his wife come visiting for the weekend. My brother and his American wife have us all over for Thanksgiving. Our home is Dutch-cozy, *gezellig;* we drink only Puerto Rican *café con leche*. It has become a tradition that we sing "Happy Birthday" in three languages, the candles melting on the cake as we make our way through the last *"hiep-hiep-hoera!"* But the English in which we speak truths and comfort is a language all our own. In our home, it is not the colonizer's language. It recognizes both Puerto Rican and Dutch feelings; its vocabulary includes both our wants and needs. We question its lapses and limitations; we laugh and love in the multiple dimensions of our hybrid, intimately constructed English. Together we confirm the truth of Adrienne Rich's statement: "The relationship to more than one culture, nonassimilating in spirit and therefore living amid contradictions, is a constant act of self-creation." Together we create family and identity, nourished by the deep-seated understanding that there is no room in our lives for the colonizing project of erasing difference or demanding conformity.

I Can Fly:
Of Dreams and Other Nonfictions

Eliana Rivero

I Hear Voices

I HAVE ALWAYS WONDERED at voices. How I have longed to speak in a deep alto, seductive in its own right, softly soothing or firmly authoritative. I envy opera singers and Motown artists; I judge people on the telephone by the way they inflect or not; I gauge character by pitch. I hate to hear my own voice on recordings, the disembodied, tinny sound of someone whom others hear like this. I redo the outgoing message on my answering system dozens of times, until I get what I think is a reasonable facsimile of my real speech.

And then there are the metaphorical voices, the personas I have fallen into along the years: my loud, Cuban slangy posture; my professional, academic stance; my American no-nonsense speech with which I deal with banks, doctors, and moderators at meetings; the soft, unimposing utterance of intimacy. My voices of inquiry, of self-empowerment, of business, of friendship, of love.

In this *testimonio* I share some of these voices with you, dear reader. One jokes casually, another philosophizes formally; still another, toward the end, engages in things of spirit. One voice sometimes sketches what another will flesh out. So please bear with me in what can seem at times a dissonant duo (or trio) of enunciations. I say this, I theorize about that, I remember, I ponder, I repeat, I tell my story for you and for me, and for all those others who think they know me, or will know me through these pages: these sounds, these murmurings of U.S. Latina life.

(Out of a tape recorder, a woman speaks; her voice is
unpretentious and conversational.)

When I was a girl between the ages of twelve and fifteen, I had two recurring dreams that were very vivid. One of them was that I could fly; I had wings. Not only did I have wings, but I could fly very high. I would always fly in my dream. Then I realized that when I was aloft, if I looked down, I could see the whole island of Cuba. I could see it all. I could also see the peninsula of Florida. I would always go — zoomp! — and jump into Florida. I would then wake up and wonder, what is this? . . . and I would dream the same thing the week after. I would always see myself flying over Florida, or the United States. I would see them as maps. This was way back in the early fifties, and there was no reason to think that anything of that sort was coming up: me flying over the United States. The other dream was that I was walking along a street, and it was sort of dark. I was by myself, and then this sinister-looking individual, a man, would follow me with a knife. I would run and run, but he would always catch me and stab me in the back with the knife. I would see myself bleed, but I would never die. I *never* died. I would be wounded, but I kept on walking. I remember the last in the series of those dreams: the man finally got me inside a house, and he stabbed me right against the door. Then he hung me on it, as if the knife were a hook. I left my body, and I looked at myself, and I was hanging on the door. I was dead, but I knew that I wasn't dead, because I was looking at myself. And then that series of dreams ended.

I thought about this a lot later, and I think that of course the crucial experience for me, the watershed experience of my life, was immigration. I was, somehow, seeing or foreseeing this in my dream of flying into the United States, from which I always awoke feeling kind of funny. And this death, or this attempted murder, took place repeatedly, but I never let myself die. I would even witness myself being attacked and killed, but I would be a survivor. I think this is very symbolic.

I had been a very privileged child, and somehow I have had to deal with the guilt of privilege. I enjoyed a great childhood and youth, in the sense that my parents — who were well off — provided me with everything: private schools, a very good home. All of a sudden, one day, I went from being this privileged young person to being a Cuban refugee in Miami. As a matter of fact, I actually had two immigration experiences. I came to the States — my parents sent me — when I was seventeen. I had graduated from high school early in Havana and was then enrolled in a finishing school, more like a junior college, in Virginia. I went there to "polish my English," or at least this is what the school officials said. So actually I was in the States during the last days of the armed revolutionary struggle in Cuba. I flew home a few days before the New Year; I was there on January 1, 1959. Then I stayed at my parents' house and refused to go back to school.

There was such an effervescence in the air, on the streets. My parents freaked out, especially my father, because he saw me as a "commie sympathizer." And it was painful to be in conflict with him, because I really respected him for what he was.

I find that my father was probably the most important single factor in my becoming who I am. I really admired his zest for life, his ongoing desire to learn, his wonderful sense of humor. Today people look at me and say "Boy, you are your father's spitting image," because I really look like him a lot.

For years I thought that I didn't have anything to do with my mother. I was telling someone recently that the first conscious thought I can recall, at around age six, was "I don't want to be like her." Part of my struggle in life was to do things just to make me into another person, not her. It was hard for me to see her so meek, so passive, so unassertive, so silent. It took me quite a number of years to realize all that she had given me that was good — her singing voice, her sweetness toward children and young people, her love for nature and beauty, the tenderness that she sometimes was able to express. I am now grateful to her for all those things that enrich my life. But it took a long time.

At first, it was my father whom I simply patterned my life after, and he had this idea that I was to do in life whatever he hadn't done. He was a self-made man, a high achiever, and totally sold on education. I was the boy he didn't have. But in spite of all the games he wanted to teach me, I wanted mostly to read books — even encyclopedias, volume after volume. Then I stood in front of my father and said, "I want to be a musician." What I really loved to do, what came naturally, was to play the piano, and my dream was to have a job at a piano bar, a cocktail lounge, playing through the night all the songs I knew for people to enjoy and maybe sing. That's what I really wanted to do. So when I was fourteen, I stood in front of my *papá* and I told him what I wanted. He said: "*¡Tú estás loca!* You are crazy! Get out of my sight, girl. *Tú lo que tienes que ser es maestra.* What you need to become is a teacher. If you want to be a professor of mathematics, say, or something equally important, do that. But you have to have a degree that will guarantee you a regular paycheck, so that no matter what happens in your personal life you can always take care of yourself, you can be independent and provide for yourself."

I went to a calendar with historical dates on it, and looked up the famous people who had been born on the same day as I had, November 7. I saw two names: one was the Cuban poet Julián del Casal, and the other was Madame Curie, the famous woman who had discovered radium in a chemistry lab where she worked with her husband. And I said to myself, "This is it. That's what I am going to be."

So in 1959 I started attending the University of Havana. My parents saw how I stayed out till very late at night, going to meetings, demonstrations, and parades, and were very troubled by my behavior. I remember trying to participate in all the political activities that were going on, but I also remember going one day to a meeting for what used to be called *"brigadas universitarias,"* university brigades, and there I sat until one of my *compañeras* stood up and said, "You don't have any right to be here; you're the daughter of rich people.

You don't have anything to do with us." I was so depressed that I decided to return to the United States. That was my second immigration.

In Havana I had started majoring in chemistry and taking courses in physics and mathematics. Until I was a junior at the University of Miami (Coral Gables, Florida), those were my majors and minors. And I studied German, because it was the language of pure science, or so I thought. It wasn't till I got sick from the vapors in an organic chemistry lab that I questioned whether I belonged there. Wouldn't I be happier in literature, which was my hobby, anyway? I ended up in a doctoral program in the humanities out of necessity, almost by default. I finished a master's degree in Spanish American literature, and much to my horror I realized that all the jobs I could get were teaching high-school Spanish. Teaching fourteen-year-olds! I just couldn't deal with that thought. I went to see one of my professors in Coral Gables and asked him, "What do you think I should do?" And he said, "Get a Ph.D. of course. Come back on Monday, and I will have a fellowship for you." I returned, and he did have it. They gave me a three-year fellowship. I finished my coursework within that time and also took my preliminary examinations, and I wrote my dissertation in one semester and one summer.

It was very difficult. My face broke out, I started getting gray hair at the age of twenty-five, I developed migraines, but I stuck it out and I finished. Most of all, I had a Scarlett O'Hara attitude: I swore I would never be poor again. The big motivating force was: I hate being poor, I don't want to be a student any more, so I am going to kill myself and finish this degree in record time. And get a job! This was my theme: GET A JOB! I actually didn't give much thought to research. It just happened: an advanced degree and a career, they just happened. Life just happened that way.

When I arrived in the United States for the second time, I was around twenty, and I didn't see my parents for the next ten years. I came to the States with five dollars in my pocket and was on welfare for a while. I was homesick and miserable, not only because I missed my family and country but also because I had tried as best I could to fit in the new Cuban society and had failed. I remember trying to go see a friend who lived in North Miami in those days, and I didn't have an extra nickel for additional bus fare (North Miami was an extra zone, beyond city limits). My family couldn't legally send me any money (hard currency couldn't leave the island). I wasn't able to go to school yet because the welfare office didn't let me: the rationale being that if I could go to school, I could work. The social worker who came to visit me told me in clear terms that the only reason I was getting any help at all was to prevent me from doing "something wrong," such as going into prostitution. Then my father managed to send me some jewelry via diplomatic pouch, and I got money by selling some of it and started attending the University of Miami.

When I arrived on campus I realized that there were special programs for

Cubans, and they helped me further with loans. I still went every month to pick up commodities, that is, food assistance items, on the program titled Cuban Refugee Aid — the fifth of every month I received peanut butter, rice, processed cheese, powdered milk, canned meat, and other goods. It was quite an experience, to go from being *la niña privilegiada*, the privileged girl, to being a Latina on government assistance programs. I remember being in Miami, speaking Spanish at a bus stop, and having an old lady yell at me, "You're in America! Why don't you speak American?" Those were hard years.

(The voice on the tape recorder becomes soft and reflective.)

I really have a hard time figuring out what the main breakdown or breakthrough points were in my life, or the points that have given me the most pain and at the same time the most impetus to go on. I remember that for years after I was divorced from my first husband I thought, "I can't decide if the breakup of a marriage — the marriage to my Cuban childhood sweetheart, the father of my child — was the most painful experience . . . or was it leaving my country?" For a long time I couldn't decide.

I have been through a series of traumatic periods and I have found that, in the final analysis, these are the points at which I have grown the most. I can name those points. I like to think about them in a series, because as I see myself now, fifty-nine years old at this writing, this is a very good time to reflect on my life. In a sense, I feel very much at peace with myself; I feel that just about all the struggles are over (at least the outer ones). I don't know what life is bringing, *y ¿quién sabe?,* but I feel that all this personal inner stuff is mostly resolved. The experience of immigration was the big watershed. Then my first divorce. And then my tenure fight.

(The scholar writes and rewrites: her voice is more analytical and formal.)

My name is Eliana Suárez Rivero, and I have lived in the American Southwest, specifically in Tucson, for the last thirty-three years. I am a professor at the University of Arizona. From being an exiled Cuban in the sixties, I turned into a "Cubacana," that is, a Cubana-Americana who has lived among Chicanos for a very long time.

I am a first-generation immigrant, who left her native country in her late teens; my parents did not join me until ten years later. Now I have a Cuban American daughter, born in Arizona, who grew up in a bicultural environment that nourished her with black beans and tacos and ethnic music; she not only eats salsa but dances to it. So I have lived at the U.S. southern border for over half my life. For a year in the late seventies I moved to a house in Sierra Vista, Arizona, from whose kitchen window I could see the mountains of Mexico on the other side. I often reflected on how wistfully symbolic it was to literally see Latin America from my own backyard.

I work in the Spanish and Portuguese Department at the University of Arizona, where I teach and do research in the areas of Latin American poetry, Hispanic women's literature, U.S. Latino literature, literary theory, and feminist criticism. I am also an adjunct faculty member in the Women's Studies Program and a member of the advisory board for SIROW (Southwestern Institute for Research on Women). Actually, I was one of a small group of women on our campus who in 1972 started working toward what would eventually be constituted into the Women's Studies Program; they called us the "Founding Mothers." In the beginning, my main interests were Latin American literature and Latin American feminisms, and I am still working in that area. But most of my research in the last few years has been headed specifically toward U.S. Latina and Latino writers.

For years I have been part of a group of Anglo feminists that has just recently begun to make appointments in what is called in my place "Women of Color" positions. For a long time I have heard university officials bemoan not having enough Latina women on the faculty, and I have been a token person for much of my career; but fortunately we are beginning to see some small breakthroughs in that respect: we have just hired a Chicana cultural comparatist in Women's Studies. I have learned much from my Anglo women colleagues, no doubt about it. And they have also given me quite a lot of support, both professionally and personally.

My academic experience includes, as well, being once a young Latina assistant professor in a group composed of mostly white males; the only two other women in a department of twenty or so faculty members were much older and Anglo, one of them emerita (only two men were Latinos). And I also had the experience of having to fight hard to become senior faculty. I called in the Feds (as university officials put it) when I was denied a promotion, and the administration finally had to allow that they had discriminated against me. I had published books and all that was needed, and still they did not promote me. The promotion went instead to a male colleague in French who had less seniority, fewer years after the degree, and fewer publications, so I had to fight. Still, in 1973 I became the first tenured Latina in the Arizona university system. And, in 1974, the first Latina associate professor. Now, as I become established as the senior woman professor in my unit, nine other women—three of them tenured—are part of our group; six of them are Latinas. Progress is on its slow way!

At present I am returning to the source, to my creative spirit, in writing. Poetry is flowing again, and I am also experimenting with incursions into the personal narrative. From a middle-age perspective I can say that this is a good time to reflect on life in general and to ponder my own construction of self and identity over the past thirty or so years. These days people ask me to speak and write about my own experiences, so I am producing a mixed bag of essays, theory, and poetry that, with any luck, will provide a fitting frame for those seemingly fragmented aspects of my life. The feminist research issues that I grapple with, and that I am still studying, are those of self-identity and representation. That constitutes the core of the work that I have done and continue to do with Latina, Chicana, and Cuban American women.

Marginality has been a way of life for me for quite some time. Borders and boundaries seem a likely metaphor for the spaces I have encountered and for the geography where I have lived. I was born in the narrowest portion of the island of Cuba, in its westernmost province: only forty kilometers wide at that point, between the southern and northern coasts. From there I immigrated first to southern Florida, a place of narrow strips of sand that separate lowlands from ocean, the United States from Bahamian and Cuban territorial waters. And for years after, I have inhabited the literal borderlands: between the barrios of southern Tucson and *la línea* between *Ambos Nogales* (one in Arizona and another in Sonora, Mexico), there is a sixty-mile space where two cultures and two languages coexist and mingle, transform themselves into a syncretic hybrid, and also—paradoxically—stand away from each other. In that space exists a vast mass of people who are richly liminal, as well as pockets of rural Western cowboy culture that partake of a Mexican component (San Rafael, Patagonia, Sonoita). All this punctuated by very Anglo, very white and upper-middle-class enclaves of retirees and artists (Green Valley, Rio Rico, Tubac).

I have recently started to represent myself as a *"fronterisleña,"* a border islander. In this way I construct my locus, my position as subject and as agent of my own existence. Subjectivity and agency, nonetheless, are also ambiguous and fluid in this territory where I exist. Sorting out the multiple layers of experience in two countries and two systems, different regions and subcultures, and playing out the diverse roles that I was called to fulfill in dissimilar cultural environments have proven not an easy task. But ease and difficulty are perhaps not the adequate terms: alienation and "lived difference" are better approximations of what I have experienced.

(Another voice on the tape; one can hear in it more wisdom, zest for life, even loving kindness.)

What has kept me going? I have thought about this a lot. I am a person who just will not let go. Period. For better or for worse, I will pursue things, any matter, to the end. What I have accomplished has been by sheer determination. This is the force that moved me.

I love my life, my profession, and even if I think I did not have the highest motives when I started out, I'll take my reasons. They have propelled me and got me where I am today. My love of learning had been instilled in me by my father, who was a man of great integrity and great strength. I believe I am strong because of him, because I patterned my life after his. I saw my mother, on the other hand, as a weak person, but lately—especially after her death—I have come to appreciate her good qualities, her nurturing. I realize all that she has given me as her legacy; for one thing my love of music, and whatever innate abilities I might have in that area. She left me her voice, and her singing, and all those old Cuban songs I enjoy to this day (thanks to her, I can follow the lyrics in the Buena Vista Social Club recordings). And last but not least, she taught me how to cook! I must say that people who come to my house enjoy my cooking. Mom's recipe for black beans is spectacular, and I still have all these cooking directions in her handwriting (copied down on onionskin paper) comprising family recipes from my grandmothers and from her. I also have Mom's pictures from the forties, when she was such a beautiful woman and had such a sweet singing voice. I am glad I made my peace with her before she left this world.

I actually come from a family of educated women; it's our tradition. Except for my mother, all the other women in her generation, my aunts and older cousins, were teachers. A couple of them had advanced degrees and were high-school principals. Even my maternal grandmother: in 1902 at the age of twenty-one, she came to Harvard to learn English in summer school, through a program sponsored by the American interventionist government in Cuba. My family had roots in Spain, through nineteenth-century immigration to the Caribbean, and my grandfather and great-uncles settled in the countryside in the eastern part of Cuba, Pinar del Río. All their children were offered the opportunity of attending high school, and most of my uncles and aunts graduated from professional schools and went on to be teachers, accountants, and businessmen. Only my mother stayed home. I have a deep love for my grandmothers, whom I see as great, strong women in their own right. I have written an autobiographical piece in Spanish, a poetic prose piece titled *Memoria de la abuela María,* in which I combine their two figures.

The other turning point in my life is more recent. One of the reasons, if not the reason, that has kept me going, and that has brought healing—actually salvation—to my life has been the unfolding of a strong spiritual dimension. This is what has saved me from what I saw as disasters, as traumatic peaks. I had been searching for a long time. I remember sitting on top of a mountain near Tucson back in the early eighties and saying to myself: "What has brought me here, to this specific space and time, in one piece? Who am I? There must be an order beyond all this, this universe must have some kind of consciousness as its source that sustains all that I see and all that I don't see. What is it?" I was looking back at my life and saw it as a series of disasters and traumas. How had I made it so far? Because not only had I survived everything, I had managed to maintain a sense of dignity, a sense that things were all right and that I was ultimately okay and — perhaps most importantly — a sense of humor. For years after that day when I sat on a rock on the Catalina Mountains, I tried to find out. I thought there had to be something more to my existence than sheer determination to live.

One Sunday morning in 1985, over brunch at a Philadelphia hotel, a friend and professional associate started to talk to me about God. I said, "I don't need this notion of eternal life. That's for other people who can't make it on their own." She smiled and replied, "I'm not thinking of immortality. I need God right here and now, so my life can be centered." Her comment hit a target deep within me; her words echoed inside me with a resonance I had never before experienced. *Y empecé a buscar.* I went through an intense spiritual search. I talked to a lot of people, in and out of the Catholic Church, which was the only spiritual space I knew of at the time.

I Can Really Fly: Life Comes Full Circle

Then in 1986 I had another one of my dreams, a very significant one. In it I heard female voices chanting, and I saw nuns dressed mostly in white who came through the back door of my house and roused me from my slumber. I was lying in bed in the middle of the living room, and one younger nun, with thick eyebrows and a sweet smile, spoke to me in perfect, though slightly accented, English. She said, "Come with me." And I answered, "Where?" She pointed up to the wall, where the other nuns had disappeared. And I said, "I can't do that. I can't fly through walls." And she said, "Oh yes, you can." I followed her, and when I reached the wall, I took a step up into midair and went right through the wall. Then we "landed" in front of what looked like an Italian Renaissance villa, made of beautiful pink marble. I went up the entrance steps, followed the nun through the front doors and inside the halls. All the rooms were empty. But we came out of the villa into a courtyard with columns and arches, and all the other nuns were there, laughing and having a good time. I noticed that there were a lot of chickens around and realized that they were roosters and hens and chicks. All this fertility inside a convent! I said to my guiding nun, "I don't belong here." She replied, "Yes, you do. You are one of us." I said, "No, I don't. I am divorced, I have a child, I have a boyfriend." She insisted, "You are one of us. Look at yourself." When I looked down at my dress, it was a habit just like my guide's. I was dressed in white and had nun's garments on. Then I woke up.

I looked for the face of the person who had guided me, this nun. I went through my history books, through religious works, and decided she looked a bit like Saint Teresa of Avila, a woman I admired very much. I kept on looking and visited all kinds of places: Zen retreat sites, Benedictine monasteries, Hindu temples, meditation centers. And then in 1988 I met the yoga master who has made it possible for my life to be transformed. She is an incredible being, and her face also looks like the nun in my dream. Her guidance and her grace have made all the difference between what my life seemed to be — uninformed pain and struggle — and what it is now, the knowledge of a higher state of consciousness that is within human reach. I visit with her as often as I can, and I follow her teachings: "Welcome everyone with love and respect. We are all One. Turn within: meditate on your inner Self, honor your Self. You are That which you are looking for . . . and so is everyone else. The universe is a garden of delight, the play of supreme consciousness. Enjoy it. Be content with what you have. Everything happens for the best. Be filled with enthusiasm! Believe in Love."

These teachings that I live by have brought me peace and contentment and a deep understanding of the profound meaning of human life. Slowly I have come to realize that it was my own face, transformed and joyful, that I saw that night in the dream. I believe I had this revelation from two great women saints in different traditions, who would point the way to a life of inner unfolding for me, an existence where I can recognize the true happiness that comes from within, because that Ultimate Source I was looking for since that day on top of the rock is inside me, as well as in every atom of the universe. It is as simple as that.

Even though I was, and still am at times, totally absorbed in the happenings of worldly life, there is the promise of my evolving into a highly conscious being, full of wisdom and bliss, unaffected by the catastrophes of the world, serene and contented in the midst of everything, and acting accordingly: with compassion, love, and respect for everything and everyone. This promise, and the great changes I see taking place in my own inner way of being, keep me going. I feel hopeful. I am glad to be alive.

I am beginning to understand how life works. The appearance of multiplicity, of diversity, veils the oneness at the still center. This does not mean that I am not troubled by human emotions; on the contrary, I realize that I can be swept away by the currents of political or personal passion just as easily as anyone. But I know better. I know it is possible to return to a position of equanimity by means of self-effort, but above all with the help of a higher power that is totally within my reach, because it is my own greatness, my very own awakened spiritual energy. It looks as if I have come to terms with many things that used to hurt or bother me. It also seems that I am who I am today, not in spite of all that has happened to me but precisely because of it. I envision my space and my inner being as a place with no partitions, no limits, unproblematized by this hybridity that is, proudly, my core. I am happy to have lived — and continue to live — in this desert where I dwell, both literally and figuratively. This is a space that bears describing in the words that Sandra Cisneros has crafted for her ethnic territory of the soul: she calls it a "homeland called the heart." In that homeland I am free to be myself, however I choose to define my being — a Latina feminist, an "outrageous older woman" (as my favorite tee shirt proclaims), knowing what my true nature really is. *Eso soy.*

II Alchemies of Erasure

Somos tan invisibles que somos visibles.
Parece contradicción pero no lo es.[1]

W HEN A WOMAN has to be made invisible, it is because she is powerful, and her presence reverberates, touching everything in its path. Whether by her beauty, her spirit, her intellect, her capacity for loving, her conscious witnessing, her creative rebelliousness-called-madness, her liberating laughter, her voice-seeking-truth, her difference, she has not gone unnoticed. Without trying, she has called attention to herself, and she is anything but invisible. She is so present, she is threatening to those who are afraid of such power. The fearful ones will do anything to destroy what makes them cower. They will diminish the woman's being, pretend she is not there, she is not important, they will make her disappear. And sometimes, for a time, their efforts will work. Sometimes she almost ceases to exist.

But there is also a tremendous power in being invisible. Some people work hard to achieve a "non-presence," the better to see, to hear, to notice, to learn. Others have invisibility imposed on them, for any number of reasons, as the women in this section testify. *Pero lo que pasa es que nos fijamos en todo a nuestro alrededor. No se nos escapa ni un detalle. Así somos cada una de nosotras.*[2]

While we may have transcended some of these histories, many times they reappear in our adult lives. The power differentials and mechanisms of betrayal and abuse do not end simply because we have managed to achieve "successful" positions. These earlier experiences helped us negotiate and survive within the academy because they taught us something about how power

1. We are so invisible that we are visible. This seems a contradiction, but it is not.
2. But what happens is that we notice all of our surroundings. No detail escapes us. That's how each of us is.

works, about how to thrive in spite of its abuses. In each of the instances that we have suffered (or witnessed) erasure, and named it, exposing and cleaning (out) the deeply painful and sometimes previously unspeakable wounds, we have learned huge lessons, we have gathered our information to ourselves tenderly and consciously. We have shared our silencing/silenced stories with each other as *amigas*. With each experience put into words, we have initiated the transmutations necessary for our own joyous well-being.

Somos tan invisibles que somos visibles. Parece contradicción pero no lo es.

The Christmas Present

Caridad Souza

THAT EVENING WAS Noche Buena, the night before Christmas. My uncle
Carlos, who lived with his wife in an apartment in the tenement building
adjacent to us, was over at our house having *unos palos de ron* with my father.
Mami was working at the theater that evening even though it was Christmas
Eve, and that was the reason my parents fought before she left for work. You
could always tell when they fought because Mami would have that rock face,
and her eyebrows, which she tweezed in a thin line and then penciled back in,
would remain arched. The effect was a look of cool disinterest, as if whatever
was going on, whatever the charges against her, really had nothing to do with
her. The atmosphere was thick with tension. Even though she tried to ignore
it, I could feel it.

There was always tension in our household, laced with a threat of violence
that seemed to lurk around every corner waiting to be ignited. My father was
an explosive man, whose rage and frustration simmered just below the surface
awaiting the smallest opportunity to be vented against his wife and six children. Mami married her first husband at age fourteen and had her children *en
escalones* so that we were all very close in age. The big kids — Yvonne at eleven
was the oldest, Eduardo was ten and already considered a "delinquent," and
Naomi was eight — were from Mami's first marriage. Her three younger
children — Tony, who was six years old; me, who had just turned five; and
Wanda, who was three years old — were from her union with my father.

My father always came home from work in a bad mood, tired and irritable.
Mami kept us quiet and away from him so we wouldn't set him off. Whenever
he was around it seems like a dark cloud settled in over the house and over all
of us. One minute we'd all be lively, animated, and happy. But as soon as we
heard the key in the front door the mood would change. We'd become somber

Rivera-Torres-Souza Family, circa 1967

and would quickly scatter to our room like mice caught in a kitchen when the lights came up. We lived with the constant fear that even our most inoffensive movements might provoke unwarranted violence against us.

We kids could always tell, by a simple look or a gesture from him, when he was about to lash out. That's how in tuned we were to him. It was necessary for our survival. My parents were proud of our public behavior. They received many compliments about how respectful and well-bred their children were. Whenever we visited the home of friends and relatives the rule was that we were to sit quietly and neatly in the living room in descending order. Under no circumstances were we to move without asking permission to do so, even to go to the bathroom. "I don't care if you piss in your pants," my father would say. We knew that if that happened we'd get hit for that, too. We were not to go to anyone's bedroom, or outdoors, or to accept food unless we got explicit orders from my father that it was okay. We were taught to respect all adults, always, and to do whatever they asked of us. If the lady of the house asked us to do something we were supposed to respond "*Sí señora*" and jump to it. Any hesitation, any movement slower than those my father interpreted as necessary, was counted as an affront to his authority. And he would exact payment later, when we got home.

Even when he agreed to let us do something in front of others, we knew what our actions should be at all times. My two older sisters, Yvonne and Naomi, learned this lesson the hard way. Once, while visiting my father's compadres in New Jersey, my sisters made the fatal mistake of allowing *comai*

Lydia to advocate on their behalf. She asked my parents if my sisters could go out to the front yard with her daughters, who were the same age. Yvonne's and Naomi's eyes lit up at the suggestion, but then they looked over to my father, who was livid at their response. He glared at them and, without looking at his comadre, said in an even tone, "Sure, they can go." My sisters bolted out of the house. The ride home was quiet, but filled with tension. As soon as the door was locked behind them, my father took off his belt and I felt the hairs on the back of my neck rise. He beat my sisters until they bled, screaming that he'd show them not to accept offers *ajenas*. My mother stood by helplessly wringing her hands. She tried to reason with him, "But Antonio, *comai* was the one that asked. It's not their fault." "Next time," he yelled, "I want them to say 'No thank you. I'm fine right here.'" My sisters never made that mistake again.

Whenever family or friends came over to the house, Papi played up his image as a gracious host. Only when we had visitors did he relax his severe hold over us enough to allow for "special" treats, like a brusque pat on the head to demonstrate affection. But when the guests left, he'd go back to treating us like shit. The contrast between my father's public image and his private behavior left me confused and scared. People always commented, "*Ese Don Antonio es un santo. Ese hombre ayuda a cualquiera.*" In public he was an impeccably polite and respectful man, making anyone feel at home with his generosity and his excessive kindness. He was considered handsome, and his height and manner of dress made people think of him as elegant. Family photos show him to be well dressed and neat in appearance in an Al Green white-suit-and-shoes-green-shirt-and-socks sort of way.

On the other hand, my uncle Carlos was quite a character. He was one of those Casanova-type Puerto Rican men who wore tight polyester pants with flowery shirts unbuttoned to reveal his chest hair and gold chain. "That's so women can see my chest," he'd tell us. He always fussed with his hair, curly and dark to match his dark eyes. He spent hours in front of the mirror primping before he left the house, to make sure his sideburns were properly brushed, his moustache was perfectly groomed, and that he was in proper style. He always managed to look like he'd just come out of the shower. And he always had a slight bulge in his pants to attest to his masculine virility. My father felt superior to my uncle Carlos and called him a "typical spik" behind his back. Papi always felt so much more worldly and sophisticated next to my mother's brother, believing that because he didn't womanize the way Carlos did, he was somehow a bigger man.

Mami worked at a theater as a cashier. Although she was only four foot ten and weighed around a hundred pounds, she could be determined when she wanted to be. Papi wasn't happy about the job, but somehow she managed to keep it despite his objections. He was certain that she'd gotten the job to have contact with other men, but Mami said he objected because he always wanted to be *detrás del culo de ella.* Papi insisted on taking her to work and picking her up every night.

That Noche Buena it got to be time to pick up Mami up from her job. Papi left Carlos watching over us while he went to get her. No one is sure why he did this. Every one knew Carlos got a little crazy when he drank. Drinking always brought out the meanness in my uncle. He'd get drunk and beat up his current wife or some relative at family gatherings. Whatever his rationale, Papi left us alone with Carlos on that Christmas Eve.

It seemed like any other Sunday night just then. We kids were settled in front of the television watching the Sunday Disney Special after dinner. There was an added anticipation in the air because it was Christmas Eve. Yvonne had been instructed by Mami to feed us a snack and put us to bed after the movie. Carlos sat on the couch behind us, the one closest to the bar. Even though we had brand new furniture, we weren't allowed to sit on the couches because we might ruin them. So Papi had us sit on the floor, lined up in two neat rows. The little kids — Tony, me, Wanda — sat up front. The big kids always sat in the back because they were bigger. On this night only Yvonne and Eddie watched the show with us. Naomi was in the bedroom we kids shared, listening to her radio like she always did when she wanted to be alone. Naomi had been branded *la rebelde,* the rebellious one, from an early age. She always got into trouble with adults because of her mouth, because she talked back. She got smacked in the mouth so often, we joked that her lips pouted permanently as a result.

At first everything was fine. We watched the Disney movie. Carlos finished the fifth of Bacardi that Papi bought for the holidays. It was only after he finished the rum that things got weird. Naomi came out of the room to get something from the kitchen and he started to eye her in that way that my friend's father looked at me the time he asked me to play with him. I watched my uncle Carlos watching Naomi, then I turned back to the television with a knot in my stomach.

Carlos called out to Naomi to come over to him as she walked back to the bedroom. Naomi was always flustered around my uncle. My mother commented once that *"Naomi parece que ve el diablo cuando ve a Carlos."* Naomi never liked Carlos because he used to pick on her, always making nasty comments about her to my mother. *"Esa, esa la vas a tener que velar bien porque esa tiene la musiquita por dentro,"* he'd say, indicating that she was going to be a loose woman.

He called to her, *"Naomi, ven acá."* She grudgingly came over and in her typically exasperated voice said, "Whaaat?"

"Búscame una taza de café."

Naomi went to get him the coffee, but not without *protesta* like she always did whenever someone asked her to do a task, muttering some complaint under her breath.

"*No refunfuñes,*" he warned her as she walked away.

She returned with the cup of coffee and served it to him properly with a saucer, spoon, sugar, and a napkin folded over neatly. It was one of Mami's new cups, the white ones with gold trim she was so proud of.

He grabbed the cup, took one sip, and said, "*Este café está muy frío. Búscame otra taza.*" Naomi took the cup out of his hands but not quick enough to avoid the intentional brushing of his hand on hers. She shot him a nervous look and left quickly to the kitchen. Eddie and Yvonne turned around just in time to see this. I looked up from where I sat and felt my stomach begin to flutter.

When Naomi came back with the second cup of coffee, Carlos again took one sip and said it was still too cold. This time, emboldened perhaps by Naomi's lack of response the first time, he tried to grab at her. Naomi jerked the center of her body away from him, "What are you doing? Leave me alone," she cried and scurried off to get him another cup of coffee. When she returned with this cup he took it, and without tasting it, he threw it against the wall, leaving a long brown stain.

"*Este café sabe a mierda. Búscame otra taza,*" he demanded. Naomi got red-faced and yelled, "Shew, get your own coffee!" and stomped off to the room. Yvonne, who always tried to smooth things over, jumped up from her place on the floor to wipe down the wall. Meanwhile, Carlos, who wasn't accustomed to being backtalked, went into a diatribe about Naomi.

"*Esa malcriá no sirve pa'na.' Por eso es que ella va a tener tantos problemas. Cuando venga tu mamá, se lo voy a decir lo mal que ella se ha portado conmigo.*"

He sputtered obscenities about how Naomi was a no-good whore, about how boycrazy she was, and about how she'd end up nowhere with seven children, no husband, and on welfare. He finally quieted down after pulling out another bottle of my father's liquor from the bar. He sat there and drank the pint of amber-colored liquid. The more he drank, the angrier he got.

I'm not sure exactly when, but at some point Carlos disappeared into the back of the apartment. No one noticed except for Yvonne who was always vigilant about us. When he didn't come back after some time Yvonne went back to see where he'd gone. The next thing we heard were her screams exploding against the quiet.

"¡DEJALA QUIETA! ¡NO LA TOQUES! LEAVE HER ALONE!" she screamed.

We all looked up from the television screen to the bedroom, then scrambled over to see what was wrong. When we got to the door we looked in. Naomi lay on one of the beds, naked from the waist down, crying. Carlos was over her, with a knee on her stomach and his hands on her shoulders, trying to keep her on the bed. Yvonne was pulling at him from behind, yelling at him to leave Naomi alone. Then everything happened real fast. Eddie ran in and grabbed Naomi by the arm to pull her away. Carlos turned around and smacked Yvonne. Eddie let go of Naomi and jumped on Carlos, who turned his attention to Eddie.

Meanwhile, Yvonne grabbed Naomi and got her pants on her. Carlos saw what Yvonne was doing and went into a frenzied rage. He turned around to grab Naomi but Yvonne was quicker, grabbing Naomi by the hand. Carlos managed to grab Naomi's other arm, and they both tugged her in opposite directions. Eddie joined Yvonne and they pulled on Naomi together. The rest of us — me, Tony, and Wanda — stared in confused horror. When it looked like Carlos might win the tug-of-war, Yvonne ran and got the bottle of rum and hit him over the head with it. The bottle shattered, drawing blood from the side of his head. He let go of Naomi and all three of the big kids fell back on their butts. The big kids got up and ran out of the apartment into the courtyard of the tenement building we lived in. Carlos followed them out, screaming that he would kill them. "I'll kill you little motherfuckers when I get you! You sons of bitches! I'll kill you all!" he yelled after them. We little kids ran out behind Carlos screaming and crying for him to leave us alone.

Yvonne was the first to get it. Carlos caught her just as she was about to go down the stairs to the street, following Eddie and Naomi. "¡Cabrona! ¡Puta! Ven acá, ¡puñeta!" He grabbed her by her long hair and started to beat her unmercifully. I watched her fall on one knee with the force of the first slap. The second slap got her on the side of her face and slammed her head against the railing so that the thud echoed off the building. The third slap made her nose bleed. Only her hand, tightly gripping the railing, saved her from going down the flight of stairs head first. We three little kids stood by, helplessly, as Carlos beat our sister. Tony, anguished by the scene in front of him, doubled over to vomit. A dark liquid came out. Wanda was screaming, "Nooooo, pleaaassse, stop!" crying hysterically. Carlos's mouth moved as he hit her, but I couldn't hear a word. All I heard was a loud roar in my ears that drowned out all the crying and screaming.

When Eddie and Naomi saw that the rest of us weren't behind them, they came back for us. Eddie looked over and saw what Carlos was doing to Yvonne. He ran to the next building to get Titi Achy, Carlos' most recent wife, to help us. After he was finished beating Yvonne, who lay in a heap at the bottom of the stairs crying, Carlos moved toward Naomi. He was in the middle of dragging her back into the apartment, maybe even to the bedroom, when Achy arrived.

Carlos beat Achy regularly, especially when he was drinking. "He's just insanely jealous," my mother would say to excuse his behavior. But this one time, maybe because he was so drunk, or maybe because he was still reeling from the knock on the head Yvonne gave him with the bottle, Achy managed to overpower him. She screamed at him, *"¡Mira, cabrón! ¡Hijo de la gran puta! ¿Qué tú te crees? Déjala a ella, ¡desgraciao! ¡Métete conmigo! ¡Vente, pendejo! ¡Métete conmigo! Dame a mí, ¡cabrón!"* Achy grabbed him by the hair and started hitting him in the stomach. That night she kicked his ass real bad, hitting him with anything she could find. It was all he could do to get away from her blows. They brawled their way back into our apartment. That was how our apartment, and everything in it, was smashed to pieces.

Still crying, Yvonne ran over to comfort Tony and led him back to the building. Eddie grabbed me and little Wanda and pulled us back into the apartment. Then he ran out to get the police. Yvonne took Tony with her up the stairs to a neighbor's house to ask if we could stay there until Mami got back. She left him there and came back down for us. Back in the apartment, Yvonne found me and Wanda huddled behind the broken Christmas tree, crying and trembling in each other's arms. Before we could get out, Achy and Carlos made their way to the front of the apartment. Carlos spotted us and came over to scream at us, "Look at this. This is your fault. Look what you did to me!" pointing to his bleeding head and crying. Yvonne looked away and inched around him so she could get us up to Doña Tere's house. Tony was curled up in a ball on the couch, whimpering softly, when we arrived. Doña Tere's daughter tried to comfort him saying, *"No llores, nene, tu mamá viene ya mismo."* Wanda and I sat on the floor to wait for our mother.

Mami got dropped off by Papi in front of the building while he parked the car. She walked into the building and noticed that our front door was wide open. All the lights were on in our apartment and the place was a wreck, like a hurricane had hit it. Broken glass was strewn everywhere, the furniture was overturned and out of place, and there was blood all over the walls and floor. She ran through the apartment looking for us, screaming, "My kids, oh my God, where are my kids? Where are my kids?" then followed the trail of blood out into the courtyard. Doña Tere, whose kitchen window overlooked the courtyard, heard her and went down to get her. After Mami found us, we went back to the apartment together.

When we got there, Yvonne, Eddie, and Naomi were all cleaning up the mess. Mami went to the kitchen to make us some hot chocolate *pa' calmarnos los nervios.* Papi showed up a long while later, having disappeared for some unexplained reason. He immediately started to rant and rave at Mami, "This happened because you went to work. If you hadn't been working this would have never happened!" He sat us down on the precious couch and started to scream at us, pacing back and forth. "This is your mother's fault, this is your mother's fault." He called for her to come out of the kitchen so she could listen to him. Apparently, she didn't come quickly enough so he grabbed her by her hair and dragged her out. The force of the jerk made her bang her head against the old piano. She looked like a rag doll in his hands, so small and vulnerable. It's the most vivid picture I have of her powerlessness against his brute strength. He yelled at her and at us, but I stopped listening to him. I think I began to dissociate from my body just about then. Why is it always our fault? Why do they always blame us? Even though Papi continued his tirade for quite some time, I never heard a word of it. I was too busy looking at a piece of shattered Christmas trimming on the floor, tracing its jagged edge with my mind's eye. After some time I looked up and noticed the broken Christmas tree, snapped off at midpoint and dangling toward the floor. Tomorrow is Christmas, I thought to myself. Merry Christmas. And the knot in my stomach, the one that has been with me ever since, tightened.

Snapshots from My Daze in School

Celia Alvarez

My Relationship to Community

THE MIGRATION OF THE late forties and fifties dislocated a critical mass of Puerto Ricans from the rural and urban working classes of the island to labor in the fields and factories of the United States. A child of this migration, I am the first-born of a seamstress and a Korean War veteran. We lived in public housing or the projects, as we knew them, in downtown Brooklyn. I was raised along the waterfront, in the vicinity of the Brooklyn Navy Yard with African Americans, Puerto Ricans, Dominicans, Italian and Irish immigrants, Chinese, and others in a predominantly poor and working-class neighborhood.

I recall once reading a *New York Daily News* article depicting my downtown neighborhood as one of the worst crime and drug-ridden communities in New York City. I tried to reconcile that social perception with the vibrant lives of the hardworking, loving, and proud people I lived with everyday. These stereotypes about myself, my community, and culture came to haunt me throughout my educational experiences.

My childhood wanderings through the streets of Brooklyn Heights made it clear that we lived on the other side of the tracks. The produce at the local Key Food was past freshness but sold at higher prices than the produce at the supermarkets of the affluent Heights. Athletic activities were limited to cement-paved schoolyards and education to hundred-year-old classrooms.

Despite these limitations, and the violence that came to permeate project hallways, there was life in this community. The transformative forces of the Civil Rights movement, the War on Poverty, and ecumenical movement of Vatican II brought hope to the neighborhood. My own encounter with these social movements was through a local Catholic Church.

Located on Front Street, St. Ann's helped to breathe life into Farragut and surrounding communities by offering numerous programs for adults and youths, such as Girl Scouts and Boys Scouts, the Cadets, the Drum and Bugle Corps, and CYO choir. The church supported a local neighborhood newsletter, as well as a community-run food and bank cooperative. Church groups organized family bus outings to state parks in Long Island and New Jersey. Church services in Spanish and English engaged local talent of all ages. We proudly sang civil rights and rhythm and blues themes, like "To Be Young Gifted and Black," "This Little Light of Mine," and "Oh, Freedom," and performed *Godspell* in church. Neither jazz dance nor gospel music nor Latin rhythms and Spanish songs were uncommon.

Trinitarian nuns — including two Puerto Ricans, Sister Thomas Marie, or Insolina Ferré as she is known today, and Sister Mary Victor — ran the Dr. White Settlement House, a local community center supporting the efforts of the parish. Additionally, the Irish priests and Josephite nuns who came to live in the community were socially conscious individuals who embraced the ecumenical and social movements of the times. They engaged the community in dialogues across race, ethnicity, language, class, and religious affiliation.

I internalized much of this critical perspective and embraced the fervor of the Civil Rights struggle for equality and justice. As a young girl I was very active in many of the social activities organized from this church, including teaching classes in homes, going from building to building taking food orders from families for the food coop, and working on the community newsletter. I recall the day my mother chastised me for exposing my political views by wearing a Martin Luther King button on my blouse and wanting to participate in the March on Washington. She feared the possible harm that might come to me for being so brazen during a period of great social and racial strife. In many ways St. Ann's gave me the opportunity to be engaged in the practice of social change at a very early age. My social activism today is deeply rooted in these years of my life.

The priests and nuns who served this church were very instrumental in my being able to navigate between my social and cultural world and that of mainstream society. I will always be indebted in this regard to Father Thomas Mannion, the pastor of the church for many years, whom I endearingly called "the old man." Even my mother seemed to understand my need to speak with the man she referred to as my "white father." Father Mannion took the time to expose us to experiences that were outside our realm of daily experience. I vividly recall being taken to dinner at Bear Mountain Inn to celebrate my high school graduation and eating for the first time sour cream and chives on a baked potato. Or another time going to a smorgasbord and eating all we could want in a restaurant in Manhattan. Or our trip to Riverdale in the Bronx and seeing for the first time green pastures within city limits.

But my most poignant memories are of my coming home from New England and sitting down with him to discuss what it was like to live in a college. In Amherst the crickets kept me awake at night and the silence was so pervasive during the day that I had to study with my radio blasting to do my papers. I often asked his advice about how to deal with the affluent college students I was encountering, whose lives were so far away from mine.

Language Was My Privilege

The question of language was foremost in my experience growing up in New York. I learned Spanish at home, from my mother and grandparents, during my early childhood years. I later sustained and developed my Spanish language abilities through my mediating role as a translator for my mother and numerous others in the neighborhood. My mother, a cultural nationalist in her own right, insisted we speak Spanish at the home, even as adults. She explicitly affirmed our Puerto Rican identity within the confines of the United States. Thanks to my mother, I am bilingual today. My father, who was in daily contact with "mainstream" society through work, brought English home. Fortunately, I had acquired both languages by the time I went to school.

I say fortunately, because bilingual education had not become a reality for many of us yet. During the early sixties, Spanish-speaking students had to "sink or swim" in monolingual English classroom environments. Many of us unfortunately sank and were unsuccessful in navigating the school system. I was continuously "privileged" by teachers for having a good command of the English language. They called attention to this ability and used it to separate me from other students, saying that I was "different."

My engagement with language was a central theme of my life and a way of positioning myself in the world. I observed how educational access hinged on knowledge of Standard English and uncovered the inequities in academic preparation between public and private schools. These insights and life experiences motivated me to further my education and seek the knowledge necessary to address the educational and linguistic needs of my community.

I also wanted to reconcile my "school identity" with my "community identity" and pursue my academic studies in a more meaningful way. I needed to reconcile the privileges and isolation of an excellent academic formation with the other sites of myself as a second-generation, bilingual, working-class, New York–born, Puerto Rican woman.

My Encounter with Race

After graduating from St. James Pro-Cathedral with honors, I followed one of my classmates to St. Brendan's Diocesan High School in Flatbush. According to her mother, the high school was known for its academic reputation. I thought going there would help me get into college, so I commuted to school an hour every day to the other side of Brooklyn. Although I had attended school with white working-class and immigrant students, this was my first experience with the middle class. It was really traumatic. I was one of four Latina students in the entire school. There were a few African Americans, including a friend from the projects who eventually transferred to another high school. I realized years later that we were desegregating the Catholic high schools at the time. Under normal circumstances, we would have been sent to Bishop McLaughlin High Scool closer to home, near Prospect Park.

For the privilege of my attending Catholic schools, my father was working two jobs — in a hospital by day and at the docks by night. My mother also went to work for a local paper factory when I was fourteen. My parents sacrificed to put the three of us through Catholic high schools. Meanwhile, numerous contradictions emerged along the way, and I found myself not knowing whom to talk to about it. I did not know how I could go home and tell my mother that that day in school I was challenged by fellow-students, who minutes before had greeted me at the door and then turned on me in a class to say, "Oh, your parents don't work. You got a scholarship to come here from downtown, but our parents pay tuition. All you people do is throw garbage out the window." Why had my academic advisor invited *me* to talk about "poverty" in her religion class that day, and I became the target of my peers' wrath? Who failed to protect me and prepare for the many encounters ahead?

Class and Academic Freedom

Four years later, with a scholarship and student loan in hand, I "legitimately" left my parents' home to attend a small private college in Amherst, Massachusetts. My father drove me the three-and-a-half hours from New York in our station wagon and I arrived at Hampshire College with all my possessions in a wooden trunk. Papi called Mami from campus, with all the news — Tita has a single room of her own. But the shock came when Papi went looking for the men's room and found out the bathrooms and showers were all coed!

It was 1972. Hampshire, barely two years old, was the UC Santa Cruz of the Five College area. Built on an apple orchard, it was known as "the farm" by most of my friends at the University of Massachusetts. A counselor in Aspira (an educational advocacy organization with offices in New York) thought I would thrive in the colleges' self-directed learning environment and recruited me. In the aftermath of the Civil Rights era, academic institutions of the cultural elite opened their doors to young, brown, working-class girls like me, and at Hampshire I thrived in the intellectual freedom and institutional privileges of the upper middle class. It proved to be the most intellectually challenging academic experience of my life.

Meanwhile, the seventies were a time to reclaim my place in Puerto Rican and U.S. intellectual history. It was a critical period in the formation of ethnic studies, bilingual education, and women's studies in higher education. I personally wanted to reconcile the dissonance between my community and academic experiences. Hampshire's alternative academic program of study allowed me to pursue my interest in the study of language, not only through course work but as an active participant with scholars in the fields of Puerto Rican Studies, Bilingual Education, and Linguistics.

I became affiliated with the Centro de Estudios Puertorriqueños / Center for Puerto Rican Studies in 1974, a year after it was formed in the City University of New York. The Centro became a center of my intellectual work from my undergraduate through postgraduate years. From 1974 to 1984 I participated in numerous research projects of the Centro's Language Policy and Oral History Task Forces and contributed to the scholarship on language, gender, and identity in Puerto Rican Studies.

Ironically, it was in Amherst that I encountered faculty of color for the first time. Roberto Márquez and Gloria Joseph significantly shaped my political and intellectual formation. As my academic advisors they saw me grow from a fledgling in their courses through the completion of my undergraduate thesis. I worked closely with African, African American, Caribbean, and Latin American faculty in the valley, including Ezekiel Mfelele, Chinweisu, Johnnetta Cole, Acklyn Lynch, Andree N. McLaughlin, Andrew Salkey, Simone Gouverneur, among others. I taught in the independent Che Lumumba School for Truth in Amherst with Maddie Márquez and Zala Chandler. I was discovering our local and global connections with each other in the Third World. I explored the connections between people of color in the United States and the peoples of Africa, Latin America, the Caribbean, Europe, and Asia. I learned to build political and intellectual alliances with scholars from around the world and contributed to public forums where they could be heard.

The Isolation of Graduate Education

Within four years I completed Hampshire's innovative curriculum and graduated with a degree from the School of Language and Communication. As part of a national competition, I was awarded a Ford Foundation Graduate Fellowship to study linguistics at the University of Pennsylvania. After having experienced intellectual inquiry in a very progressive academic environment, I was hit over the head with the conservative individualism of Penn and the hierarchical structuring of graduate school.

In the Department of Linguistics I studied the ethnography of speaking and sociolinguistics with the gurus in my field. However, I constantly had to fight off their stereotypical conceptions of my cultural and academic identity. As an

Ivy League student, I was not a member of the "underclass" that represented "the community" to them. Yet I was Puerto Rican enough to be told not to do my dissertation on the Puerto Rican linguistic practices if I wanted to be legitimated as a scholar in my field. I struggled to reconcile these contradictions, reminiscent of my earlier experiences with "academic privilege" in grammar school and high school.

My place and legitimacy within (and outside) the university were constantly challenged and I struggled for many years with these issues in isolation. I wanted to do research that was socially responsible and to position myself differently from the way my dissertation advisor related to his "subjects," but I had no mentors to follow. He would send us out to do field research and say, "Well, go to the Puerto Rican community in North Philadelphia and collect this data for me." I didn't relate to my community that way, so feelings of angst constantly boiled up inside me. As a graduate student I was caught in the middle, between the interests of the university and my community. I wasn't in a position of power to understand or to determine what happened to the material I collected. I wanted to analyze bilingual language practices, so I went to Stanford University for a year to work with a specialist in Spanish sociolinguistics. After completing my doctoral exams at Penn, I developed my dissertation research topic on the bilingual language practices of Puerto Ricans in New York.

Coming Around Full Circle:
Highlights of an Academic Career

I returned to New York in 1980 to work at the Centro de Estudios Puertorriqueños at CUNY and contribute to the research on code-switching among Puerto Rican bilinguals in East Harlem. By the time I left the Centro in 1984, I had situated my interest in narrative within oral history and gender studies. While completing my dissertation, I worked in the grants office of the Ms. Foundation for Women funding grassroots women's organizations nationally. In 1985 I organized a panel of working-class women of color for Forum '85: the United Nations global meeting of women in Nairobi, Kenya. These activities outside academia paved the way for my future cross-cultural work with women nationally and internationally. The years 1987 and 1988 were pivotal years in my professional development: From our project on women in the migration to New York, *"El Hilo que nos Une"* was published by the Centro and the *Oral History Review*. I was finally able to integrate my commitment to community within my scholarship and reweave myself into our collective history. I completed my dissertation and received my doctorate from the University of Pennsylvania. I was also appointed to a tenure-track position at Columbia University Teachers College in the Bilingual-Bicultural Program.

Teaching at Columbia was in many ways the fulfillment of a life's dream. I engaged graduate students, who were bilingual/multicultural practitioners of elementary and secondary education, counseling psychology, and international education, in the social and theoretical applications of sociolinguistic research. I felt I was giving back to community, preparing educators to address the linguistic and cultural needs of multicultural populations in the schools and the world. In addition to teaching and advising graduate students across the disciplines, I contributed to the writing of Title VII grants that provided partial and fully funded scholarships to master's and doctoral students in programs across the college. By my fourth year I was on service overload as one of two nontenured faculty running an academic program. Like many Latina women in the academy, I was torn between my commitments to community and myself. The straw that broke the camel's back was when I was asked at the end of a successful fourth-year review to become director of the program during my fifth year. My colleague was going to take a sabbatical the year before I was to come up for tenure. I realized then that my research interests (a key component to my evaluation for tenure) as a faculty member were not going to be protected by the institution, so I painstakingly left New York in 1992.

A colleague had informed me of a new women's studies department in Phoenix that was recruiting faculty to develop a program with national and international cross-cultural perspectives. Building on my research on Puerto Rican women, my desire to do comparative Latina feminist research, my activism in women's forums globally and nationally, as well as my participation in interdisciplinary, race, class, and gender curriculum reform, I applied for a tenure-track position in Women's Studies at Arizona State University West. I embraced the challenge of creating an innovative upper-division liberal arts curriculum in a public institution that served community college graduates. The transdisciplinary intellectual emphasis of the institution resonated with my undergraduate experience. I was excited about building a new Women Studies department that put national and global diversity at the center of the curriculum. What I had not anticipated was the insurmountable resistance to developing a Women's Studies department that had been situated on the margins of the academic curriculum.

I relocated to the Southwest with the hope of connecting more directly with Chicanas in the region. Coming from New York, I participated in the formation of the Comparative Latina Feminist Working Group and the new Puerto Rican Studies Association. Both created opportunities for a more sustained dialogue among Latina feminists. Fueling my interests in gender and education, I worked on a comparative analysis of Puerto Rican and Chicana women in higher education with Dr. Gloria Cuádraz, my colleague in American Studies. Once again, I encountered the invisibility of Puerto Rican women in the literature. I began to collect oral histories of an intergenerational group of Puerto Rican women who contributed to American academic life in the post–Civil Rights era. Today *Intersecting Lives: Puerto Rican Women as Community Intellectuals* is on its way to being published by Temple University Press.

I was awarded tenure and promoted to Associate Professor of Women's Studies in the spring of 1999. Along the way I had been told to "keep my eyes on the prize" but rarely discussed "the price of the ticket" for admission. What did it mean for us to dare to cross — not once, but continuously, and at times simultaneously — the borders of race, class, and gender that today still perme-ate American higher education, despite increasing global interdependency? Receiving tenure was a turning point for me. It gave me reason to pause and reflect on some contradictory feelings and thoughts that I want to voice as my gift to you:

How have I dared to develop my mind, without selling my soul?
What has been the cost to my heart and spirit along the way?
What price have I paid for my 1954 birthright to an equal education?
What marks of institutional abuse imprint my body after all these
years? Why is it that even after mastering the ivy nuances of the academy, I am not heard?
How dare you render me invisible, and not give credit where credit is due?
Will I ever be human,
or always constructed through socially tainted lenses?
In the name of diversity,
why would you rather teach about my experiences
than be with me in the same room?
A luta continua.

Point of Departure

Mirtha N. Quintanales

"¡MIRA, CARI! ¡Ya estamos llegando! We're almost there!" The girl's eleven-year-old brother tugged excitedly at her sleeve, coaxing her to look out the window. It was an old propeller plane — no rugs on the floor, no courtesy meals, no lights flashing at them to comply with regulations. Caridad leaned toward the boy and glanced over his shoulders. The small square of plastic was scratched and dusty, but yes, she could make out the flat stretches of land breaking the blue monotony of the sea below. The sun was beginning to set. She smiled at him, nodded in agreement, and settled back into her seat.

677-2857. She repeated the number to herself for the hundredth time since their departure. Then, like an old familiar ritual, she followed with the inventory: the gold earrings, Mami; the inkless fountain pen, Papi; the small Swiss watch that doesn't work, Abuelita: the thin ring with the tiny garnet, Tía Manuela. She reached nervously into the right pocket of her red cotton jacket. It was still there, Grandpa's buffalo nickel. She felt its contours and rubbed it vigorously. It was the talisman against her mounting fear. "I can use it to call if no one is waiting for us. I can, I can . . . " she muttered to herself, closing the ritual in earnest self-affirmation.

She promised herself that she would tell Pablito nothing about the possible complications, about her doubts. Why worry him? He seemed full of a child's sense of adventure. Unconcerned. Only hours earlier Caridad had been the older sister by only two years. But now the critical choice had irrevocably widened this small age gap between them. She felt herself aging rapidly. "You choose Cari, you are the oldest. You choose for yourself and your brother."

Her father's words had twisted themselves into a giant knot and settled next to her heart, invisibly pushing against and seemingly rearranging the

Mirtha Quintanales, Havana, 1956

surrounding organs. "*Es un riesgo, mi hijita,* it's a risk. If you leave, you may never see me or your mother again. If you stay, you may never be free to live the way you may want to live." His swollen, reddened face had signaled a warning: don't say anything that could make father cry. He had never considered the possibility of this snag in his plans. Mother was turned away by government officials at the last moment, right there in the airport, without previous warning. Critical of parents who were sending their children alone, "*a lo loco,*" he would have never forced a family separation. Caridad had measured her terror against his painful attempt at being fair. "*Yo sé, Papi,* I know. It's okay, we'll manage."

The knot had dislodged itself and traveled downward. She preoccupied herself with its trajectory, now and then catching a glimpse of her small body being hugged and fondled. Passed from crying relative to crying relative until the very last minute before entering the "*pecera*"—the glass-windowed enclosure that held travelers of all ages for hours until the final routine search before departure. It must have been 8:00 or 9:00 in the morning.

The gradually thinning crowds on both sides of the "fishbowl" had been her only clue to the passing of time. The authorities within had attempted to restrain her high-spirited brother, but had finally given up. He walked about freely, mingling and conversing with the waiting passengers. She had not moved from her seat nor spoken to anyone, her self-absorption interrupted only by occasional nods and half-smiles in acknowledgment of her family's sustained, quiet presence beyond the glass.

At last it was time to go through security. Caridad and her brother waved their last good-byes from afar and walked up to the line that had slowly formed against the back wall of the room. A child, perhaps six or seven years old, stood in front of them. A young *miliciana* approached him, turned him around and unfastened the thin gold chain hanging from his neck. The boy's crying startled Cari, breaking through her numbness. She immediately curbed the impulse to touch her own jewelry. Will she remove my watch, my earrings, my little ring? She wondered.

But the militia woman didn't notice them. She only motioned for Caridad and Pablito to step into an adjoining corridor. Suddenly Cari remembered the fountain pen she had tucked into the front of the white button-down blouse under her jacket. Her father's pen, perhaps his last gift to her. The thought of it being seized brought on a surge of energy and a renewed interest in the immediate proceedings. "I will not let anyone take it," she told herself. "No one." Firm in her resolve, an image of herself as a clever smuggler emerged to give her confidence in the face of impending danger.

Caridad and her brother were separated and she was led into a small room crammed with metal shelves, chairs, and tables. She figured it must have once been a large closet. A second *miliciana* instructed the girl to take off her jacket. While the woman busied herself filling out a form, Cari modestly turned her back against her, followed her order, and carefully but swiftly removed the pen from her blouse, clipped it on her jacket, folded the jacket, and laid it down on a chair nearby. The militia woman frisked her and told her to put the jacket back on. Cari reversed the earlier procedure, hiding the pen in her blouse again. Before dismissing her, the woman looked through Caridad's shoulder bag, removing a ballpoint pen, a blank school notebook, a small envelope purse, and, despite the child's loud protest, two thin paperback books of José Martí's poetry. Cari had temporarily lost track of the knot in her body, the exigencies of the moment demanding her total attention.

She joined her brother in the luggage inspection area. They shared a single large suitcase that now lay open before them, nearly empty. They were each allowed to take five items of street clothing, five pieces of underwear, socks, one pair of shoes. Their mother had decided against dresses for Cari, carefully selecting matching skirts, blouses, and blazers that could be combined into more than five outfits.

A middle-aged male customs official eyed Caridad's clothes with suspicion. "There are more than five things in here," he snapped at her, pointing to all the articles he had identified as "girls' things." "Yes, but some of them go to-gether," she argued with him, undaunted by his harshness. "A skirt, a blouse, and a blazer are equivalent to one dress. See?" she sorted through the clothes, selecting the appropriate items to illustrate her point. "Besides," she challenged him, "what do men know about fashion?" Having practically grown up in school uniforms, Cari knew practically nothing about fashion. But like any thirteen-year-old Cuban girl, she was aware of Cuban men's fear of having their masculinity questioned by their being too familiar with women's things.

Clearly annoyed, the customs official momentarily backed away from the children, muttering something under his breath. Outsmarted by a child. Cari was terribly pleased with herself. Giving only a perfunctory look through Pablito's clothes, the man was about to close the suitcase when he noticed a pair of boy's shoes. A smirk on his face, he lifted the high-top sneakers by their shoelaces and flung them behind him onto a long wooden table. An extra pair of shoes was an extra pair of shoes. They were even. There was nothing more Cari could say. But all in all, they had fared well. Caridad and her brother were ready for boarding.

It was already dark when Cari and Pablito settled into the large Chevrolet station wagon parked outside International Arrivals at Miami's airport. Everyone had come to meet them: Tía Nidia, Tío Tomás, their two children, cousins Tommy and Ricky; Tomás's niece, Nela; Rubio, the blond cocker spaniel. From the wagon's trunk area, nine-year-old Tommy reached into the back seat, tapped Cari on her shoulder, and handed her a stick of Juicy Fruit gum. Smiling at him she took it, unwrapped it, and put it in her mouth, quickly pressing her face against the car window. She was not quite ready for conversation. Soon the children's animated chatter and Tío Tomás's unabashed cursing at the long line of cars barely moving ahead of them receded into the background. Again Caridad was alone with her thoughts.

Cari and her brother had walked through U.S. Customs without delay, their luggage allowed to pass uninspected. No one had spoken to the children, only signed them instructions. After Customs, they had been led into a crowded reception area. Perhaps over a hundred children and a handful of adults had been gathered there. For several minutes that seemed to stretch into eternity, Caridad and Pablito had waited, frozen in place, for their relatives. Tía Nidia and Tío Tomás had finally appeared at the doorway, walked in, and unceremoniously grabbed the children and their suitcase and pulled them out of the room. The hugs and kisses would not come until later, when the family had met outdoors, safely away from the crowd.

For Caridad, the great relief of seeing the familiar, friendly faces had been marred only by the realization that the majority of the children left behind would not be met by relatives. This she had understood by overhearing snatches of conversation in Spanish — key words like scholarships and special family homes, sponsors and shelters. Cari had shuddered at the thought that she and Pablito could have been among them. After all, Tía Nidia and Tío Tomás may have chosen to return to Cuba shortly after the triumph of the

Revolution. Hadn't Tío Manolo and his wife, Tía Maritza, and their children packed up and sold their home in Hialeah and moved back to Havana only three months after Batista had fled the island? "Mami and Papi may have decided to send us off alone whether or not we had family here to meet us," Caridad reasoned. "Hadn't other parents done that? What would have happened to us? What will happen to the kids in the airport? Where will they go, for how long? Who will they go with, how will their parents be able to find them, will their parents even look for them at all?"

Cari's jaws suddenly felt stiff and sore. She hadn't chewed gum in years. She thought it funny, though, how her hard, aching jaws were affecting the rest of her body. It seemed to be rapidly turning into stone. "You must be hungry, no?" Tío Tomás, sitting behind the wheel, turned around searching for the girl's eyes, a smile of conviction on his face. "I hear there's no food . . . " "People are not starving in Cuba, Tomás," Tía Nidia broke in, her voice angry but restrained. "*Yo quiero un sándwich de jamón y queso—a ham and cheese sandwich, Tío Tomás,*" Pablito requested eagerly and loudly. Dismissing his wife's comment with a curt "*¿Qué tu sabes, chica?* What do you know?" Tío Tomás straightened himself on the seat, held on tightly to the wheel with both hands, looked sharply ahead, and picked up speed. "Okay, kid, a ham and cheese sandwich and lots more goodies coming up. Let's stop at the supermarket and get some groceries." The children cheered, except Caridad. Caridad had not spoken a word since the family left the airport.

The bright neon lights inside the Grand Union made Cari's eyes water. Grabbing a shopping cart, Tío Tomás took over Tía Nidia's official role of food shopper. This was, after all, a special occasion that called for the "man of the house" to take charge over the wifely duties of lesser moments. "*Aquí los hombres también hacen las compras, quiero que ustedes sepan*—men here also do the shopping, I want you to know." Tío Tomás told Cari and Pablito, though he seemed to be talking to himself. "And we're Americans now," he added emphatically. "*Yo no, ¡qué vá!* Not me, no way," Tía Nidia retorted.

Ignoring her words, Tío Tomás instructed her to mind the kids and walked away, pushing his cart. Tía Nidia's face tightened as she grabbed a shopping cart of her own and told the children in no uncertain terms to behave. She rolled the cart away and the five youngsters followed her without protest. Caridad watched Tía Nidia mechanically select the food items and arrange them carefully in the shopping cart: bread, butter, cheese, eggs, chicken, vegetables, and fruits. The little unit, moving through the aisles under her command, eventually met up with Tío Tomás.

His cart was filled to the top with bags of potato chips, jelly and peanut butter jars, boxes of doughnuts and cookies, bags of jelly beans and chocolate candy. Pablito couldn't contain his excitement in the presence of such bounty and broke away from the ranks to inspect it. Tía Nidia didn't say

Point of Departure 189

anything as Tío Tomás affectionately stroked the boy's hair. The family had finished shopping.

The house was exactly the way Cari remembered it from her last visit three and a half or four years earlier. The large living room with the unpolished but immaculately clean marble floor. The old, faded, but well-cared-for couch and stuffed armchairs. To the left of the living room, the dining area crammed with the dining table, unmatched chairs, and a china cabinet. A breakfast counter separated the dining area from the smallish kitchen beyond. Readjusting the travel bag on her shoulder, Caridad pushed the other suitcase all the way to the bedroom she would be sharing with fourteen-year-old Nela. Nela followed her into the room.

She had been living with the family almost a year now, having been sent alone while her mother, her stepfather, and younger stepsister had remained back in Cuba, their future plans uncertain. "The kids are a pest and Tío Tomás and Tía Nidia don't let you do anything fun. You'll see." Having uttered her welcoming remarks, Nela want over to the her night table, opened its drawer, and pulled out a nail file. Suddenly, loud, unintelligible speech accompanied by movie sound-track music brought the two girls out of the bedroom into the living room. "It's just the TV," Nela said, bored. "Is there TV in Cuba? I can't remember," one of the boys asked Pablito. Pablito, insulted, was about to punch his cousin when Tío Tomás intervened, grabbing his arms in midair. "Don't be silly, Tommy. Of course there is TV in Cuba. Come on, kids, no fighting now. Let's eat."

Caridad looked at the sandwich fixings, the bread, the fruit, the sweets. She opted for a glass of orange juice. "Aren't you going to eat something?" seven-year-old Ricky, who had been watching her, asked, puzzled. "All this good stuff. You gotta be crazy!" The other children momentarily stopped their sandwich-making activities to stare at the girl but quickly returned to their business. "*Pero ¿cómo no vas a comer, Cari?* How could you possibly not eat? Look at your brother," her uncle tried to coax her. But Caridad would not bring herself to touch the food. "I'm just not hungry, Tío, and Pablito, well, he's always been a glutton."

Nela, Pablito, Tommy, and Ricky, their plates full, settled down to eat. Tío Tomás grabbed a beer from the refrigerator and Tía Nidia, standing by the stove, poured steaming dark rich coffee from the espresso coffee pot into a large, brand-new thermos bottle. It was one of her old habits, Cari noted. Making sure that the coffee stayed hot until she was ready to mix it with hot milk to make *café con leche,* Tía Nidia's staple.

"*Bueno, Cari, y ¿cómo dejastes a la gente por allá?* How did you leave the folks back home?" Tía Nidia asked her niece from across the room as she closed the thermos bottle. Not waiting for an answer, she continued talking. "*Tú vas a ver, tus padres se van a aparecer cualquier día de estos, cuando tú menos te lo esperes.* You'll see. Your parents are going to show up one of these days, when you least expect them." "Tía Nidia, how kind you are," thought Cari, not saying a word. But her stiff body momentarily relaxed.

Nela and Caridad cleared the table and helped Tía Nidia with the dishes while the boys and Tío Tomás moved into the living room to watch the rest of the movie. "Three people at the sink are one too many." Nela happily excused herself and joined the others in the living room. Tía Nidia and Caridad were finally alone. They had always liked each other immensely—favorite aunt, favorite niece. "Really, Cari, how are the folks back home?" Tía Nidia asked, her wet hands affectionately stroking the girl's cheeks. This time she paused to hear the response.

"She smells just like Mami," thought Cari, "feels like her too." Caridad looked up at her aunt's fierce but loving green eyes. "Cat eyes," Cari used to call them. They stood out in stark contrast to Tía Nidia's suntanned olive skin—darkened by hours of labor, transforming sand into a green garden under the hot Florida sun. Tía Nidia was considered the beauty of the family, but that label had not spared her from having a hard life. "They are well, Tía, but Abuelita, Grandma, says she's not leaving as long as any of her children remain in Cuba. And that's final." Caridad barely caught her aunt's deep, heavy, but nearly imperceptible sigh.

Everyone had gone to sleep. Caridad, lying in her bed, stared into space. Moonlight, or perhaps the light from a street lamp, illuminated portions of some objects in the bedroom, casting shadows on others, giving them an odd, unfamiliar look. She could pretend to be elsewhere. A magical land, perhaps. The sound of the crickets outside, clear, sharp, and sweet, seemed like chanting. "Crickets are really little night angels God has sent to keep me company," Cari told herself. She remembered when she had first slept in this house, years before. Grandpa had paid for her trip to Miami to visit the family. It had been different then. She had felt safe. Away from the bombs and the fires and the riots in the streets of Havana, she had been able to sleep, a welcome respite from the worrisome nightly vigils: "Will Papi make it home from his studies at the university?" "Will Mami and Papi be safe on their way home from their visit with friends?"

She did not feel safe now. She had a strong premonition that a very long time would pass before she would feel safe again. "Mami, Papi," she pleaded to the memory of them. "Please come soon. Please come soon." Remembering her father's last words to her before her departure, she addressed him in the dark: "I hope I chose the right thing, Papi. I hope I chose the right thing."

New Haven, Connecticut, 1981

Point of Departure   191

Another Way to Grow Up Puerto Rican

Liza Fiol-Matta

IN 1956, DURING THE week of my fourth birthday, my family joined thousands of other Puerto Ricans in the mass migration from the island. I have often wondered how it would have been — and what I would have been like — had I lived in Puerto Rico during the eight years we were away, following my father from one posting to the next. My memory of our departure is that documented in my father's photographs taken from the deck of the ship: the nondescript dockside buildings in San Juan, the city growing smaller as the ship pulls away, El Morro fort looming above us then becoming tinier until Puerto Rico is only a spot against the horizon. The brass band that greeted our ship as it moored in New York that summer (also captured by my father's Konica) was small compensation for that memory of the slowly receding coastline of the island we had left behind.

That my family has never spoken about those years as a migration story parallels the silencing of the Operation Bootstrap migration story and its aftermath on the island. It is not difficult to understand how our situation must have seemed different from that of the displaced agricultural workers leaving the island by the thousands in those years. First, my father's career in the Army was certainly not considered migrant work, and second, given our family background and my parents' educations, had we stayed on the island my family would have been part of the growing professional class. Nevertheless, the Puerto Rican migration of the fifties seems like a shameful untold family secret, collectively silenced and denied. How could it be otherwise? The reality is that over one third of the Puerto Rican *familia* was sent away during the Operation Bootstrap furor, which promised the island quick economic development.

For ten years my family lived on a succession of Army bases in Arkansas,

Texas, Colorado, and South Carolina. The only contact with the communities outside the bases happened in the string of Roman Catholic parochial schools I attended. I recall always having to juggle identities. At school, at Girl Scout meetings, and in the homes of my friends I spoke my perfectly enunciated English and behaved "American." At home, as in so many Puerto Rican families in the armed forces, my parents spoke Spanish to us, while, as our time in the United States progressed, their children began to speak Spanish less and less. What I knew was different about my family, however, was the dramatic way that the duality of citizenship played out daily in front of us—not as an abstract political proposition but as an everyday reality. You see, my father's fierce loyalty to the stars and stripes, demonstrated by his decision to make a career out of military service, was paralleled by my mother's strong, outspoken, and passionate commitment to the nationalist cause of Puerto Rico's political independence.

I am sure that what facilitated my entry into the "American" world outside was that I behaved, looked, and spoke just like my schoolmates. In other words, I was white, Roman Catholic, and spoke accentless English. These facts overrode a very singular fact of difference: Puerto Rico was always at the center of our daily home life. Though we were enrolled in Catholic parochial schools in town, our family friends were the other Puerto Ricans stationed at the base. We spent weekends picnicking with them, celebrating births and birthdays, holidays and promotions, eating Puerto Rican food, dancing to Puerto Rican music, and speaking in rapid, loud, funny, passionate Spanish. My maternal grandmother made yearly visits and, for the month or so that Abuela stayed with us, the house would fill with things from "home." In those days before there were Goya sections in every supermarket and tropical fruits in the "exotic" bins of their produce departments, Abuela's luggage would hold the treasured smuggled plantains, yuca, and achiote for *pasteles,* the pigeon peas for her *arroz con gandules,* the salted codfish for *bacalaítos,* a jar of her secret *sofrito.*

In the Catholic schools I attended, as my father was transferred from one posting to another, I learned the mixed messages of selfhood and power, class and race hidden in the curriculum of English-language immersion. At Loretto Academy in El Paso I learned that the less I associated with "the Mexican girls," the better (that is, the more "American") I was. At Pauline Memorial School in Colorado Springs I learned that the better my English, the better my relationship with my teachers. At St. Joseph's in Columbia, South Carolina, the better I memorized lines from my reader, the greater the distance from my mother. It was not until years later, when I heard my father talk about St. Boniface in Fort Smith, that I learned that other Puerto Rican kids had attended a different, segregated school. We played together on weekends but could not share the intimate details of children's lives — stories of teachers we hated or loved, tests failed or passed, school bullies and school friends. My family, evidently, had passed the "white" test.

I was thirteen in 1965 when my father was stationed in Korea, and my mother brought her eight children back to live in Puerto Rico. Because my immersion into U.S. culture and language had been so all-encompassing, I had to deal anew with identity issues. The outside world, which I had previously learned to negotiate so well by speaking English and by assuming American behavior and thinking, became Puerto Rican. The process of my reimmersion into Puerto Rican culture began through my identification with the extended family with whom I was interacting for the first time. I stumbled through Spanish with Abuela and my mother's sisters; each visit to my father's parents brought me into a world of Spanish *zarzuelas* and stories of a Puerto Rico I had never known. Until that time, my life had been tidily divided into an American public world and a Puerto Rican private world, but my new life in Puerto Rico unexpectedly became a complex, conflicting cultural jumble. In the family, I fought to convince my cousins that I was not the *americana* I appeared to be; at the military-run high school I now attended, I struggled to establish my Puerto Ricanness, my otherness. In both cases, I was embarrassed to find that I was not as bilingual as I had thought. Ironically, returning to Puerto Rico, whose existence had given me so much comfort and identity while growing up, only made me feel more like an outsider.

I became conscious in adolescence of how being different from white mainstream America meant constantly educating it about oneself. It was painfully obvious that some of my schoolmates' parents accepted me into their households because I did not seem Puerto Rican to them — I did not "look Puerto Rican," I did not speak English "like a Puerto Rican." Too many conversations with these adults — negotiated carefully because I so often felt that my father was being judged by my actions and reactions — revolved around why I did not call myself Spanish instead of Puerto Rican despite my "obvious" (to them) European ancestry, despite being (to their minds) so different from "those people" whom they met on their excursions outside the sheltered worlds of Fort Buchanan and Ramey Air Force Base.

I remember how often I internalized my anger and played the "good girl," all the while imagining what my mother would have told them and wishing I possessed more of her fire and patriotic righteousness. Instead, I sat at their dinner tables, making sure to leave food on the plate so there would be no comment on the table manners of Puerto Ricans. I measured my speech and became precociously conversant with all sorts of issues to disprove that Puerto Ricans were loud or stupid. I recall seething with anger and frustration whenever someone uttered the inevitable "you don't look Puerto Rican," knowing that they really did not want to know about me or my culture or my history. They needed to think I didn't "look Puerto Rican" — so they could justify their children's friendship with one of "them," so they could in two years' time go home and say, "You know, there are still some Spanish Puerto Ricans."

It was during those years in a U.S. armed forces high school that I came to a conscious understanding of the political and racial issues that separated me from the American culture that I had partially assimilated in the early years of my life. As did many during the late 1960s, I became immersed in the literature of the Black Power and Young Lords movements in the United States. Though my reality was far from that of the urban ghetto life in the United States that gave birth to both, these movements articulated the contradictions that I carried within. As the daughter of a Puerto Rican U.S. Army officer, raised on military bases, I was deeply affected by the duality of my citizenship and the incompatibility of my loyalties. It became obvious that, for my own survival, I needed to choose between being American and being Puerto Rican. Others, I know, negotiated this duality differently, but I just could not be both. In those Cold War years marked by the turbulence of Vietnam, the urgency of the struggle for Puerto Rican independence, and the rabid anti-communism that demonized any attempt to think outside the colonial strait-jacket, being Puerto Rican and seventeen meant choosing against my father. And I did.

El Beso

Ruth Behar

Todo lo que guardé se me hizo polvo;
todo lo que escondí de mis
ojos los escondí, y de mi propia vida.
Everything I hid turned to dust;
everything I hid I hid from my
own eyes, and my own life.
DULCE MARÍA LOYNAZ, *Poemas sin nombre*

THE FIRST BOY to put his tongue in my mouth was Puerto Rican. I remember his tongue touching my tongue and then plunging down my throat so fast that I feared I would choke. I was so stunned I hardly had time to react. We were on the beach and we nearly slipped to the ground from the effort, but he managed to catch me in his arms before we both fell. The sun was low in the sky. The ocean had fallen silent. I remember his tongue was cool and that I sipped from it as if it were a fountain. He tasted of smooth sand, mint, and blooming young manhood.

I think I was twelve or thirteen; he was just two or three years older than me, but I thought of him as much, much older. And definitely more "experienced." Boys, I was being taught by my mother, would always know more about those things than girls. Boys had to know more because they were boys. In developing into men they would need to have sex, *la cosa del hombre* required it, *no sé si entiendes, mi niña,* but they can't hold themselves back, if they don't have it, they will go crazy, they will explode, so don't tempt a man, because he can't stop himself, it's *la cosa,* their *cosa* is like that, it's not their fault, they have to have it, so say no, say no, remember, say no before things go too far. *Trata de entender, mi niña. No te dejes. Dí que no.* Don't let them convince you. They don't have anything to lose. *La que pierde es siempre la mujer. No te olvides de eso.* Wait, wait until you find *un hombre bueno, un hombre que te quiera de verdad, un hombre* who doesn't want you just for that. *Ten cuidado,* okay? Be careful.

Counterposed to this message of fearing sex and withholding from sex to save yourself for the good man who would love you enough to put a bridle on his animal needs, I would watch jealously in years to come as my father educated my brother in the ways of desire with laughter, humor, and brash joy.

On lazy Sunday mornings, after brunch, my father and my brother would lie together in bed, my father sharing with my brother his stash of *Playboys*, whose hiding place in his night table I had long since discovered. As my father looked at the pictures with my brother, he seemed to say: For you this legacy, *mi niño*. Because you are a boy, for you a taste of all the delicious fruits of a woman's body. Soon they will be yours to squeeze and smell and savor and let drip from your lips like the sweetest and juiciest of mangoes.

I don't remember how I met the Puerto Rican boy who gave me his tongue to taste. I know he was Puerto Rican from Spanish Harlem, but I don't remember his name or what he looked like, except that he was skinny and long-limbed and had thick jet-black hair. I had no idea where he was staying or who he was with. All he knew about me was that I was Cuban and lived in Queens, in upwardly mobile Forest Hills, where we'd moved recently, and that I was a chubby girl, desperately ill at ease in my red two-piece bathing suit edged with a sad blue ruffle, with eyes already cloudy from reading too many books, and so pathetically innocent about the pleasure my body was made for that it made you want to cry. We'd meet on the beach, kiss, and ask no questions.

Our kissing took place in Miami Beach, in July, when the sea grows warm as a steam bath and the hotels on Ocean Drive drop their rates by half. My parents and their friends in *El Grupo*, all Cuban Jews who had formed a tightly bonded network during the early years of immigration to New York, had begun in the late 1960s to make enough money that they felt they could afford a vacation. Someone found out that summer was the low season at the Ocean Drive hotels, whose better clients preferred to winter in the sun, and decided that the Surfcomber Hotel offered the best deal—two meals a day and two double beds and the kids stay free and a lifeguard to watch them at the pool.

Off we'd go, five *Grupo* couples and their children, to burn our skin to shreds in the cruel summer sun, drink hot pink *mamey* milkshakes, remember Cuba, and forget how hard and gray life was in New York. The *Grupo* fathers would all come for a hard-earned two weeks of vacation and then they would depart, leaving behind their bathing suits and donning their business suits to go back to work in New York and keep earning the money that allowed the *Grupo* mothers to stay for an additional two weeks in Miami Beach with the children. How free and easy were those two weeks without the fathers—no scoldings, no demands, no tensions, no arguments. How happy they looked, Miriam, Zelmi, Fanny, Nina, and my mother, lounging around the pool, their bodies slick with suntan oil, their breasts pouring jubilantly out of their bathing suits and no man to tell them, *oye, estás enseñando muncho,* their nails painted, and not a care in the world, ladies of leisure as they might have been in Cuba had the revolution not dared to interrupt their lives so impolitely. And we *Grupo* children, how gloriously wild we were allowed to be during those fatherless two weeks, jumping in and out of the pool, no one admonishing us about how we were going to get paralyzed for not waiting long enough after eating to go swimming. It was during one of those blessed weeks when the *Grupo* mothers were alone with us that I began to learn how to kiss like a woman.

But my education was cut short. One afternoon, just after a kissing session, I climbed back to the pool area from the beach and saw my mother and brother watching me. They had strange looks on their faces, but I waved hello and tried to act nonchalant. My mother didn't waste any time getting to the point. Where had I been? Why hadn't I told her I had a boyfriend? she demanded to know. What do you mean? What boyfriend? I asked, in a vain effort to feign ignorance. Giggling at first, she said that my brother had seen me with the boy and he'd told her about it. She didn't believe him, so he said, "Okay, let's spy on Ruty," and the two of them spied on me and she saw me, saw me with her own eyes kissing the boy, clear as day. As she told me this, she broke out in a roar of laughter. Both she and my brother laughed so hard watching me, she said. It was all they could do to cover their mouths, that's how funny it was. Had I really not heard them?

I had heard nothing. Now I had heard too much. I was ashamed and angry and vowed never to trust my brother. Or my mother.

Wiping away her laughter tears, my mother asked, "*Y ¿quién es el muchacho?*"

Who was this boy? I hardly knew. I hardly wanted to know. "He's just a boy I met," I said.

"*No parece* Jewish," she said.

I shrugged my shoulders. "He's Puerto Rican."

"*¿Puertorriqueño? ¿Estás loca, Ruty?*" Her face became deadly serious, as if I'd just said the boy was from Mars or was contaminated with some rare form of the bubonic plague that had survived the Middle Ages. "Thank god your father isn't here," she said, putting her hand to her chest and sighing.

"And what's wrong with him being Puerto Rican? We're Cubans, aren't we?" I exclaimed, feeling very clever.

"*Pero Ruty, tú que eres tan inteligente, tan* smart. *¿Tú no sabes* that we're Jewish? You're too young to be kissing any boys, *pero ¿cómo pudiste besar un puertorriqueño? Ay, Ruty, un puertorriqueño, ¡por tu vida! Ruty, ¿tú no sabes cómo son los puertorriqueños?* They have dirty minds. *Solamente quieren una cosa.* They want only one thing from girls. *¿Cómo te dejaste, Ruty?* And you're so smart. *No lo puedo creer. Menos mal que tu padre no está aquí. Te mata si está aquí.* Please, don't ever see that boy again. If your father finds out, he'll kill me too for not stopping you."

Only later would I understand fully the depth and consequences of the prohibition my mother gave voice to that July in Miami Beach. Only later would I learn that one of my aunts, in Cuba, had run away at fifteen with a sailor who wasn't Jewish, causing my paternal grandmother to mourn and tear at her hair as if her daughter had died. Only later would I see how my grandmother looked at me with solemn eyes as I held in my lap the great-grandchild who had come of her daughter's union, for which she had so grieved. The great-grandchild had come from yet another taboo union, between her grandson and a beautiful brown Costa Rican woman. Only later would I see how my grandmother kept looking with those solemn eyes when the little girl, my cousin, brown like her mother, rose from my lap and I smoothed out the wrinkles left on my silk dress. Only later would I learn from an aunt on my mother's side of my family, who grew up in a small town in the Cuban countryside, that she'd been shipped off to Havana when her parents, my great-grandparents, the only Jews in the town, discovered that her flirtation with one of the local boys was getting "too serious." Only later would I understand how we were Cubans, yes, how we spoke Spanish, yes, and ate black beans and rice, and got nostalgic for Cuba in Miami Beach, and how, yes, we'd have ended up in Hitler's ovens had we not been saved by Cuba, but how nevertheless our belonging to the Jewish tribe made it impossible for that whole world that had nourished us and given us life to have any place in our longing, our desire, our hunger to drink from tongues and bodies that had not been branded by the yellow star. Or if we dared — as my aunt had dared — to welcome those tongues and bodies with our own tongues and bodies, then it was at the cost of bringing to the Jewish tribe unbearable suffering, grief, a loss so deep that it was unto death. Only later would I understand why I had always claimed a Latina identity so hesitantly, with such painful self-hatred, fearing that I did not deserve the love or respect of those Chicanas and Puertorriqueñas and Cubanas who accepted me, who claimed me as one of their own, when I didn't feel worthy, because I knew, knew it in the heaviness of my heart, that I'd been brought up not to get too close to their men, not to mix with their kind, to keep separate.

I had planned to disobey my mother and keep seeing the Puerto Rican boy, somehow, secretly, when we returned to New York at the end of that July vacation in Miami Beach. In his hand I'd placed a folded piece of paper with my name and address and phone, so he'd find me, so he'd come for me from Spanish Harlem. So he'd take me away from the posh Ashkenazi Jewish neighborhood of Forest Hills, to which my father, a dark Sephardic Jew who was constantly being told he looked Puerto Rican, had moved us. Had moved me when I'd entered my teens, trying to keep me safe from the Latino boys and black boys who were moving into our old Queens neighborhood. But the Puerto Rican boy who put his tongue in my mouth never called, never came to Forest Hills looking for me. He was forbidden fruit, which I'd never taste again.

The Prize of a New Cadillac

Yvette Gisele Flores-Ortiz

For Ruth Behar and Gary B.

SEPHARDIC LOOKS AND Ashkenazi heart. But I was too young to know the complications of loving a Jewish man.

I was sixteen years old, walking home with my mother from the grocery store, ashamed someone might see us. Why did people never walk in L.A.? We were so visible without a car. Ashamed someone might hear us, why did mother have to speak so loud in Spanish? Everyone would know we were foreigners, wetbacks, like the kids used to call me in South Central. But now here we were, in the white lands of the San Fernando Valley of the 1960s, before the *pupuserías* arrived, before the low-riders, and home-girls came to my high school, long before drive-bys and brown faces posturing with pride and attitude. Then it was just me, *una mosca en leche,* my mother used to say.

And then I saw him, but he had seen me first. His seventeen-year-old Ashkenazi heart fell in love with my Latinidad. Mother, always afraid, tensed as she saw the young man and his friends approach. *¡Ay Dios mío! ¿Qué querrán?* Don't worry mother, we are in the white lands, you need no longer be afraid when young men approach. Mother, these young men are white, relax. Unspoken conversations, like most Mother and I had.

He offered to help carry our grocery bags. I smiled quietly inside my heart. He had noticed me! And then I had a thought, an echo or a fragment of a remembered conversation. I don't know where or when I heard it, *"Los judíos son buenos maridos."* My mother's voice *sembrada en mi cerebro,*[1] transmitting the story of Luisita and Abraham. *La tía panameña y el judío bueno.* Abraham, the Jewish refugee who fell in love with the eldest daughter of an orphaned family of eight. Abraham who came from Europe with nothing but hopes and

---

1. Jews make good husbands. My mother's voice took seed in my mind.

dreams and offered to help Luisita raise her siblings, because he too had fallen in love with her *latinidad*. He understood her sorrow; he was an orphan too of the First World War. My mother told me Luisita remained very Catholic, thanking Jesus daily for her Jewish husband, while Abraham continued to wait for his Messiah. But he was such a good man! *"Hija, ningún panameño se echa esa carga encima. ¡Ese judío es un santo!"* Perhaps mother was right; no Panamanian would assume the responsibility of marrying a woman with no money and seven siblings. I suppose that is why the family considered Sandy Abraham a saint. And I remembered all this as Gary walked next to me.

But I was too young to know the complications of loving a Jewish man. We met the summer before I entered high school; he helped me enroll and negotiate the maze of academic tracking. Once again, because of my Spanish surname I had been placed in the "basic track." My mother, who spoke no English, with Gary at her side, invaded the registrar's office and demanded I be placed in the academic track. I was.

Gary, who walked me to and from school, who understood I was not allowed to date unchaperoned, who took my cousin along to the movies, who explained to me the mysteries of algebra, Gary who gave me status because he was a senior, Gary who picked the university I would eventually attend, Gary who awakened in me desires I did not know a sixteen-year-old could have, Gary finally worked up the nerve to take me home to meet his family.

I did not know then why the three L.A. blocks between his apartment and mine seemed so long on that hot autumn day. It never occurred to me to wonder why his parents lived in an apartment in that end of town, instead of in the hills where my other Jewish classmates lived. I never asked, he never told. And on we walked those three long blocks. A beautiful blond woman opened the door. She seemed so young to be a mother, mine always looked so old. She was elegantly dressed, and in the middle of the day. Her polite smile could not hide the coldness in her eyes. What were you thinking and feeling, Mrs. D.? I never would have broken your son's heart. But I did not know then what it meant to you, for your son to love a gentile.

We enter his apartment, elegantly furnished, orderly, clean. I did not know it, but I had crossed an invisible class divide. He asks me to follow him to his room. I am horrified. No proper Latin girl goes into a boy's room unsupervised, but before we reach his door, his grandma approaches. She looks just like a grandma should, I think. She is short and round, come to think of it, she almost looks Latina. She speaks a language I do not understand, but one word sticks in my mind: *"Shiksa!"* she screams in horror. *"Shiksa!"* I do not know then what the word means, but I feel the sharpness in her tone, her disapproval, no, more than that, her fear.

He navigates me into his room, closing the door, his face red in anger and embarrassment. He tries to explain that she is a Holocaust survivor and afraid of those who are different, afraid of losing him, the only grandson, to a gentile. Deep in my heart I understand, and I know it would be futile to tell him about Luisita and Abraham. Outside his room we can hear his mother's voice, on the phone to her husband. She is crying, "We are in the San Fernando Valley, for goodness sake. Why did he have to fall in love with her?"

We lie on the grass, next to each other, watching the clouds parade, he takes my hand and whispers, trying to hold back laughter, "I love you, my *shiksa.*" Later he confides that his parents offered a prize if he were to break up with me, sort of a combined graduation and drop the *shiksa* present, a brand new 1968 gold Cadillac.

I never felt entitled to be angry. I suppose I understood his family's need to preserve tradition; but I don't think I quite understood then the threat that I posed. I was a brown girl in the whitelands. What sense of power could I possibly have? I also remembered the tragedy of Luisita and Abraham. Despite their love, their life together was filled with pain: three disabled children, one son killed accidentally, one daughter tortured in Guatemala. There were whispers in the family, maybe it was a punishment from God. "*Castigo de Dios, nena.*" But which God, whose God?

We did not break up. Gary had too much principle and adolescent spite. But it was never the same for me after that. Three years later, when we met again in college, we would take drives in his three-year-old gold Cadillac. Within its spaciousness he taught me how to smoke, and within its comforts we revisited the adolescent passion we once felt. And then we would laugh, but I really wanted to cry. One word had ruined the innocence of teenage passion. We never made love when we were in love.

Years later, a letter from him found me. I was already a married professor, mother of two. He was now a doctor and wanted to see me. I never responded. I was afraid that after so many years he would not find me worth the price of a new Cadillac.

La Tra(d)ición

Latina Anónima

¿CÓMO DECIR LO *que nunca se ha dicho?* How to give voice to the unspeakable? *Me miro en el espejo y escucho el diálogo interno entre la niña buena y la adulta enojada.* I see my reflection in the mirror; the good child within speaks to the angry adult.

— *Pero no le digas a nadie, que se van a enojar.* Don't tell anyone, they'll get mad.

— *¿Quién se va a enojar, y por qué no?* Somebody needs to get angry. (But who do I hold accountable after nearly thirty years of silence?)

— *Pero no fue tan serio. A otras mujeres les han pasado peores cosas.* How does one compare the relative violations women suffer? I am silenced by the possibility of comparison.

— *Eres muy bella, una de las más lindas de la familia. Tu tía quiere que te examine. Tengo entendido que tus períodos son irregulares. Sígueme a mi consultorio . . .*

I am alone in the doctor's office, my father's illegitimate brother, the one grandfather sent to medical school to assuage his guilt, while my father, the first-born, had to struggle financially all the years of his life. *El tío que no era tío, pero que era médico, y nos atendía sin cobrar.* The uncle, who was not my uncle, but who was a doctor and never charged.

— *No seas tímida. Quítate la ropa, estamos en familia. Necesito hacerte un exámen pélvico. ¿Sabes lo que es eso? ¿Qué edad tienes?*

— *Dieciocho.*

— *¿Tienes novio?*

— *Sí.*

Tradition/betrayal. In Spanish the word "betrayal" (*traición*) is embedded in the word for "tradition" (*tradición*).

— *¿Te gusta? ¿Lo quieres?*

— *Sí.*

— *¿Has tenido relaciones sexuales?*

— *No* (I lied; the proper Catholic girl, I could not tell him I had had sex. I wondered if he could tell. And why was he asking me this, anyway?)

I feel his hands touching me, it doesn't feel right, but I don't know, he is the doctor *y mi tío. Y a mí no me enseñaron a cuestionar a los médicos, ni a ningún hombre,* come to think of it. His hands explore the depth of my vagina, he breathes more heavily, I shut my eyes and tune out his voice . . . but I can still hear.

— *Eres muy bella, una de las más lindas de la familia. Qué lástima que vives tan lejos. Pero tus labios son muy chicos, y tu cerviz no es normal. Tendrás problemas al parir.*

And his fingers continue to explore my sacred places, arousing me, exciting me, and my body betrays me, between the terror and pleasure, he wins and I explode.

— *¿Quedaste con deseo?*

I fail to answer. He leaves the room. Defiled, *desacrada, sucia,* and ashamed, I dress and leave the room. He smiles and waves good-bye.

I don't feel the ground beneath my feet. I board the bus. I climb the stairs. My tía awaits.

— *Y ¿cómo estaba el doctor?* (She never openly acknowledges he is her brother). *Y ¡tan buen doctor que es! Y no te cobró, ¿verdad?*

— *No tía, se lo cobró a mi padre.*

But it was me, in fact, who paid, an adolescent woman who could not defend herself. It was not my fault he was the bastard child of my grandfather, one of many anyway. I did not cause his pain. But now we are forever connected. He continued the legacy of incest, one more woman victimized in our *sagrada familia.* He also robbed me of the will to go to medical school. *Pero la lealtad a la familia y el miedo y la vergüenza* silenced me.

Pero ahora the voice screams from the other side of the mirror.

You had the audacity to ask if I had been left with desire! *El único deseo que me quedó fue de matarte, y de esconder mi dolor, hasta este momento.*

No tenías derecho a hacer lo que hiciste. No tenías derecho a robarme algo tan sagrado.

No tenías derecho de sembrar en mí la vergüenza. Cargué tu culpa, desgraciado, me eché la culpa a mí, por no saber, no anticipar, no desconfiar. Me eché la culpa por ser joven, inocente. Me eché la culpa porque tú me usaste.

Pero es tu culpa. No tenías derecho de tocarme, a erotizarme, a ensuciarme.

Sin embargo, no ganaste. En mí no lograste tu venganza. Parí hijos, disfruté al hacer el amor. Pero yo tampoco gané. Cuando el sexo es arma de violencia, y el poder se usa para el mal, no hay ganadores. Mantuve tu secreto y mi silencio me hizo tu cómplice. ¿A cuántas más les has hecho lo mismo? ¿Cuántas más caminan por el mundo sintiéndose sucias porque violaste tu privilegio y poder de médico?

Pero no soy tu víctima. Contigo aprendí la desconfianza, pero también aprendí a protegerme mejor.

Y ya no guardo el silencio ni protejo tu secreto. Y espero estar viva cuando tú mueras.

Between Perfection and Invisibility

Latina Anónima

"WHAT DID I THINK I was doing in academia?" I thought as I was in the middle of a seminar during the first semester of graduate studies. "What do I think I am doing here, in graduate school?" I continued to ponder. It was a Ph.D. program. I had just completed my B.A. and had been encouraged by my professors to apply to their own Ph.D. program; at that time they did not have a master's program. I had become accustomed to performing very well academically. After some difficult consideration, I decided to take the challenge. The vast majority of the graduate students in the seminar had already completed their M.A.'s elsewhere, and was well prepared for these advanced studies. I could have sworn they were speaking Russian, Greek, anything but a language I could comprehend. As the semester went on, my self began to slowly vanish. I would soon become invisible. Although I knew I was physically there, attentively listening, taking in as much as I possibly could, I also knew that I was the only one aware of my presence. Completely ignored in a silence, I was growing numb. I asked myself, "What the heck do I think I am doing here?" *¡No les entiendo!* I don't know what's going on in the classroom.

As I took a walk on the beach at twilight that evening, I thought of how privileged I felt about living close to the ocean. Coming from an arid area, I could fully appreciate the freshness of the ocean breeze, *el rocío de las olas contra las piedras,* the oranges, golds, and violets of the sky reflected on the water. They momentarily soothed the feelings of isolation. I don't have anyone to really talk to about this emptiness, this sense of invisibility, fragmentation, and alienation. An unthinkable thought crept up within that existential instance: what difference would it make if I were to walk into the ocean? As I began to feel the waves splashing against my thighs, the ghosts of my female ancestors splashed my face with memories I could not ignore, memories that had been erased by others. You're really foolish. I bet none of the women in your family have ever been caught in this existential moment, forgetting everyone else. Get out of it! I knew my mother wouldn't have done it, much less my grandmother. What are you doing? Gazing at the small shimmering stars in the vastness of the darkened sky, I wondered, why am I caught in this twilight zone between perfection and invisibility?

Feeling caught in the borderlands of perfection and invisibility was not new to me. My recollections of growing up in a small border town were filled with demands placed on me to be a role model for others. As the eldest child in a family of nine, I was expected to set *el buen ejemplo*. I always felt compelled to be close to perfection. Mistakes by my younger siblings were my responsibilities as well. I paid dearly not only for my mistakes but for theirs as well. My own mistakes were *imperdonables*. I had to always strive for perfection. As far as I understood, I had to achieve it or suffer humiliation before everyone present.

As the warm sand on the beach mixed with the hot end-of-the-summer desert sands, a shivering sensation electrified my spinal cord. That first moment of invisibility appeared before me in the deep blue waters. I was entering, for the first time, my kindergarten class. Later my mother would tell me of my joyous anticipation of finally getting to attend school. According to her, I had been impatiently waiting to go to school since I was about two years old! Well, the day had arrived. It was straight up our street, ten blocks. I was going to a new place where I was going to learn many new things, get school supplies, and, most importantly, get to check out new books at the school library. So after waiting your entire life, you finally have the opportunity to go to school, my mother teased.

But something extremely strange happened. That first day of school, I could not, for the life of me, understand what was going on. All of the kids were being instructed to go into the classroom, my mother said good-bye, and then I began to hear strange sounds. We were seated. Way beyond many bopping heads, I could see a very nice-looking woman in her late fifties. Stupefied, I could not believe that it was she who was articulating all those strange sounds: Whatacatmetskicosklekntlsedjfosw aeijraoisd. What was going on?!

As the days were going by, I knew I was becoming invisible. I couldn't understand what was happening to me. At home, I had an important role: I was the eldest. I was five; my sisters were four and three. At home, I was Ms. Big Sister, in charge. Of course, I was always to be in control. I was responsible for my younger bratty sisters. Why was this new place, school, causing so many of my friends so much grief? Why were kids pushed outside the classroom and made to stand there without speaking when they had been using words that all the other kids could understand? Why were kids crying silently, heads bowed?

In the early 1960s, education in our border city was entirely in English. Most teachers were recruited from other areas of the country and, unfortunately, most if not all were monolingual. It was total emergence: sink or swim! I knew that because my mother insisted that I go to school, I had to. Putting in at least twelve hours at work kept my father very distant in our lives. There was one thing he was severe about: whether we liked it or not we had to go to school. It became extremely difficult for me to know that I was spending a pretty good part of my day in a place in which I knew I was in real space, in real location, yet I was floating, in nowhere land, in limbo. I was not a happy camper. This world was totally indecipherable to me. Where was I going with this? That handsome woman at the head of the class was slowly becoming a distorted sight. Those frightening, harsh sounds emitted from her mouth were incomprehensible bombs thrown in our direction. Day in and day out, that consistent bombardment began to take a toll. Battle fatigue. Whose idea was this? What I wanted was to learn, not to be muffled. If you cannot take in, you cannot give out. I was bewildered and silenced.

That was precisely what I was experiencing again when I began the graduate program. I knew back in kindergarten that I never wanted to be in that situation again, and yet here I was. It had taken me three years of my early life to finally become a citizen, a member of a class. During that entire time I was silent. I was absorbing, taking in all I could. Finally I was able to become an A student, top in the class. Three years of my life: I just felt that total loss!

I decided to go back to the source. I wanted to know about the women in my family. I told my grandmother, "*Aquí tengo la grabadora,*" and I pretended to turn the imaginary recorder on. Of course, she would not tolerate my recording her. "What kind of intrusive gadget was that!" I was the only one in the house who was really interested in her oral narratives.

Going away to college became my way out of the small town and the home in which I could not get away from not performing as *la perfecta*. I had to prove I could make it at the university even though it was such an alienating place. I went to a small school, where the majority of the student body was graduate students, instead of attending the state university with most of my friends. I felt I was out there in the middle of nowhere with a lot of white students, although there was a critical mass of students of color. I had to deal with a lot of the conflicts of belonging to student organizations. There were a lot of drugs, sex, power struggles, gender struggles, racial struggles for my taste. Having been raised in a rural area in a very protective family did not prepare me for the urban university. I knew I had to stay out of the struggles in order to survive: no social life for me until I got my B.A.! I had gone to a high school that could barely secure yearly accreditation. There I was again; I felt I barely knew how to read and write satisfactorily. I had never heard the word "psychology" as far as I knew. We were given such an inadequate education.

And yet I had been an excellent student, by my school's standards, and I had excellent grades. My parents had demanded that I be in school every day of my life. At that moment I was convinced I had received straight A's virtually for my attendance. And that was how I was able to make it out of that small rural town. I never had this sense of education, in the institutional aspect, as valuable. Ideas, yes. Narratives, theory, analysis, making connections, *filosofía* . . . that fascinated me! Intellectualizing, theorizing about experiences, that's what interested me! And the conversations I would have would be with the women in my family, especially my mother. All I wanted to do when I finally made it to the university was to make up the twelve years in which I had not received a decent education and learn absolutely everything I felt I had missed. So I didn't have one discipline in mind. The first courses I took in college were beyond me. I almost failed one of them. That was one tragic moment! I could not understand how on earth I could have gone from feeling extremely brilliant in high school to not grasping what was going on in the classroom, again! How could I have gone from being a mature, self-reliant, independent, role-model seventeen-year-old back in my hometown to a scared, insecure, alienated college student? I was invisible in my new space. The linguistic sounds I heard were suspiciously incomprehensible. The nuanced articulations of the white middle-class students felt like bricks thrown at my face. The bruises silenced me once more. I felt split, dismembered. At home I had been precocious, my young mother's confidante, I could think very clearly, well, and I was focused. I could be everyone's mentor, model, guide. I had made it to the university and I was nonexistent. In some fleeting moments of existence, I was to find out I had an accent, that I was a woman of color, that I was a Chicana, or should be. Yet I knew I had to survive, because I also knew I could never go back home. My mother asked me why. "Because I want to have opportunities you never had." She smiled, "I taught you well."

When I met the person who was to become my *compañero,* I made it very clear that I was a person to be respected, never to be told what to do. I had to be in complete control of my own person. I intended to be financially independent. My intelligence was not to be questioned: my integrity as a thinking human being, honored. Open communication was imperative. Sharing of experiences was to be an integral part of our relationship. We had an idyllic relationship during our student days. He became part of the essential support system that made my graduate studies possible.

What enticed me to stay in graduate studies? Since I was cognizant of my inadequate elementary and secondary education, I felt I deserved a college education. In the first four years of my college life I learned to read and write fluently in English. And I intended to learn how to do it well! However, there was this nagging uneasiness about expressing myself in English. Why did it feel like an artificial experiment? I felt translated, not fully captured in that language. After completion of the graduation requirements, I felt the need to attempt to understand that irking linguistic displacement. I was fortunate enough to be at an institution where one of the first Spanish courses taught from a sociolinguistic perspective was offered. I finally realized I could not command the English language until I came to terms with the insidious erasure, on the part of a weak educational system, of my native tongue, Spanish. Reclaiming my native tongue becomes part of re-membering my self. But I didn't do it alone.

The institutional support that made it possible to reach the Ph.D. came from the Chicana/o professors who were blazing trails for the new generation of graduate students. I had the great fortune to work with one of the best sociolinguists and theorists in the country. This professor took a group of us under her wing, became *la mamá de los pollitos,* as some would joke. We were trained to conduct research, grapple with theoretical problems to "make sense" of both canonical and noncanonical texts, and approach all our academic probes with fine-tuned critical-analytical skills. Her standards were extremely high, her demands "ruthless" (we sometimes complained) but always attainable. From early on in the program, she expected seminar papers of presentable quality (as in conferences). Virtually single-handedly, she made it possible for us to attend conferences, hone our ideas and papers, write and rewrite throughout the years until we produced publishable articles. Intense collaborative critical assessment was a requirement. Soon I was to learn that we had become a highly privileged group due to our mentor's invaluable support while she was undergoing her own tenure process. Surely we constituted a severe overburden beyond the excessive institutional demands placed on her. We not only survived but thrived in that collaborative space she had us develop.

Articulating the personal moments of invisibility has got to be one of the most challenging exercises I have undertaken. I must admit it creates an eerie sensation of *desnudez verbal ante el público,* at best. The critical consideration is the forum. If disclosure of ingrained fears — due to distorted conceptions of perfection insidiously imposed through various processes of socialization — serves as a minimal basis for a potential student to identify with, it will have been worth the effort.

Diary of *La Llorona* with a Ph.D.

Gloria Holguín Cuádraz

IN THE MIDDLE of my four-and-a-half hour stretch of driving from the *desierto del Valle Imperial* to the Valley of the Sun today, the tears start dropping, slowly — arriving with an almost familiar comfort. I just said good-bye to my mom and four generations of *familia*. And here I am, returning to my life of solitude, with my liver-brown dog, Tito (named after Tito Puente of course!), curled up on the front seat, and my dubbed tapes of salsa and classical music on the floor, when I think to myself, "I feel like the *Llorona* in that damn legend!" At that moment, the words for this stream-of-consciousness poem started to flow. And suddenly, despite the questions I have asked over the years, such as, "What do all those Mexican figures like La Malinche and La Llorona have to do with me?" I make a connection.

The Educated *Llorona*

llora
en silencio
dropping *lágrimas*
onto the beautiful
brown curvature of her belly
no por los niños que perdió
pero
por los niños
que nunca tuvo.
And for the children
she consciously gave up.

Nationalist ironies
Los aztecas

le quitaban el corazón
as an offering to the Gods
ahora
le sacan su corazón
by failing miserably
and perhaps intentionally?
to love her.

She cries now
a woman nearing forty
for the absence of affect
in her daily life.

No es que no agarra
un abrazo
here and there.
But that's just it
they are only here and there
like the rare bristling of leaves
on a hot summer day
en el desierto del valle.

She weeps
año tras año
for having to
build and sustain her own temple.
"The Temple of Tenacity"
she calls it
so that she can guarantee
herself pillars of support.

La Doctora Llorona cries
about everything in her life

The absence of someone
to greet her at the airport gate,
por ejemplo,
serves as a
constant reminder.

No one is there
the room / the house
is empty . . .
Day after day after day.

Even the checks and balances
on her value system
all of them
incumbent
contingent
dependent
on *Dra. Llorona*'s
own will.

She cries
because the things
that make her cry
are no longer the things
she used to cry about.

It is futile
to talk to someone
about her woes.

The phone is merely
a means
for temporary
unfulfilling
respite.

Respite from the dailyness
of solitude
eggshell solitude
scrambled with doses
of delusions
and diminishing dreams.

Solitude.

The only thing
that now gives *Dra. Llorona* solace. . . .

Afterthought: The irony is that sometimes I'm not even connected to my
solitude. But, in this respect, I feel content in my knowledge that "it could
be worse." I know far too many *compañeras* who exist in a totally numb
state to survive their states of solitude. So I guess the fact that I'm still conscious of it and struggling with it is some relatively healthy sign of sanity.
I wonder.

The following are entries I wrote before and after I wrote this piece. I share these with the hope that my words will resonate for others and perhaps remind you that we are not so alone.

December 11, 1982
Quiet despair / trying to convince myself I'll survive
the silence / got to get rid of the silence

Quick! Put the TV on, the radio
click the lights on / turn on the computer
water to boil
I wish the phone would ring

Why don't we get credits for our class
in isolation? / isn't even recognized in
the department / yet it's such a major part
of the curriculum

Spring 1987
We picked up our t-shirts today! Several of us (Chicana graduate students and faculty members) have decided to make a statement. To whom, we're not quite sure; and actually, we're not really sure who would care. But in our own way we're obviously trying to find some humor in how we all seem to be living our lives. We ordered hot-pink t-shirts, etched with a small heart in the front with the name of our group, "*Solitas* Club"; on the back of the t-shirt we have black, velvet-cased letters that read "*¿y qué?*"

I guess the literature on "resistance to oppression," à la Caulfield, would suggest this is our way of resisting the "larger social forces" creating our conditions of solitude. I would rather quote Ntozake Shangé, who said "You've gotta dance to keep from crying."

November 22, 1989
I woke up today thinking, "It's historically, structurally, and politically impossible for my male counterpart to exist."

December 14, 1989
I have a dear Chicano male friend, who jokingly talks about belonging to the "*Nadie nos quiere* club!" I have something to add to that, at least in terms of how it pertains to Chicana faculty. We belong to the "*Nadie nos quiere querer* club."

October 1992
pero qué ruido trae
el silencio

Can one have an anxiety attack
over silence?

pero el silencio es dulce
es la soledad, the solitude
that envelops
like a hawk
around its prey.

It is unconscionable for someone
to feel so alone.

August 8, 1994
Tonight, I realized
that I feel fully qualified
to write the modern-day version of Paz's *Labyrinth of Solitude*
. . . from "La Chicana" perspective.

Almost 12 midnight [no date]
Another full moon. Funny, my writing is so little tonight — and so faint. Must reflect
my aura — my energy.

La Llorona had a good cry tonight
Her wails filled the
four walls
Didn't think a human
could cry like that
at least,
solely for herself.

Could *La Llorona* be going *loca?*

August 8, 1995
I'm hearing from too many people who "need" me — who need my strength.
Of all things, what makes them think I have the fortitude to deal with all their misery?
    This is another dimension to the life — the daily life — of the educated

Llorona. Because she's alone, people around her feel the liberty to extract from her emotional constitution for their own comfort and psychological needs. She—the educated *Llorona*—is supposed to feel perfectly okay about being the appendage in everyone's life—the someone who is there, especially for married heterosexual women whose needs at some junctures become so great they conveniently call their single (always accessible) friend when they desperately need someone to talk to. But where are they when I need them?

The last two days have been painful reminders. First, I get a call from X— recently divorced, her only child just left for college and here she is calling me because for the first time in eighteen years she's having to think about being alone! She's having a hard time living alone for the first time in her life. Suddenly, she can give a moment of reflection to what and how people who live alone go about constructing a meaningful life. She must really be in the thick of it because she even said, "Gosh, you can go a whole day without talking to anyone." What can I say? Welcome to my reality. I know I sound resentful—but I prefer to think I'm being observant! Where are they and where have they been in my daily struggles with solitude? Where are they when I, once again, have to plan and dread being alone for yet another holiday? To feel unloved for yet another birthday? They were all too busy—back then—to think about me—or to give me a call.

Yet I'm supposed to be here now, with open arms, ready to embrace yet another one into the world of solitude.

If I have energy reserves,
perhaps its because I earned them.
You want me to give you clues as to how to make your life work?
and how to make it feel worth it?
Alone?
My advice is expensive.
Any sense of self I have has been at great cost
and it's simply not available for distribution

April 6, 1996
I find some comfort in knowing I am not alone. There's a whole cadre of women—other educated *Lloronas* of the twentieth century, who had the historical audacity (and ovaries) to become thinkers. We are historical apertures, unwanted in our times, and adultresses to our culture and class.

Welcome to the Ivory Tower

Latina Anónima

THE GRADUATE EXPERIENCE is mortifying for probably most women. My entrance into the Ivory Tower went beyond the elitism, competitiveness, or insensitivity we often find in the culture of the academy. I nearly abandoned my intellectual vocation because of the ugly mix of sexism, racism, and neglect. I had to find my own path with mentors who were just as junior as I.

I entered graduate school in 1973, fresh from an excellent education at a small, private liberal arts college. Although I was nervous, the challenge of entering the best department in my discipline in the country excited me, as I had always done well in school. I arrived at the university full of hope and immediately called a well-known professor in the discipline with whom I intended to work. I assumed that he would be as glad to work with me as I looked forward to working with him, as he was a pioneer in Chicano Studies, my intended field. When we finally spoke on the phone, he refused even to meet with me. He explained that although his work was within the discipline, he was burned out by the politics of my department and he refused to work with any students unless they were from his own department. I was taken aback—there was no one else in my department whose research focused on Chicanos. I was cast adrift.

Nevertheless, I made my first appointment with my summer advisor. Since I had received a minority fellowship, I was selected to participate in a faculty mentor program where I would work closely with a senior member of my department, both of us receiving a stipend. Although his research expertise was totally different from my interests, I assumed he could guide me, and I cheerfully explained my own research interests. He asked to read my senior essay, which had focused on Chicanas. The essay wove a critique of the field with a theoretical formulation to guide my future research and called for politically engaged scholarship. My college advisor had praised my work and I was proud of it. The professor and I met the following week and he suggested we talk over lunch, hot dogs purchased from a stand near the department. Too polite to refuse the junk food, I joined him and we sat in the sun. "Well, let me start out by saying that I don't like people like you who come from ethnic studies," he blurted out. Acknowledging that it was unfair to judge a senior essay as if it were graduate work, he then proceeded to do exactly that. I choked down the greasy food as he rained denunciation on the manuscript and engaged in racial polemic rather than scholarly assessment. I drove home feeling demoralized.

Our required theory course was a veritable who's who in the discipline. Each student was required to make copies of her weekly paper for every other student in the seminar, much to our anxiety. A subtle but real hierarchy emerged early on in which the students who were most laudatory of the great scholars were praised, while the rest of us with critical comments became the troublemakers. In the middle of one early sharp debate, the professor intervened in the discussion: "If you want to change the world, then leave academia. The academy is the place for objective analysis by scholars unsullied by politics." By the end of the quarter our original perspectives had become blurred into bland, noncontroversial commentary that assessed various scholars' "contributions." More distressing, it became clear that the troublemakers were students of color and/or feminists and that we were sanctioned for speaking our minds. By the end of the first term I was so miserable that I considered transferring to another department, and I actually took out the forms to do so. A dear friend reminded me that this was one of the best departments on campus: "It's no better anywhere else. If you transfer now, all your work this term will be lost. Do what you have to do to meet their requirements, and be political elsewhere." So I began a strategy of choosing my battles, engaging in confrontation only if I thought it was appropriate. To this day I say that she saved me for the discipline.

I began forming a support network, helping to found a Chicana feminist collective and joining a mixed-gender reading group on Chicano Studies. Over time I struck up friendships with several white feminists and feminists of color, who had their own incredible stories of professorial insensitivity. And within the department I became a quiet student, aware that my views were seen as marginal to the discipline.

Despite my deepening alienation with the department, I passed my first-year exam, garnering praise for my skillful defense of my dissertation research, and handling one cranky senior professor's baiting questions with aplomb. The professor who approved my dissertation prospectus the following year characterized me as "more theoretically oriented than most graduate students." My fears of failure were beginning to subside.

Then I inadvertently became pregnant. This set off a debate within the department — could I keep my fellowship? Some professors actually said that I had decided to pursue a family rather than a career. To its credit, the department in the end established a policy of allowing women graduate students to retain their support even if they became pregnant. One professor chuckled, "We practically came out in support of motherhood and apple pie," oblivious to my embarrassment at the attention to my fertility. None of the male graduate students whose wives were pregnant or who already had children were subject to such scrutiny.

When I returned from conducting field research, I eagerly joined the department's dissertation seminar. My advisor suggested that I seek out another professor, one of the few women in the large department. I had avoided her previously because I had heard too many stories about her exploitation of graduate students — free gofer work, even serving dinners in her home. After we discussed my research, I realized that she couldn't be much help, but I pretended to be interested in her ruminations. As I was leaving, she asked, bluntly "Why haven't you come to see me sooner?" The implication was that I had passed her test, and now I should pay homage before she would deign to work with me. I made up something about knowing how busy she was, and besides her research was not very close to mine. As I walked out of her office, she said "Shame on you!" then spanked me on the butt and quickly closed the door behind me. I stood there totally stunned. I could not believe that this had actually happened. The irony is that if it had been a man, I would have reacted instinctively and probably would have belted him.

So I went back to my advisor, a man whose own research was worlds apart from mine. From a wealthy family and with pedantic bearing, with his pipe and pince-nez, he was the only faculty member on whom I could count to read my work and give me critical feedback. The ironies were piling up.

I arrived in town to get my dissertation cover page signed by my advisor. I was impatient and frustrated. I had moved to another state, following my partner whose part-time job was supposed to support us while I wrote my dissertation. I was pregnant again and the child would be born by cesarean section, the due date in the middle of the term, so finding a job myself would be out of the question. I spent that year learning discipline and how to write on my own. I carefully mapped out my schedule for writing the chapters and managed to produce four chapters in six months. I dutifully sent off each one to my advisor but never heard from him except a message through a fellow graduate student: "Tell her to keep writing." Unsure that my work was any good, I did. I ran into a fellow graduate student at a party and confided that I was having a difficult time writing. "Maybe you have nothing to say," he commented, and advised me to get involved in other projects. (This person has never finished his dissertation, so perhaps he was projecting his own anxieties?) So I struggled on by myself, showing my work only to a few trusted friends whose feedback was invaluable. When I finally finished the first draft of the entire dissertation, I proudly put it in the mail to my advisor three days before my son was born. Many weeks later my advisor responded, and it was not clear that he had actually read the whole dissertation since he had only a few minor editorial comments. I traveled to the university to get his signature. After quickly signing the form, he invited me to lunch at the faculty club. His self-satisfied grin suggested that he thought I would be honored.

I arrived on time and pretended that I hadn't noticed that I was the only female, the only nonwhite, and the only nonelderly person in the club. I feel like I'm in an old folks home, I thought to myself. My advisor opened the conversation by inviting me to call him by his first name. Ah, this is a coming-of-age ritual, I thought to myself. He proceeded to "review" my graduate career: "When you arrived you were so green," he noted. During the course of my research, he said, I had changed. I had totally departed from my original project and did life histories with women. And I took risks and included a discussion of my political activism with my subjects as part of the text. "You know, you really *became* a *Chacahna* while writing your dissertation," he observed. I blinked and looked at him in disbelief. You have absolutely no idea who I am, do you? I thought to myself. I guess that's a good thing, I rationalized to myself afterward. It probably saved me a lot of grief. Later I heard through a friend that in the letters of recommendation he had written on my behalf, he actually said that it was unclear what my contribution to my field would be. The kiss of death for an academic job. I stopped asking him for letters of recommendation.

I managed to land a postdoc and temporary job I found through my own Chicano and feminist networks. I began presenting my work at conferences in both areas and blossomed with the support of my peers and those barely more senior than I. We formed our own professional associations and caucuses within the disciplinary association, and I found a place where my work was valued. My children, who give me a wonderful, daily sense of the meaning of work and love, were another source of support as I constructed a life apart from the academy.

Then I applied for a job I really wanted. It was in an interdisciplinary department full of progressive people. When asked why they were interested in me, the most senior professor in the department said, with some puzzlement, "Because of the quality of your work." He did not realize that this was the first time anyone had ever said my work was good without equivocation.

It was so refreshing. And this department encouraged faculty to teach about power relations and inequality in all forms. I had found my niche. However, the search dragged on and I was getting worried. Since students were allowed to evaluate candidates and voice their opinions, they were privy to the faculty's assessment of the candidates and reported what my colleagues said about me. "We were disappointed with the pool," the chair of the search committee had said. I decided I didn't want to hear anymore. Finally I received a mysterious phone call from the departmental secretary. Could I meet with the faculty tomorrow morning, early? "There are a lot of ways to interpret the meaning of this meeting, but please keep it confidential," she said. I had no idea what to expect.

I arrived at the meeting and the group, all men and virtually all white, announced that from the field of 130 candidates they wanted to offer me the job. They were used to proceeding by consensus, however, and had not been able to reach consensus on this decision without some compromise. They needed to inform me of their critiques of my dissertation. Although I was familiar with criticism/self-criticism as practiced by left groups, I was puzzled by this unorthodox process in offering a job to a candidate. But, interested in the job, I gamely agreed to participate. It quickly became clear that this was not like a dissertation defense: every time I tried to defend or explain my work, I was cut off. They accused me of arrogance in not citing scholars they thought important, flawed theoretical formulation, problematic presentation of my research, on and on. Some points were appropriate, but many were totally without basis. I became flustered and defensive and very angry. By the end of the two-hour session I was reduced to tears and totally humiliated. They wanted me to think about their critiques and then give them my response to the job offer. They knew that I had another job offer at a very prestigious university, and they wanted to be honest with me about what they thought of my work. How could they know about the other offer? I had only received the verbal offer myself late the previous night and had told no one.

I went home and cried my eyes out, devastated. My partner ranted: "This is incredible! You should sue their asses. You should take the other job just to spite them." Then it clicked. This was a strategy to get me to accept the rival offer so the department could make an offer to the second candidate. So I dried my eyes, reapplied my makeup, and went back to campus and carried on like nothing had happened. I'll be damned if I let them get to me! I thought. Every man in that group, with the exception of the department chair, later apologized or expressed regret about what had happened in the meeting. With great chagrin, the senior member, who later became a respected mentor, said, "I never thought that it would get out of hand," and explained what had happened: the department chair was a personal friend of the second candidate, who was the lover of the chair's best friend, an influential scholar who had written a letter of support for her candidacy. The chair wanted to appoint her to keep in the good graces of his colleague. Little did my colleagues know that I had been sexually harassed in the other department at the other university that made me an offer, and during my interview had been asked if I would be willing to become chair of the department within a few years, that is, while an assistant professor. The prestigious university was offering me academic suicide, so that offer was never much of an option. Later, after I settled in, I swallowed my pride and approached the chair and asked for his concrete suggestions on how to improve my dissertation as I revised it for publication. He reiterated his previous points and made a telling comment: "You have to approach your work as if someone were coming at it with a knife. You have to defend your vulnerable points." I set my resolve to prove the faculty's low expectation wrong, even if it meant I would have to work twice as hard.

It is no wonder, then, that I'm annoyed when conservatives suggest that people of color somehow have had an easier time because of affirmative action. As I train my own graduate students, mainly women, I take care to be the mentor I never had and to give them support to find their own voices. When they are frustrated with professors who won't read their work, don't take them seriously, pull *movidas* for political reasons, or assume that they are not committed to their careers, I assure them that you can survive academia and still keep your integrity. Knowing where you come from is key to maintaining your balance in the face of institutional violence, along with nurturing alternative venues of support. These have kept me going all these years.

I Still Don't Know Why

Latina Anónima

I HAVE NEVER, NEVER spoken to anyone about this, but I was the victim of very aggressive sexual harassment when I was in graduate school. The perpetrator was one of my major professors. Until recently, I still had nightmares about this part of my life.

In these dreams, the common denominator is a feeling of utter disgust, of physical revulsion. I see this man again, always dressed in a dark suit, coming toward me with pleading eyes. He wants to embrace me, and I recoil violently (I always scream at him): "Don't you dare touch me!" I hear myself shouting while I put distance between us, close doors, escape. Sometimes his wife is in the dream, smiling like a classy lady, dressed in pink, unaware of the sordid secret. I wake up with the enormous relief of knowing that they are both dead now, that this cannot happen again, that I am safe. And also I awaken with the acid taste of revulsion in my mouth.

I felt so powerless when this was happening years ago, and at the same time so trapped into vulnerability. He would call me on the phone and invite me to his office, where he had a couch, and I would go. Or he would invite me to lunch to talk about literature, and what he really wanted—this was explicit—was to take me to his bedroom. I tried to talk to some of my fellow women students about it, and they wouldn't even acknowledge the problem. A couple of female students, who were also the victims of advances by other professors, and I went to see the provost at our university and expressed concern about these male professors we had, and he laughed us out of the office. In a very nice way, of course.

What has bothered me all this time is that I felt horribly guilty, because I gave in: I actually had a relationship with one of my professors in graduate school. For years I felt tainted, dirty, and a willing victim. I don't know why I consented to this relationship. Many times I asked myself, "Why am I doing this?" I admired the man, because he was such a talented intellectual and writer, but to this day I really don't know why I didn't run away from him. I still feel this terrible discomfort when I think about that time of my life, which was also so intense with the pressure of finishing a doctoral dissertation and getting a job. I think he really used me, but sometimes I have the sinking feeling that I used him too. I also have come to understand that I was very lonely and in need of someone to dialogue with. Some of the deep reasons for my consent are being revealed now, years later, as very human. At the time, I was wrenched by the feeling of belonging nowhere; only intellectually could I claim some space of my own. No family, no country, no moral support. And this man validated me as a person and as a fledgling scholar, even if he also pursued me for his own needs.

It's good to talk about this "dirty secret," even without names, because I have blamed myself for so long. It has been only by talking to other women that I have realized that I suffered at the hands of someone who abused his power in an academic setting. And I wasn't the only one with this particular man. Promptly after I told him I never wanted to see him again — after my oral defense of my dissertation, after I had a job — he started on another young doctoral student. And she also gave in.

What is it with these powerful males? I hate to think about what we have been put through. He was Latino to boot. And his victims were of any nationality or culture. It has been very difficult to overcome this pervasive guilt of mine, that I was really the cause of this episode and not the victim. Nobody talked about sexual harassment in those days, and of course the men went undisturbed about their dirty little games.

I still don't know why. I still can't understand fully why these things happen. Especially because I know that, throughout the years in classrooms and in offices, a student will come along who will seem attractive, intelligent, eager to spend time and energy with us. But as far as I know, women professors are not that prone to engage in relationships with students. Or is it that we are more discreet in how we reconcile power and vulnerability?

The academic women I know who have become involved with students have been quite careful in extricating themselves from conflicts of interest. Most of all, they are not "shameless pursuers" of flesh but acquiesce to consensual relationships without exercising the boldest prerogatives of power. Most of all, I have known them to be sincerely motivated by deep affection.

Human emotions and needs being what they are, however, the subject of love and sex on campus has been explored only tenuously, at best, for women professionals, let alone for Latinas. We are keenly aware of our extreme vulnerability and of the witchhunts that would result.

As for our past, it was a way of life in the hallowed ivy halls during the years we were in graduate school. Why some of us succumbed to the dirty power plays, I still don't know.

Lessons Learned from an Assistant Professor

Gloria Holguín Cuádraz

IN THE CONTEXT of your department:

— You are expected to remain silent, especially in department meetings when issues of a moral, ethical, or political character come up. Despite the fact you have traveled mountains, swum rivers, and leaped flying buildings, demonstrated your aptness, ability, wit, etc. to earn your Ph.D., don't assume the union card grants you a right to have a voice. In fact, just in case you think you're entitled to have a voice, you better find something else to feel entitled to.

— Try not to observe or care that senior faculty do the least amount of work.

— Whatever you do, do not expect that your colleagues will think collectively about the good or vision for the department.

— Be prepared for the young white men in the department to receive higher rankings for merit pay than you get, even though your record is comparable (and of course, your service is triple what all of them have, combined).

— The biggest character trait you need to develop as an assistant professor is SELFISHNESS. Remember, no one else, no cause, no political conflict, no humanitarian emergency, not even your own family, is more important than whatever you have going on for the next few lines on your vitae.

— Despite the fact everyone will tell you to say NO more often, be prepared to PAY if you say NO.

— Expect that a cloak of secrecy is the underlying rule with respect to just about every significant or insignificant decision made at the departmental level. If you dare to articulate what you know everyone else knows, sitting in those departmental meetings, you will offend their ever-so-genteel culture of "appropriate" behavior. Before you know it, you yourself are participating in the culture of secrecy so crucial to academic existence.

Lessons on "Our Own Men"

— Warning: Now, first things first, realize that in their views, you may appear to them as a "young th'ang" who thinks she knows a lot, but really doesn't, because you see, you haven't "fought the wars" they have. You don't have those illustrious stories of having "shamed the administration" or having "mobilized the community." Hence, any questions you raise about the merits of their decisions or any presumptions about their "strategies" will not be received gracefully.

— Realize that RUMORS are the best weapons and artillery "our men" have to use against you. Similar to the ways in which white women involved in the Ku Klux Klan utilized "whispering squads" to mount economic boycotts and defeat black businesses in Indiana, you can count on some of your men to engage in this kind of fabricated, paranoid warfare against you and others who dare challenge their authority.

— Beware: any and all family dysfunctionalities you thought you might have been running away from when you decided to pursue your Ph.D. will only be duplicated for you via the rhetoric of *"la familia"* — in meeting after meeting.

— Be prepared to notice how the women who are acknowledged publicly and validated by the men are not only those who are male-identified but, moreover, those who stare blankly into space — seeing nothing and hearing nothing.

— Of course, be prepared to find out that you will be represented by "our men" on countless occasions to which you were never privy. In other words, representation without consultation will be the modus operandi.

— Even when your work is in similar areas of expertise, do not expect any of "your men" to engage you in an "intellectual" conversation about your work, much less be interested in collaborating with you. Don't bother to be puzzled by this; you will only waste good brain cells.

— Finally, expect that any criticisms or observations you voice publicly will either be infantilized (attributed to your junior status) or genderized (attributed to your special needs as a woman) and will therefore be largely ignored.

Don't You Like Being in the University?

Latina Anónima

Journal entries

OCTOBER 1

First month at my first university job, fresh out of graduate school, hotbed of student radicalism. First service assignment to the committee that sets policy on financial aid. Good. Minority students need support. First meeting in a building on the fringes of campus. I arrive late, lost, mouth apologies with breathless charm. I'm the only woman, Spanish surnamed, the junior-most member of the committee, one of two voices from the margins. The other is an African American scientist . . . male . . . tenured . . . composed. Chair of the committee is a fair-haired professor who seems like an alright guy; his scholarly interests include black male writers.

Chair explains our charge: to "streamline" support packages for incoming minority students. The special categories to increase diversity are problematic, we're told. Part of a quota system. Fair-haired chair thinks we can maintain the category for the gifted top 5 percent. I'm trying hard to keep cool, maintain professional decorum. Today can't help it. It just comes out: "That's just another elitist strategy to reproduce privilege! We need to make quality education accessible to a broader cross-section of minority students. This campus is so homogeneous, my god!" Take note: when your chest tightens and your voice jumps above alto . . . chill the shrill, kiddo. Black colleague zeroes in on the charts; questions the method for gathering the statistics. Damn! Gotta learn that technique, but I hate statistics.

OCTOBER 15

Just learned how inappropriately I've behaved in my new professorial role. First cocktail party this afternoon. Sunny afternoon . . . new faculty cordially invited . . . party hosted by the ADMINISTRATION. Feeling out-of-class and terrorized. Breathe deep and walk through the "Office of the Provost." Smoothly mingling crowd of administrators and faculty, all senior to me, all totally comfortable with each other. Fast, find a shy soul and disappear into a darker corner of the room. Trying to be a good girl and appear when summoned, eh? Late afternoon sun streaming through the geometrically beveled windowpanes, kaleidoscopic crystals dancing over the whole affair.

Five steps over the threshold, I'm intercepted from the side by an outstretched hand. It's Fair-haired Committee Chair. "Nice to see you! Come, have a drink." His mouth stretches out to the corners of his cheeks in smooth, perfect tension. He finger-steers me slowly, deftly, over toward the table.

"You know, I've been wondering, don't you like being in the University?" "Sure I do. Why do you ask?" Coy answer. I'm disarmed, fumble a nervous laugh. This bastard has maneuvered me into female paralysis. Irony and quick wit not my forte. Shit.

"Well, you seem so upset in the committee." He feigns a coy counterstrategy, absolutely sure of himself. His blue eyes pin me to my spine. One deft snipe and he's branded me with a red question mark. I wonder if others can see it. How long will I have to wear it? How long will I remember that question?

JUNE, SIX YEARS LATER

This year I came up for tenure. Fair-haired Committee Chair got promoted to Dean, empowered to brand me once again. He submitted my work to a second outside review. He claimed "quality of scholarship," but he and I know. . . . Too contentious; always upset; too strident an advocate for minority access to this prestigious, gentile institution; not his team player, wouldn't even play with him. . . . So, I won't gain permanent entry myself. Fair-haired Dean continued his scholarship on black male writers and his rise through the ranks.

Temporary Latina

Ruth Behar

No one wanted the temporary job of acting director of Latino Studies while they searched, yet again, for a permanent director of the program. It was a humid day in early August and I was sitting with my colleagues in the program, all of us in shorts and t-shirts, around a hodgepodge of metal office tables. I had come to the meeting with some regrets, leaving my mother and my grandmother to wait for me at home. They had flown in, my mother from New York, my grandmother from Miami, for my son's fifth birthday party. We were enjoying our days together; my mother was busy stuffing my freezer with blintzes and stuffed tomatoes, and my grandmother had found relief for her chronic back problems sleeping on the futon in the guest room. I had vowed not to respond to any interruptions. But they phoned me at home several times and insisted the meeting was urgent and wouldn't take long and if I cared about the future of Latino Studies I should be there.

All heads are bent as if in prayer. The Anglo-American woman professor who heads American Culture, of which Latino Studies is a subunit, breaks the silence. If we don't appoint a director today, she says in a lamentful tone, the program will not be able to continue. The senior male faculty, obvious choices for the job, bow out quietly; they are going to be on leave during the coming year or have other pressing commitments. The eyes turn briefly to the non-tenured Chicana, Cubana, and Cubano professors, but we all realize it's not right to burden them with the job. And then I feel the eyes landing on me. "How about you, Ruth?" the chair says. My colleagues sitting next to me smile encouragingly, while a senior colleague, an Argentino who's held the job before, looks at me with sympathy. Before I can think of how to answer, my Chicana colleague whispers, "Do it. You'd be great. Don't let the program down."

Recalling how my university refused to hire me as a Latina, first because I'm Jewish, and second because Cubans no longer count as a needy Latin group, I feel an urge to take the job, to be Latina with a vengeance. I picture myself coming into the office wearing a Carmen Miranda headdress, or piling jewelry like thorns around my neck in the style of Frida Kahlo (who no one seems to remember, in this moment of Fridamania, was half-Jewish).

I steal a glance at a colleague who is a puertorriqueña and an associate professor like me. She's knowledgeable and would be the perfect choice for director, I think, wondering why her name hasn't come up. I'm not sure what to make of her expression. Everyone's eyes are still upon me. I realize I haven't answered yet. "Maybe Frances and I could do it together, as codirectors" I say, not quite sure whether to phrase my sentence as a question or a hesitation. Frances pauses and then says, "That would be fine, but I'm going to be on leave in the fall." It hadn't occurred to me to say from the beginning that I wouldn't be able to take the job for the same reason. "Actually, that's my problem too," I now say. "I'm going to be on leave for the year." A sigh of despondency fills the room and I hear myself adding, "Well, maybe we could each give up a little of our leave time. For the sake of the program. But only if there's no one else who can do it."

As soon as I'm done speaking, our chairwoman brightly pops out of her seat and says, "Good, so you'll think about it?" I nod my head and Frances nods hers. It dawns on me that a maybe in this context is a roaring yes. The heavy air in the room, whose only window faces the computer center, seems to lighten, as though a breeze were blowing in from the Caribbean. People edge their seats back, waiting for the signal to leave. The decision has been made, it seems. Now I'm worrying about what I've gotten Frances into. Her baby, I realize, is only six months old. She needs to get writing done and so do I. We're both going to be on leave, just like the men, but somehow, in our case, that disclaimer seems to carry less weight.

The chairwoman calls the meeting to an end and rushes toward us and hugs us joyously at the same time like a bridal couple. She tells us she realizes it's unfair for us to give up our leave time and that she'll try her best to see if there's anyone else who can do it. Of course we both know that she won't find anyone else, but with our good Latina manners we politely thank her all the same.

And so begins a year in which two women supposedly on leave from their academic obligations give up several hours of their time a week trying to maintain the strengths of the program and introduce some new energy. Our first action is to change the name of the program from Latino Studies to Latina/Latino Studies, in obvious support for the Latinas in the program and for the many Latina writers and artists whose work we admire. This meets with some criticism. We are told by the chairwoman that the names of programs can't be changed just like that; things need to be discussed and viewed from all sides and voted upon democratically and approved at various bureaucratic levels, but informally and provisionally we may use the new name.

We are not discouraged. We decided to start a series of Friday lectures by Latina and Latino faculty and students in order to build a sense of community. And we begin to think more ambitiously, of building a library of important books and essays, of offering funding to students to do research, of having essay contests, of inviting outside speakers, of organizing a retreat for the Latinas, but immediately we learn that the program is pathetically underfunded. And we learn it is underfunded because its intellectual existence needs constantly to be justified before the administration and our colleagues, some of whom feel — though they won't dare tell you in so many words — that the program's main purpose is to serve as a counseling service for those Latino and Latina students brave enough to set foot in the "Harvard of the Midwest."

In the end, I never do get to sport the Carmen Miranda headdress or weigh my neck down with crucifying jewelry in the style of Frida Kahlo. Office life doesn't lend itself to zany exoticism or high drama. The only departure from the everyday drabness comes on the Day of the Dead, when a Chicano artist we have invited sets up an altar complete with candles, candy skulls, and pink and yellow paper cut-outs of dancing skeletons.

In the director's office I set up another altar in the corner in memory of my comadre Pancha, from Mexico. Her eyes, foggy from cooking tortillas on an outdoor fire, didn't see the car that killed her one morning as she ran across the highway to catch a bus. I use a bright red scarf with the imprint of the Virgin of Guadalupe as a background and place on the table a picture of my comadre, some bananas and bread, a lime wooden car driven by skeleton figures, and a can of Coke (*porque a mi comadre le gustaba su Coca*). I leave the altar up all year. As I sit talking to students or signing letters, I feel my comadre's smoke-filled eyes resting on me in that office with the gray metal desks and chairs, where the bookshelves stayed empty.

I am glad to be around the small but vibrant group of faculty and students — mostly Latinas — who care about the program. At the Friday seminars I find a community where I can hear thoughtful and sometimes heated debates about identity politics, feminist conflicts, stereotypes of the Latino community, and the geographies of difference between American Latins and Latin Americans. As I listen, I realize that I've been hungry for such talk for a long time.

But it pains me to realize that some of those colleagues who participate most passionately only have visiting positions or lectureships. There is a Colombiana professor who teaches Latino film courses and an Argentina professor who teaches courses about Latino health issues, and both of them are always on the edge of their seats, waiting for their positions to be renegotiated from year to year. The Chilena professor who pioneered a course about U.S. Latinas and has taught for twenty years at the university as a lecturer in Spanish wonders whether she can rightfully identify as a Latina because of her middle-class background. How do I tell her that she became a Latina the day she arrived on this side of the border and was told her Latin American degree was worth nothing?

Yet I understand her predicament. I too am always wondering: do I, by calling myself a Latina, take away the "real" Latina identity of someone who needs to claim that identity for her very survival, self-preservation, and self-worth? Yet why should my colleague, or I, feel that our Latina identity is somehow optional? That we are temporary Latinas? Our Latina identity is not a garment that we choose to wear or discard at will. And yet we are often made to feel that way.

At stake is the question of who counts as a Latina or a Latino; in current affirmative action terms, you have to be Chicana or Chicano, or Puerto Rican, to qualify. Lately, two of my colleagues in Latina/Latino Studies, a Chicano (who is a convert to Judaism) and a puertorriqueña (who is married to a Chicano), have begun to put pressure on the university administration to redefine the meaning of Latino and Latina, so that fellowships can become available not just to Chicanos and puertorriqueños but to a broader range of needy students, including Guatemaltecos, Hondureños, Salvadoreños, Peruanos, and working-class Cubanos (of whom there are many from Hialeah and elsewhere who contradict the "success story" Cuban stereotype).

While I agree with my colleagues and support their efforts, I feel that out of respect for the struggles of Chicanos and puertorriqueños in this country, I, as a Cubana, cannot be the one to lobby for such expansions of the meaning of Latinidad. It would be an act of terrible presumption, an erasure of history. I must acknowledge the preferential treatment that was given to Cuban immigrants relative to other Latinos because of our symbolic capital during the Cold War as refugees from communism — although many Cubans will tell you that the only reason we got the red-carpet treatment was because the United States "owed it to us" for abandoning the Cuban insurgents at Bay of Pigs.

In truth, our individual Latino ethnic identities in this country have always been a function of our positions relative to the different histories of U.S. colonization in our home countries. Indeed, as the United States grows increasingly xenophobic, the border is being closed to Mexicans crossing over in search of honest work at the same time that the red carpet is being pulled from under the feet of Cubans still fleeing Fidel Castro. In recent years we have watched Cubans desperately seeking to cross over to the United States on leaky rafts. What difference is there any more between Cuban *balseros* and Mexican *mojados?* Clearly, as far as the dominant society and the U.S. government are concerned, we are all part of the same Latin horde that is threatening to overrun the country with the Spanish we can't seem to rub off our tongues and the dizzyingly hot salsas we both eat and dance.

Under these conditions, our identity as Latinas and Latinos will need to become stronger. Acknowledging a common Latinidad defined from within as a form of resistance, rather than from without as a form of negative stereotyping, is a step in a healing process. Our wounds arise from the genealogies of distrust and hatred that divide our various communities and that we have inherited along with the riches of our diverse cultures. Acknowledging a common Latinidad is a refusal to reproduce those genealogies that only pour salt on our wounds. It is a desire to give ourselves a chance to know one another as human beings and not as the absurd little boxes we are obliged to check off on the United States census. It is a process of learning to recognize the differences in our national origins and privileges while being able to identify compassionately with each other's sufferings and longings. All of us, in pain, loss, and grief, have carried the "other America" on our backs to these United States of America.

Latina/Latino Studies offers us a waiting room at the border where we can put down our string bags and suitcases and boxes, straighten our backs, and together stand tall, so we can cross over to the other side. Being involved in a program of Latina/Latino Studies I come to see just how many common experiences I share with others whose backgrounds, according to administrative categorizing, would seem to be different from mine. Many Latina/Latino students are the first in their families to be studying for an advanced degree, and they have a gentle, unassuming manner, a seriousness of purpose, and a profound vulnerability that touch me deeply. In their midst, I am reminded of my own beginnings, and my own struggle to become an educated woman.

When a Chicana student, in a shaky voice that is trying to hold back tears, tells me about how a professor insinuated that if he lent her his unpublished writings about a particular topic, she might plagiarize them, it is all I can do not to cry with her. I can't say to her, "Don't take it personally," because she's hurt to the bottom of her soul, and because I remember my own hurt when I was told by a professor, who thought she was being "objective," not to bother taking any more courses in philosophy because I lacked the appropriate "mental nature."

After our last Friday seminar is over, I am approached by a student I know only from seeing her at Latina/Latino Studies events. She stops me at the door and tells me she's been wanting to ask me how I feel about being in the program. For the past year she has assumed I'm not Latina. I, on the other hand, have assumed that she is Latina. "I'm half Philippine, half Anglo," she tells me. "And I work on Puerto Rico. I'm dark, so I sort of look Puerto Rican." I tell her that I'm Cuban. "Oh, so you're a Latina?" she says, obviously surprised. I don't give her a chance to ask about my name or any of the other things that make my Latina identity suspect. I go ahead and complete my confession. "But I'm also Jewish," I say, and quickly add, "so I never feel totally authentic."

This encounter, coming at the end of a long year of administrative work for which I discovered I am definitely not suited, was both deeply troubling and illuminating. It made me wonder yet again: am I just a temporary Latina? A part-time Latina filling a space until the full-time Latinas can come on board? The student, assuming from my name or looks that I was a non-Latina co-directing a Latina/Latino Studies program, had, curiously, expected to share a common bond with me. And I, in turn, had made assumptions about the student's identity based on her looks and the fact of her participation in Latina/ Latino Studies. Sadly, I had played into the racial and racist stereotyping game, and, worse, I had internalized the university administration's view of our program as a counseling service rather than as a serious academic discipline. It hadn't occurred to me that the student might not have been Latina because I expected that only "a real Latina" would have intellectual interests in Latina/Latino studies. Not only did I take it for granted that the student, being brown-skinned, was a Latina, I took it for granted that her color made her more authentically Latina than me.

Afterward it bothered me that I had felt obliged to apologize for being Jewish. Why should my being Jewish compromise my Latina identity? Haven't we gone beyond the authenticity contests of the past? Haven't we accepted hybridity and mixed identity and mestiza consciousness?

The problem is that current racial ideology in the United States classifies Jews as "whites" and Latinas/Latinos as "people of color." In the course of assimilating successfully into American society, Jews have become "whites," along with other European groups, like the Irish and the Italians, who earlier in the century were viewed as "nonwhite." Latinos and Latinas, on the other hand, have maintained, at once freely and forcibly, their claim on difference within American society, a difference that may include but is not limited to color. As a Cubana, and therefore a Latina, I'm presumably a person of color. Yet I'm equivocally of color, because middle-class Cubans of the first emigrant wave are thought to have "made it" enough to become "white." But as a Jew, certainly, aren't I a white woman? I'm equivocally white, too, it turns out, especially if I listen to those Jewish critics who invoke the recent historical memory of our racial otherness as people of color, lest we forget too quickly how we were viewed only half a century ago, and how, indeed, we are still viewed by neo-Nazi groups today.

All of this is very ironic for me, because the reason I came to be born in Cuba is that my grandparents could not enter the United States in the 1920s because of racist quotas that sought to curtail Jewish immigration. Seventy years ago, my grandparents were not "white enough" to be granted entrance into the United States. Yet, in Cuba, where the turn-of-the-century white ruling class worried about the rise of the black population on the island, they were welcomed as white Europeans. Being white is always relative to how the "dark other" is constructed. Now, two generations later, having come to the United States with symbolic capital as a Cuban refugee from communism, I am "too white" and "too Jewish" to be authentically Latina.

I remember how a Jewish American colleague laughed and sarcastically said *Mazal Tov* to me when he heard I'd become codirector of Latino Studies. American Jews always have trouble accepting the Cuban part of my identity. They think it's a joke. They can't believe it's real. They want me to just be Jewish and be done with it. Not to complicate things. To finally admit to my "essential" identity and stop kidding myself about being Latina. Yet another ostensibly well-meaning but much more vicious assumption was voiced by a different Jewish American colleague, who said I was just like her, and that I was too successful to be a Latina—as if not being successful is the definition of a Latina!

It is precisely in such situations, which seek to turn me into a temporary Latina, when I most fiercely take hold of my Latina identity with all the determination of the Virgin of Guadalupe crushing the ugly snake underfoot. The ad of my childhood was "You don't have to be Jewish to like rye bread." So who says you have to be Catholic or Mexican to invoke *La Guadalupana?* I say: Any success I've had has come not in spite of my being Latina but because I am Latina—a Latina who grew up with a belly filled with black beans and rice, a Latina whose prayers, when she remembers to say them, for the gifts of light, bread, and wine, are always uttered in Hebrew with the cadences of the Spanish her banished Sephardic ancestors stubbornly kept speaking, even in their exile.

Dispelling the *Sombras,*
Grito mi nombre con rayos de luz

Inés Hernández Avila

Erasure, *el hecho de borrar la vida de alguien, hacer como que nunca existió, como que nunca estuvo, nunca pensó, nunca habló, nunca cantó, nunca bailó, nunca tuvo, ni tiene, presencia en la historia de su pueblo.*[1]

Momentos cósmicos que borran, revelando traiciones.[2]

— "If I don't acknowledge you, you don't exist. If you don't exist, I don't have to recognize your work, or your worth. This is especially important if I want to take sole credit for any ideas you might have had, as I incorporate them into mine. It is also important if your ideas impinge upon mine in such a way, were I to admit this, I would have to alter my own interpretations radically. I have gained positive attention for my analyses, so your ideas would disturb mine, and cause me to share the light of notice. I will therefore turn my back on you. Anyway, your name is not as known as mine, I have a more widespread audience, it is easy to ignore you. I am building my own reputation, and I am at the point of being able to anoint persons into being. If I say you exist, then you exist, but only when I say so."

— "If I recall your name and speak it, it will create a link with me now. It will remind people I knew you, I was close to you, it may remind them how much I love(d) you. Even though we (along with other *compañeras y compañeros*) made history together, my relationship with you is (was), to me, utterly personal. You are (were) a part of me, so it is enough that I am named when the story is told. You are the silent, intimate part of me that I will keep to myself. Surely you understand."

— "You are a woman. What you do, what you think, cannot be as important as what I do, what I think. Besides, . . . you did not give in to me, you did not

Dispelling the Shadows, I Shout My Name with Rays of Light

1. The act of erasing someone's life, pretending as if she never existed, as if she was never there, as if she never thought, she never talked, she never sang, she never danced, she never had, nor does she have, a presence in the history of her people.

2. Cosmic moments that erase, revealing treacheries.

let me have my way with you. I could have given you anything. I could have ensured that your name would be recorded. That you are forgotten is no one's fault but your own. You made your choices *y te chingaste.*"

— "You are a woman. Women are extensions of men. They carry out the grand ideas that come to men, so that men do not have to worry themselves with such mundane aspects of struggle. Men, after all, are the leaders, as everyone knows. It doesn't matter that we have worked side by side, thinking together, organizing together, visioning together. In my mind, you have always been below me. Don't tell me you didn't know?"

Testimonio de una desaparecida

At a Modern Language Association meeting many years ago, I met a white woman who is recognized for her scholarship on Native American women's literature. In conversation with her, she discovered that I am Nez Perce and Mexican. In an unabashedly condescending tone she then commented, "Oh, you're one of those." I said, "Excuse me?" She said, "Oh, well, you know, you're Indian if you're at an Indian gathering, and Mexican if you're at a Chicana gathering." I responded furiously to her, yet I know her comment represents a largely held suspicion of persons who are Native American and Mexican, as if the very union of my parents was an intentionally subversive gesture meant to disrupt neatly positioned structures of culture and power. In the face of such a threat, the ranks close to oppose admission.

I have found my voice silenced by both Native and Mexican/Chicana individuals and organizations. The message, directed to me overtly, through the chilling process of erasure, is that I cannot belong to both communities. This message does not surface so much in my families, although in my Mexican family there is clearly a discomfort at the idea of "Indianness" (Indian-hating is alive and well in Mexican/Chicano and Latino communities). My dad's family, those who even broach the subject of "Indians," don't really know what "Indian" is. In recent years, moved perhaps by my work in Native American Studies, a couple of my relatives from Texas have sent my mom presents with "Indian themes." Their eyes cannot discern what is beautiful and what is horrid in Indian representations, so what they have sent is replete with ugly stereotypical images of Native people. My mother has been left speechless by these gifts, as have I, at the same time we realize that these relatives were sincerely searching for a present-day connection with us. My Mexican family had their Indian heritage erased from their midst during my great-grandparents' generation. My great-grandmother, my father's father's mother, is said to have been *"pura india,"* but no one knows anything else about this dreaded identity. Upward mobility could not include an Indian presence.

The all-too-familiar equation resounds deeply in many, many Mexicans: *India = Bruta, Estúpida, Tonta, Pata Rajada,* or the even more fearful *Bruja, Diabla.*[3] The other side of this infuriatingly predictable and tiresome coin is the romanticized version of the Noble *India,* the arch *curandera,* the one attuned to the earth and issues of the spirit, although this is not a common image among the majority of Mexicans or Latinos today. It is certainly not an image sustained by my Mexican family. It is sustained, to a large extent, in Chicana/o intellectual circles, however, wherein those of us who are identifiably Native come to represent *"las cosas del espíritu,"* at the same time there is little regard for our intellect, as if the two, the mind and the spirit, are inherently disparate, and even antagonistic, entities. Since I do work with spirit, for some people *se les ha hecho fácil borrar de un golpe mi trabajo intelectual.*[4] "We'll ask Inés to do the blessing, that will be her part of the program."

Borrándome, me borran como si fuera un suspiro en el aire, nada más. En la comunidad chicana, junto con la razón, a veces mano a mano con la conciencia, la ignorancia también camina abiertamente.[5] Not just with respect to me, but in regard to anyone or anything that disturbs essential definitions of raza. I feel the ignoring in my core, *en mi corazón. "Tú no tienes el análisis que queremos. Te atreves a insistir en ese algo que dices que es la fuerza de los pueblos indígenas de las Américas. Dices que las comunidades indígenas no requieren misioneros ni de la derecha ni de la izquierda, que tienen perspectivas de soberanía y autonomía que podrían servir como base de una nueva visión milenaria. Te tenemos que borrar. Además, no quieres ayudarnos a imaginar rituales, y autonombrar líderes espirituales, no importa si muchos de ellos están peligrosamente perpetuando viejos patrones de opresión. Lo único diferente es que andan vestidos de aztecas, y pretendiendo una nueva mexicanidad. Nos exiges que hay actualmente conocimientos indígenas muy profundos que están a la mano para estudiar, pero requieren mucha disciplina para lograr. Eso es demasiado difícil. Te tenemos que borrar."*[6]

So many erasures and incredible ironies. What might be surprising is that Mexicans are as hated by many Native people as Indians are hated by many, if

3. Indian=Brute, Stupid, Dumb, Poor and Barefoot, or . . . Witch, Devil
4. it's been easy for them to erase, with one blow, my intellectual work
5. Erasing me, they do so as if I were a sigh in the air, nothing more. In the Chicana/o community, along with reason, hand in hand with consciousness, ignorance walks openly.
6. You don't have the analysis we want. You dare to insist upon that 'something' you say is the strength of the indigenous peoples of the Americas. You say indigenous communities don't need missionaries from the right or the left, that they have perspectives on sovereignty and autonomy that could serve as a basis for a new millennial vision. We have to erase you. And furthermore, you don't want to help us imagine rituals, or self-name spiritual leaders, no matter that many of them are perpetuating old patterns of oppression, the only difference is that they're dressed as Aztecs, and pretending a new Mexicanness. You insist to us that there are actually profound indigenous knowledge-systems that could be studied near at hand, but to become well-versed in them requires much discipline. That's too hard. We have to erase you.

240   Inés Hernández Avila

not most, Mexicans. This hatred, manifested as an intense aversion, an over-powering repulsion, was set in motion intentionally as a measure of control through the colonial project; it has been systematically enforced ever since, "casting" people in roles antagonistic to each other on the basis of blood and culture. "You're not Indian enough. You speak Spanish. Why? You talk about your Mexicanness. Why? You're tainted by *mestizaje,* even though you identify as a Native woman of this hemisphere. It doesn't matter, we will erase you. You will not be considered a Native writer, if we can help it. It doesn't matter that many of us who accuse you are mixed bloods ourselves, some of us Mexican, too, like you, but we won't admit it. It doesn't matter if you have a real family base on the reservation, sometimes more than many of us. It doesn't matter if you walk with your head held high, your mother's daughter, tall and proud of your Indianness. We will still erase you, because you will not erase your Mexican father, your Mexican culture, you will not stop speaking and singing in Spanish. You insist on calling attention to the Indians in Mex-ico, in the South. Why? They are not as real as we are. We erase you."

And, sometimes *mujeres* do to each other what we accuse the men often of doing to us. It is outrageous enough when many of our *hermanos,* our male colleagues (not all), do the unfortunately expected, casting their patriarchally trained *ojos* out into the world to engage in their assessments of our peoples' *situación(es),* and in the breadth of their scope, only see themselves and other men like them as actors/players/leads. These are the unequivocal *machistas,* the ones whose "handsome little masculine heads" articulate the lofty ideas, but who can't figure out, for the life of their helpless, less-than-ingratiating-little-boy selves, how to do the detail work that translates the lofty ideas to empirical reality, and what's more, who remain almost completely unaware that there are any details to be worked out, until some woman (or many women), tired of being credited only as supporting cast, when they them-selves have also actually contributed to the lofty ideas, remind(s) them, in no uncertain terms, that there is work to do. It is bad enough that after thirty years of so-called people's struggle, there are still so many men (and even women) who do not have a clue that "people" includes women.

What's worse is when we women do unto each other what we would not, under any circumstances, have done unto us. When we do not give each other credit for our work, our *palabras,* our voices, when we pretend a sister has not written or accomplished something because it is easier to act as if she doesn't exist. If her work is recognized then it has to be dealt with, it has to be considered as part of the overall production and discourse. I have had Chicana and Native women scholars, intellectuals, treat me with devoted friendship, and yet, as they pursue their own work, they ignore mine, as if I had not spoken, as if I had not written. I have had an esteemed Chicana colleague tell me proudly that she acknowledged me in a published article, only to find out that the recognition is to me as a friend, a *"comadre,"* and I am named in a footnote by my first name only. It is not that I don't value her friendship, but the erasure of my full name, to me, is an erasure of my engagement in intellectual work. For those of us who work as intellectuals, writers, artists, organizers, in academia, or in the larger community, we know how hard it is to have visibility. We are the ones naming, and we should be naming as many names as we know, for it is our power to recognize. If we do not explode the clouds that surround us, dispelling the shadows, so that our faces can be seen, our voices heard, and our bodies of work known, who will do it?

Y luego, the most violent erasures. There are the erasures *que nacen de la falta de conciencia,* but then there are the ones que *nacen de la maldad y la cobardía, los que hacen sangrar el corazón, cada gota llorando la desolación,*[7] causing the spirit to go so deeply inward that it is impossible to speak. The body, upon such an offense, wants only invisibility, as the mind takes in the magnitude of the betrayal, and the spirit wails in anguished silence. There have been these times for me, these erasures of my presence, these articulations of my insignificance as a human being, as a woman. I will mention just one story. In the early eighties, when I told my movement friends I had been physically beaten by a respected and supposedly *firme* veteran organizer, the men to whom I turned, my face and body covered with bruises, told me they wouldn't get involved because it was clearly a personal matter. This same man had raped me previously, when I was recovering from surgery and helplessly drugged with pain medication. When he got off my lifeless body, he told me, "You have an interesting style." My mind and spirit went so far away from my body to escape, as much as I could, the consciousness of his violation of me that I could not even speak of the rape for years.

I ended up moving out of this town, where I had been a recognized community activist and organizer, and he stayed, above reproach. I am quite clear that his actions against me were eminently political — *de una u otra manera me iba a chingar,* because otherwise he would have to deal with me as an equal. We were both involved in the Native American and Chicano communities, we were both recognized voices. A major advantage he had over me was that I am a woman and, during that time, a single woman (a mother, also, but in terms of my presence in the community, I did not have a man, a husband, a partner, to back me up). *Dice el dicho, "El hombre no pierde como la mujer."*[8] As a single woman, living a fairly complete life in the Chicano/a community during that time, asking no one's permission for my comings and goings, any woman's

---

7. There are the erasures that are born from a lack of consciousness, but then there are the ones that are born from malice and cowardice, the ones that make the heart bleed, each drop weeping the desolation.

8. The saying goes, 'A man doesn't lose like a woman does.'

issue I might raise (or any single woman might raise) was immediately personalized, because my single status, my freedom of movement, made me suspect. *¿Quién me mandaba andar sola y libre?*[9] I got what I asked for. Single women got what they asked for. This is what the men, and probably many of the (married) women, thought. It was not hard, then, for this man to exercise his *táctica para desaparecerme.*[10] My voice had to be silenced, my presence had to be erased. I had to leave so that he could stay, representing what went on between us as my wanting him and not being able to have him. This is the information that has come to me over the years. He says my story is a lie meant to hurt him out of spite.

Transmutations and Awakenings

It has taken me a long time and much dedication, but I have found myself again, *y me tengo tanto cariño.* The path has been arduous, *porque ha sido un camino de (re)conocimiento, un camino hacia la conciencia de mí misma, de todo a mi alrededor, ésta es mi meta, adonde se me es posible. Ser consciente físicamente, emocionalmente, intelectualmente, espiritualmente es un reto tremendo en esta vida, en esta tierra. Para mí, ser humana es el trabajo de amor más grande que me toca mientras tenga cuerpo, mientras tenga vida.*[11]

I am no longer struck dumb, no longer mute in shock, frozen in fear, immobile from pain, stilled with outrage at the erasures that are born of ill will, of hatred, of violence. My voice is with me now *constantemente,* strong and vibrant. I am caring for my body like I never have, building its strength, its courage. *Cuando contemplo mi vida, sé también que no todo ha sido doloroso. Me pongo a reflexionar sobre los tiempos pasados, y encuentro muchas instancias de felicidad y victoria. Es curioso como algunos momentos quedan grabados mucho más que otros.*[12]

Many years ago, I used to sing with a group known as the Conjunto Aztlán in Austin, Texas. I never officially rehearsed with them, but I would frequently sing onstage with them during performances. I was the only woman in the group, and the audiences appreciated me being there, or so they told me often.

---

9. Who told me I could go around alone and free?

10. strategy to make me disappear

11. . . . I have so much love for myself. The path has been arduous, because it's been one of coming to know myself, a path toward consciousness of myself, of everything around me, this is my goal, to the extent that it's possible for me to achieve. To be conscious physically, emotionally, intellectually, spiritually is a tremendous challenge in this life on this earth. For me, to be a conscious human is the greatest work of love that I can do as long as I have a body, as long as I'm alive.

12. When I contemplate my life, I know also that not everything has been painful. I reflect upon past times and I find many instances of happiness and victory. It's curious how some moments stay recorded much more than others.

Even so, I always noted how some of the men seemed to think me in some way irrevelant. I'll always remember one occasion when we competed in East Austin for a music award at a *conjunto* festival. We won first place, and the trophy was given to our group. The men took the trophy apart and gave a piece to each of the men, but nothing came to me. They reserved the most prized part of the trophy, the eagle, for one member of the group who was very respected not only for his music, his arrangements, but for his consciousness and work toward social justice. A short while after this happened, he walked over and presented the eagle to me. I don't know if any of the rest of the group ever realized he had done this. Perhaps he could have made a more public confrontation with them about their dismissal of me. That's true. But at the time, I was content with the more private *reconocimiento* from him, since I, too, respected him and considered him a brother. I used to tease him and call him *"Conciencia,"* so for me it was fitting that he would make this gesture of acknowledgment to me. This eagle is still with me, too.

Lo que se borra vuelve a reaparecer, estoy segura. La energía que niega, que tapa, que ignora, que esconde, que miente, simplemente no tiene la misma fuerza, el mismo poder, la misma riqueza vital que la energía que afirma, que destapa, que reconoce, que descubre, que revela. La energía que borra es una energía de muerte. La energía que reconoce es una energía de vida.[13]

¿Y yo? Yo sigo el *Gran Movimiento del Cosmos y de la Tierra,*[14] dancing my body into laughter, my smile embracing me in exhilaration, embracing the world in joy. *Con mi sonrisa alumbro al mundo, mi cuerpo meciendo al son de una ranchera tejana. Hace ya muchos años escribí un pequeño poema que me sirve de conclusión. Dice así:*[15]

Y tú ¿quién eres?	And you, who are you?
¿De dónde vienes?	Where do you come from?
I have not given you	I have not given you
permission to exist.	permission to exist.
Soy quien soy	I am who I am
Soy de aquí	I am from here
Y soy porque	and I am because
yo digo	I say so
Es todo.	That's all.

13. What is erased reappears, of this I'm sure. The energy that denies, covers up, ignores, hides, lies, simply does not have the same strength, the same power, the same vital richness that affirms, uncovers, recognizes, discovers, and reveals. The energy that erases is an energy of death. The energy that recognizes is life-giving.

14. And I? I follow the Great Movement of the Cosmos and of the Earth.

15. With my smile I illuminate the world, my body swaying to the sound of a Tex-Mex love song. Many years ago I wrote a short poem that serves me as a conclusion. It goes like this:

Biting Through

Latina Anónima

I WAKE UP NERVOUS, depressed. Make myself some coffee and come sit at my desk. Throw the *I Ching*. "What has happened to me? Why have I grown so passive in the past few years? What has rendered me so helpless that even minor tasks of daily life appear to be insurmountable problems?"

Hexagram #21: "Biting Through." "Someone is doing you an injustice. . . ." Someone is acting dishonestly toward you; perhaps even criminally. . . . You, or friends, or a third party is knowingly behaving dishonestly toward the other or others, causing unhappiness and grief. . . ."

What does it mean? How do I interpret this message? There is a knock on the front door. I get up to answer it. On my way there I run a comb through my hair and button the robe that barely covers me. It is a neighbor. She's shaking, her voice cracks. I can't tell right away whether she is truly upset or whether this display of emotion is merely for effect. I decide quickly that it makes no difference. She has come to complain about my friends across the hall, to "warn," as she tells me, all of us. I fight the impulse to respond, to tell her off, set her straight. I want to know what she knows, what she thinks . . . know thine enemy.

We are compatriots. I have known this, of course, but having her here, face to face (our first encounter), finally makes her presence in this building real to me. I feel nauseous. *"Tú estabas ahí anoche, ¿verdad?"* "You were there, in their apartment, last night, right?" "Those women, or *whatever they are,* don't have a schedule. They are up at all hours banging typewriters and throwing who knows what else around. They don't have a time to get up or a time to go to bed. I bet they're asleep now. They say they don't understand Spanish. I want *you* to tell them that I've complained to the super, that I've complained to the landlord and that I'm going to complain to the police."

I want to grab her and shake her hard but decide that she's not worth that kind of intimacy. The thought startles and frightens me. I say to myself that I am making a big thing out of nothing. Come on, don't I know about troublesome neighbors? There's at least one in every building. And haven't I witnessed much greater displays of homophobia? I don't say a word to her. Having nothing to push against, she loses her bearings. She obviously had not anticipated my response. I watch her waver, stumble over words. She knows she's talking to an empty body. I have gone away and she doesn't know where to find me. I am above her, sitting on the doorframe, my knees drawn up, my arms around them. I wait for her to leave.

Reluctantly, I come down from the doorframe, dreading re-entry into the body that closes the door and turns the key. I don't want to feel the pain. There is a minor struggle, resistance. But the body pulls me in. Irresistible magnet. I am back in and confused. I want to talk to somebody. It is too early to call anybody. I am alarmed. It hurts too much. I feel unsafe. There is no one to hold me. I'm making a big thing out of nothing. I am overreacting. When am I going to learn to deal with this kind of situation? The *I Ching* says: "The dishonesty being perpetrated on you has not yet gone far enough to be serious or irreversible. . . ."

"If you act now, reconciliation is possible. . . ." I have nearly forgotten how to act. Reconciliation. I don't understand. I look at the clock. It is 11:30 already. Don't know where the time has gone. I have to get dressed and go out. I have wasted several hours. Self-indulgent. Irresponsible. Every day there is something wrong. Every day I split myself in two, spend hours putting myself together again. This is a shameful way to live. "Shame," says the dictionary, is a "painful emotion caused by a strong sense of guilt, unworthiness, or disgrace. . . ." "To live" means "to have life, to continue to remain alive. . . ." Obeying the laws of nature, my body, already in motion, remains in motion. Suddenly, I feel grateful, very grateful, for those laws. To live, to have life, despite it all, to continue to remain alive.

Sand from Varadero Beach

Ruth Behar

For Jaime, the only socialist in the family,
who died on September 15, 1995, in Israel.

Grandiose,
that gesture
of piling sand from Varadero Beach
into a plastic cup
to bring back with me.

But I'm a tourist,
watching myself act the part of the exile.
I know that for me
that sand
is just sand.

And as I'd expected,
when I unpack the sand
in my Wedgwood blue house
on a sunless morning in Michigan,
it looks as tacky as the coffee mug
with the curved crocodile tail handle
that says Cuba, though it was made in Taiwan.

No need to worry.
I will turn even that sand
into something refined,
something bearable to look at.
I'm the kind who's quick to frame pictures,
quick to put them on the wall,
so I can forget they are there.

Rebecca Behar, Ruth's mother,
on her honeymoon in Varadero, 1956

I know exactly which jar
I must put the sand in —
the little hexagon jar
that held the English jam
Mami sent me years ago for my birthday,
nurturing, as always, my pretensions.
It arrived in a handwoven basket
covered with cellophane,
and there were shortbreads too
and a pale green porcelain tea cup
with pine cones embedded on the edges
that I drank from every morning
until it slipped from my hands.

In its glass jar
the sand looks quaint enough
on the bookshelf.

I don't bother with it any longer
and a day comes when the cicadas gasp
and become ghosts in the trees.

Autumn is anxious to begin.
You see the leaves bracing themselves for wind and silence.

Mami flies in from New York.
We haven't seen each other
since we ate roasted vegetables and mozzarella
in a Soho restaurant in late spring
during her lunch hour.
That was all the time I had for her.
When the tears bunched up in her eyes,
I asked the waiter for the check.
She walked with me to the subway,
descended, too, and waited for me
to go through the turnstile.
Then she climbed back up to the street.

Afterwards, we let a whole summer pass
like a thief between us.

The truth is
I want to punish her
for loving my father
more than I think is good for her.
Today, when I need to give her the news
that Jaime has died on the kibbutz,
I realize I'm the punished one
because I've missed her terribly.

Here, I say in Spanish,
look what I brought you,
a jar of sand from Varadero Beach.
Touch it, says Gabriel, her grandson,
in English. Nana, did you know
it's the softest sand in the world?
She dips her thin-nailed fingers in the sand.
Yes, she says, I know, I know how soft it is.
And I can't remember in which language she says that.

Speaking Among Friends:
Whose Empowerment, Whose Resistance?

Luz del Alba Acevedo

You are the friends that I chose for myself,
the word that I want to proclaim.
— CESÁREO GABARAÍN, *You Are the Seed*

THIS IS A STORY of friendship and betrayal, of despair, resistance, and empowerment among feminist scholars. Remembering it brings pain but also affirmation. Pain, because the friends I chose for myself proved to share some of the same prejudices as the enemies we constructed. Affirmation, because in this painful journey of reflection among my Latina friends, as well as in some recent works by other feminists, I found that my experience is not isolated. I hope that in politicizing my personal experience with institutional feminism, this *testimonio* ("the word that I want to proclaim") become the source ("the seed") of empowerment for others enduring prejudice and isolation.

My encounter with academic feminism in the United States came at a time when both the women's studies and ethnic minority movements had succeeded in compelling the university establishment to become more representative of the growing sociocultural diversity that characterizes North American society. The challenge was, and continues to be, to confront and overcome ethnocentrism by transforming the undergraduate liberal arts curriculum. Although the United States does not have a national curriculum, the debate on curriculum transformation has become a political and ideological terrain in which diverse groups compete and struggle for the inclusion of their voices in the production of knowledge. The recognition, affirmation, and validation of the cultural attributes that make us different from one another have become important elements in these projects of curriculum transformation.

In this contradictory context of conflict and resistance, multicultural celebration and empowerment, Women's Studies departments have adopted "diversity projects" as part of the curricular agenda for the twenty-first century that amount to mainstreaming minority women's studies projects. These projects include adding minority women's experiences as topics of discussion in introductory Women's Studies courses; substituting the plural "feminisms" for the singular "feminism" in academic discourse; and hiring faculty who embody the trilogy of race, gender, and cultural/ethnic diversity.

The implementation of diversity projects within feminism have had important theoretical and methodological consequences, as well as pedagogical and administrative ones. They provide a space for questioning the essentialist premise on which Women's Studies is based. The theoretical challenge they present is not about discovering what a woman is but discovering "who we are as women," since the multiple definitions of womanhood are determined by the intersection of our experiences and social locations. This theoretical quest has created a tension between giving meaning to our own personal experience and explaining the plurality of identities that are constructed through specific social relations of class, ethnicity, sexual preference, age, life cycles, religion, etc., which are formed in diverse cultural contexts. This questioning has reshaped the feminist view of a global feminist "sisterhood" and opened up the possibility for initiating a multicultural and transnational dialogue among women concerning their identities, feminist perspectives, and political practices. This dialogue, in turn, serves as a basis for rethinking, from different sociocultural and class localities, the political practices and power relations involved in theorizing feminism and understanding *latinidades*. I believe that this process of knowledge building, anchored in women's *testimonios*, will empower the voices of difference in the Women's Studies academic experiment with multiculturalism.

I want to share my experience to show the politics of historical conflicts and ideological contradictions between feminism and race/ethnicity within the context of diversifying the Women's Studies curriculum. My intention is to critique the use of power, authority, and resistance in our intellectual and social practices as feminists. My goal is not to dilute my experience in a discussion of the merely personal but to bring the personal experience to the level of the political and ideological debate where the meaning and significance of the "other" gets constructed.

Testimoniando en resistencia

I began this dialogue, which I believed to be among friends, by raising questions about the specificity of my position and contribution as an island-born Puerto Rican middle-class heterosexual mulatta woman professor of women's studies, in shaping the diversity project advanced by a Women's Studies department with a predominantly white and lesbian view of the world.

Having taught courses on Puerto Rican and Latina women as a graduate student, I became a professor in a Department of Women's Studies in the 1990s. My first assignment was to be the instructor of record for an introductory course on "feminisms," a course, that according to the newly adopted university guidelines, met the "values and diversity" requirements of the curriculum. This course was organized and taught by members of a teaching collective, which included a group of students and one or two faculty, who worked together to design and coordinate the course, "Introduction to Feminisms." The student facilitators were primarily responsible for selecting topics and readings for the class, preparing the class outline, presenting class material, leading class discussions, designing assignments, and evaluating and grading students. Each section of the course was taught by a team of two or three students of the teaching collective with the support and assistance of a faculty member, not necessarily a participant of the teaching collective, who served as the instructor of record. The student facilitators, however, had a degree of autonomy and academic responsibility that was not the norm in the university. The instructor of record assisted student facilitators when classroom discussions got out of hand and served as a "shock absorber" when student and parent complaints about the class were subject to administrative scrutiny by university officials. With this pedagogical model, the power relations between professor and student were shifted to the student facilitators.

As an instructor of record for "Introduction to Feminisms," my role was that of a detached observer, a role that I assumed with naive enthusiasm. I saw this as a unique opportunity to relive my experience as an undergraduate student, devoting myself to the task of reading and studying the materials used in the course. I had some mixed feelings, however, because I was entering into a situation where my agency was constrained by the imposition of boundaries negotiated in a collective process in which I had no part. My participation in this "collective" course became an intense process. I experienced some strong emotions and feelings of alienation, indignation, and resistance. I read narratives that did not represent my existence, I listened to the all-encompassing dominant discourse of the predominantly white women students, voicing anger, indignation and hostility against the dominant white male discourse. Yet I felt that my experience as a Latina (Caribbean, Puerto Rican) and a heterosexual were obliterated by the totalizing appellative "woman." While both the students and class facilitators devoted themselves to the process of discovering who "we" (they) were as women and the sources of "our" (their) oppression, I discovered that for the students in this class, my identity was invisible and my experience nonexistent in their "map" of knowledge and power relations. I was a missing person whose experiences were only to be found at the borderlands of knowledge; I was the "other." From the margins, I became an observer of a process that reflected the tensions of the race and ethnic divide in feminist theory and practice in the United States. That is, of a process of producing knowledge that seeks to understand differences among women while simultaneously remaining within the discursive framework and perspective of those in a position of privilege and power. What for the students was a process of empowerment turned out to be a process of resistance for me. Through their process of empowerment I began to feel resistance to knowledge and pedagogies anchored in a homogeneous, universalistic, and ahistorical understanding of who we are as women.

I broke my silence of "detached overseer," hoping to cut the distance between me and those who had thus far defined my identity as a woman while condescendingly ignoring my existence. In teaching another core course, "Women's Perspectives," there was a significant shift in the power relations between the Women's Studies students and me. I moved from being invisible to being the "visible minority" professor, that is, the authority figure in the classroom. This made me an object of great curiosity and some resentment, curiosity surrounding all that was different about me: my accent, the color of my skin, the rhythm of my gestures, my "colorful" clothes. Immediately following the curiosity about the exotic, the folkloric, the "other," I found resistance. The resistance came mostly from students who were white, middle class, and lesbian, who felt the challenges of being confronted with racist and classist views in Women's Studies. These students resisted the inclusion of multiple voices and nondominant discourses as a central component in the study of women's experiences. During class discussions of the diverse experiences of nonwhite and poor women of different cultural backgrounds, I repeatedly listened to some of these students say, "The problem of 'those women' is not race, they are oppressed because they are 'women.'" Others, referring to African Americans, remarked that "their poverty was due to the fact that they are women," while others questioned the frequency of our discussions on race: "Why are we talking about race? We should be talking about sexuality." The comments reached the level of gossip in the halls, "If we are going to go around the world looking for the sources of oppression of 'those other women,' then 'Intro' should be a class that offers a safe space for coming out of the closet."

Soon my classes began to attract Latinas and Latinos, African Americans, Asians, and white women, lesbians, heterosexuals, and even a few male students. I became an atypical professor in the Women's Studies milieu. My classes were not simply a "safe space for coming out" but a terrain of contestation about the complacent assumptions of the advocates of diversity. Reductionist arguments about the oppression of women and minorities were critically examined and *everyone* was called upon to question and critically examine their social locations and determinants of their multiple identities in a racist, homophobic, and classist society. I quickly discovered that the intellectual investment of my students in learning about women was shaken by a historically and culturally grounded understanding of difference among women's social locations and positionalities. In a sign of appreciation for the introduction of new perspectives in the study of women, some white female students majoring in Women's Studies remarked in a letter sent to the department, "She is very passionate about the subject she teaches and passes that on to her students." Another wrote, "She was able to maintain a significant level of discussion that expressed very diverse points of view in a way that was respectful of each student." An Afro-Caribbean male wrote, "Your teachings allow us to re-examine and re-evaluate a variety of experiences in our lives," while a Latina student said, "She clarified complex issues without oversimplifying and used examples relevant to our experiences."

On the contrary, most of the comments made by the white, radical feminist students, predominantly lesbian, revealed a one-dimensional intellectual point of reference within Women's Studies and a set political agenda for feminist practices in academe. I heard students commenting that "the objective of Women's Studies courses is to affirm sexual differences," "provide a safe space for coming out," and "build a network of support for lesbians." It became clear to me that these students did not want to engage in dialogues on the intersection of gender, race, ethnicity, and sexual orientation that could lead to a critique of the use of power and authority between and within genders. These students, and even some Women's Studies faculty members, were uncomfortable sharing the academic space conquered by the women's movement and feminist practice with "minority" women. The students and faculty who espoused such views seemed to have developed a sense of ownership over the women's movement agenda that pretended to dictate to all the other women the terms, conditions, and degrees of inclusion of our different experiences. This, in spite of arguing that the space for teaching Women's Studies had been conquered on behalf of all women.

I soon realized that by introducing a discourse on differences — grounded in the analysis of social relations that structure and organize inequalities based on gender, race, ethnicity, and sexual orientation — I was challenging the static and celebratory notion of diversity "added" to the Women's Studies curriculum. I was unsettling the power relations that maintained white privilege in the governance of a Women's Studies department and I was empowering students from diverse sociocultural localities and sexual orientations. By refusing to assume the discourse of sameness, I subverted the role assigned to me as the token Latina who was supposed to accept being the vacuous embodiment of the Women's Studies diversity project. Instead, I became the affirmation of difference, *la mujer puertorriqueña mulata y heterosexual* who taught Women's Studies and openly challenged the intellectual project and institutional practices of the first and second wave of feminisms in the United States. My oppositional politics made me the target of feminist struggles in an unsuccessful attempt to recolonize my body and my mind, my whole self. The battle over the ideological and political meaning of diversity among feminists started with the purpose of domesticating "difference" (Latina, African American, and Asian women) and setting the example for disciplining noncompliant women.

At Women's Studies faculty meetings there were discussions on issues of exclusion and inclusion concerning the feminist participation in the diversity project. The faculty was composed of two Puerto Ricans, two African Americans, and about twelve white women among whom there were three lesbian couples. At one meeting, someone raised a crucial question: Who defines diversity? The very formulation of this question in such terms revealed a desire to create a new "master narrative" of diversity. It revealed a view of the world intended to subsume differences into a unifying discourse of "the diverse." The answers to that question reflected the predominance of the white women's discourse. In this discourse the core view of diversity would be concerned with understanding issues of sexual orientation, while relegating issues of race, class, and ethnicity to the margins. The search for an answer trapped us in a game of identity politics (sexual politics vs. racial and ethnic politics) and derailed the focus of our academic debate from the analysis of the construction of multiple subjectivities and the complex formation of cross-cultural identities to an individualistic, and ahistorical, understanding of difference.

The substantive theoretical questions underlying the game of resistance were not considered. These were: What are the theories of "gender," of "race," of "class" operating in Women's Studies that were determining its practices in terms of knowledge building, pedagogy, and personnel? What were the assumptions about "woman/women," and how do these affect its practices? How were the standards of teaching and research set and validated? Nevertheless, the unfocused debate uncovered racism, homosexism (heterosexism is usually the norm in other contexts), and classism in academic feminism. My stand in the debate over the critique of the all-encompassing category of women, the unproblematized notion of difference, and the challenge to the political agenda of sexual correctness unleashed a power struggle masked by differences in race and sexual orientation among women faculty. The resistance to the inclusion of new and rigorous knowledge and pedagogies, grounded in the study of difference, soon translated to discriminatory institutional practices against minorities.

In a document proposing a master's program in Women's Studies, the

Puerto Rican, African American, and Asian women professors were lumped into the category of "women of color," while the rest of the faculty were identified by name. The "women of color" category was not defined in ideological or political terms. It was used for classification purposes to "codify," to "other" professors in the department according to a totalizing racial criterion that disregarded and devalued our professional identity in our working environment. As part of the "women of color" group, my name, academic credentials, and expertise were erased by a homogenizing category, ironically, used in opposition to white women who retained their personal and professional identities. I found myself boxed in an alien feminist agenda that counted my presence as a necessary gesture of inclusion and multiculturalism devoid of any reference to issues of racism and exclusion. This practice made me realize that I was assigned the role of a second-class citizen and was only tolerated as a silent and subordinate partner in the diversity project. This behavior was certainly contrary to my ethical standards, feminist academic principles, and commitment to diversity, equality, and justice for all of us who believe in Women's Studies education. I felt that the practice of labeling and codifying difference was an exercise of power that amounted to discrimination against the Puerto Rican, African American, and Asian faculty with the object of controlling our input in the diversity project curriculum. I brought this issue to a faculty meeting where I faced silence, resistance, and indignation from my colleagues. As the untenured Latina, I had dared to trespass the unstated hierarchical boundaries among women.

This act of discrimination was formally reported to the head of the Office of Affirmative Action, a feminist active in the governance of Women's Studies, who responded to my complaint, replying, "I do not think that you want me to intervene. How would you feel if a friend of yours scorns you? You should plan an activity that can contribute to the understanding of these issues and get Women's Studies faculty involved." Without a second thought, the head of Affirmative Action had brushed aside my white colleagues' illegal behavior and ignorance, thrusting on me the onus of "educating" them in matters of race. This solution, in my view, masqueraded that the Office of Affirmative Action served only the interests of a group of "corporatist" women bent on holding onto positions of power within the institution and perpetuating reductionist, racist forms of feminism. The Office of Affirmative Action became a sword pointed at me rather than a shield to protect me from racism. I soon found myself on a collision course with a powerful clique of white, upper-middle-class women, whom I labeled "corporatist feminists" because of their power-oriented views and undemocratic style of governance.

On academic and political grounds, I rejected all attempts at "domestication" by a biased-mentorship program. I chose not to surrender my intellectual production, academic achievements, and intellectual contributions to the scrutiny of mentors alien to my experience. The mentorship program in Women's Studies was designed to reproduce the same mentality and "ways of knowing" of a generation of white, middle-class academic feminists, well entrenched in the power structures of the university. The mentor/mentee relationship was characterized by an asymmetrical power relation that subjugated the mentee to the ever-demanding desires of the mentor to conform to a status quo. The mentor would discipline mentees with the threat of nontenure, while "colonizing" their intellectual work. I discovered that mentors used the academic brokerage of the "underrepresented classes" (minorities) to climb the administrative ladder to positions of institutional power in the name of the diversity project. The mentees were trained to become insiders through a process of reward and punishment that required their active participation in the devaluation and exclusion of other minorities (outsiders). This meant that minority women were pitted against each other in order to foster academic struggles rooted in the ideological and structural dynamics of white dominance in Women's Studies.

My critique of the way in which the mentorship program was implemented made me the object of power abuses designed to put me in my place and bring me to order. I was construed as a "problem." In the discursive construction of that imaginary identity, oppositional binaries were activated to wipe me out of the terrain of feminist knowledge and women's political action. My academic work and my teaching were devalued, as if I were a racist white male. I became the target of a witch-hunt designed to punish me, to make me hurt, and make me pay for my intellectual and political transgressions. My scholarship was devalued for critiquing the theoretical and pedagogical canon prevalent in women's studies. My academic contributions were disrupted in order to prevent me from speaking out against the power abuses by an institutionally entrenched feminist "clique." I was portrayed as the unruly illegitimate daughter of feminism, an unfaithful and undeserving Latina sister who formed part of a group of disposable people in academe. I went from being the token Latina needed for the diversity project to being the "troublemaker," the traitor.

By demonizing me and devaluing my academic achievements and intellectual and professional contributions, a hostile working environment erased my identity as a Puerto Rican middle-class heterosexual mulatta woman professor. I became the target of intellectual defamation and personal persecution. These took the form of anonymous threatening letters and telephone calls. In a clear attempt at character assassination, a flyer attributing to me the characteristics of a mentally disturbed person was distributed to the faculty of my college. One of the perpetrators of these hostile acts was arrested for making harassing calls to my house, and a restraining order was issued against this so-called "progressive," "pro-diversity" faculty who was part of the feminist/diversity coalition. All these acts of intimidation, humiliation, and vindictiveness were made while the same feminist coalition used the Office of Affirmative Action to fabricate a case of sexual harassment against my husband, also a faculty colleague. This case collapsed for lack of evidence, yet it was part of the punishment delivered to me for speaking out of line.

I was further declared a public enemy of Women's Studies in a letter signed by the Women's Studies faculty. The letter alleged that I was part of an anti-feminist education conspiracy that was preparing the terrain for the future retrenchment of Women's Studies faculty. It was addressed to the patriarchal figure of the university's president and sought to elicit an investigation that would "take appropriate disciplinary action" against the attackers of Women's Studies. In a perverse twist of feminist politics, this letter attempted to cover up a campaign of harassment and hostility rooted in a desire to repress diversity by presenting the corporatist feminists as the "victims of political attacks." In a typically male fashion, the corporatist feminists were resorting to institutional retaliation as a means to intimidate and silence me. It was as if I had broken the silence from an abusive family and deserved to be punished for speaking out against feminist "sisters."

I answered the corporatist clique's renewed threats and innuendoes in a public letter, stating:

[. . .] I am *not* attacking Women's Studies. I believe in multicultural feminist education based on rigorous scholarship and critical thinking. That is why I challenge the political practices that have taken the pedagogical and intellectual substance out of feminist education. As I said at the beginning of this letter, *I belong to a generation of feminist scholars whose work is guided by high ethical standards, an open critical perspective, and academic substance, not by feelings of fear, hatred and desire to punish.*

As a feminist scholar, I believe as well that the university, as a site of feminist education, must be an open and democratic space for the free and uninhibited exchange of ideas.

Through this eye-opening academic experience, I discovered that the white corporatist feminist concepts of woman and sisterhood embodied hierarchical power relations with centers and margins. And that the apparently unified discourses constructed around multicultural power-neutral understandings of diversity remained a contested terrain for ideological debate and political practice. I was punished for challenging whiteness and uncovering the misguided centrality of sexual correctness in the feminist agenda for the diversity project. I believe that my experience of inclusion in the feminist multicultural project shows that, in the name of supporting women, a new form of antifeminism has been instituted in women's studies, an antifeminism that, by incorporating the voices of difference, suppresses the meaningful research and theoretical work that is outside the normative boundaries of mainstream feminist scholarship.

Testimoniando con Poder/ Politicizing Personal Experience

As I see it, this *testimonio* represents a catalyst for comprehending and politicizing my experience with feminism. The anger and indignation that sustained my political resistance to the academic and institutional aggressions inflicted to silence my voice, suppress my thinking, and erase me from the map of knowledge was transformed into a source empowerment for anchoring my critique and emerging perspectives on feminisms and Women's Studies.

My battles of resistance coincided with a process of self-affirmation and intellectual empowerment. As I was subjected to psychological battery and ostracism by a white corporatist feminist clique, The Latina Feminist Group embraced me and provided the intellectual and emotional shelter in which to reflect on a painful experience as I was living through it. The solidarity of my Latina peers provided an extraordinary intellectual and political environment in which to foster a process of empowerment. Notwithstanding the common denominator *Latina,* this was an extremely diverse group of women not only culturally but in terms of sexual orientations (heterosexual, bisexual, and lesbian), ages, life cycles, spiritual beliefs, academic experiences, and political views. This made the group a challenging terrain for contestation. It served as a space in which to confront our own biases and internalized sources of oppression, sexism, and racism, as well as to face the breaking points and empowering experiences in our lives that shape the multiplicity of identities each of us represents. We listened to each other's *testimonios* but the power of each story and its resonance with some of our own experiences inevitably made each of us ask ourselves questions about how we know what we know and reflect on the meanings we have constructed out of the knowledge we have built. For example, through the *testimonios* on sexuality, I was able to rethink and politicize the nature and extent of the "body politics" that was engaged in my own experience with academic feminism and the project of diversity during the 1990s in the United States. A diversity of lived sexual experiences, of views about sexuality, the meaning of the Latina "body" and what is constructed from it were central issues in some of the *testimonios.* But these discussions on sexuality were always aimed at validating our differences (as heterosexuals, bisexuals, lesbians), rather than imposing a sexually correct vision of each other. And this process of validation was achieved without giving a hierarchical interpretation to diverse sexual identities and avoided the construction of a dominant single view of women's sexuality by a particular group. In this process I realized that the contention surrounding the discussions on sexual difference and body politics is not rooted in what sex is but in what sex is for; it is about who regulates sexuality and for whom. In my view, this is a political issue of power between and among genders for the control of minds, bodies, and souls and the elaboration and imposition of a particular dogma of body politics. This was at the center of the struggles I lived through with lesbian and white feminism over the definition and institutionalization of diversity in academe.

At a methodological level, my *testimonio* was more than a balm to heal a wounded soul and an instrument to anchor new knowledge. *Testimoniando con poder* became a useful political strategy. It kept me centered on the fundamental theoretical issues and political practices and the development of a truly multicultural feminism that had been challenged by my involvement with the diversity project in Women's Studies. My theoretical understanding of the intersection of gender, race, class, and sexuality in constructing diverse women in a multiethnic society was constantly reshaped by the experience I was living. I was not indifferent to anyone but had to contextualize and historicize my experience to bring it to the level of the political. I had to tell my story repeatedly, with all its complexities, in different academic, political, and legal forums in order to move away from the oppositional categories into which I was boxed, obfuscating the understanding of difference in my knowledge-building agenda. As I gave my *testimonio,* its political strength uncovered unseen intellectual adversaries, gained new feminist friends, and strengthened old friendships. The intellectual exchanges and political discussions over pieces of my *testimonio* contributed to focusing my political lens and to constantly reshape the strategy I would follow. In turn, the outcome of these strategies became the source of a new story in my *testimonio.*

As I kept my *testimonio* alive, other women (students, colleagues, and friends) broke their silence and began giving their own *testimonios,* sharing similar experiences of erasure. At a time when my personal safety was jeopardized by the intensified campaign of harassment, letters of attack, and anonymous threats, Latina and white women abandoned their work and private spaces to provide support and companionship. We broke bread and talked about politics and theory, and about life and friendship. Recounting my experience of violent threats and physical intimidation allowed the opportunity to affirm difference, establish friendships, and develop commitments and cooperation between us, women in the margins of corporatist feminism. This process of mutual empowerment and feminist reciprocity, forged through the politicization of our *testimonios,* provided the basis for political solidarity, intellectual collaboration, and personal empathy among women with different academic expertise, of diverse races, ethnicities, sexual orientations, ages, and religious identities.

Power relations did emerge in our Latina feminist group, but these *nudos de poder* (nodes of power) could be loosened and united through a process of collaboration and polyphonic negotiation of difference without compromising the validation, understanding, and affirmation of diversity. We did not avoid confrontation and we acknowledged our ideological disagreements and looked for other ways to understand the strength that comes out of difference.

My experience with institutional feminism as a Puerto Rican middle-class heterosexual mulatta woman has raised intriguing theoretical questions and analytical puzzles for further research: How do we theorize difference? What is the conceptual language that captures the complexities of difference without diluting the singular experience of the diverse? How do we construct a feminist multicultural critique to counter processes for the recolonization of women's intellectual identities and knowledge building? How do we understand power struggles among women within difference and across difference? What are the implications of feminist power struggles for bridging alliances, building coalitions, and political practices?

My personal experience, the methodological discussions among the Latinas in this volume, the dialogues with white lesbian and heterosexual American feminists, and the literature produced by other Latinas and non-U.S. feminists have made me realize that the discourse of global sisterhood provides the ideological support for an ethnocentric feminist agenda. Sisterhood as a model for invoking feminist solidarity and rallying women's political support needs to be historically scrutinized and politically challenged from the standpoint of multicultural difference and how the "other" women get constructed.[1]

In the process of telling our stories and reflecting on our *testimonios,* my experience in participating with the Latina Feminist Group cannot be described as one of sisterhood but of friendship. I did not experience women bonding on the basis of shared victimization by a common enemy, nor a sense of sisterhood that sought to avoid conflict and minimize disagreement. What I experienced was the kind of friendship built through disagreements, critical discussions, and caring constructive arguments directed to enrich rather than diminish and discredit our personal lives or work. This experience led me to imagine an alternative framework to sisterhood as a model of feminist solidarity. Such a model has to be anchored in friendship and based on strength derived from women's different experiences, socioeconomic diversity, plural-

1. María C. Lugones (1995) and bell hooks (1997) presented the concept of friendship as an alternative to the concept of sisterhood as a framework of women's political solidarity.

istic political practices, and multicultural identities. The group dynamics that emerged as we were *testimoniando* taught me that friendship requires good listeners, the capacity to empathize with the experience of the other, and the acceptance of the autonomous character of the other without giving up your own separate and individual self and experience. Friendship ties among groups of women ought to be sustained through empathy with the other, the friend with whom we establish a promise to understand the particularities of our identities, the diversity of our experiences, the complexity of our realities and to unlearn the biases, prejudices, and stereotypes we have constructed about each other. As friends, a mutual commitment to confront our internalized sexist (heterosexist, homosexist), racist, and class-biased ideologies must emerge to transform pervasive perspectives and lay the foundation for truly political solidarity.

A view of women's solidarity as friendship, as opposed to sisterhood, could afford the possibility of reconstructing relations among women within a pluralistic and heterogeneous context that confers centrality to sociocultural differences. Therefore, the understanding among diverse groups of women found through friendship and solidarity relations does not presuppose the existence of unanimity or consensus on which to establish support. Since friendship is not an unconditional relation of inequality among sisters, the space for dialogue is always a contested terrain for building feminist alliances and multicultural coalitions that rely on mutual commitment to eliminate diverse sources of women's oppression, to engage in egalitarian politics, and to struggle for social justice. The political practice in a friendship paradigm should aim at the creation of a political project that constructs identities forged on politics rather than from politics based on identities that tend to defend and perpetuate inequalities among women. Friendship as a model of relationships among women should be based on respect for difference and sustained on the basis of a constant negotiation and renegotiation of shares of power, not subject to rules that define rights and responsibilities along the lines of unequal sisterhood. The solidarity that emerged among us on the basis of friendship has the possibility to open and democratize the political base of feminism across our *latinidades* and beyond.

III   The Body Re/members

Positioned as survivors of multiple violations, we offer the narratives in this section to document the shame and silence induced by institutional, social, familial, and interpersonal injustice. The body speaks in languages left unread. Indeed, the body encodes the *agravios,* the assaults that sometimes lead to numbness and alienation, to depression and despair, to a desire for an endless night of sleep.

Our stories document how women's bodies are damaged by the ravages of institutionalized racism, by the patriarchal structures that accord privilege on the basis of gender and class, and by the sexism and heterosexism that forbid love and silence desire. Our stories and poems chronicle how even the earned privilege of women of color, *las princesas,* only buys us time, for the structures of racism and patriarchy support the oppression of brown women by oppressed brown men. Further, our cultural mythologies encourage women to protect men by keeping silent. To maintain our sanity and perform our culturally mandated roles, we may abandon our bodies, suppress our rage and pain, bearing witness to our own pain.

Forced by circumstances, we struggle to survive. Broken by our parents' love or the violence of a lover, our spirit may be compromised. But the body remembers, and once we reconnect to it, through depression or imposed violence, we must heed its message.

As we give testimony, our bodies awaken, revealing our *llagas* (wounds) and our joys. Our stories celebrate the awakening of our bodies as we also acknowledge the cost exacted because of our gender, race, class, and sexuality.

Healing begins as we begin to re/member the violations, as we give voice to the atrocities committed in the name of love, and as we name the traumatic events that marked our lives. As we make our secrets public, we reclaim our bodies and our spirits.

Reading the Body

Norma E. Cantú

Start with a literal exegesis
And thereby refute all metaphor.
¡calla boca!

The historical record reigns supreme:
battle scars, accidental burns, scraped-knee scars;
surgeries: appendectomy, hysterectomy, mastectomy.

Birth marks destiny.
And I wonder at the state of limb and joint
at three, thirteen, thirty.
Examine teeth and hair to discern age;
look for skin's sun signs — spots and lines tell the tale.
— *palitos y bolitas* uniquely etched.

Then consider metaphor — decipher choices
written in blood: children borne or not.
Breasts that suckled lovers / infants,
feet well-shod or well-heeled,
work-roughened or smoothly manicured hands
Nun's hands, ringed in gold.

Read the lessons of ages writ in parable
upon sagging flesh,
the seven ages (or nine lives) would speak tomes.

Finally, deconstruct
the gendered
racialized mind

in patterns rich and plain
clearly stamped upon a haircut
earringed lobe, nose or nipple;
tattoos, birthmarks,
test the script
with the language of bones, of skin.

The body speaks in tongues
far more eloquent than mere words:
A flushed cheek, a sweaty palm,
the scent of menses and of sleep.

Characters of a known code:
A fading ever-widened *vacuna* scar on the arm.
An aging *viruela* pockmarked face.
The blue threads of varicose veined legs.

Yes. The body speaks in languages left unread,
and you can only marvel
at the message, literate only in your own.
Awed by stories told by thighs and lips
or the ugliness of the littlest toe.

Missing Body

Caridad Souza

THE OTHER DAY I woke up and realized that my body was missing. It was MISSING IN ACTION. What has happened to my body? Where did it go? It used to be attached to the rest of me, but I haven't seen it for so long that I worry it may never come back. Looking down at the ground the other day I noticed my feet. They were bare and I looked at them really close for the first time, not thinking about anything in particular. Then something amazing happened. I actually saw my feet. Right then I noticed that they didn't look quite as slender as I remember, that they had some lines on the arches I had never noticed, that they had some deep veins. My eyes moved slowly up to my ankles, then to my shins, and finally settled on my knees. I had to stop there. I couldn't go on because I got too anxious. What I found in my body's place is not what I remember as mine. Where is the body I remember? And why does the one in its place frighten me so? Was that other body just a figment of my imagination? How did I exist in it? How have I managed without it. Did I always exist just outside my body, watching it from afar? I've been living outside my body for so long I'm not sure how to make it back. I want to be back inside my body. I miss it.

Thinking back, my body must have gotten lost sometime during the late eighties. I hadn't noticed its absence until just recently. You see, I get so caught up in the day-to-day struggles to survive, to achieve, that I haven't noticed how long it's been gone. Yet the scars I bear are the markers of a body that once existed. But I don't seem to be able to conjure up the history of that body either. Whenever I try, I draw a blank. It frustrates me because I want to remember my body, but there is a void in my memory where my body should be. And without that memory I fear I will not recover my body. What part of this war is my body a casualty of? Was it that graduate school professor who suggested trading mentoring for sexual favors? Was it the flashbacks of sexual violation that began while I was studying for my comprehensive exams? When did my body become community property for all the men in the neighborhood, the street, the world, to gawk and leer at, and grab at, and fondle whenever they wanted? Here I can't even summon up the memories of a body that belongs to me. What kinda shit is that? How is it that my body can be assaulted time and again, day after day? Like the time that neighborhood man hissed as I walked by: "*Oye nena, déjame chuparte esos coquitos,*" so effortlessly destroying months of work building whatever twelve-year-old confidence I could muster about my changing body. I felt so dirty and ashamed about my body after that, especially because I wore my sister's new silk shirt that day, the one with the low neckline. For the first time since they'd appeared I wasn't ashamed of my breasts. After what he said I didn't want to leave the house for a whole week.

Male attention has never really been flattering to me. All the unasked-for leers, the unsolicited gazes, the unwanted eroticization of my body have always felt like assaults. Is that how my body began to fade? Did my body begin to wane around the time I was ten and my great-uncle, who was dying of cancer, demanded that I sit next to him on the bed so that he could touch me? Was it when that beloved family friend slipped my ten-year-old body a note while I watched television with all my siblings, telling me to go to the bedroom and take off my pants? I was so scared of him that I wouldn't go anywhere near him for years. He always made me feel like a small, caged animal, the way his eyes always traveled up and down my body when he thought no one was looking. It wasn't a shock when years later I heard he raped his nine-year-old daughter. It made me wonder how responsible for her pain I was because I kept silent about him.

Was the exact moment my body began to disappear the time my friend's brother, who I always thought of as a homie, decided it was his turn to have a shot at me? Since when does physical maturity signal that your body is available to any man at any time, regardless of your interest in him? How many times before I started to feel numb, before I began to erase my body? How long before I stopped looking at it? When did my hips start to spread? How did my breasts grow so? When did my waist disappear? When did my pain start to show on my body?

I've learned to speak with my body about the atrocities it's witnessed, all the invisible marks left by too many leers, too many eyes on my breasts, unwanted hands on my body. People only see the surface and never think about what lies underneath, all the damage that's been inflicted on this body. They never imagine the pain, never ask about it, even when I hint. That kind of silence assists in my erasure. Every pound, every patch of cellulite, every stretch mark on this body has a story behind it and the name of an assailant on it. The assaults have been relentless, yet nobody's ever noticed. Every time my assailants hammered away at my body I added extra layers of protection. Sometimes it makes me feel powerful, these layers. I've lost my self in the process. This kind of torture has been slow, methodical. I'm not allowed to show the pain I carry around inside, so I let the outside speak. It's taken ten years to lose my body and to acknowledge that it's been gone. Will it take another ten to get it back?

It's been so effortless to transfer these lessons to my new lifestyle in the academy, to continue the abuse on my body so easily. The academy reinforces all the lessons I've learned living as a working-class Puerto Rican woman in the United States. It's been an excellent training ground for the abuse. The way I am compelled to work myself ragged, into the ground, the lack of sleep and nutrition to meet deadlines. All the subtle ways I allow my body to be abused. This body has become a libation for all the assaults I've endured, a wall against all that pain. None of that has been effortless. The pain hasn't gone away. It just sits here awaiting another avenue of expression.

Malabareando / Juggling

Liza Fiol-Matta

I

mírenme. soy malabarista por excelencia.

en una boca mastico dos idiomas.
con una lengua acaricio los alfabetos.
si se quedan me verán tirando al aire "la cultura"
mientras sostengo otra en el arco de un pie levantado.

mírenme de cerca. me ofrezco como espécimen de laboratorio.

(el exilio sabe a periódico mojado.
la tinta se me corre de la boca
manchándome la barbilla mientras mastico.)

2

sombras nada más entre tu vida y mi vida

¿de qué vale el exilio si no nos hace
mirarnos más de cerca?
sombras nada más entre tu amor . . .

y las vidas sombras son.

3

cuando a mí se me muere alguien, se me muere allá.
se me muere y se vela en Ehret. se me llama por
teléfono. se me dice. se me entierra sin mí.

esto de vivir acá me sabe a esquela.

el exilio me sabe a periódico mojado
y me suena a timbrazo de teléfono.
¿lo cojo? ¿no lo cojo?

¿Halo? Hello?
(si me hablan de muerte me muero.)

1

look at me. I am a juggler *par excellence.*

in one mouth I chew on two languages.
with one tongue I caress their alphabets.
if you stay you will see me throwing into the air "my" culture
while I balance another in the arch of my foot.

Look at me closely. I offer myself as a laboratory specimen.

(exile tastes like wet newspaper.
the ink runs down my chin
staining it as I chew.)

2

shadows, nothing more, between your life and mine
Of what use is exile if it does not make us
look at ourselves more closely?
shadows, nothing more, between your love . . .

and lives are but shadows.

3

when someone dies on me, they die "over there."
they die and are watched in Ehret. I am called on the
telephone. I am told. they are buried without me.

this business of living here tastes like an obituary.

4

exile tastes of wet newspaper
and it sounds like a telephone ringing.
should I answer? should I not?
¿Halo? Hello?
(if they speak to me of death I will die.)

Migraine / *Jaqueca*

Norma E. Cantú

Talking mouths spew lights into infinity
like sparklers on Fourth of July
and with black-hole acuity warn of your approach

I ignore it all and with the force
of machete blows at 60 mph you arrive:
forehead, temples, neck, my very being
smashed with waves of pain
overwhelming the calm ridges
of my brain

I lie in darkness
within the proverbial pit from pole to pole
light is searing pain,

You win.

De las bocas que hablan salen estrellitas hacia la infinidad
que con la agudez del universo
presagian tu llegada

Sin embargo no presto atención, y con la
fuerza de un machete a 60 mph me
golpeas la frente, las sienes, el cuello,
el mismo ser
atropellada por olas de dolor
que se vierten en las calmadas rutas
del cerebro

La obscuridad alivia
dentro del abismo proverbial
la luz es dolor pugnante,

me vences.

The Wart

Daisy Cocco De Filippis

THE DAY SHE NOTICED it for the first time, Clotilde Ramírez stared at it as she would have a two-headed cat. "*¡Qué raro!*" she muttered to herself, not sure of what to make of it. She had not seen it before. It had somehow escaped her scrutiny. She could not imagine why except that mirrors were not on good terms with her those days. Andrés had not noticed it either. But there it was. Bigger than anything she had ever seen, protruding from her back, boldly escaping the constraints of her brassiere.

As luck would have it, every time Clotilde thought she might "do something about it," life got complicated. First, it was her feet. Of course, she had to deal with that first. It had become so painful to walk on them that Clotilde decided to visit the podiatrist. His prescription of anti-inflammatory pills and ice packs proved more of an illness than a cure. The second day of being "medicated," Clotilde found herself covered with blisters and blotches. One look in the mirror convinced her that she needed to put on her sunglasses. She dared not venture out lest the neighbors think the dark circles under her eyes were caused by some "unmentionable" family secret.

The podiatrist was at a loss, he said. He had not seen anything like the reaction to the medicine Clotilde's body had produced, he explained. The cure for his cure, steroids, produced a weakness in Clotilde's immune system that precluded any visit to the dermatologist for a year. So the wart continued to grow, reminding Clotilde of its presence, especially at nighttime when every turn to the right produced a slightly pulling sensation that at times was accompanied by very slight bleeding.

Meanwhile, life continued to happen to Clotilde and to her "growth," as she had come to call it tenderly. But just as suddenly as it had come and Clotilde had taken it into her life, Clotilde found herself one morning unable to look at it, to touch it, to feel its presence in her bed. As she dressed to keep her appointment, Clotilde could not look at her back. For the first time she realized that it had become tired, bent over. Her round shoulders, a source of much pride in the past, had lost their sex-appeal, she commented to herself.

The visit to the dermatologist brought a new set of challenges. Unaccustomed, perhaps, to having patients grow warts on their backs, the dermatologist was at a loss to produce a patient's gown. Instead, Clotilde, quite conscious of her sagging shoulders and bent over by the weight of her "growth," barely managed to cover herself with the disposable sheet provided her by a very eager dermatologist's assistant.

It seemed to Clotilde that the woman could not stop talking. The topic of her harangue was impatient patients. Individuals, unlike Clotilde, who did not extend courtesies or wait for the professional staff to be ready. She also confided in Clotilde that her "growth" was not one the likes of which the doctor's assistant had ever seen in her many years of professional life. As they readied the tools of their trade, the doctor and his assistant chatted casually. Before Clotilde could say "*concho,*" after feeling a slight prick and then a burning sensation, the "growth" had been removed.

Clotilde turned around just in time to see what the doctor was holding in his carefully rubber-gloved hand: it was wrinkled, brownish-pink, round but slightly flattened. "*¿Qué raro!*" she thought, "Is it possible? Have I . . . have I really been carrying a testicle on my back?" Clotilde was careful to keep her thoughts to herself. A number of days went by but seldom was there a moment when she did not reflect on the extraordinary life of her recently departed "growth."

The morning came when Clotilde could look at her back in the mirror again. For the first time in a while, she found her skin supple. Her round shoulders were proudly held back, as she hummed to herself. Clotilde thought for a moment, for one long moment. Then with a movement of new found determination, Clotilde Ramírez opened her closet and began to pack.

Why My Ears Aren't Pierced

Ruth Behar

for Iris, because she wanted to know

When I was born
so they tell me
in Cuba
Papi wouldn't let my ears
be pierced.

"Mira ¡está completica!"
She's complete, all of a piece —
Look at her little feet!
Look at her little fingers!
Look at her little mouth!

*"Una muñequita de carne
y hueso,"* he exclaimed,
tears flooding his eyes.
A doll of skin and bones. . . .
Please, don't ruin her, please.

How well he knew already
that when I grew up
and became a big bad girl
he'd hurt me
to the quick.

And so I am grateful
for that first kindness
when I was little
and he thought me perfect,
cared enough to spare me pain.

This is why, Iris,
I haven't pierced my ears.
My ears without holes,
you see, mark the time
before I broke my father's love.
Before my father's love broke me.

Night Terrors

Latina Anónima

MY EYES FLUTTERED open. Dark all around. My sisters slept in beds next to mine. The only sound was heavy breathing nearby. Something was wrong. *What was happening? Daddy?* His large hand pushed into my panties and touched me. He smelled like beer.

"Don't make a sound."

I was a good girl and always obeyed Daddy. He was a large man, dark as a wild pony and just as mean. He lowered himself into the bed, on top of me. He penetrated my thin, nine year old body. I whimpered, afraid.

"Shut up!" he hissed.

I always obeyed Daddy. If we were bad or disobeyed, he would yell at us or hit us. *Why is he doing this? Isn't this wrong? It hurts. Where's Mommy? What if my sisters hear?*

The questions raced through my mind, but I remained silent. The pain became unbearable and I could no longer contain myself. I began crying, tears flowing down my cheeks. I was so ashamed. He touched me there. Worse yet, I disobeyed Daddy. *What would he do?* I was terrified.

"Shut up!" he hissed. "Don't tell anyone."

Then he slowly slipped away, leaving me stunned and confused. *Was I a bad girl? What did I do to deserve this?* Then I remembered the time a few years back when Daddy noticed my flat breasts, and I had covered them in shame. The next morning he pretended that nothing had happened. I knew I was supposed to say nothing.

Daddy visited me at night several times after that. I began to look for clues that he would come. I learned to read his face and body, noticing when he was angry or frustrated. I watched my mother for signs of conflict. I became a light sleeper, awakening at the slightest sound. When he came home drunk, I went to bed in dread. And I became a quick study. I learned that when he tried to penetrate me, if I started crying right away he would get nervous and leave. Once, when Mom was in the hospital having a baby, he made my little sister sleep with him. I wondered what went on.

The last time Daddy came to my bed in the night, my mother woke up and entered the room just as he was leaving. My body tensed.

"What are you doing?" she asked, her voice tight.

"Just checking the kids," he said, casually, as if he ever did this.

There were no more night visits after that.

I was asleep in a large bed with my two sisters. We were startled awake by my father's yelling. Mom was crying.

"Stop it. You'll wake the kids. Leave me alone."

Something was wrong. He had been drinking again. I was ten years old. We were living in a cheap motel at the edge of town. There was nothing to do. We had brought few toys and there was no playground, only a dusty parking lot with battered cars and white trash families down on their luck. We stayed there for weeks. Daddy had a job, but he drank away his paycheck. We didn't have enough money to move into a real house.

"Fuck you, bitch. God damned son of a bitch. *Hija de puta,* shut up. I said shut the fuck up!"

"Leave me alone!"

"Don't tell me what to do, you fucking bitch. Shit. Look, you woke up the kids."

He beat her again, slapping and punching, in his rage tearing off her blouse. Her bare breasts flopped around. We stared, horrified, ashamed at her exposed body. She wrapped her arms around her chest, trying to cover herself. "Leave me alone," she pleaded, then she wept quietly, humiliated.

"Ah fuck you, bitch."

He stalked away into the other room and turned on the TV, muttering under his breath. Soon he "tanked out," as we came to call it, and everything got quiet. My sisters were crying softly. I looked around and noticed the sky through the window. The stars watched, blinking, mute.

My parents had been arguing on a cold winter night. Everyone was tense and went to bed early. Suddenly we heard a commotion on the front steps. I ran out in my nightgown. Daddy was beating Mom again, slapping her on the head, face, all over her body. Mom cried, "Leave me alone! I'm leaving. I can't take this any more. We live like animals. I can't take it anymore." I froze, panicked. If Mom leaves, what will we do? I would be responsible for everything. I silently pleaded with God, *Bring her back. Don't let her go.* My father pulled her back into the house by the hair. "If you ever try to leave again, I'll kill you, you fucking bitch. If you get away, I'll find you and kill you." The next morning, Mom's face was red and swollen, and there were bruises on her arm and face. There was an eerie silence as we got ready for school.

Mom never tried to leave my father again. My sisters and I learned to jump and please my father. When we saw him coming home, we turned off the television, picked up crying babies, cleaned up the clutter, slipped into our rooms. I stopped inviting my friends over. We became isolated, only able to play with other children when Daddy was gone.

As I came into adolescence, I came to hate my body, especially when my breasts developed at an early age. My father would notice when I wore shorts, and would slap my butt as I walked by, or fondle my breasts when he caught me alone. Although now I realize that I was slim, in those days I felt fat because of my developing curves — I was too womanly for a girl. I wanted to disappear.

I retreated into books and became an avid reader. I would walk to the public library every week (one of the few places I was allowed to go on my own) and would check out stacks of books. I waited every day for the afternoon newspaper and read it from cover to cover. I came to love stories of romance, faraway places, clever sleuths, warrior women. Reading was the only escape.

I was fifteen, naive, with few prospects for earning money. So I accepted a job to baby-sit for a woman I hardly knew. She lived in a back cottage on the edge of town. Her son was a toddler and would sleep most of the time, she promised. It was hot and I was just beginning to appreciate my woman's curves, so for the first time I wore a low-cut blouse. It was nighttime and I settled in to read in the dim light — Edgar Allan Poe's "The Raven." The poem was haunting and gave me the shivers. I noticed little creaking noises and the shadows made the dingy room seem spooky. I jumped at a knock on the door. There were two men, one the woman's boyfriend. They were Mexican *cholos*, dressed in plaid Pendleton shirts and baggy pants. I explained where they could find her. "*Orale, esa.*"

A short time later I was startled by a noise out back and realized I had not locked the back door. I rush to lock it when suddenly the door jerked open. One of the *cholos* pushed into the room, grabbed me, and threw me against the wall. The other watched, excited.

What's happening? What is he doing?

I screamed and he banged my head against the bathroom wall. Somehow I managed to run into the bedroom. He caught me, slapped me on the face several times, then threw me on the bouncy bed and tore open my shorts and ripped off my underpants. "No!" I screamed, trying to wrestle away. He held me down and put his hand over my mouth. *I couldn't breathe.* I panicked, then realized he could kill me in an instant and I went limp. Everything seemed as if we were in slow motion. I noticed the baby had stopped crying and stood in his crib watching, wide-eyed.

This isn't really happening. It's just a bad dream. I'll wake up in a minute. I want my Mommy. Blackness engulfed me. He quickly undid his pants and penetrated my ninety-pound body as I came to. It hurt too much, and I squirmed away. "Put it in," he hissed, then slapped me on the face. "I said, put it in!" I hesitated an instant, about to say no. I braced myself for the blows that would surely come. But there was a knock at the door. *Thank God!* I pulled up my shorts and ran to the door.

The neighbors had called the police when they heard my screams. I was never so glad to see anyone in my life. I rushed to one cop, hugging him, but he pushed me away. "He raped me," I said in a small, hoarse voice. I wasn't sure if that was the right word for it. The police handcuffed him and began searching the cottage, leaving us standing there side by side. A small crowd gathered at the edges of the light, staring at me, barefoot, clutching my shorts about my waist. I felt so humiliated.

"*¡Díles que soy un amigo!*" he whispered.

I avoided his eyes. He wanted me to say he was a friend.

He spat out, "*Si no le dices que soy un amigo, regresaré y te mato.*"

I edged away as I realized he had threatened to come back and kill me unless I pretended we were friends.

"You fucking bitch, you scratched me all over."

I stole a glance at his hands and arms. I did that? Then I flashed on Mom's warning, "*M'ija,* if you're ever in trouble scream as loud as you can." I don't remember scratching him or even screaming.

Feminists call the criminal justice system the "second rape," but actually I endured several assaults. The police took me to the station, where I was met by a woman officer. I had to tell the story several times, first to her and then to other male officers. Did I know the man? Did I invite him in, they asked. Of course not. "Was there fluid all over your legs?" I was puzzled. Fluid? While I had learned the mechanics of reproduction in school, ejaculation was a foreign concept and it took me a while to figure out what the officer was really asking. Finally they took me into another room for photographs of my black eye, bruised and lacerated face, and tattered clothes. When I saw myself in the mirror, I was shocked. The lump on my head throbbed.

Then the physical exam. Lying on my back, nude, freezing cold with only a sheet to cover my body. Bright lights, faces in blue caps and gowns standing around me. "Spread your legs, young lady." I had never had a pelvic exam and began to cry. *It hurts.* I struggled to pull away and the nurse held me down. No one bothered to explain the procedure. The doctor was a big man, built like a football player with huge hands and a patronizing manner. He stuck his finger in my vagina and it hurt like hell. "Aw come on, little lady, it doesn't hurt that much." They gave me a shot for possible venereal disease. After the ordeal was over, I overheard a *gringa* nurse saying, with disgust in her voice, "It shouldn't have hurt that much." Did she think I was faking it?

Facing my parents was the next feat. Mom was upset, her first questions: "Did you know him, *M'ija?* Was he your boyfriend?" *I can't believe it!* Daddy asked the same thing. "No, I didn't know him." We rode home in silence.

The next day I looked up the word *rape* in the dictionary and confirmed that indeed, that is what had happened to me. There was a short article in the local newspaper, without my name. I winced when I saw it, knowing that people would figure out who it was. I was right. My girlfriend asked for confirmation. People were talking about it. Only bad girls got into such trouble.

This was August, no school, so I had plenty of time to think. I was emotionally devastated, numb, my spirit broken. I asked myself over and over again, *Why did this happen to me? What did I do to deserve this? Why had I worn that blouse?* And more troubling: *Why had God abandoned me in my time of need?* I slowly and painfully came to the realization that no God would allow this to happen. I lost my faith in an all-powerful God. I attended church as usual, but it felt empty. I berated myself for not being more careful. *Why didn't I check the locks? Why hadn't I taken a sister along? Why had I worn that outfit?* Most eerie and puzzling of all, *Why hadn't I listened to my inner voice?* As I had dressed for the baby-sitting job, a thought had flashed through my mind, *What if something were to happen?* I dismissed it immediately as a weird idea. Later I chided myself for not paying attention to this thought. Had it been a warning?

It turned out that the rapist was an acquaintance of my father's. One night, drunk as usual, Daddy told me this, anger in his voice, as if somehow I had hurt *him.*

"People are talking. They say I have no control over my family." He got angrier and worked up. I didn't understand what he wanted from me. To recant my story? Then he made a threat: "I'll tell him where you live. He'll come back to get you." I sensed this was an idle threat. *How could you think such a thing? What about what happened to* me?

There was enough evidence to prosecute. Did my parents want to pursue the case? Daddy declared he wanted "to fry the son-of-a-bitch." After all, this was *his* daughter. The district attorney looked startled at my father's anger, then explained the limited possible penalties if the man were convicted. The point of his case would be my youth, and I realized that I would be on trial as well. He carefully instructed me about how to present myself in court. I was to dress in a modest way, nothing too revealing, and not too much makeup. No problem, that was how I always dressed.

The trial itself was brief. The jurors, all white, scrutinized me as I took the oath. I had to convince them that I was a good girl. The prosecution began with my school record, the grades I received, the activities I was involved in, my regular attendance at church. At one point I had to tell the grade expected for every course I was taking—all As and one B—and the jurors nodded approvingly. Then I had to draw the cottage, pointing out the location of all the events, and narrate what happened. There was a puzzling question—"Where were his hands?" I thought for a while, then shrugged, "I think somewhere near my shoulders."

The defense's questions centered on two things. "Why did I stop screaming and no longer resist?" I explained my thought processes, how at first I couldn't believe this was happening and then I was afraid that he would smother me, but the defense attorney pressed. Finally the judge admonished him, "She wasn't just lying there waiting to get raped." I felt horrible inside because in my mind that is exactly what had happened. The other question was whether I had ever seen a penis before. I couldn't say I had seen my father's penis, so I lied and said "No." *What do I say? I can't tell them the truth.*

"Then how do you know that he put in his penis? What color was it?"

"Brown."

"How do you know that was a penis?"

I was in a quandary. I couldn't admit the truth, that I knew what a man's penis looked like because I had seen my father's, but I was certain that the defendant had inserted his penis. I hung my head in shame. "I don't know."

I left the stand thinking that I had lost the case, feeling utterly miserable. The judge ordered a break, and in the bathroom, my mother admonished me. "Don't cry so much, *m'ija*." Apparently, if I appeared too distraught, I wouldn't be credible. I dried my tears and put on a stoic face. The argument made by the defense, I found out later, was that he had not penetrated me with his penis but with his finger. Stupid defense, since it was still forceful penetration of a minor. The rapist was convicted and sentenced to an indeterminate sentence: three to twenty-five years.

After the sentencing, the district attorney had a little talk with me. I shouldn't feel as if I had done any wrong. It was the rapist who was a horrible man. I choked at any response, desperately wanting to believe him. *Bless you*, I thought, *bless you*. He was the only person who ever told me it wasn't my fault. Despite his counsel, I felt completely empty and soiled. I knew that any dreams I had of a marriage in white were ruined—no man would want someone who had been used. And even though the rapist had been convicted, I knew that I would carry the stigma.

That night Daddy came home drunk, as usual. He sat me on his lap and told me that he was sorry about what had happened. He began to blubber and eventually cried. After his behavior throughout the whole ordeal, I was cynical. *"How do you expect me to believe you, after all this? Why didn't you believe me when I said I didn't know him?"* I got away as soon as I could. This is my only memory of my father holding me with tenderness.

I deliberately tried to forget all of these events and get on with my life. I hoped time would erase the trauma.

Twenty-five years later I was a parent with a daughter who was fourteen years old. She was staying out late and going places on her own, and she told me stories of flipping off men who harassed her on the street. I worried about her safety and decided that for her fifteenth birthday I would take her to self-defense classes. I was determined that nothing like what had happened to me would happen to her. I was so proud of her strong kicks and loud yells. In the middle of a lesson on averting a chokehold from behind, I had a flashback about a brown Pendleton shirt. I got woozy, couldn't breathe, and came home and crawled into bed, sobbing as I remembered the rape. I realized that even if the rapist had served a full sentence, he would be out of prison. I developed severe back pain and couldn't return to the classes. Finally I went to an acupuncturist for relief from the pain. While I was under treatment, she quietly asked me: "What are you avoiding? Your body is your best friend. It's trying to tell you something." I winced at the new-age language, but then I looked down at my chest and had a momentary vision of churning black clouds, a violent storm that would suck me in and drown me. Utter chaos. I realized it was time to confront the demons.

As I began therapy and talked about my father and my childhood, it felt like ripping off a huge, thick burn scar that covered my whole chest. Each telling felt like I was ripping the scar an inch at a time, it was so painful. I was drowning in sorrow, rage, and self-blame. I felt ugly and fat. Over time the therapist taught me a powerful reconfiguration: I am not a bad person. I am a survivor, not a victim. In each incident of abuse, I did what I could to protect myself. I cried and stayed out of my father's way; I screamed and fought the rapist, and then I testified so that he was convicted. And, when it was necessary, I let go and saved my own life. Through therapy, I also recognized my mother's unseen power. The summer after the rape I had told her about the night visits. "I thought something like that was going on," she said, remorseful and sad. Even though she had little control over my father, in her own way my mother also helped to stop the night visits, and I am grateful for that. And I learned that the shame I felt toward my body reflected the abuses imposed upon me.

I also sought comfort through reading and found knowledge a powerful tool for recovery. I learned to name what had happened to me. Men are violent toward women out of their own rage or sense of powerlessness. Women are usually raped by men within their own racial group. Pedophiles, batterers, rapists, and alcoholics often do to others what they saw or what was done to them as children. My father was a very sick man. Despite these men's own pain, there is no excuse for what they did to me. The rapist's punishment by no means compensates for the trauma I experienced.

Despite these insights, the night terrors continue to haunt me. I have recurring dreams where I am a child in my parents' home. My father is telling me what to do and I feel powerless. I still have occasional nightmares about dark men chasing me. It is nighttime and I am desperately trying to get away from them, to get home. I run and my legs become rubbery, failing me. "I see a volcano inside you, ready to explode," the therapist said, and she encouraged me to write down what had happened. It would be a year before I could take her advice.

These words began literally in the middle of the night. I awoke from an uneasy sleep where I had dreamed about my father, again. I stumbled to the computer and wrote nonstop about the first night terror, unable to even look at the words on the screen. It was a year before I could reread them and begin forming coherent sentences.

When memory is repressed and then returns, there is often a liminal space between recall and imagination. I asked myself over and over again, did this really happen? Did it happen like that? I kept these little stories hidden away, too ashamed to show them to anyone. Even today, my family does not talk about this, the silence remarkable. It wasn't until our Latina Feminist Summer Institute that, with the support of other women, I found the courage to tell these experiences out loud. Through the telling, when *las mujeres* immediately believed me without question, any doubts about their truth disappeared. It did happen like that.

At Baca I realized, for the first time, that the wrong touch makes me cringe. Another woman told how she refused to be touched by anyone, and I realized that I, too, jump when someone I don't trust touches me. Baca is where I also realized that disclosing family secrets touches a raw nerve, evoking waves of guilt and worry. And I realized the power of denial, where we doubt our own experiences. Later at home in my partner's arms, I cried, "It took me all these years to figure this out." Baca will always remind me of women's power, of the love and trust we had for one another as we gave testimony about our lives.

Writing these stories for others to read has been difficult. I still cry every time I read this *papelito*. Though memories recorded here came to me slowly at first, after Baca they turned into a flood of feelings and images. It became *necessary* to write them down, to channel the torrent. As I crafted the memories into stories, I took control over the narrative and felt some empowerment by telling them from *my* point of view. The process of writing has been a lancing of the wounds, and some of the hurt was transposed into healing. As I cleanse myself of sadness and anger, I contemplate the possibility of forgiveness toward these men, but I'm not there yet. In a loving relationship with a man I am recuperating myself as a sexual person and beginning to *feel* the insights I gained through therapy. I am learning to love my body and see it as a source of wisdom rather than betrayal. To hasten the healing, I surround myself with love and beauty.

La Princesa

Latina Anónima

HIS CAR PULLED INTO the driveway. I was crouching behind my neighbor's car, waiting for him to enter the house. As soon as I heard the door slam shut, my heart racing, I ran to the end of the block. I remember feeling the wind in my face and my backpack, carrying students' exams, slumped against my right shoulder. All my senses were alert. It was past dusk and all I could think of was "Where can I go?"

I spotted a bus and jumped on it, shaking, as I slipped some coins into the box, trying to pretend—that everything was fine.

I had finally left him for good. Memories jarred my otherwise numb state.

It was Christmas Eve. We were celebrating it quietly, with a roaring fire, a small "charlie brown" kind of tree, and an abundance of gifts to exchange. I opened package after package—of clothes he had picked out for me. Meanwhile, I lost count of his drinks. Later that evening, I soaked the sleeve of my new coat, stained with blood from the busted lip he had added to my evening's "gifts." I wondered how I would hide the bruises on my left temple and the cuts on the lower left corner of my lip from the friends coming over the next day for tamales. I remember, most of all, looking in the mirror the next morning, not recognizing my own eyes. They were completely vacant of all emotion.

As the bus made stop after stop, I remembered the two years' worth of incidents, apology after apology, promise after promise. I clung to the memory of when I finally snapped, of the moment I knew I would *plan my escape*. It was toward the end of the relationship. By this time I was getting "bold," verbally challenging him when he questioned me, not caring if what I said provoked him. By that time I had finally figured out that no matter what I did, he would find reason for violence.

I entered the house, carrying bags of groceries, placing them on the table. He questioned me, asking me why I had gotten the wrong kind of sausage. He had asked for hot links and I had bought Italian sausage. He wanted me to return to the store and get the ones he wanted. I didn't like the fact that his tone of voice was in the form of an order. "Go back to the store and get the RIGHT *kind," he screamed. I refused and told him, "I'm not going." He shoved me, from one room to another, beginning his tirade of intimidation. When we entered the living room, he pushed me to the floor. I feigned that he had hurt my back, as a way of keeping him from continuing. Not knowing whether he had really hurt me, he kicked me. He kicked me while I was down on the floor. I was no better than a dog. That's when I snapped.*

That's when I knew that whatever it took I would leave this animal and keep him out of my life forever.

Over the next few months, as I recovered in the safety of my mother's home, I kept asking myself, How could this happen to me? Only a few years before, I had been special. My picture made Spanish-speaking newspapers, announcing my fellowship award to attend graduate school. My entire history, up until this point, had been laced with validation, awards, and recognition for my academic achievements. And at home, I had been loved and cherished. How could I have reached the point that I would accept the slightest form of physical or emotional violence to my person? The question remains today.

As I sought ways to heal and understand, I did what every good academic does. I went to the library. I punched in the words "battery," "domestic violence," and "women" into the computer. Based on her research and interviews in *The Battered Woman*, Lenore Walker developed a typology of characteristics and types of women who tend to become victims of domestic violence. In these pages, I found a description of "the princess syndrome." The princess, Walker explains, is shocked by her confrontation with violence. So sheltered, protected, and revered has she been and so unexposed to any kind of violence in her life that when she encounters someone violent, she is in a state of shock. With no experience of invalidation and feeling intense personal criticism for the first time in her life, the princess believes she can "do right" by the perpetrator and change his opinion of her. Like the other types of women, she endures all the typical cycles before leaving the batterer.

With hindsight, in contextualizing my circumstances, it would be an understatement to say that there were competing tensions in my life at the time. They culminated to create ripe conditions—even for a former homecoming "princess," literally—to enter and come to know a sphere of violence far too many women experience. Ideologically, I had failed to reconcile the family expectation that I marry and have children with my pursuit of an advanced degree and my identity as a Chicana feminist (the ironies prevail). I thought I could have both. Hence, when I connected with this man I was still trying to be a "good girl" and find that husband everyone expected. Yet I was in a graduate program that was brutally competitive, alienating, and disempowering. Looking back, I realize that my self-esteem was at an all-time low with respect to my graduate studies and that I was no longer looking to the institution, or academic processes, to nourish my sense of self. Thus, it was no surprise that when I met this man I foolishly looked to him as someone who would make me feel that I was special.

During pensive moments, I've developed a theory for *princesas* of color. *Earned privileges* in a given life cycle only buy us time. The structures of subordination will get even the achievers. Those who think they might have escaped find themselves — like countless other *princesas* of color — treated just as women. Today the memories of this time in my life seem surreal. I do not identify, much less connect, with the experiences I've just recounted. It's as if they belong to someone else. But they don't, and instead they are tucked away in what I like to call my *caja de llagas,* my box of scars. I do, however, use the memories to move myself into using my voice. By remembering the contents, I remember to speak.

Forced by Circumstance

Norma Alarcón

to be a woman I've had to live
far from your scent
far from your calloused lips
and smoke-stained hands

The day I left
I heard the miscrack of a wishbone and
longed to pull your flesh off every rib,
putting off a kill I felt fated to fulfill
I held back   I held back
gestures   glances   even sounds

I've had to let you go   to evoke my name
though your face follows me
reminding me of the unsaid

Enveloped by the silence of a mushroom cloud
I left with cardboard boxes arm in arm and
joined the endless lines of hapless immigrants
who gather up their threadbare breath and walk

I've walked everywhere
I've walked everywhere you've walked
Following your tracks on pressed down dirt
I've lived inside your every move
your every thought

Forced by circumstance to be a woman
I've lived far from your scent
though your face follows me
reminding me of the unsaid

Let Me Sleep

Latina Anónima

THE POLICEWOMAN searches through all my drawers, under the mattress; she empties the Tylenol and Excedrin bottles, finds the few Percodans that are left and takes those too. I have awakened to the sight of paramedics and police officers in my little bedroom; I feel the arms of one of the paramedics tense as he lifts me to the stretcher. The building superintendent is in the hallway, his wife peering from behind their door. I silently protest being carried away from my home. How the hell have they found me? How could they have known? During the longest shortest ride in the ambulance to the hospital two blocks away, the blond policewoman rides in the back with me and another paramedic. I try to tell them I am fine, but my mouth is cotton, dry, choking me. I wonder what time it is, what day it is, what does it matter.

In the emergency room the young crew surrounds me. What did you take? How much? How many? When? Who is your doctor? Who do we call? My mouth is still dry, my mind taking in the clock, oh, 1 A.M., lying in the bright lights so different from my darkened room, hearing the clanging of metal on metal, the cold air of the room bruising my face. I just want to sleep. I want to say, Let me sleep. One young man brings in a tube, a metal pan, a hypodermic needle, we are going to put this through your nose to reach into your stomach and pump out what's left. Through my nose, up my nostril, they push and I bleed. My way was so bloodless and neat, but now I am covered in my blood, and still the tube does not go through. A young woman comes to help, she prods the tube into my bleeding nostril, the pain is searing but I am mantra-like chanting silently my comforting tuneless chant "death and dying, death and dying, death and dying'" and am neither resisting nor helping them push this impossibly large green plastic tube into my nasal passage. I am sure I will die now of asphyxiation. Whatever. I will accept whatever.

In the slot next to me a man has been brought in. He is white as a corpse I think to myself. He looks gay, a Christopher Street clone. His mustache and dark hair remind me of my friend Matthew, and I think, oh, no, it can't be Matthew. But then I am told to open my mouth, that I must swallow the green tube, that my nasal passages are too thin, oh, I think, even in this I am a failure, but I am more concerned for the man who is lying next to me, the curtain has not been run all the way, I can see that they are going to try to revive him with those electrical machines I know only from television, his face, which will remain in my mind forever, is solemnly peaceful, they are not trying to stick a tube into his nostrils, I gag and throw up blood, they are scraping my throat now with their green plastic tube, I try to talk but cry instead, the blood nauseates me, but I think, they are doing this to make sure that I never do this again, they are making it hard so that I will be scared to do this again, but I am angry and swear that I will go home and next time I will not fail, they cannot scare me, and I look at the man in the other bed, and his body jumps from the electrical impulses they are sending through his limbs, and they yell again, and zap him with electricity that does not awaken him. And I think, god, he probably didn't even want to die, he probably didn't even want to die. And then I feel the tightening in my stomach, something has made its way there and scrapes and burns and I want to scream "why him?" but my mouth tastes of blood and vomit and plastic and the sour taste of the pills I have swallowed, and green bile green liquid comes out of me through that tube and I know that it will soon be all over for me, and I try to will the man alive but they have left him there, silent, pale, alone and I am being filled with gray tarry liquid, I am being fed charcoal through the tube, I want to cry out in frustration but I am exhausted and I am still alive.

At 3 A.M. they advise me of their intentions to admit me into the psychiatric ward. No, I think. I will die there. I do not want to die there. No, I say, I want to go home. Sign here that you are being released on your request. I sign. The dead man is still lying in his little corner of the emergency room. My blouse is bloody and my mouth is dry from the charcoal. I walk out the door into the city streets and walk the two blocks home. My door is unlocked, my clothes are scattered, the medicine cabinet has been emptied, I remember the blond policewoman, she was thorough, she even found my backup stash. I set the alarm clock for 7:30. I have a nine o'clock class to teach. I lie down on my bed again and sleep.

Depression

Mirtha N. Quintanales

A balloon inside of me
Expands
The past haunts me
In unexpected letters
And mysterious phone calls
Today is visited
    by yesterday
   Tomorrow will be
      by today
Searching for the origins of trouble
I gulp down history
Karma in great swallows
My body grows slow and heavy
In vain I try to start anew

New York City, Fall 1982

Desde el Diván/Testimonios from the Couch

Yvette Gisele Flores-Ortiz

DE LA MISMA *manera que el continente América ha grabado en la topografía de su tierra las invasiones, los agravios, robos, asaltos y desacros, mi cuerpo, tu cuerpo, su cuerpo recuerda violaciones a sus derechos humanos.*

In the same manner the American continent has recorded in her geography the invasions, assaults, robberies, and desecrations it has endured, my body, your body, her body remembers all the human rights violations it has suffered.

She is a young woman, a successful attorney, who experiences shortness of breath and anxiety attacks:

"I can't breathe, I can't swallow, I feel as if a weight lay on my chest. *No me salen las palabras cuando quiero hablar. Algo bloquea mi voz,* invisible hands encircle my neck, tightening, pressing, choking, until I can no longer think, feel or remember, until I have no voice to tell."

She is a college student who suffers from bulimia:

"I cannot eat, my stomach is all in knots. I threw up again this morning. I don't know why I awaken to dreams of snakes and dragons. I feel as if I have been eating chalk. I have to purge, whatever this is inside me must come out."

She is fourteen, on the threshold of womanhood:

"The nightmares returned again last night. I felt a presence in my room. My mother said it must be *el diablo* because I wouldn't go to church on Sunday. I cannot tell her that her God and baby Jesus abandoned me a long time ago, *y la virgencita,* she would not understand, *ella fue una virgen,* mother, *¿que no?*"

Her family thinks she is going crazy because she has joined a gang and no longer attends school:

"The voices returned, they told me I was bad, naughty, *la puta, la mala, la culpable, la que lo hace hacerme daño.* Daddies don't hurt their daughters, it must be something I did. I know he loves me, he told me so. He said this is special between us and nobody must know. I don't think this is special, but if I told, would I be believed? My *prima* wasn't, and now everyone avoids her. Besides, it would break my mother's heart, so I better keep quiet. Promise me you won't tell, please."

She can't concentrate at work; of late she has been unable to perform to her own standards in her very demanding professional career:

"The headaches, so many voices trying to escape, so many *gritos que no pueden salir de mi garganta, mi estómago, mi alma. Silencio, quiero silencio, quiero silencio, el silencio eterno. Quiero morir.*"

She is twenty-two years old; her professors and mother worry. She is absent-minded and appears at times to be depressed:

"I saw flying penises in my room again; they danced around the ceiling fan. His face was at my window. So was mine, a disembodied mouth, open, unwillingly receiving his hardness. But that is not my mouth, and that is not his dick. They fly around the room, unattached. They meet in the darkness of my room, while my baby sister sleeps next to me. My real mouth is shut, tight, as I sleep. His body is in his room, sleeping next to Mom. Only his dick visits my mouth at night. Everything else sleeps."

She has been in therapy several years and now feels ready to tell:

"When he would come in to my room, late at night, when everyone else slept, I would look out my window. I would look at the stars and count them. I would imagine I was atop a pyramid about to be sacrificed, another virgin to another male god. Because when he came in me, he tore out my heart."

She has been in the United States a short time, having fled the violence in her country and family:

"*Tengo una relación muy íntima con la depresión. Somos mejores amigas,* I can always count on her. She comes to visit if I am about to feel happy, if perchance I am attracted to someone, but especially if my guard is down and I am about to trust. She comes to remind me that it is not safe, 'watch out, go inward, pay attention, listen to your internal voice *que te previene.*' *La depre me acompaña, me cuida, me protege,* don't even think of asking me to give her up. She is the only one who doesn't lie."

Coworkers complain that she is angry and has an attitude problem:

"You ask me what I feel. You have a fucked-up sense of humor, *doctora*. Feel is an f-word, a four-letter word. I don't feel, I don't fuck. That is something done to me. I am merely the receptacle of their rage / sperm, *su esperma-rabia. Soy la cogida, la jodida, la Malinche*. That is what they say anyway. Who is they? *Los cabrones, los que luchan por la causa,* wearing their berets, *los políticos, revolucionarios, pinches cabrones. La única revolución que saben hacer es la destrucción de mi cuerpo y mi alma.* They speak *pinche movimiento y causa,* but they are takers not givers. You ask me what I feel. You have a fucked-up sense of humor. What do I feel? OK I'll tell you. *Carnalismo* sucks."

She self-mutilates, carving into her body the words "I remember'":

"Why do you want to know what happened to me? I don't want to remember. Leave me alone in my darkness, it does not matter that I cannot enjoy the tenderness of a potential lover, that I cannot trust the possible authenticity and sincerity of a potential friend. I am fine in my aloneness. No one can hurt me if I don't let them in. No one can touch the essence of my being, it is too buried beneath the layers of hurt and violation. I don't want to remember, leave me in my darkness to find my own light."

She is a community activist, a successful organizer:

"A white sister mentioned that I did not appear to be angry enough. The nerve. What does she know about my anger. I don't get angry like a white woman. I get angry *como Chicana. Bueno, al menos así lo hago yo, me trago la rabia, escribo poemas, y rehuso morir.* Survival is the best revenge. I don't scream, I don't yell, I write. *¿Cuál fue el vato que dijo que el* pen is mightier than the sword? *Bueno, al menos así lo hago yo.* I tell my brown sisters they don't have to take it. *Si el familismo y toda esa pendejada patriarcal te oprime, pues a la chingada. Si te llaman vendida, pues a la chingada también. Mejor vendida que cogida.* My words, *mis poemas,* propose a different *familia,* a different *comunidad. Y si los vatos* want to join us, *órale. Si no,* see you later, *carnal. Pero no me acuses de destruir la familia, carnal. Estudia tu historia, carnal.* Your male gods failed you. You laid down the sword, you let us be raped. Don't ask me to sacrifice myself for you. Been there, done that. *Chale, vato,* fight your own battles."

She is a professor with a Ph.D. in social sciences and another in masking her pain:

"You ask me why I do what I do, why I teach, and write, despite the disapproval of colleagues who should support me, of an institution that does not care, where I am often invisible? I write because I must, because I have the privilege of education, the power of my words. Because there are too many sisters out there who cannot yet use their own voice. So I collect their stories, they are the pillars that hold me up, when I stand before my students, when I give a talk, and when I sit down to write. My *tías* were mediums, and I conjure their essence when I sit down to write, because I need their voices to counter the silencing echoes of hegemony, patriarchy, and *lealtad*. I write and work within the walls of academia because I must, because I can, *porque puedo y porque quiero*. I teach and I write because the words transform my rage, my pain. Because when I teach and write, I give voice to my body, and my body remembers."

Como América, el continente, su cuerpo, mi cuerpo, tu cuerpo is living testament of endurance, survival, transformation.

Look at us, I invite you. Can you tell, which one of us was not violated? Which among us is not a survivor of multiple atrocities? *Pero ni el rapto, la violación, el maltrato físico, la violencia espiritual, psicológica, emocional, ni el incesto nos ha destruido.* Look at us, I invite you. Your institutions will not destroy us. If you keep us out, we will find another way to make our voices heard. We know, we remember, we speak, and we hold you accountable.

These are the collective voices spoken, heard and written in a safe space in California. They are not fiction. They are offerings from us to you, because the body remembers, and the soul finds its own voice.

Telling To Live:
Devoro la Mentira, Resucitando Mi Ser
Inés Hernández Avila

I REMEMBER HOW a molestation memory stalked me for over forty years until a healer woman helped me with it. She told me she could see how the memory was placed in my psyche by a distant relative who was the perpetrator to make me believe I was the dirty one, the nasty one, the one to blame. As she talked to me about what she was seeing, my body reverberated forcefully and gratefully. Upon hearing the truth, I cried hard as the *tormenta* around me began to clear. For the first time since the molestation had occurred, for the first time since I was four years old, my tears and the rage I did not know how to name connected with their source, and I was free of an implanted and distorted memory that had shamed and silenced me all my life. With the freedom to speak and the ability to name came another level of rage I have had to learn to heal, because I am certain the molestation affected my perception of how I, as a female, should be treated for much of my adult life. As I felt the rage surface, I reconnected with the energy of violence, of violation I knew as a small child, memories of being overwhelmed with a need to hurt, a need to turn on someone or something more vulnerable than me, to yell, to kick, to release the seemingly unconscious fury I was feeling. The fury, I see now, was my signal that I was alive and, at the level of spirit, supremely conscious of the depth of the offense and betrayal to my being. It has taken me a very long time to piece my life's experiences together in a way that addresses the intricately complicated narrative my body has recorded, and I have had to pass many *pruebas* along the way.

My first husband was an abuser. He constantly humiliated me verbally and reduced my self-esteem to nothing, till I thought I was going crazy. Then he beat me badly when I was two months pregnant with my second son. I told him that if he ever touched me violently again, I would leave him (it is ironic to me that the physical act seemed more violent, when the violence to my spirit had already been devastating). When he hit me a second time, weeks later, I didn't do anything (the first time I had tried to push him off of me), but the next morning, after he left for work, I phoned my parents and told them to come for me and my baby son. I never went back. I was four months pregnant. I know that these experiences affected my relationships with men for more than twenty years. I often suffered degradation, violation, and rape, at some level thinking I deserved mistreatment. Even though outwardly I was known as a strong woman organizer and cultural worker for the community, inside I was empty. In public, my writer's voice always spoke up on behalf of women, while I listened to an internalized voice that told me I would never be good enough at anything, and no one would ever love me. It was only when I began to work on myself, to search for my integrity and truly care for myself that I was able to resuscitate my voice, and feel my own power and beauty as a woman, as a human being. Then finally I was able to recognize and accept a partner, a soul mate who truly loves me, a husband who is my life's companion.

Testimonies. Stories. Life stories. In the beginning it is hard to speak, to write, to tell of abuse in the first person, because the first assault is on the spirit. When we suffer violence, the wound degrades the spirit, and when the spirit is hurt, a space is opened for shame to enter, and the blame of self can begin to weave a blanket of silence. This silence is not the silence of inner peace or contemplation, it is not the silence of fulfillment and self-love. These silences are good and necessary for the spirit; they represent the time we take to be with ourselves, *calmadamente, cariñosamente*. The other silence, caused by terror, fear, guilt, and self-loathing, is the silence of control and domination. All the cultural conditioning we receive as *mujeres* (not only within the Latina/o and indigenous communities but in society as a whole) dictates to us the need to keep up appearances, to not let anyone know of the abuse. To break the silence makes the family look bad. To admit the shattered foundations makes the community look bad. To call attention to the internal contradictions makes the social organization look bad. Better to pretend that all is well. Better to fabricate a unified front. Better to lie.

Pero la mentira dura hasta que la verdad llega. As more and more *mujeres* stand together to tell our truths and to give *valor* to each other's stories, we call the lies for what they are. We do not destroy our communities. The lies destroy our communities. Over the generations the lies have caused us to deceive only ourselves. In front of our young people and our children who see with the eyes of their hearts and know when justice is not served, we keep up appearances at their expense. We create the lies they might continue unless a miracle occurs to help them not fall into the same patterns. Truth is a miracle. Knowing our own truths is a miracle. Truth comes from knowing our own selves with such a tender and profound intimacy that we can surely trust our intuition. We can surely trust our bodies, in each reverberation and tremor, because we have embraced ourselves with utmost love, *pasión,* and delicacy. We have the right to answer the following questions for ourselves: Who am I? What am I about? What do I want to accomplish in this life on this earth? What is it that fulfills me? When am I the most happy? What is it that makes me laugh? How shall I be true to myself? Telling the truth defeats the hierarchy of domination by creating miracles. Each truth telling makes the next time easier. Each miracle reconnects us to ourselves, to our source, to life itself, and to our visions for ourselves.

In each cell of our bodies the violations leave their imprints that can make us forsake our creative powers as women. These imprints affect our memories, especially when they begin to erase any self-esteem we have and cause us to see ourselves only as *mujeres malas.* The memory of the violations we have suffered is tremendous enough. The memory of being judged and rejected by our loved ones when we tell our stories can add another heavy layer of pain to our load. Sometimes we have to stand alone, apart from our families, if they are unwilling to understand. In such times, at all times, having our own certainty is crucial. We must nurture every cell of our being. We must look within ourselves and find our beauty. We must recreate ourselves with much, much love. As we uncover our complexity as human beings, we find that each of us must come up with our own answers regarding the many facets of our selves.

Nuestra compañera escritora pensadora Gloria Anzaldúa has said, *"Hay que distinguir entre lo impuesto, lo heredado, y lo adquirido."* As Latinas and Native women, what has been imposed on us, what have we inherited, and what have we acquired? These questions point to a history that encompasses us all, a hemispheric history, a global history that is textured by the differences of class, race, ethnicity, gender, sexualities, nationalities, cultures, and homelands. How do our personal histories intersect with each other as *mujeres,* and with the collective histories of our communities, however we define and distinguish those communities? How do we process the cumulative effects of our individual and social histories upon ourselves and our past and future generations? Which tools of analysis are critical to the re-search and recovery of our selves and our peoples? As we strive to be conscious human beings, we situate ourselves more and more concretely as agents of history. The moment we reject being objects, we begin to be subjects of our own destinies. The path of consciousness is hard but joyful and often paradoxical. Sometimes we might feel lonely, but as we pursue our answers we continuously discover that we are not alone. Each discovery adds more light to the path, allowing us to see and be with others in solidarity. Each piece of sifted information helps us figure out the puzzles, personally, collectively, globally. Once begun, there is no turning back. To forsake consciousness is to forsake being human. Being conscious is being a seer.

We are living in a social political climate in the state of California and in this nation that is increasingly and dangerously repressive for Latina/o and indigenous people. In the face of a growing and dehumanizing war on our communities, how can we struggle for social justice for our children and each other if we are subjected to violence daily as a fact of life within our own intimate circles? How can we struggle on behalf of our whole communities when many in our communities do not see us as part of the whole, as worthy of a voice and a place? For the sake of ourselves and our people, we must take a stand as warrior women. The first stand must be for ourselves as women and for the children, *los inocentes*. The only way for us to be able to respond with strength and clarity to the assault on our communities is to work from within to confront and heal the assaults on our selves. No movement can last if its foundations are rotten, or its clarity compromised by a refusal to transform what holds us back as individuals, as families, as communities. As *mujeres*, we know what holds us back. It is no secret and it never has been. In our hearts, in our spirits, in our bodies, we have known full well what is wrong, even when our subjugated minds tried to convince us otherwise, even when we did not yet have the words to name the causes of the wrongs. Patriarchy. Misogyny. Sexism. Racism. Classism. Homophobia. Ageism (Cultural) Nationalism. Religious fundamentalism. It has been easier in the activist community to raise these issues against mainstream (colonialist/imperialist/hemispheric) America. It is much harder to raise these issues as they apply to ourselves. I have been met with outrage when I bring them up. I have been challenged, "What about the five hundred years of colonization?!!" I have answered, "We all know that, it's the easy part, what we won't admit is the damage that has been done internally, by ourselves, to our women, our children, and our people."

We must be prepared to face rejection even by our own loved ones when we stand up for ourselves to tell our stories and name our truths. We might also happily learn who in our families stands with us. Regardless, we must give ourselves credit for the good we have done for ourselves. As we heal, we tenderly regather our selves in our totality as physical, emotional, intellectual, spiritual, creative beings. As we refine our strategies of survival and transformation, we realize how to know and show compassion and forgiveness, to ourselves first, then to others. By loving our bodies and our minds, we do honor to our spirits and our hearts. Moving through the grief and the anger, we find the laughter, the smiles, and the female creativity and power that belong to us. I cannot say enough on behalf of laughter and its wonderful life-giving power against the energy of guilt, judgment, contempt, hostility that is thrown into the space of someone who is recovering from abuse. As we recreate the delicately strong fabric of our lives, we must always remember: *Tengo valor.* I have value and I am brave. *Tenemos valor.* We have value and we are brave. May the stories be cherished and sustained.

IV Passions, Desires, and Celebrations

I N THIS LAST SECTION we culminate the process of telling our histories by rejoicing in the vital energies that have made it all possible. We have arrived at a particular point in our *testimoniando* where we relish affirming who we truly are.

We became inspired to explore diverse genres while expressing the humor, the beauty, the spirit, and the sensuality that are both our legacy and our personal constructions. These pieces are very "Latina," and yet they are simply human, and richly female. We reminisce about our coming out as writers, we enjoy the ecstasy of physical love, we tell about the pleasures of working with other women of our tradition. We reflect introspectively on how our destiny brings us to self-knowledge, and we relate the struggles of coming to terms with our own subjectivities. These stories, poems, and essays are a paean to life, to having walked on the edge and through the fires of conflict. Not only survival but also personal fulfillment and variable degrees of marketable success are the fruits we have reaped as we journeyed through immigration and diaspora, as we navigated the perilous seas of academic conflicts, as we danced in the glory of creative realizations or shed a tear for our losses.

In the testimonies offered by autobiographical fiction, by our stories and our poems and our journals and our essays on living, there is a thread of passion that links us to perseverance. It also links us to the faith we have in ourselves and/or in something intangible that some of us call divinity and that others among us would not know what to call. The joys of discovery are similar to the satisfaction of having done our work well, and perhaps we should say that we are proud of our lives: after all, why not celebrate our own making?

Variety abounds from "*La Cosa*" to "Everyday Grace" and in vignettes of

Latina lives where writing, geography, or sexuality are contemplated. Music, culture, and secrets of our innermost selves are revealed in the practice of gathering our testimonials. There is mischief and magic in these pages, in these expressions of Latina lives that give voice to our memories, to our relationships with people and with events. These are, we repeat, relationships of sustenance and symbols of our having become who we are.

There is a toast in these voices, to ourselves and to our becoming, a rich tribute to our different *latinidades femeninas y feministas*. A Pan-Latina party for all! Our written version of those nights at Café Baca in the Colorado mountains.

And last but not least, as some of us suggested in the beginning, this is where our love meets itself, and where we dance in all varieties of movement. We hope the reader might feel inspired to dance with us.

Shameless Desire

Aurora Levins Morales

I SLIP AWAY FROM my lover to meet you in deserted parks. Whenever we come together again after an absence, I am a little shy, but how your presence intoxicates me! In minutes I am high as a kite. All these years and infidelities and you have never once wavered, never gone out of reach. You are the most dazzling lover, the one with the sweetest, most knowledgeable touch, the one who gets all my jokes, remembers my shiest thoughts, cherishes me the most unabashedly. At night, in your arms, I dream the best dreams, those dark and shining revelations from which art and poetry rise like fire. You are the one who insists on the best for me, who puts her foot down when enough is too much and gets me out of the corner into which I have once again backed myself. No one is more loyal and I have no secrets from you.

I am not supposed to love you like this, to gloat that I have you, to rejoice in every moment alone with you. You are supposed to belong to someone else. You are female, so I must not love you as if it matters. You are Latina, so I must not take you seriously, as a force in this world. You are Jewish, so I must not cherish and trust you. This is what they try to tell me. But I lust after you night and day, love you in the moments when I am most afraid to love, want you with me more and more, every day, ever more intensely.

You are the one I have been told it is most shameful to want. No one is as forbidden. No desire more ridiculed. Such transgression! Such delight! Such trembling as I claim you before others. How many officious people have tried to part us. What force has been used, what invasions and tortures, what atrocities committed in a vain attempt to crush our love.

How glorious it is, here among my *hermanas,* to be able, at last to openly admire your fineness, boast about your courage, graciously acknowledge how much you have given, accept praise on your behalf. *Querida,* each day I become more worthy of your trust, more determined to put you first, to care for you the way I have cared for those other lovers, so much less reliable. Here and now, before all these *gente,* I proclaim it. I am the love of my own life, and I will cherish and defend me against slander and disrespect, violence and erasure, in sickness and health, in favor or out, come hell or high water, until death does me scatter, amen.

La Cosa

Ruth Behar

for Mami

My mother taught me to be afraid
of *la cosa*
between your legs
to run from it
like the plague
not to look in that direction
because that meant I wanted it.

She wanted to be sure
I got through school
became someone
before I let myself
go mad with yearning
for *la cosa*
between your legs.

Years and years
when I wanted
and wanted *la cosa*
between your legs
all I could do was flee.
I am remembered as the woman
who was gone when you awoke.

I guess I should
thank you, Ma, for your concern
and for my credentials.

I'm a professional woman now.
I have a house, a good job,
a bank account, and a computer.

And the *cosita*
between his legs —
I have that too.

Boleros: A Very Melodramatic Musical Performance

Eliana Rivero

(PLEASE IMAGINE *a stage with a big boom box and a large video screen. The woman acting this out, namely me — the narrator, yours truly — speaks and sings in different voices: to the audience, to a friend. On the screen, a black-and-white slide show of ballad crooners, couples dancing, the faces of great boleristas, Latino MTV style.)*

I admire the Cuban American Gloria Estefan very much. You know I am her fan, and I hope to see her in concert pretty soon. She is a gutsy woman with great determination and spiritual insights. And what a voice! As if that were not enough, she owns two Dalmatians named Ricky and Lucy (Ricardo)! I am so proud of her.

Mostly, I like her *boleros,* the ballads she sings with a deep voice that talks of love and pain and, sometimes, delusion:

"I'm not giving you up" (yeah, well);

"*Hablas de mí*" (you kiss and tell, what a fink);

"The heart never learns" (it sure doesn't);

"*Con los años que me quedan*" (many years left, I hope).

They bring me back to the early sixties on L Street in *El Vedado, La Habana,* when I used to listen to La Lupe belt out her unforgettable torch songs at *El Gato Tuerto.* (The One-Eyed Cat. What a great name for a nightclub!)

And a few blocks away, on La Rampa Boulevard, Frank Domínguez at the piano was singing his "feeling" numbers:

(with piano accompaniment)
En el hechizo de tu mirada había ternura,
y en el encanto de tu sonrisa tibia dulzura.
Pero el destino marca un camino que nos tortura,

y entre mis brazos quedó el espacio de tu figura
Y desde entonces te ando buscando para decirte
que como un niño, cuando te fuiste me quedé llorando.

Allow me to give you my own version of these lines:

"Bewitching gaze, full of tenderness, charming smile with warm sweetness. . . . But destiny has other plans, and points to a torturing road; my arms are empty, now that you went away. I still look for you, to tell you that I cry like a child when I think of you" (*¿qué melodrama, no?*).

Talk about passions. It seems that life is an interminable succession of *boleros,* ballads to be danced when one is happy or sad, drinking rum, wine, or nothing, just sitting around musing about the pain of rejection.

S/he inspires this music, these lines. He (or she) writes the songs. S/he listens. They dance, all of them. A Latino tradition, mixed in with other cultural strains. The hurt and sadness of rancheras, tangos, country western, the blues: everything we have listened to and liked, rolled into one. From Gardel to Lucha Villa, from el Benny Moré to Gloria going through Anne Murray and Aretha Franklin: what a tradition. "*¡Que siga la tradición!*" *como canta la Estefan.*

And then there is *Contigo en la distancia,* by César Portillo de la Luz. Now *that* is a classic. I play it often on the piano ("With you in the distance," isn't that appropriate?), and I think of your voice, your eyes, your look. Two, three, five stars appear in the early evening sky: it's not the same if you are not around. I remember Ernesto Cardenal's poem:

Si tú no estás en Nueva York,
en Nueva York no hay nadie.
Y si tú estás en Nueva York,
en Nueva York no hay nadie más.

Again, my own version: "If you are not in New York, there is nobody there. And when you are in New York, there is nobody there." (*But now you are really in New York, and I am somewhere else. To tell you the truth, I want to be in California forever, by the ocean we love.*) You are so proud that a poet wrote these things for you, that someone translates them (even though you don't like to read them). But you *do* like the idea of being "immortalized"; you appropriate the names of fiction to suit your reality. "*Lo tuyo es mental,*" what a trip you're on (I must admit that Celia Cruz is *not* a great *bolerista,* although I say this line of hers here). You believe that all those who walked through your life would die for you gladly, relishing their pain because it kept them connected to a stubborn, bewitching woman with intense eyes (*pero chica, "sólo cenizas hallarás de todo lo que fue mi amor,"* as Toña la Negra used to say, my love for you has turned to ashes).

I actually don't believe all the words in the *boleros,* but they make sense to forsaken lovers. They cry, they reminisce, they want to sing of inexpressible emotions: the torment of love as the rumor of honeybees, stinging your heart. The hidden song of the mourning dove (*¡qué romántico, Dios mío!*). You laugh at these, you rationalize, while you also experience moistness in your eyes. You don't want to commit for life because you might be, well, bored, and what then? Guitars strumming and *boleros* to sing of your *perfidia,* your leaving *sin decir adiós.*

(*"Mujer, si puedes tú con Dios hablar, pregúntale si yo alguna vez te he dejado de adorar"* — I have never stopped worshipping you, God can tell you — is this by Luis Alcaraz or Agustín Lara?)

It's difficult to talk about *boleros* to someone who doesn't really experience the words. The Spanish that rolls off the tongue like *mamoncillos,* or *quenepas dulces,* or *pedacitos de mango* — bits of tropical fruits. This is a language that you think you know, but it escapes you, because you own a body that is really denied speech, you keep it silent, immovable, untouched by other discourses.

This very song, or play, I wrote at the (computer) keyboard, brings back nights on the Caribbean, but you are so far away. The one by Portillo de la Luz, *rey de los boleros,* surfaces again:

> *No hay bella melodía si no la escuchas tú.*
> *Es que te has convertido en parte de mi alma,*
> *ya nada me conforma si no estás tú también.*
> *Más allá de tus labios, del sol y las estrellas,*
> *contigo en la distancia, amada mía, estoy.*

What words to listen to when one is sitting *en la noche antillana,* Caribbean night, warm and luminous, full of white shadows and breezes! Or when one is really so far away that only memories persist in the distance, forbidden love, sleeping in the arms of unreachable dreams.

"You have become part of my soul, nothing is enough if you are not there. Beyond your lips, the sun and the stars, I am with you in the distance, beloved." Wow!

In this loud silence, I keep on writing lines as if they were lyrics (or I actually copy lyrics as if they were lines I invent) to tell you what my heart is murmuring now, what it used to feel for you, what is no longer a reality. I go after the mirage of water in the desert, as I used to when we were traveling together on the road, and *boleros* were playing on the radio.

> *No sé si aún la quiero, pero tal vez la quise.*
> (I don't know if I still love her, but maybe I loved her)
> *¿Cómo no haber amado sus grandes ojos fijos?*
> (How could I have not loved her large, quiet eyes?)

(And what would Neruda think of my quoting his poem in the context of *boleros?* Well, at least it is a *"canción desesperada,"* a desperate song like the others. What luck.)

Pelicans flew then across the Pacific shores, and perhaps you love them now as you did before. I remember you looking at their reflection on the window panes, birds of static flight and enormous patience. You smile when you turn fully to see them, your feet run to meet the waves and the wings, you take your shoes off and run into the ocean:

> *Como espuma que ardiente lleva el caudaloso río,*
> *flor de azalea,*
> *la vida en su avalancha te arrastró.*
> *Y hoy para siempre quiero que olvides tus pasadas penas*
> *y que tan sólo tenga horas serenas tu corazón.*

"Like that ocean foam (or so I say) oh azalea blossom, the river of life swept you in its wake. Let me help you forget your sorrows, let your heart have only serene moments" (Wow again!).

> *Quisiera ser la golondrina que al amanecer*
> *a tu ventana llega para ver*
> *a través del cristal.*
> *Y despertarte, muy dulcemente si es que estás dormida,*
> *a la alborada de una nueva vida*
> *llena de amor.*

"I want to wake you up, like a bird looking in your window at sunrise — if you are asleep, I will wake you up sweetly, to the dawn of a new life full of love."

(Yeah, well . . . still, do you remember when I played this on the keyboard for you, and you blushed?)

Los Panchos (*Epoca De Oro* album), above, sound like nineteenth-century poets. Swallows and all. Their *Flor de Azalea* tells the tale of a man (I guess) wanting to save a woman (I guess) from her life of trouble. Swallow indeed. *Hay que tragarse todo el* speech (this pun is untranslatable). And we have to swallow all the swallows, the bitterness, keep on living, although trying not to forget the sweet nothings so we don't totally drown.

A veces pienso que la vida es una sucesión interminable de boleros.

Yeah, I really think sometimes that life is an unending chain of songs. Ballads that leave a funny taste in our mouth.

(white and red flowers projected on the screen)

Gardenias from Daniel Santos, *ilusiones (flores rojas) de Gloria Estefan* about the love that will surely return even if he left for another woman (*"Volverás,"* *Mi Tierra* album).

(show a slide of Gloria as she appears on the cover of that album, dressed like a torch singer from the forties)

Years go on and we keep on dreaming about unfulfilled love, galleries of song that the music of the golden oldies or the silver nineties repeats again and again, *como un disco rayado.*

"Show me the way back to your heart": *Destiny* CD.

(Please do. Or better not: "Your love is bad for me," *Cuts Both Ways.*) Formulas for living, on cassette.

Life is a scratched record, going back time and again to the same narrow groove, where the words echo and echo *como en los boleros.* It cuts both ways. Our love is like a knife, it cuts both ways (it plunges into my heart). *Y uno sigue y sigue cantando, hasta que se le acaba la voz.* Until the end we sing, then our voices die out. Like in the *boleros* of old, the ballads of new. . . .

Give me a break, will you? Stop the music. . . .

This melodrama is a sassy slice of Latina life, in and out of classrooms (and nightclubs!) . . . and you'll say: she's quite the party animal, this profe. . . . But not really: I just play the music, I witness the dance that never stops. It's a potent metaphor, don't you think? So: I really wanna sing the poems and dance the *boleros* until the last curtain call. . . .

(all lights out)

A Working-class *Bruja*'s Fears and Desires

Norma E. Cantú

SOME OF THE ISSUES that I have faced as a Chicana in the academy are really tied to the way the community I grew up in shaped me and prepared me for life. My fears as an adult are rooted in fears in childhood. My experience is not unique: if one grows up working class and becomes a relatively well-paid professor, certain issues are bound to come to the forefront.

The Subconscious

I recently became aware that I have what could be called a behavior problem — one I am ready to grapple with now but which I didn't even know existed in my youth. It wasn't an analyst who told me about the role of the subconscious to protect the self above all else; it was a friend who stayed with me for a five-week summer session and who in late night tea-sipping *pláticas* shared with me her own defense mechanisms. At that time, I was unaware that I too subconsciously behaved according to patterns designed to protect me. My protective mechanism came to the forefront not too long ago on a trip I took with two good friends. Because we were on a cruise and in close quarters for a week, even I noticed how erratic my behavior became as the week progressed. I began to pick on anything no matter how insignificant as a point of argument. Suddenly, I understood what the pattern of behavior meant, a pattern that one of my close friends referred to as the "professor syndrome." I have tried to monitor my behavior now that I am aware of it, and I am still trying to understand what exactly triggers it. The closest I have come to an explanation is that my subconscious senses danger as I get too close to someone. When that someone is a lover, the reaction reaches gigantic proportions, and we end up fighting all the time, until I leave. I have developed the protective mechanism so well that even when friends become close, I immediately turn ugly to keep the person at bay. In retrospect, I can see that it has already caused me to lose some good friends and several lovers. I am too perfect for anyone, or no one is perfect enough for me. The layers of programming must be incredibly thick and numerous, for I have not yet managed to change my behavior. As I get older, the fear of spending my life alone grips my imagination, and I become even more determined to do something about this trick of my subconscious that is doing, after all, exactly what I myself have programmed it to do.

I must say that the "professor syndrome" seems to work very well in the academy; my colleagues all seem to act that way, too. Could it be that we are protecting ourselves? A colleague once explained that he would never form close friendships with coworkers, and I was appalled. But now I think I understand what he meant. The potential for betrayal is too great. But then, whom do you trust?

Spirituality vs. Religion

I have an altar at home where I have placed special items — photographs of my family, a bit of sand from a special beach in Mexico, a swatch of hair from the *trenza* I cut off when I finished my dissertation, a red ribbon that bound a special gift, and other odd items. Before the framed image of La Virgen de Guadalupe, the same one my grandmother revered in a similar altar in her home, I burn *copal*, light candles, say a prayer, and I find a peace that comes from within me.

I often say I'm not religious but that I am spiritual. What I mean by that is that although I attend the Catholic Church rituals and feel a special devotion to the Virgin of Guadalupe, I do not consider myself religious, only spiritual. I have an uncanny psychic sense that I link to spirituality. I meditate and have for a long time felt that there are guardian spirits — angels? — protecting me. When I was mugged recently, the feeling was so powerful I even heard a voice telling me to not fight it and to give the attacker everything he wanted. The first time I sensed this I was a child and later I thought I had made it all up, but now I am aware of how the guidance only comes when I need it and that it is an intimate knowledge that has no rational explanation. Because of this, I am reluctant to talk about it with anyone at the university or with whom I interact in a professional manner. I am afraid people won't understand and will think I am delusional or that I need psychiatric help. I have confided in my sister and a couple of close friends, people who know me well and who understand how disturbing it is even for me to have these feelings because I am so rational and so left-brain dominant. I believe in reincarnation because of strong evidence in my own life of its existence. I have had strong dreams and experiences that have led me to believe even before I had read or studied the belief. Once in Europe, I was walking down a street and had the sensation that I had been there before, and I could tell what was around the corner. I freaked out and didn't tell the people I was with. I have witnessed too many unexplained phenomena to glibly discount such events. I know there is something there and that I am a part of it. I am not frightened of it, but I am scared of what people will think when I tell them of my experiences. Some friends and I joke about being *brujas;* I find the thought comforting, although I also then feel like a fraud — I don't even know any incantations, just the one for cleansing a house; I don't do any healings, although if pressed I probably could do a healing for *mal de ojo* or for *susto.* One of my greatest fears is that I will become mentally ill, although I have no basis for this fear.

Abandonment

Because my father went to work away from home when I was newborn, my analyst tells me, I have abandonment issues. What this has meant for me is that I have always left my lovers: left on sabbatical, moved to another town, another job; in effect, I abandon the object of affection before I am abandoned. I recognize it as a pattern, but one that I'm not sure I can or want to change. When I first thought about this pattern, I resisted the revelation, yet it made perfect sense — for about ten minutes. Then I thought of how even though my father had left for a few months in my infancy, he didn't desert us and I never felt abandoned; in fact if anything I have usually felt that my family was too much with me. *Entre familia,* with all my extended family around, I don't think I had too many instances of solitude for the first twenty-five years of my life, which may be why the next twenty-five have been full of long periods of solitude in my travels and in my personal life in general. I live alone, I often travel alone, I rejoice in my solitude; it gives me the most productive writing time. So maybe my analyst wasn't totally on the mark after all, at least when it relates to lovers.

But there is another part of this conundrum: does my family feel abandoned? Yes, I believe so. Being an academic has in some ways distanced me from my working-class family. It has taken many years of reassurance to convince my parents, especially my father, that I have not "forgotten where I come from." My father, a laborer, has very little notion of what it is that I do as a professor. Although they are extremely proud of me, I don't think my siblings and my parents understand my constant travel to conferences, my irregular working hours, or what it is I do other than teach. At first, it was hard for me, as a brand-new assistant professor, to reconcile my non-working-class position with who I am, the first-to-go-to-college daughter of laborers. Now, after years of agonizing that I was not doing enough for that community that had nurtured me and formed me, I have to admit realistically that no, I do not share that life anymore, but I also know that my allegiances are still with that group, and that that is who I am, that is where my heart and soul reside. I have learned that being a professor and belonging to a working class are not exclusive, in spite of the awareness that obviously my economic status places me in a much more favorable position: my class formed me and is still with me even though my position in society as a professor at a university allows me freedom and resources I would never have as a factory or agricultural field-worker. Do I ever regret going on in academia instead of staying at my office job where I was already better off than most of my family and neighbors? No. But I do believe that at the time I was making the decision I did feel I was betraying my community by going away, by growing away. Partly the feeling came from subtle and not so subtle messages from coworkers in the office as well as some members of my family who felt that I was odd, strange to want so much education and not want to be married. At least, that is what I perceived they perceived. But, no, there are no regrets, in fact I now know that I would not have been as effective a community organizer without the *papelito* that confirmed to the world that I was somebody. In spite of the fact that I knew I was somebody without the Ph.D., the powers-that-be in my community did not see me—I did not exist in any real viable way until then. Armed with the *papelito*, I could be appointed to the public library board, I could organize a literacy campaign, I could be the conscience for my colleagues and a role model for my students. And indeed I have been and thereby have served my community in many more ways than I would have if I had never been to college, or never gone on to graduate school.

Aún

Yvette Gisele Flores-Ortiz

Aún
después de tanto tiempo
our eyes can meet across
the filled spaces of a room
and we both know
without speaking
that history
is stronger than desire
and familiarity
more powerful
than lust

The Names I Used to Call You /
The Names I Do Call You

Eliana Rivero

The Names I Used To Call You

When sparks were flying
        I retreated from your Latina fire
                and looked at my guilty hands:
I said what I said
in the rush of the liquid moment,
                knowledge
        and slow frustration
coming to the surface.

Still, I pointed reddish fingers
and I called you
by all those words
                I didn't really know:
you staked your territory
with
        quite sharp weapons.
I retreated,
        offered only the resistance of time.

And then I called you, silently,
by all those other words
                that my tongue turned around
one by one,
like thin chocolate wafers
                drenched in fruit.

They melted on my lips before they reached you:
you really had no way of knowing
                        those syllables I uttered to myself.

I wondered
how you would look at me
                if I said them out loud,
those other names I used to call you
in my dreams.

                The Names I Do Call You

I'm pleased to say
I don't retreat from battle anymore.
I don't care
                if you burn me
with your fiery tongue
and all those words
                that I still find incomprehensible.

Your very name
                those syllables
gather the liquid wetness of ripe fruit
but your voice can be caustic
                like sour lemons,
worse than acid tamarind
                your tongue.

So in spite of my nurturing instincts
                I have begun
to call you on your war.
I now stand up to your defenses,
unleashing my very own Latina fire
                right in front of your face:
you smile
        you begin to retreat
you celebrate
that I am also
        (or can pretend to be)
a feisty woman
        like the aunts in our dreams

I am your mirror
        in oh so many ways.

Plátanos and Palms

Rina Benmayor

I didn't grow up *en el trópico*[1]
el trópico grew up in me.

I came home from a trip to Jamaica
obsessed with plantains
infatuated with palms
those ragged roman candles
shaggy medusas in the sky
climbing the hills of my landscapes
decorating contours of my shores.

They seduced conquerors.
Ever heard of a colony
without *plátanos* and palms?
That's why indianos[2]
gone home to Spain to die
built mansions with their fortunes
giant *palmeras* planted at the door
nostalgias de América,
their tropical coat of arms.

Plátano is the Spanish name of the banana or plantain tree. Palm trees are variously called *palmas* or *palmeras*. In Spain, *plátano* is also a common name for a species of elm.
1. The tropics
2. Spaniards who went to the Indies, the Americas, and returned rich men to retire in their native towns and villages.

I once had a majestic palm tree
outside my office window, second floor,
my own latticed shelter
gracefully standing guard;
but I never had the light
to grow a *plátano* at home
morning translucence
of banana leaf greens
scalloping, soaring
plunging to the ground.

Instead, I have images —
paintings, postcards, photos,
midriffs of the globe
palmas reales cubanas[3]
polynesian coconut groves
tall silhouettes of memory
breaking open my apartment walls
exuberancias opacas[4]
in this dazzling city of stone.

New York, July 1996

3. The Cuban royal palm, which is the tallest of the species and has a characteristic bulge in the trunk.
4. Opaque exuberances

Three Penny Opera
or Eve's Symphony in B Minor
Daisy Cocco De Filippis

Act I — Scene from *La Forza del Destino* — Scherzo

AURELIA GOT UP that morning convinced that this was her day. She could at last face the world and say: "Yes, darlings, didn't you know. I am she, the author who can rename the world, recreate realities and leave all better off from having experienced my work."

Aurelia's "surprise" was months in the making. Not even Chita, her *manita* who knew even about the first time Felipe had touched Aurelia's breasts, had been told. Aurelia had played the scenes to herself many times over. Even the slightest gesture had been rehearsed in front of her faithful and quiet mirror. Having mastered how to feign an air of casual indifference she had seen so often at poetry readings, Aurelia felt ready.

For weeks the local papers had heralded it "the event of the year." To Aurelia, the upcoming conference represented the New York Marathon. She ran at the lonely distance of the unabashed and undisputed front-runner. That Saturday she was early to rise, convinced that on her coming-out day even the humblest of tasks deserved to be honored. She walked the dog and washed her hair, painstakingly blowing and curling it just enough to ensure the shiny and bouncy elegance it was known for, even as far as her aunt Lydia's neighborhood, twenty blocks away.

Eleven o'clock came quietly. Aurelia pulled from her closet the beige suit she had carefully chosen because it denoted assertiveness without giving offense. Her silk scarf, multicolored and soft, caressed her neck, gently reminding her of the possibilities of this transformation. Methodically, she placed her treasures in the half-moon flowered bag she had managed to save enough to buy at Macy's semiannual sale. Everything about her person spoke of careful elegance and gentility. One by one, her dearest objects found their way to the inside of her bag. Her gold-cased Ultima II Dark Rose lipstick nestled next to a black and gold Cross pen. Her florentine wallet, whose filigreed drawings had inspired countless verses that had found their fate at the bottom of her secret drawer, rested comfortably next to the house keys. All that remained was to place in it the folder holding a neat sheaf of typed pages. Aurelia hesitated, but only for a moment. "There, now it's done," she said as she took one last glance in the mirror before running out.

It was three o'clock. Aurelia had been sitting for two hours before she realized how small the community center's lecture hall was. She had not been aware that so many men in her community were interested in writing. The round of speeches appeared endless. Her sweaty palms and pounding heart began to get in the way of any enjoyment. Aurelia had a vague sense of discomfort. She twisted, turned, trying to avoid a stiffening of the neck. After twenty minutes of listening to him, Aurelia could not figure out why the disgruntled, skinny man with the cane continued to drum up new ways to vituperate anyone in the community who had not recognized his genius. Compelled by a sense of brotherhood with this victim of misunderstanding, many other writers lined up, rallying before the rejuvenated, enraged philosopher to reiterate that in New York Dominican males were indeed voiceless. Feeble attempts to bring the discussion back to the issue of literature were dismissed as out of place.

It was six o'clock. The time allotted for the youngest writers to introduce their craft to the community had finally arrived. No introductions were necessary. All one needed was a manuscript and the presence of mind to stand up and read it. Aurelia got out of her seat feeling small, worn out, clammy. No longer sure of sustaining an aloof air (it seemed hours since her last curl had gone softly limp), she looked down to notice her skirt's defiant struggle to maintain gentility. She advanced, folder in hand, grateful that at last her turn had come. Slowly but steadily she marched on, past the bold, imposing poet. She looked ahead to realize that she still had to get past the thick row of men whose voices blocked the entrance to the podium. Stopping to take a deep breath, Aurelia considered alternatives. One look around, a firm grip on her folder, and an imperial toss of the hair were all she needed before stepping up to the podium.

Act II — Scene from *Un Ballo in Maschera* — Adagio

There is an arrogant air about an independent woman. It is the sort of pride paid for in blood, I am told. I wouldn't know it because, you see, I am one of those plants who manages to bloom, thrive, and spread in the shade. African violets, they keep telling me, grow in the semishade. Now, there's a flower.

They are the sort of weeds that are used to demanding and getting respect. I also understand that many of their kind are thriving and prospering in middle-class comfort. This is not the case with cacti. Those wretched creatures reject touching, don't require painstaking care, and somehow manage to spring up even in the harshest of settings. The minute I saw Martirio I recognized a cactus.

Dressed in black and cloaked in pink she entered the room a half hour late. Her artistically casual hairdo gave the impression of somehow having achieved a life of its own. Everything about her spoke of contempt for the trivial, for the inane habits of those not painstakingly engaged in a cause. Nothing in her demeanor betrayed her origins. Even her accent was difficult to trace. The only thing I, Flor, the African Violet from Queens, could tell was that she belonged to an uniquely Manhattan mold of academic "revolutionary." I immediately spotted one of those independent spirits typically identified by their preference for black, matched only by their passion for silver and/or trinkets bearing the unmistakable stamp of the third world.

There we were. We measured each other, trying to understand. I, the easily identified Latina, masquerading in white middle-class opulence, feeling compelled to be the bearer of the hope that the American dream was within grasp of my disadvantaged Latino students. She, clearly the product of middle-class Europeans, who, as she acidly explained, had descended from a ship, mimicked the dress of a poor Central American peasant. The irony was hard to bear. Determined to carry on business as usual, I proceeded to conduct myself as the mistress of ceremonies of the Spanish Honor Society. I spoke of tradition, order, virtue, and love for *la madre España*. Martirio followed up with a rather lengthy dissertation, I thought only matched by the voluminous bundle of papers she carried. There was clearly an attempt to give visual evidence of solid and weighty scholarship. She spoke with passion of an old theme: literature at the service of the State. Mercifully for all, the afternoon ended.

That afternoon we went on our separate ways. Each one of us convinced of our proper place in the great scheme of things in this universe, like cacti and violets.

Act III — Scene from *Le Nozze di Figaro* — Allegro

Dinner had been accomplished. Left alone in the kitchen, Dominga Martínez faced the inevitable pile of rejected, sadly abandoned morsels of what was planned and heralded as a true gastronomical delight. Dominga proceeded to make some order of the habitual postdinner chaos. The dog lingered, charming spoilt creature, not quite satisfied, hoping to catch any droppings.

Drying up, tidying up, had its own discreet sort of charm for Dominga. It was the ideal moment, as no one was known to drop by at this most inconvenient of times, for reminiscing, day-dreaming, and basically reflecting on the ponderous questions of the reasons for living, the price of sausage this week, and any sort of fantastic ideas she might have about her neighbor's not-too-certain sex life.

Sex . . . now there was a word not easily uttered in her family circle. Dominga thought of her own life. Daniel, her man, was aging now, yet every inch of her body ached for his touch. Dominga's own body, blown into quite an unrecognizable bundle of joy, countless pounds too joyous, as some of the catty tongues in the neighborhood were known to whisper. Yet all these clear-headed facts had not deterred Dominga from lust.

Relentlessly, Dominga continued to dream. How much like a five-and-dime novel it all sounded. Proper young women of her day went into marriage open-eyed, understanding that passion was not part and parcel of respectable life. Yet for Dominga, the sight of Daniel's somewhat imperfect body, neglected by years of what he called the "good life," which usually meant too much eating and drinking a bit more than what was considered proper, made her ache even more for his every imperfection.

The rhythm of Dominga and Daniel's life together had been marked by a series of somewhat discordant, slightly off-key notes, sort of a "Für Elise" played valiantly at amateur's night at the conservatory. Daniel had turned out, quite charmingly, slightly unsatisfactory, as they used to say. Big dreams, big splurges, resurgences of rather fleeting affluence had become their way of life. Yet, to Dominga, Daniel was a true dream maker. He opened for her hidden doors to the world.

For years, Dominga and Daniel traveled, drank, and wondered at every step about the meaning of it all. Their pockets usually emptied quite quickly, and they would return to the drudgery of earning a living. Steady work had always been out of the question. Restless and adventurous, Daniel plunged into business deals that had taken up quite a bit of his time. He had used as a down payment his youth, infrequently remembered asset, no longer available.

And yet Dominga lusted for him. She spent endless days dreaming of possible moments of erotic expansion that in her younger days she had not dared to reveal. With the passing of the years together, these dreams had become their own guilty secret; one which Dominga and Daniel could never share with anyone.

Descubrimiento(s)

Celia Alvarez

Encontré a Puerto Rico en tu corazón,
    en el medio del desierto.
Barreras católicas,
    cárcel patriarcal.
Descubrimientos,
    de nuestros lazos comunes
        con Borinquén, la isla del Edén.

Nací una nena católica, como tú,
Envenenada,
    por la iglesia que imprimió su sello
        sobre nuestros cuerpos y corazones.

Nenas buenas,
    buscando cariño y amor.
      Corazón abierto,
    dulce reclamo de pasión.
        Zánganas,
    abandonadas
      sin protección.

Amor de hombre,
    una distorsión.
Nos comieron vivas,
    sacando cuerpo de corazón

Objetos
     de sus deseos
         hambrientos,
             sobrevivimos . . .
    llenas de pecado
         y sin salvación.

Del sexo,
    "no se hablaba."
y si lo hiciste,
    "lo dejaste."
Su mera existencia
    lo valorizaba,
         sin responsabilidad.

"El hombre lo necesita,
         y tú, se lo tienes que dar."
    "Los hombres son como los perros
        o nenes,
            que los hay que cuidar."

Mientras tanto,
    cargamos en el rostro
        una mancha sucia,
        . . . carnal,
    "por haber metido mano"
    en nuestro santuario corporal.

La vida nos engañó
y caímos,
asfixiadas,
en las entrañas del género.

Seguimos siendo
nenas buenas
    hija, hermana, mujer . . .
Abuso espiritual
    apagando
        la luz de nuestra niñez.

Protegidas por secretos
    hombres que "nos quieren"
padres, amantes, maridos,
    amigos, hermanos, primos,
    tíos, abuelos
        y sarcedotes también.

Y nadie pregunta:
    "Nena, ¿cómo tú estás?"
    "¿Qué te pasa?"
        cuando aparece la desilusión.

El catecismo,
    . . . una prisión.
El abuso,
    involucrado en secreto
    enterrado por el silencio
apaga nuestro espíritu,
    inocente.

Nacidas con la mancha de plátano,
    y el sello de la iglesia católica,
internalizamos
    a la "virgen" María
    y a Eva, en su jardín.

Virgen o puta
    en un mundo misógino
    . . . sin beneficios.
acumulando puntos
    para el infierno.

Qué liberación
encontrarte ¡mujer . . . !
    Me cogiste de sorpresa,
        levantando
        la neblina
        de un sueño malo.

¡Qué despertar!
El toque de tus ojos
    abrieron puertas
    cerradas
    en mi corazón.

¡Espíritu libre!
me resucitaste de la muerte
          el día que te declaraste mía
          mil gracias,
          ¡mi moriviví!

Entre Nosotras

Latina Anónima

For Latinas who like to please

SHE'S WHAT I would call my "type." You know, the kind of woman who makes me swoon and feel giddy and who steals my speech. She's sorta tall, around 5′ 8″, a light brown, and has one of those shapely bodies we call "*cuerpo de guitarra*" in the Caribbean. Her breasts are full, the nipples so dark they look like little chocolate daisies in a vat of caramel cream. A slender waist and flat stomach spill out into broad hips and one of the nicest, fullest, jutting Puerto Rican butts, the kind you never see on television but that I love so much. Sensual is the only way to describe how her long ample thighs round off the rest of her curvaceousness. Just looking at her gives me cottonmouth. A real femme in her manner and disposition, she is, for me, exquisitely soft sexiness personified. Even when she's angry with me and tells me off she manages to be sweetly sensual. Her sexiness is framed by a wonderfully inquisitive, creative mind that carefully analyzes things in a calm way, considering the whole picture and all the possible angles, so different from my own strident, abrasive intellect. Her short cropped hair accentuates her femininity. Those dark brown eyes shine with a piercing intensity. She is somewhat quick-tongued too, but only around her political views. And she doesn't let anyone get over on her. Womanish, I think it's called. The combination of strength and tenderness gets me every time. Every time.

Stretched out on the bed she contrasts nicely against the orange sheets. After kissing her mouth long enough to make both her nipples stand, I focus my attention on her breasts. I love to lick her breasts, so deliciously soft and firm. My tongue begins in its usual place down by the crease that separates them from her chest, working its way up toward the middle. Beginning with broad, long strokes I lick all the way up to her nipples, alternating with small, hard bites. Erect, her nipples taste like smoke and ash with a slight hint of honey (almost like an afterthought). Grabbing one nipple with my lips I concentrate my licking on it, pressing down on it like a button. Then I suck it really hard. She moans and I'm not sure if its from pain or pleasure, or both. Her acknowledgement stirs me, sending a stab of desire shooting through me. The sound of her voice plucks the imaginary chord that connects the tip of my tongue to the tip of my clit, making it quiver. I feel a tightness between my legs. I move down toward her stomach. She tenses up and lets out a yelp when my mouth traces the curve of her waist. At her hip I pinch a fold of skin between my teeth, then roll it gently in my mouth. Here she tastes like sweet creamed butter. I suck on the skin slowly, methodically. Then I bite her there, on her hip, and let go slow enough to tease her with my tongue. She moans again.

Using my nose as a guide, I rub along her outer thigh all the way down to her knees. My head moves up between her legs, my own body draped along the lower half of the bed. It's early morning and there is enough natural light so that I can look her over up close. I marvel at how pretty she is, how neatly and daintily her folds envelope the rest of her sex. She's got one of those two-toned pussies, a lovely plum color on the outer lips and a burnt rose color on the inside. Her scent, a mixture of salt and sea water, rises to tickle my nose. I tease her again, nuzzling the inside of her thighs. Then I move slowly up to her lips, taking them both gently into my mouth as if they are her tongue, staying there for just a little while longer to savor them before I move on to the area where the hair is thickest. I press my mouth on her mound, first with my tongue flat and wet, then slowly working my way back down toward her slit. Using the tip of my tongue, I lick in small circles moving closer and closer to the center. Pointing my tongue, I glide it softly along the fleshy part of her lips, then between her folds where I concentrate the pressure.

The heat coming off her body urges me on. Her clit peeks out arrogantly from under its hood, demanding that I take notice. I grab it using both my tongue and my lips and pull, sucking softly at first, then with more pressure, surrounding it with my entire mouth. The taste stings me. She flinches and I hear her say, "What are you doing to me?" Her naiveté about her own body always astounds me. I increase the pressure, building up her sexual tension, then letting it subside several times. Rubbing my tongue on the sides of her clit, then massaging back across it, I stick one, two, then three fingers inside her, into her wetness. I continue to suck on her clit. "*Así, así . . . Ay, qué delicia,*" she murmurs as she encourages me to move in and out rhythmically with her own hand. She lets out a soft gasp, "Ahhh." Shyly at first, then more eagerly, she begins to move her hips to our rhythm until she goes rigid. When she cums I can feel her throbbing on my lips, feel the pulse against my mouth. I lap up that precious trickle, enjoying the tanginess of her fluids. Finally she's let me taste her, really taste her! Her taste, like her scent, becomes permanently fixed in my mind. I will carry it with me always. As I begin to move away from her clit and back along those wondrous folds, she smashes herself on my mouth. "Mmmmmm, mmmmm mmmmm, mmmmm, uhmmmmm," she purrs as she arches her back. Her response makes me smile against her. I love when she does that, when she shows me how much she relishes my kisses, my tongue, my mouth on her. I love it when she lets go of her prissy, middle-class island-Puerto Rican inhibitions enough to *saborear este placer entre nosotras*.

When I look up at her there is a hunger in her eyes. They have that hazy, unfocused look that tells me she's somewhere else. Reaching down to pull my face up to hers, she lets her tongue greet mine. She kisses me deeply. Later, while we lay wrapped around each other she quietly says "No one's ever kissed me there," pointing to her hip. I frown. "*Qué tragedia, cariño.* You should be kissed everywhere." How negligent her lovers have been. It's such a shame that she has not been kissed properly, that no one's wrapped their tongues tenderly around her hips or thighs. It seems such a shame that no one's licked her around her waist, down her back, across her shoulder blades, hard first, then softly with different textures and intensities. That no one has kissed the space where the back of her thighs meets her butt. It's amazing to me that no one has thought to celebrate her in this way.

How lovely to have witnessed her reticent abandonment to her own pleasure. After weeks, months, of discussion and debate, of frustration, she's finally let go enough to enjoy herself. I've been patient. The butch in me secretly wants to believe that the reason she's finally let go is because I have a magnificent tongue and great technique. But I know that it's really because she's finally coming to terms with her sexual self; that she's really just more comfortable with her own pleasure in woman-sex. Maybe she's finally unlearned some of the catechism lessons on guilt, restraint, and grace. Or maybe it's just that we have not been together like this for a few weeks, and we know this indulgence of ours must end soon. Things will be different. We will both go on with our lives, with our responsibilities, leaving behind these stolen moments of respite we have found in each other. These are such rare moments. I ask no questions. I just enjoy their simplicity. And I make of them small celebrations that I store away for strength and perseverance, treasures to be taken out only in those more desperate moments when the war outside becomes too overwhelming.

Pisco and Cranberry

Eliana Rivero

(Puerto de Valparaíso, Chile)

Sweet and juicy
   its inviting redness tantalizes my tongue,
it makes me
   want to put my finger right inside
        and stir things up:
the rim is wet
    round like an open cavity,
   moist like my dreams.
A garden of unearthly delights opens,
   promises the bliss
hidden in its liquidness,
      seductive as in no other country,
sensuous like saliva
   like sour lemons
    like surrender.

I succumb to temptation
    as if days had no ending
no aftermath
    as if only the drinking of this sexy juice
offered by a woman
    had any meaning.

Much later
   the tartness stops me:
too risky, I realize,
    much too intoxicating

this indulgence.
        Still
                the rim is beckoning
                        for me to put both lips around it,
                                or run my tongue inside its secret,
to bring new life to hardened flesh,
        to get drunk
on reddish moonlight magic.

When I finally stop
                (don't be mistaken)
        my quite feeble restraint
                has little to do with virtue.
It just so happens that I dread hangovers:
        the absence of such sweetness,
                the withdrawal of such a tender drink
makes me tremble like an abandoned ship,
        like a sailor
left at the tavern by a laughing lover.

De lo que es Amor, de lo que es Vida

Inés Hernández Avila

POETRY REPRESENTS TOTAL freedom for me. In other places I must acknowledge certain protocols that may or may not have an affinity with mine. In my poems, the protocol is mine, I give myself the license to say what I want, how I want it, *y así es.*

> *La única bandera que yo amo*
> *es la libertad*
> *El único anhelo que yo tengo*
> *la verdad*

> The only flag I love
> is freedom
> The only yearning I have
> is for the truth

I can fall in love with the sound of a voice.

It is beautiful when a person knows how to sing in such a way the world opens for the embrace of her or his voice. Whether the song is an honoring song for the land, for the deer, for the bear, for the eagle, a love song, or a song of social conscience, I am taken back to the beginning of time and forward into eternity, as I feel the life-giving intonations penetrate me and shower me with blessings.

There are many voices that move me deeply, as they fill the universe with their beauty and power, connecting ancient times with the future, uniting the heart of the earth with the heart of the cosmos. My Nimipu grandpa Tom, Ukshanat and his son, my uncle Frank; the late Paiute elder Raymond Stone; the Conchero elders, María Teresa Mejía Martínez, Cruz Ibarra Hernández,

Miguel Alvarado, and the late Emilio Alvarado; *mi compadre* Felipe Molina *y mi esposo* Juan, *cuando están cantando los maso bwikam,* the Yoeme deer songs; my Chiapaneca friend (who is Tojolobal Maya), Roselia Jiménez Pérez; *los maestros de la nueva canción,* Atahualpa Yupanqui, Violeta Parra, Gabino Palomares, Amparo Ochoa; of the Tejano singers, the Bernal brothers, Tony de la Rosa, Esteban Jordán; of the Norteño singers, Bronco y Los Tigres del Norte; *las maestras de las canciones de amor, que son tantas, como* Ana Gabriel y Paquita La del Barrio. The list could go on! All I know is I must have music to be whole, I wake up with songs, and I love to sing.

> *Oigo una voz que derrumba los años*
> *de las sombras aparece un canto*
> *reconocido*
> *de repente la voz está por donde quiera*
> *y en cada momento escucho*
> *las tonadas del ayer*
> *hechos presentes*
> *alumbrando las huellas*
> *que me traen hacia el futuro*
> *y en cada huella está una flor*

> I hear a voice that makes the years collapse
> From the shadows a familiar song appears
> Suddenly the voice is everywhere
> and in every moment I hear
> the music of yesterday
> brought into the present
> lighting the tracks
> which take me toward the future
> and in each track there is a flower

"México lindo y querido." Mexico vibrates with a sense of justice, movement, and profound love. Since January 1, 1994, the official beginning of the Zapatista uprising, there is something powerful in the air. *Los zapatistas mostraron su valor, manifestando su conciencia y compromiso en el nivel local e internacional, y nos dieron valor a todos los pueblos indígenas de las Américas.*

When I am in Mexico, I feel alive in a way that is hard to do here in the States. I go often, for many reasons, one of which is to work with *La Asociación de los Escritores en Lenguas Indígenas,* persons who are conscious, thinking, participating, and planning the next millennium (even with all the *pleitos y desacuerdos cotidianos que surgen de vez en cuando*). Here in the States so many people are trying to hold on rigidly and desperately to the past, and to patterns that are life-denying. I am tired, and I know I am not alone, of justifying my existence and proving my intelligence. I am tired of the racism that is so transparent, and the emperors with no clothes.

The new day is upon us, the songs are strong, the voices are clear, and the actions conscious. *México es un centro de estas transformaciones que se están llevando a cabo. Tiene una energía tremendamente poderosa, y le tocó tenerlo. Voy allá a sanar, a encontrarme, a sentir la tierra sensual, y dejar que ese sol y esa luna me inunden con fuerza y vitalidad.*[1]

> "*Dime ¿qué me diste prieta linda!*
> *creo que me tienes enyerbado*
> *Porque todo cambia en esta vida*
> *Sólo mi cariño no ha cambiado*"

> "Tell me, what did you give me, beautiful dark woman?
> I think you have me bewitched with herbs
> Because everything else in this life changes
> Except my love for you which does not change"
> (from a popular Mexican folksong)

As a child, and throughout my adolescence, I frequented the Mexican movie theater El Teatro Rey, delighted to find role models representing dark, Indian-looking beauty in women actors/singers like Flor Silvestre and Lola Beltrán, the first attracting me with her confidence in her own beauty and sensuality, shown in the sweeping *miradas* of her *ojos coquetos,* and the delicious ways she moved and talked; the second drawing me to her because of the way she established her presence, standing tall, head held high, beautiful cheekbones, deep strong voice with a raw edge.

When I moved to California in the early eighties, I happily became very involved in Native ceremonial gatherings in the state. Often when speaking to elders in the Native community, I would be told, "You're sure a pretty Indian girl." One woman elder would look at me, and simply say, "Those eyes." I cannot say enough about how those statements made me feel. As a grown woman, I still felt their words like a sacred aromatic salve healing my body, my mind, my spirit and heart, taking me back to an innocence of early childhood and bringing me forward again to be whole.

---

1. Mexico is a center of these transformations that are taking place. The country has a tremendously powerful energy, and it is fitting. I go there to heal, to find myself, to feel the sensual earth, and to let Mexico's sun and moon inundate me with strength and vitality.

Ven a mí, quiero sentirte dentro
quiero que me atravieses todo el cuerpo con
tus labios
quiero que me hagas sentir mujer
Llévame a los límites del universo
al océano de las estrellas
Regálame tu sonrisa con tu cuerpo entero
Que nuestros dedos se entretejan
Que nuestras piernas se entrelacen
Que nos estrechemos entre las cobijas del
cielo
Riéndonos con los ojos y
suspirando calientito con amor

Come to me, I want to feel you inside
Cover my whole body with your lips
Make me feel my womanhood
Take me to the limits of the universe
To the ocean of stars
Give me your smile with your whole body
Let our fingers be interwoven
And our legs entwined
Let us stretch ourselves amongst the blankets
of heaven
Laughing with our eyes and
Sighing warmly with love

Las que me conocen saben quién es mi esposo. Es un hombre sincero, digno, bueno e inteligente, a good-heart, and gentle man. *Estoy tan agradecida por tenerlo como mi compañero de vida, algo que nunca me imaginaba después de tanto sufrimiento, tantos trastornos. De descendencia mexicana, nacido en Los Angeles, su papá de Michoacán, su mamá de Sonora, él se identifica como Yoeme (Yaqui).*

"Where You Are, You Might Hear This Song—
Look Around in the Direction of Her Who Loves You"
Poem for Juanishi, after a Nez Perce love song

The *Yoemem* spirit was strong when you were born, *compañero mío*
From the stars the Old Ones sent you to walk the earth
You were a favorite of theirs from many lifetimes ago
They knew you would let them speak through you
In ceremony they come through

Old Spirit you
Old Spirits them

When you sit down with the *hirukiam* to sing
they see how you lovingly hold your raspers
They see how you make the sacred space for yourself
and for your instruments
They help you sing the *maso bwikam*
They sit down with you to listen to your songs
They smile because you make their spirits happy
so they shower you with blessings from above
They know you are full of love for them
your mother's people
your ancestors
and so they bless you in this life
You open the ears of your heart
and they open the eyes of your spirit
To see and hear *saila maso,* your little brother deer,
You are one with the song
You are one with the dance
and for this I love you

With the same hands by which you hold the *hirukiam,* you hold me
With the same voice by which you sing the *maso bwikam,* you speak to
    me
In the same way you open your heart and your spirit to *seyewailo*
you open your heart and spirit to me tenderly, lovingly, powerfully
In the same way you are one with the song
you are one with the dance
You are one with me
So I send you this song in thanksgiving
for your love and for your spirit.

My youngest son says he often thinks of me as a sister, as well as a mother. I
understand his point of view. I was a young mother, and my sons are eleven
months apart, so when they were small, people sometimes asked if they were
twins. I probably spoke to them more as if they were my equals than my
children, which has its pluses and drawbacks. They grew up with me in the
Movimiento, their childhood games mimicking what they saw me doing in my
daily life, "putting up posters for Raza Unida" on our apartment walls, doing
teatro presentations about Villa and Zapata. They could not watch television,
even cartoons, without me commenting on the subliminal messages, the im-

plicit indoctrination embedded in the programming. I made many mistakes, the most significant of which was not realizing the most obvious: the struggle on behalf of the people begins at home. The struggle for self-determination begins with the individual. In some ways it is a miracle that my sons walked these paths with me and came out whole, and I know that this wholeness has come with a price.

I have called them my Quetzalcóatl and my Huitzilopochtli. My oldest one is the gentle one, the artist/poet/builder, the one who seeks the path of wisdom for himself and for his children (he is also a Grizzly Bear coming from his Nimipu grandma's side). My youngest one is the warrior, the sun dancer, the strategist, the one who seeks the path of liberation for his family, for the people. The weapon of the first is his creativity, the weapon of the second, his intellect; both base their responses to life in their intelligence, nurtured by my parents, and me, and shaped by their life experiences, some of those joyful and some deeply painful. As I watch them proceed on their life's path as men, my heart is full with love and pride.

Tengo tres nietos, two boys and a girl. When my oldest, my first grandson, was born, within minutes of his birth I went to him at the "baby room" of the hospital and softly sang him two songs in his little ear, one from *la tradición Nahuatl, un canto a la Madre Tierra,* and the second one, a song for the oldest bear couple from the beginning of time. *Así empezamos nuestro camino de abuela y nieto.* My affinity with him is sure. He calls me his "radical granma" and says he wants to be like me. When he was about nine years old (he is almost twelve), he told me and my husband how he appreciates our sense of play. He says it is because we still have "child spirits."

My youngest grandson is the image of his father, with his father's generous, loving heart and sense of fairness. Like his father he knows how to communicate with his eyes, with silences.

My granddaughter is a wonder to me. Because she is female, I tend to worry more about her. The socialization process of this consumer society is so violent, it can kill the artist at a young age, erasing forever the crucial gift of imagination. I cringe with each Barbie doll, each baby doll she has, or every "trapping" that catches her with its faddishness. When she offers to help in the kitchen (at the age of seven), I don't know whether to be glad she is willing to share in the work, or alarmed because she is already setting herself in the role of serving. I want her to grow with certainty and love for herself and to create what she chooses.

Being a daughter of the Ancient Coyotes, the First *Pareja Coyote,* I must say a word about the life-affirming energy of humor and laughter. I am awed by

Native peoples from throughout the hemisphere who not only value humor but in many, if not most cases, uphold the need for humor as a vital principle of their belief-systems. The ability to laugh, not in ridicule but in amusement, at oneself, at situations, at anything and everything, even what is considered sacred, in a way that acknowledges the potential for the absurd, the ridiculous everywhere, is considered to be an admirable and necessary quality, one that has the power of taking the edge off what is overly serious, or grief-ridden. Humor is one of the major ways Native people have been able to survive these more than five centuries of *desastre*.

Y qué bueno que soy hija de Coyote, ya que él/ella siempre, siempre resucitan, aunque hayan sido masacrados, violados, hechos garras, arrastrados por los más horribles lugares. (A veces también se ofrecen, sabiendo bien el final que les espera.) Vuelven a vivir, a tenerse confianza en si mismos, a reír y gozar.[2]

Una de las lecciones más grandes que he aprendido en mi vida es ésta: Nada es imposible y todo es posible. En el mero momento cuando dices, "No puede ser," sí puede ser. Por eso, una de mis expresiones favoritas es "¿Quién te manda?" Así es. ¿Quién te manda? ¿Quién me manda? ¿Quién nos manda? ¿Qué de raro tiene que somos como somos, siendo que somos seres humanos?

Esto sí me lo enseñó Coyote.[3]

Dancing is my prayer and my passion, *la manifestación de mi voluntad de vivir, entonando mi ser con el ritmo precioso y sensual del cosmos.* It is my articulation of the sacredness of life's renewals.

En Oaxaca, en el Zócalo hace poco estaba escuchando música de marimba, cumbias sabrosas llenando el aire, acurrucando sensualmente los espíritus de cada quien. La gente se había formado en una media luna, parejas, familias, individuos, grupitos de amistades, todos haciendo de ese momento una preciosa curación al alma. Sentí las notas penetrando cada célula de mi ser. Casi me moría por bailar, pero nadie bailaba. De repente un señor pobre, alto, delgado, piernas largas, se me hizo caribeño, apareció en el centro, dejándose llevar por el ritmo, sus pasos marcando el son

2. It's a good thing I'm a daughter of Coyote, since he/she always, always resuscitate, even if they've been massacred, violated, torn to shreds, dragged through the most horrible of places. (Sometimes they offer themselves, knowing full well the end that awaits them.) They come back to life, to once again have confidence in themselves, to laugh and know joy.
3. One of the greatest lessons I've learned in my life is this: Nothing is impossible and everything is possible. In the very moment when you say, "It can't be," it can be. That's why one of my favorite expressions is "Who do you take orders from anyway?" That's it. Who do you take orders from? Who do I take orders from? Who do we take orders from? What's so strange about us being the way we are, given that we're only human beings? This for sure is what Coyote taught me.

del cosmos. ¿Su pareja? La tierra misma, toda la Creación. Bailaba entregado, con los ojos casi cerrados y con una fluidez exacta, una sonrisa estrechándose por su cara. Así es como quiero pasar de este mundo al otro, bailando de esta manera.[4]

4. In the plaza in Oaxaca I was listening to marimba music, delicious cumbias filling the air, sensually soothing everyone's spirit. The people listening formed a half moon, couples, families, individuals, groups of friends, and we all made of that moment a precious healing of the soul. I felt the notes penetrating every cell of my being. I was dying to dance but no one would. Suddenly a poor man, tall, slim, long-legged, who seemed to be from the Caribbean, appeared in the center, giving in to the rhythm, his steps marking the dance of the cosmos. His partner? The earth herself, all Creation. He danced in surrender to the music, his eyes almost closed, with such a precise fluidity, and a smile stretching across his face. This is how I want to pass on from this world to the next, dancing in this way.

Eating Mango

Liza Fiol-Matta

Her cousins laughed wickedly
as the drops of sticky mango juice
trickled down their "American" cousin's cheeks.
Try as she might, her teeth
couldn't pierce the thick yellow skin.
The plumper end of the mango slid
in the palm of her hand
threatening to slide down her neck and into her blouse.
So, she gripped the wet pit
tightly, while its juicy pulp
scraped against her lips.
Finally, her girl cousin —
the one with hair bobbed like Jackie's —
showed her how to bite off a small round piece
of the rind at the top, how to eat
the exposed meat slowly, how to keep her hands
clean, gripping the mango
by the bottom half still covered by rind.
Miraculously, the skin
gave away cleanly.

Over time the taunting stopped, and
mango began tasting sweeter.
Everything was new that summer
when her aunts and uncles and cousins
became more than just photographs, and
the island seemed to burst in a frenzy of color,
smell and taste to welcome her home.

Everyday Grace
(Excerpt from a Diary)
Mirtha N. Quintanales

MANHATTAN
March 14, 1996, 10:00 A.M.

HAD A GREAT EXPERIENCE yesterday. I was on a very crowded bus on my way home from the Columbia University area. It was around 5:00 P.M. A woman and a little girl of about five years of age got on the bus. I think the woman was probably the child's nanny rather than her mother; she was dark, the child had very fair skin, and the dynamic between them was decidedly not familial.

I saw that a seat behind the driver was about to be vacated, and since the woman with the child evidently could not see it, I tapped her lightly on the shoulder and pointed to the now-empty seat. As the woman moved toward the seat the little girl, who from the very start seemed to be wearing a sign with "Trouble" written all over it, immediately began to whine and complain that the person who had just left the seat and was waiting for the bus to stop was "blocking her." Before the bus had come to a full stop, the child pulled away from her adult companion and darted to the area by the driver, almost falling.

The girl's nanny managed to get the child back into the empty seat, but not without effort. The girl squirmed and slithered and complained, complained, complained. This hurt and that hurt, this was bad and so was that. "You hurt me," she accused her companion. "It's your fault." The woman didn't say much but accommodated the child into her seat. At some point she must have whispered something to her. That was all. No scolding, no scenes other than the one the little girl was putting on for all of us. I was puzzled by the nanny's reaction, mostly because the child's words, attitude, and behavior had sparked a surge of what I felt was a justifiable anger within me. My peace was being disturbed.

A young woman who was sitting nearby gave me a look as if to say, "She has her hands full with that child." A moment later she glanced toward the nanny and said to her, "I know, I have one of my own." The young woman spoke with understanding, empathy, a feeling of accepting recognition. There was no evident emotional "charge" either in her voice or gestures. I was still angry at the bratty child.

Yet, suddenly and unexpectedly, there was a shift in my awareness that allowed me to observe myself with detachment and reflect upon my response to what was going on around me. I realized at that moment that the child herself was angry. I had been so caught up in my own responses that I hadn't even considered the child's feelings or the possible reasons for her attitude and behavior. It was difficult for me to maintain the state of detachment from my own anger, but compassion for the girl emerged and won out.

The possible reason for my anger began to become less relevant a concern as I became detached from anger *itself*—the child's or my own. As that happened, the girl almost miraculously calmed down and by the time she and her nanny got off the bus she was perfectly quiet and sweet and I, still in state of detachment, felt kindly toward the child.

I didn't think much more about the incident until earlier this morning when I woke up. It occurred to me that in some way *I* was that little girl. That the little girl had been showing me something, teaching me something about myself. Perhaps when I was her age I didn't have outward tantrums like she did, but inside I had experienced and still experienced anger, dissatisfaction, and the occasional desire to blame others for whatever befell me.

However, as I began to write down this experience, I had a deeper insight. It became evident to me that the "issue" here was one of "identifying with" and "becoming attached" to emotions and states and thoughts and behaviors and incidents, etc., and not just a matter of hanging onto psychological baggage from the past. It was now clear that it doesn't really matter who or what triggers these states, emotions, thoughts, and behaviors or incidents, or, for that matter, whether they "happened" in the past, are unfolding in the present, or are imagined for the future. It is the identification and the attachment that brings up the discomfort or that, more accurately, disturbs my peace of mind, pulling me away from, rather than bringing me closer to, the serenity of my inner Self. To practice detachment, to be able to live with such detachment. Like the sages and the saints. What a great life that would be!

One more recollection. At some point during the crowded-bus incident, the little girl and I looked at each other straight in the eyes. There seemed to be a silent and mutual understanding that we were both "in this" together, one of life's little plays. The cast also included the kindly woman who most generously gave me a clue about what was really going on, and the child's nanny who selflessly accepted the heavier responsibility of physically looking after the child.

I didn't fully understand our parting at the time, but as the little girl and her companion got off the bus, I had the peculiar sensation of seeing, with non-physical eyes, the little girl take a bow for her performance as some part of me silently applauded her and thanked her with much gratitude. Even as I write, I still feel very grateful toward these fellow travelers who were so willing to teach me and for the grace that fills my days. Every day there are so many wonderful experiences, so many insights and teachings, so many small and not-so-small miracles. So much grace. Everyday grace.

Tenemos que Seguir Luchando

Patricia Zavella

TIRED AFTER A LONG DAY in Valencianita, *un ranchito de mil personas en Guanajuato, México,* John Borrego and I headed back to our hotel in a rented Volkswagen bug. It was clear why *burros* were still a source of transportation here, for even the bicyclists had to walk their bikes, the road was so bad. We offered a ride to Señora Gómez, who, with her young son, was walking to catch a bus on the highway. We told her we were studying the effects of food processing on the local region and had interviewed women about the community literacy project. *Muy amable y animada,* she got excited and launched into her life story. Within twenty minutes, she presented a rapid-fire narrative about how although her husband *era machista,* the literacy project had changed her life. Sharing their life histories with one another, she had gained *confianza* with the other women in the village, and confidence to speak up for herself: *"Escribimos nuestras historias, y fue lindo."* Her voice broke as she noted that many of the women faced similar problems: *"Fíjense, todas tenemos casi los mismos problemas."* After effusive mutual *agradecimientos y despedidas,* expressions of gratitude and good-byes, we dropped her off and I turned to John and joked: "Whew! She just gave us her *testimonio,* didn't she? I should have whipped out the tape recorder."

As part of a project investigating food processing and its globalization from Watsonville, California, to el Bajío, in Mexico, John, my friend and colleague, and I have been conducting life histories with people of all classes in both regions. We are finding that the migration of Mexican workers to the United States, the demise of food processing in California, and movement of U.S. capital to Mexico are linked. These processes illustrate how U.S. and Mexican agricultural economies form a binational system of production for specialized market niches and generate complex changes in both regions.

As we interviewed workers in the rural villages in the Bajío, we inadvertently came upon the literacy project. Told beforehand that some U.S. professors would be coming by, the women were understandably formal at our arrival. However, our relaxed demeanor, Borrego's quirky, self-effacing humor, and my sympathy about women's issues quickly put them at ease. "*Ustedes son* chicanos," they noted, signifying that our liminal status included both North American privilege and bonds with them as descendants of Mexicanos. We got on famously.

They didn't realize how meaningful our exchange was for me. This was my first "real" trip to Mexico. Although I had spent time in many border cities, this was my first extended stay in the center of the country. Despite poverty conditions that wrenched my heart, everyone, whether bourgeois owner or humble peasant, was kind, generous, gracious. And there was riotous color everywhere, bougainvillea, lacy jacaranda trees, incredible churches, from the baroque to simple, displaying magnificent beauty. Regional music seemed to play in every shop, and artisans filled the cobblestone marketplaces. And the Spanish language — melodious, poetic — gave me such pleasure. I came to love Mexico in all its diversity, and these women helped set the stage.

In exchange for helping us set up interviews, they asked us to take oral histories of their project, organized under the auspices of *Programas Laubach para América Latina* (PLAMAC), which has provided literacy and basic education for over thirty years.[1] They arranged a focus group that was to include six young women who worked in local food-processing factories, but it eventually included about twelve women and assorted bystanders who joined the conversation. We sat around the dirt plaza in front of a small grocery in the cool evening light. Shy and unaccustomed to speaking in front of a group, each woman haltingly told her story about working in the factories. With each telling, however, the women lost their *vergüenza* and became bolder and more critical. By the end of the evening, the women engaged us in a heated discussion, voicing their frustration with limited local job options for women, with the *machista* men, and with California immigration politics. "Why don't they want us? We only want to work!" They insisted that we answer their questions and give advice about how they could better their lives. I was impressed with their transformation from demure to assertive young women in the course of an evening of collective *testimonios*.

Later, we did individual life histories with several women who had worked

---

1. Guillermina López, "Proyecto Tinaja de México: Una Experiencia de Educación Popular Campesina," in *Alfabetizar para la Democracia*, El CEAAL y el Año International de la Alfabetización, María Eugenia Letelier, et al. Ed. César Picón, Programa de Alfabetización popular del CEAAI, pp. 83–109.

Guzmán Amezquita and their children in Valencianita, México
(l–r) Micaela Amezquita, Asunción Guzmán Amezquita, María de los Angeles

in *agroindustria,* including three sisters who were organizers of the literacy project. Eager to tell their stories, they showed us their archives, a photo album, and documents related to the project, as well as their own creative writings. It was clear that *las testimoniantes* sought an audience beyond our interviews. They wanted their story to reach the United States, and thus they shared their *testimonios* with us, revealing painful personal experiences and triumphs.

The village of Valencianita is located on the outskirts of Irapuato in rural isolation. The only road to the main highway is of recent construction, built over steep terrain crossed by creeks. In the summer the rains make the roads impossible to use and the *pueblitos* are cut off. There is no sewage or drainage system, although they do have running water, electricity, a small elementary school, and a chapel. High unemployment or part-time jobs leave many very poor. Those who do own land have small *milpas* with lackluster crops because they have few resources for fertilizers. Men lounge all day on dusty street corners, and there is significant migration from this region to the United States. Some homes have dirt floors and jerry-rigged electrical outlets. A small grocery store provides credit and occasional essential purchases that cannot wait for the weekly trip to the outdoor market, and serves as a social gathering

place as well. Adult illiteracy rates are high, and even those who have completed elementary school often have trouble writing.

The expansion of food processing provided jobs predominantly to young
women, although widows and older women with few resources also seek jobs.
Thus women often find themselves the sole or major support of very large
households. The young women were proud that they contributed to their
families' well-being and aware that if they were to marry and leave their families would suffer. Older women are also in vulnerable situations, often the
major source of support for their families even when husbands or sons work
because their wages are inadequate. However, the jobs paid minimum wages,
and workers' families lived in poverty in the rural areas. And, as women
continually reminded us, the men felt threatened by women's increased independence and departure from being solely *amas de casa*. Gender conflict could
be seen in the jump in domestic violence as more women sought full-time
employment, or in abandonment as men left for *el norte*.

The women's literacy project took hold within this historical context. Projects of PLAMAC normally target youths fifteen or older. They begin with a
community assessment of the major social problems and develop a plan for
addressing them, including providing basic education and job-related training. Often literacy serves as a consciousness-raising process, as youths gain
technical and analytic skills. The organizers engage in periodic self-reflection
so as to ensure that the participants themselves define the goals and strategies
and analyze the changing political and economic context in which they work.
PLAMAC uses a *metodología dialéctica,* a Freirian process where the participants' knowledge about their daily life forms the basis for theorizing social
action and, on the basis of self reflection and new theorizing, constructing an
evolving political praxis to address the conditions in which they live. There
were twelve communities in the local region with PLAMAC projects.

In the case of Valencianita, the local women initially approached PLAMAC
themselves, requesting help in learning to read lyrics so they could sing at
church. Once the women had basic literacy, they decided they wanted to learn
dressmaking. Eventually they established a cooperative store for selling sewing supplies and clothing the women had made. When they assessed their
goals and realized they could not compete with the local *maquiladoras,* the
women then decided that they wanted help with health problems. A major
problem was the unfortunate deaths of children from scorpion bites because
indigenous antidotes had been lost and the village was too far from medical
care. Workers at PLAMAC provided the health training while the women
approached local state authorities to secure resources for a community medicine chest to deal with medical emergencies, complete with a trained *promotora
de salud*. One of their sources of pride was a wall-sized mural that provided

basic health information about how to avoid intestinal illnesses. Eventually the ongoing training included alternative health remedies such as using local herbs, and the women periodically would go on long walks to gather herbs and train the girls about their use. Perhaps the most radical goal was providing family planning, where women were given contraceptives without their husbands' consent. The organizers proudly showed us records indicating which women had taken such a bold step, secretly taking birth control pills.

The *promotora de salud* for the project, María de los Angeles Guzmán Amezquita, or "Ange," had worked in food processing between ages of eleven and fifteen, then lost her job and went back to school, completing *la secundaria* and then health training, after much struggle. She described her commitment to this process of self-education and women's ability to help themselves: "*Si yo aprendí, tiene la gente que aprender. Tengo que enseñar porque siento que es mi obligación.*"[2]

In 1994 the gravity of the national crisis was such that the group wanted a project that would counter the villagers' demoralization. They decided on a savings program where each woman would bring a *peso* to each meeting and the group kept track of the growing balances. To join such a program was a major economic commitment in a time of economic crisis, and sustaining it took collective discussion and mutual support in the face of men's criticisms that women could not handle such an enterprise. At the end of the first year, which coincided with Christmas, the women saw their collective work pay off in their ability to purchase holiday gifts for their families. Convinced of their value, the women started new savings programs, and by 1995 there were fourteen *grupos de ahorro* with a total of 350 participants in Valencianita, mostly of women although a few included men and youths as well.

The women's successes were not totally unmitigated. They took pains to give us a list of slights the local Partido Revolucionario Institucional (PRI) authorities had displayed toward the village, ranging from not providing adequate medical supplies to removing previously donated furniture. Ange told us the story of how she had run for delegate but lost because the villagers would not support a woman.

In their fourth year of operation, the women reflected on what would entice the youth to read and write, and they decided that local history would be interesting. Thus they began an oral history of the community, focusing on politics, the struggle for land, and the role of women. They designed the project themselves, conducted oral histories with elders, and used them to write *un discurso* for public presentation. They decided such an event required a solemn occasion, so they organized a celebration of *16 de Septiembre,* Mexico's

2. "If I could learn, anyone can learn. I have to teach because I feel its my obligation."

Independence Day. They staged a reenactment of the *Grito de Dolores* (the ceremonial call for independence) symbolizing Mexico's declaration of autonomy from Spain. The PLAMAC organizer recalled the significance of this event, where nearly everyone participated, and the success of the festival brought emotional celebration as well: *"La gente — emocionadísima. Tocaron las campanas, tocaron la música mexicana. Todas las señoras de los grupos se organizaron un puesto de comida con pozole, enchiladas, todo lo que es típico de nuestra región. Y luego la gente empezó a bailar, a disfrutar de la fiesta. Creo que no hubo una sola familia que no haya estado presente en la fiesta."*[3] The women were *haciendo patria,* constructing a nationalist collective identity that gave them great pride.

In this highly politicized effort, however, everything became open to contestation: who would participate, open the ceremony, lead the *Grito?* Since the event had been organized by women, the local PRI delegate refused to participate. After much debate, they decided that one of the organizers, Asunción Guzmán Amezquita ("Chuncho"), should enact the *grito,* disrupting traditional gender expectations. Chuncho recalled how stepping forward helped her claim a sense of personal empowerment for recuperating the lost history of the village: *"Fue conmovedor. Me gustó mucho realmente hacer eso. Porque hacía 25 años que no ocurría eso, de que dieran el grito de independencia. Fué muy bonito y mayormente cuando recuperamos la historia del rancho. Porque, pues, los viejitos ya se están acabando."*[4] The success of the event gave the women more room for celebration, and, soon thereafter, they started a new project. With the help of a local community organizer and lecturer, they offered a weekly radio program focusing on women's issues. In preparation for the radio program, the women had written their individual stories, which had galvanized the solidarity that Señora Gómez remarked upon.

Our third visit to the village coincided with the second annual *16 de septiembre* celebration, so we were introduced to everyone, guided through the activities, and got to know the organizers better. To their delight, we had come *no más para visitar* — just for a visit — and brought *regalitos.* They loved the photographs of them and tee shirts with designs of the alphabet in the shape of animals, which John had found in a Watsonville nature center. The women prepared a mole dinner and gave us gifts as well, crocheted doilies they had made themselves, and sang *corridos* they had written to document their history.

3. "The people — very emotional. They rang the bells, played Mexican music. All of the women from the groups organized a food booth with pozole, enchiladas, everything that is typical from our region. And later the people began to dance, to enjoy the festivities."
4. "It was very moving. I really liked doing that. Because it has been twenty-five years since we had done that, that we reenacted the call for independence. It was very beautiful and especially when we recuperated the history of the village. Because, well, the elders are leaving us."

They entreated us to come back for the village's *día del santo* in the spring, to see for ourselves how life had been transformed through their project.

Over time we became aware of tensions among the women organizers that had been left out of the collective narrative of contesting male dominance in politics, overcoming adversity in the face of few resources, and constructing a woman-centered collective identity. Although the term *feminista* never came up, *las mujeres* were rightly proud of their work and women's sense of community they had constructed despite the tensions among them.

Testimoniando can be a powerful tool for *concientización,* as we have seen in sites as disparate as El Barrio in New York, therapeutic settings in California, or Latina feminist spaces in higher education. Women gain insights about how their personal circumstances and pains mirror those of their *compañeras,* and they gain a powerful framework for understanding their collective source of subordination. In giving their life histories to Chicanos from *el norte,* the women from Valencianita waged the battle to position themselves as political subjects and make the narrative their own. Perhaps this explains their urgency in telling us their stories in an extraordinary public setting, in private interviews, or even within the confines of a twenty-minute ride in a bouncing Volkswagen bug. *"Tenemos que seguir luchando,"* remarked Señora Gómez when she got out of the car. We must continue the struggle. It is only now, telling her story in sites far beyond Valencianita, that I understand the prescience of her words.

Not long after our meeting with Señora Gómez, in the middle of an intense bout of field research where we had done several life histories with women, the organizers brought us to a local carnival. Although it would stay for only a few days, and the rides and treats were quite modest, the villagers were excited. Surrounded by clamoring boys with flashing grins, John began giving away his coins, delighted by their enthusiasm. I wandered off with Ange, chatting about how nice it was to see some recreation for the children. She pointed to a cloudy set of stars in the sky and told me it was the comet Hale-Bopp. As we marveled at its beauty, we wondered if the comet was visible from my house in California, and then I had a flash of insight. This is why I do this work, for the human connection.

Later that evening I reflected some more in my field notes. "Field research is really traveling to other social worlds (sometimes literally close to home), hanging out with people I like, listening to stories, and tracking down the pieces of a giant puzzle. Every observation, conversation, interview, document or study adds another piece of information." The most challenging part of my work is to render all of these *testimonios* into a narrative, theorize about their meanings in ways that the subjects would recognize, and make women's lives accessible to larger audiences. I take pleasure in the writing itself, despite the never-ending challenges, and am pleased to leave publications that others can use in their own work. And then I teach classes where my students hunger for compelling readings about the complexities of women's lives. I have the pleasure of introducing my students to the process of creating and writing based on the stories of others or their own *papelitos guardados*. I cannot imagine doing any other type of work. *Y aunque tengan sus propios desafíos, mujeres como éstas me animan para seguir la lucha y los placeres en mi trabajo* — and even though they face their own challenges, women like these inspire me to pursue the struggle and the pleasures in my work.

Select Bibliography

I. Latina and Women of Color Mixed-Genre Anthologies

Acevedo, Luz del Alba. 2000. "La cara multiforme del sexismo en la contienda electoral del 2000." *Diálgo* (October): 23.

——. "Género, política y primarias: ¿hará el género diferencia en las elecciones del 2000?" *Panorama 21* 2, no. 2: 46–51.

Anzaldúa, Gloria, ed. 1990. *Making Face, Making Soul/Haciendo Caras: Creative and Critical Perspectives by Women of Color.* San Francisco: Aunt Lute Foundation.

Asian Women United of California. 1989. *Making Waves: An Anthology of Writings by and about Asian American Women.* Boston: Beacon Press.

"Bearing Witness/Sobreviviendo, An Anthology of Writing and Art by Native American/ Latina Women." 1984. *Calyx* 8, no. 2.

Behar, Ruth, and Juan León. 1994. "Bridges to Cuba/Puentes a Cuba." Special issue of *Michigan Quarterly Review* 33, nos. 3–4.

Bell-Scott, Patricia. 1991. *Double Stitch: Black Women Write about Mothers and Daughters.* New York: Harper and Row.

——. 1994. *Life Notes: Personal Writings by Contemporary Black Women.* New York: Norton.

Boza, María del Carmen, Beverly Silva, and Carmen Valle. 1986. *Nosotras: Latina Literature Today.* Binghamton, N.Y.: Bilingual Review Press.

Castillo-Speed, Lillian, ed. 1995. *Latina: Women's Voices from the Borderlands.* New York: Simon and Schuster.

Cocco De Filippis, Daisy. 1988. *Sin otro profeta que su canto: Antología de la poesía escrita por dominicanas.* Santo Domingo: Biblioteca Taller No. 263.

——. 1992. *Combatidas, combativas y combatientes, antología de cuentos escritos por dominicanas.* Santo Domingo: Taller, Publicación del Instituto del Libro, Librería Trinitaria, Cámara Dominicana del Libro.

——. 1993. "Singing to the Beat of Their Own Drums: Dominican Women Writers." In *Gender, Culture, and the Arts: Women, the Arts, and Society,* ed. Ronald Dotterer and Susan Bowers. Selinsgrove, Pa.: Susquehanna University Press.

——. Ed. and principal tr. 2000. *Documents of Dissidence: Selected Writings by Dominican Women.* New York: CUNY Dominican Studies Institute.

Cocco De Filippis, Daisy, and E. J. Robinett, eds. and trans. 1988. *Poems of Exile and Other Concerns: A Bilingual Selection of the Poetry Written by Dominicans in the United States.* New York: Ediciones Alcance.

Cocco De Filippis, Daisy, and F. Gutierrez. 1994. *Stories from Washington Heights and Other Corners of the World: A Bilingual Selection of Short Stories Written by Dominicans in the U.S.* New York: Latin American Writers Institute.

Cole, Johnnetta B., ed. 1986. *All American Women: Lines That Divide, Ties That Bind.* New York: Free Press.

Espíritu, Yen Li. 1995. *Filipino American Lives.* Philadelphia: Temple University Press.

Etter Lewis, Gwendolyn, and Michele Foster, eds. 1996. *Unrelated Kin: Race and Gender in Women's Personal Narratives.* New York: Routledge.

Fernández, Roberta. 1994. *In Other Words.* Houston: Arte Público Press.

Galindo, D. Letticia and María Dolores Gonzáles, eds. 1999. *Speaking Chicana: Voice, Power, and Identity.* Tucson: University of Arizona Press.

Geok Lin-lim, Shirley, Mayumi Tsutakawa, and Margaret Donnely. 1989. *The Forbidden Stitch: An Asian American Women's Anthology.* Corvallis, Oreg.: Calyx.

Gómez, Alma, Cherríe Moraga, and Mariana Romo-Carmona. 1983. *Cuentos: Stories by Latinas.* New York: Kitchen Table/Women of Color Press.

Harjo, Joy, and Gloria Bird, eds. 1997. *Reinventing the Enemy's Language: Contemporary Native Women's Writings of North America.* New York: Norton.

Heyck, Denis Lynn Daly. 1994. *Barrios and Borderlands: Cultures of Latinos and Latinas in the United States.* New York: Routledge.

Horno-Delgado, Asunción, Eliana Ortega, Nina M. Scott, and Nancy Saporta Sternbach, eds. 1989. *Breaking Boundaries: Latina Writing and Critical Readings.* Amherst: University of Massachusetts Press.

López, Tiffany Ana. 1993. *Growing Up Chicana/o.* New York: Avon.

López Springfield, Consuelo, ed. 1994. *Puerto Rican Women Writers: A Special Issue. Callaloo* 17, no. 3.

Moraga, Cherríe, and Gloria Anzaldúa, eds. 1981. *This Bridge Called My Back: Writings by Radical Women of Color.* New York: Kitchen Table/Women of Color Press.

Ramos, Juanita, ed. 1994. *Compañeras: Latina Lesbians, An Anthology.* New York: Routledge.

Rebolledo, Tey Diana, and Eliana S. Rivero, eds. 1993. *Infinite Divisions: An Anthology of Chicana Literature.* Tucson: University of Arizona Press.

The Women of South Asian Descent Collective. 1993. *Our Feet Walk the Sky: Women of the South Asian Diaspora.* San Francisco: Aunt Lute Books.

Trujillo, Carla, ed. 1991. *Chicana Lesbians: The Girls Our Mothers Warned Us About.* Berkeley, Calif.: Third Woman Press.

Vigil, Evangelina, ed. 1987. *Woman of Her Word: Hispanic Women Write, Revista Chicano-Riqueña.* 2d ed. Houston: Arte Público Press.

II. Single-Author Autobiographical Writings by Latinas and Women of Color (fiction, poetry, essay, autobiography, memoir, and hybrid forms)

Alvarez, Julia. 1992. *How the García Girls Lost Their Accent.* New York: Penguin.

——. 1996. *The Other Side/El Otro Lado.* New York: Plume/Penguin.

——. 1997. *Yo.* New York: Plume/Penguin.

——. 1999. *Nothing to Declare.* New York: Plume/Penguin.

Anzaldúa, Gloria. 1987. *Borderlands/La Frontera: The New Mestiza*. San Francisco: Aunt Lute Books.

Brant, Beth. 1985. *Mohawk Trail*. Ithaca, N.Y.: Firebrand Books.

———. 1991. *Food and Spirits*. Ithaca, N.Y.: Firebrand Books.

———. 1994. *Writing as Witness: Essay and Talk*. Toronto: Women's Press.

Campbell Hale, Janet. 1993. *Bloodlines: Odyssey of a Native Daughter*. New York: Random House.

Cantú, Norma E. 1995. *Canícula: Snapshots of a Girlhood en la Frontera*. Albuquerque: University of New Mexico Press.

Castillo, Ana. 1992. *The Mixquiahuala Letters*. New York: Anchor.

———. 1994. *Massacre of the Dreamers: Essays on Xicanisma*. Albuquerque: University of New Mexico Press.

Chrystos. 1995. *Fire Power*. Vancouver: Press Gang Publishers.

Cisneros, Sandra. 1984. *The House on Mango Street*. New York: Vintage.

———. 1991. *Woman Hollering Creek and Other Stories*. New York: Vintage.

García, Cristina. 1992. *Dreaming in Cuban*. New York: Ballantine.

García, Diana. 2000. *When Living Was a Labor Camp*. Tucson: University of Arizona Press.

Harjo, Joy. 1990. *In Mad Love and War*. Middletown, Conn.: Wesleyan University Press.

———. 1994. *The Woman Who Fell from the Sky: Poems*. New York: Norton.

Hogan, Linda. 1990. *Mean Spirit: A Novel*. New York: Ivy Books.

hooks, bell. 1996. *Bone Black*. New York: Holt Rhinehart.

Levins Morales, Aurora. 1998. *Medicine Stories: History, Culture and the Politics of Integrity*. Boston: South End Press.

———. 1998. *Remedios: Stories of Earth and Iron from the History of Puertorriqueñas*. Boston: Beacon Press.

Levins Morales, Aurora, and Rosario Morales. 1986. *Getting Home Alive*. Ithaca, N.Y.: Firebrand Books.

Martínez, Demetria. 1994. *Mother Tongue*. Tempe, Ariz.: Bilingual Press.

Mohr, Nicholasa. 1973. *Nilda*. New York: Harper and Row.

———. 1985. *Rituals of Survival*. Houston: Arte Público Press.

Mora, Pat. 1998. *House of Houses*. Boston: Beacon Press.

Moraga, Cherríe. 1983. *Loving in the War Years*. Boston: South End Press.

———. 1993. *The Last Generation*. Boston: South End Press.

Obejas, Achy. 1994. *We Came All the Way from Cuba So You Could Dress Like This?* San Francisco: Cleis Press.

———. 1996. *Memory Mambo*. San Francisco: Cleis Press.

Ortiz Cofer, Judith. 1990. *Silent Dancing: A Partial Remembrance of a Puerto Rican Childhood*. Houston: Arte Público Press.

———. 1993. *The Latin Deli*. Athens: University of Georgia Press.

———. 2000. *Woman in Front of the Sun: On Becoming a Writer*. Athens: University of Georgia Press.

Pérez, Emma. 1996. *Gulf Dreams*. Berkeley, Calif.: Third Woman Press.

Ponce, Mary Helen. 1993. *Hoyt Street: An Autobiography*. Albuquerque: University of New Mexico Press.

Rose, Wendy. 1993. *The Half-Breed Chronicles*. New York: Random House.

———. 1994. *Bone Dance: New and Selected Poems, 1965–1993*. Tucson: University of Arizona Press.

Santiago, Esmeralda. 1993. *When I Was Puerto Rican*. New York: Vintage.

———. 1997. *America's Dream*. New York: HarperCollins.

——. 1999. *Almost a Woman*. New York: Vintage.

Serros, Michele. 1993. *Chicana Falsa, and Other Stories of Death, Identity, and Oxnard*. New York: Riverhead Books.

——. 2000. *How to Be a Chicana Role Model*. New York: Riverhead Books.

Silko, Leslie Marmon. 1981. *Storyteller*. New York: Little, Brown and Company.

——. 1991. *Almanac of the Dead*. New York: Simon and Schuster.

——. 1996. *Yellow Woman and a Beauty of Spirit: Essays on Native American Life Today*. New York: Simon and Schuster.

Tapahonso, Luci. 1993. *Sáanii Dahataal/The Women Are Singing: Poems and Stories*. Tucson: University of Arizona Press.

——. 1997. *Blue Horses Rush In: Poems and Stories*. Tucson: University of Arizona Press.

Torres, Olga Beatriz. 1994. *Memorias de mi viaje/Recollections of My Trip*. Albuquerque: University of New Mexico Press.

III. Other Creative Writings by Authors of This Book

Cantú, Norma E. 1995. "Letters Home/Letters from Home." Occasional column of poetry and prose in the monthly *LareDOS* (January 1995–present).

——. 1996. *In Short: A Collection of Brief Creative Nonfiction*, ed. Judith Kitchen and Mary Paumier Jones. New York: Norton.

——. 1997. "Bailando, Cantando," "Las diosas," "Decolonizing the Mind," and "Fiestas de diciembre." In *Blue Mesa Review*, no. 9, and in *Cruzando Fronteras: Literature from the Borderlands*, ed. Pat Smith. Albuquerque: University of New Mexico Press.

——. 1998. "Capirotada: Stirring Prose." In *Cooking with Texas Authors*, ed. Deborah Douglas. College Station: Texas A&M University Press.

——. 1998. "Decolonizing the Mind," and "Trojan Horse." In *Floricanto Sí: A Collection of Latina Poetry*, ed. Bryce Milligan. New York: Penguin.

——. 1999. "Excerpts from *Canícula: Snapshots of a Girlhood en la frontera.*" In *Aztlán and Viet Nam: Chicano and Chicana Experiences of the War*, ed. George Mariscal. Berkeley: University of California Press.

——. Forthcoming. *Soldiers of the Cross: Los Matachines de la Santa Cruz*. College Station: Texas A&M University Press.

Fiol-Matta, Liza. 1980. "Cassandra Curses Her Deaf Protectors," "A Halo Breaks Sometime in This Formation," "Three Performances," and "One Ends by Hearing Voices." *Signos* 1, no. 1: 24–25.

——. 1981. "Her Eyes Dialogue Slowly," "Cycle," and "Cuentos Chinos." *Reintegro de las Artes y la Cultura* 2, nos. 1–2: 12.

——. 1982. "Las mujeres del pueblo mudo." In "Siete Poetas Boricuas en los Estados Unidos [Seven Puerto Rican Poets in the United States]," selected and introduced by Efraín Barradas. *Areíto* 8, no. 29: 27.

——. 1994. "Blanca (from Julia Rodríguez, MSW)." *Callaloo* 17, no. 3: 803.

——. 1996. "De 'yerbas malas,' la diáspora boricua y la isla caribeña." *Diálogo* (April): 24–25.

——. 1998. "Poems of the Mute Country." Seven Poems and Commentary. *The Peace Review* (fall): 351–56.

——. 2000. "Poética II," "El discurso del político," "Malabareando," "Violeta," and "Elegía." In *Conversación entre escritoras del Caribe hispano*. Ed. Daisy Cocco De Filippis and Sonia Rivera-Valdés. New York: Centro de Estudios Puertorriqueños.

Hernández-Avila, Inés. 1992. "Body of Mine, Body Be Mine." *Blue Mesa Review* no. 4: 30–38.

——. 1993. "In Praise of Insubordination, or, What Makes a Good Woman Go Bad?" In *Transforming a Rape Culture*, ed. Emilie Buchwald, Pamela R. Fletcher, and Martha Roth. Minneapolis: Milkweed Editions.

——. 1995. "Enedina's Story." In *Latina: Women's Voices from the Borderlands*, ed. Lillian Castillo-Speed. New York: Simon and Schuster.

——. 1995. "Relocations upon Relocations: Home, Language, and Native Women Writing." *American Indian Quarterly* 19, no. 4: 491–507.

Levins Morales, Aurora. 1981. "And Even Fidel Can't Change That." In *This Bridge Called My Back: Writings by Radical Women of Color*, ed. Cherríe Moraga and Gloria Anzaldúa. Watertown, Mass.: Persephone Press.

——. 1983. "El bacalao viene de más lejos." In *Cuentos: Stories by Latinas*, ed. Alma Gomez, Cherríe Moraga, and Mariana Romo-Carmona. New York: Kitchen Table/Women of Color Press.

——. 1991. "Dancing on Bridges." *Bridges: A Journal for Jewish Feminists and Our Friends* 2, no. 1: 42–43.

——. 1991. "Vivir Para Tí." *The American Voice* 23: 24–39.

——. 1992. "Tsu got vel ikh veynen." *Bridges: A Journal for Jewish Feminists and Our Friends* 3, no. 1: 74–77.

——. 1994. "Hurricane." *Callaloo* 17, no. 3: 804–7.

——. 1994. "A Remedy for Heartburn." In *In Other Words*, ed. Roberta Fernández. Houston: Arte Público Press.

Quintanales, Mirtha. 1981. "I Come with No Illusions," and "I Paid Very Hard for My Immigrant Ignorance." In *This Bridge Called My Back: Writings by Radical Women of Color*, ed. Cherríe Moraga and Gloria Anzaldúa. Watertown, Mass.: Persephone Press.

Rivero, Eliana. 1983. "En el lugar que corresponde," "Salutación: Ave," and "Gloria." In *Woman of Her Word: Hispanic Women Write*, ed. Evangelina Vigil. Houston: Arte Público Press.

——. 1984. "Huachuca," and "Going West." In *Bearing Witness/Sobreviviendo: An Anthology of Writing and Art by Native American and Latina Women*. Special issue of *Calyx* 8, no. 2: 22–23.

——. 1986. "Anticipo," "Presagio," and "Para alguien que no sabe cantar." In *Nosotras: Latina Literature Today*, ed. María del Carmen Boza, Beverly Silva, and Carmen Valle. Binghamton, N.Y.: Bilingual Review Press.

——. 1995. "North from the River, South Inside." In *Daughters of the Fifth Sun: A Collection of Latina Fiction and Poetry*, ed. Bryce Milligan and Angela de Hoyos. New York: Riverhead Books.

——. 1995. "Tanta agua bajo es(t)os puentes." In "Más allá de la Isla: 66 creadores cubanos." *Puentelibre: Revista de Cultura* 2, nos. 5–6: 35–39.

IV. Literary Criticism on Latina Writings

Alarcón, Norma. 1981. "Chicana Feminist Literature: A Re-vision Through Malintzin/or Malintzin: Putting Flesh Back on the Object." In *This Bridge Called My Back: Writings by Radical Women of Color*, ed. Cherríe Moraga and Gloria Anzaldúa. Watertown, Mass.: Persephone Press.

——. 1997. "Traddutora, Traditora: A Paradigmatic Figure of Chicana Feminism." In *Dan-*

gerous Liaisons: Gender, Nation, and Postcolonial Perspectives, ed. Anne McClintock, Aamir Mufti, and Ella Shohat. Minneapolis: University of Minnesota Press.

Benmayor, Rina. 1989. "Getting Home Alive: The Politics of Multiple Identity." *The Americas Review* 17, nos. 3–4: 107–17.

Cantú, Norma E. 1995. "Los Matachines de la Santa Cruz de la Ladrillera: Notes Toward a Literary Analysis." In *Feasts and Celebrations in North American Ethnic Communities,* ed. Ramon Gutiérrez and Genevieve Fabre. Albuquerque: University of New Mexico Press.

———. 1995. "Margarita Canseco del Valle, Escritora Fronteriza." In *Las Formas de Nuestras Voces: Chicana and Mexicana Writers in Mexico,* ed. Claire Joysmith. Mexico City: Universidad Nacional Autónoma del México.

Cocco De Filippis, Daisy. 1987. "La mujer dominicana y el quehacer literario." *El Diario/La Prensa,* 1 March 1987, B8–B9.

———, ed. 1988. *From Desolation to Compromise: The Poetry of Aída Cartagena Portalatín.* Santo Domingo: Ediciones Montesinos No. 10.

———. 1988. "Indias y trigueñas No Longer: Contemporary Dominican Women Writers Speak." *Cimarrón* 1, no. 3: 132–50.

———. 1993. "Singing to the Beat of Their Own Drums: Dominican Women Writers in 1980s." *Gender, Culture, and the Arts: Women, the Arts, and Society,* ed. Ronald Dotterer and Susan Bowers. Selinsgrove, Pa.: Susquehanna University Press.

———. 1995. "Aída Cartagena Portalatín: A Literary Life." In *Moving Beyond Boundaries: Black Woman's Diaspora,* vol. 2, ed. Carole Boyce Davis. London: Pluto Publications.

———. 1996. "Dominican Writers at the Crossroads: Reflections on a Conversation in Progress." *The Latino Review of Books* 2, no. 2: 2–8.

———. 1996. "Enigmática transparencia: Reflexiones acerca de la literatura dominicana en los ochenta." *Vetas* 3, no. 15: 15–23. Reprinted in *The Latino Review of Books* 3, nos. 1–2 (1997): 16–21.

Fiol-Matta, Liza. 1988. "Naming Our World, Writing Our History: The Voices of Hispanic Feminist Poets." *Women's Studies Quarterly* (fall/winter): 68–80.

———. 1994. "Puerto Rican Women Writers of the United States: A Critical Reading of Critical Fictions." In *Gender and Puerto Rican Women: Presentations at the Third Encounter of Women Researchers,* ed. Alice Colón. Río Piedras: University of Puerto Rico/Centro de Investigaciones Sociales.

———. 1996. "De 'yerbas malas,' la diáspora boricua y la isla caribeña." *Diálogo* (April): 24–25.

———. 1996. "Writing the Self in a Changing World." *Women's Studies Quarterly* (fall/winter): 100–112.

Hernández Avila, Inés. 1995. "Relocations upon Relocations: Home, Language, and Native Women Writing." *American Indian Quarterly* 19, no. 4: 491–507.

Lomas, Clara. 1989. "Inés Hernández Tovar." In *Longman Anthology of World Literature by Women, 1895–1975,* ed. Marian Arkin and Barbara Shollar. New York: Longman.

———. 1989. "Mexican Precursors of Chicana Feminist Writing." In *Multi-Ethnic Literature in the United States,* ed. Cordelia Candelaria. Boulder: University of Colorado Press. Reprinted in *Estudios: Chicanos and the Politics of Community,* ed. Mary Romero. Oakland, Calif.: Cragmont Publications.

———. 1989. "Sylvia S. Lizárraga." In *Dictionary of Literary Biography: Chicano Writers,* ed. Francisco Lomelí and Carl Shirley. 1st series. Detroit, Mich.: Gale Research Company.

———. 1992. "Leonor Villegas de Magnón." In *Dictionary of Literary Biography: Chicano Writers,* ed. Francisco Lomelí and Carl Shirley. 2d series. Detroit, Mich.: Gale Research Company.

———. 1993. "The Articulation of Gender in the Mexican Borderlands, 1900–1915." In *Recovering the U.S. Hispanic Literary Heritage,* ed. Ramón Gutiérrez and Genaro Padilla. Houston: Arte Público Press. Reprinted in *Cultures D'Amérique Latine Aux Etats-Unis: Confrontations et Métissages,* ed. Elyette Benjamin-Labarthe, Yves-Charles Grandjeat, and Christian Lerat. Bordeaux: Université Michel de Montaigne, Editions de la Maison des Sciences de L'Homme D'Aquitaine.

———. Forthcoming. "Beyond Icons: Reconstructing the Feminist Agenda of Jovita Idar." In *From Guadalupe to Malinche: Tejana Writers.* Austin: University of Texas Press.

———. Forthcoming. "Nina Otero Warren." In *Dictionary of Literary Biography: Chicano Writers,* ed. Francisco Lomelí and Carl Shirley. 3d series. Detroit, Mich.: Gale Research Company.

Rivero, Eliana. 1982. "Nota sobre las voces femeninas en *Herejes y mitificadores:* muestra de poesía puertorriqueña en los Estados Unidos." *Third Woman* 1, no. 2: 118–21.

———. 1985. "Hispanic Literature in the U.S.: Self-Image and Conflict." *Revista Chicano-Riqueña* 13, nos. 3–4: 173–92.

———. 1989. "From Immigrants to Ethnics: Cuban Women Writers in the U.S." In *Breaking Boundaries: Latina Writings and Critical Readings,* ed. Asunción Horno Delgado et al. Amherst: University of Massachusetts Press.

———. 1990. "(Re)Writing Sugarcane Memories: Cuban Americans and Literature." In *Paradise Lost or Gained? The Literature of Hispanic Exile,* ed. Fernando Alegría and Jorge Ruffinelli. Houston: Arte Público Press.

———. 1993. "Escritoras chicanas: Fronteras de la lengua y la cultura." In *Hispanic Culture on the Pacific Coast of the Americas: From Chilenos to Chicanos,* ed. Grínor Rojo. Long Beach: California State University Press.

———. 1995. "Cuban American Writing." In *The Oxford Companion to Women's Writing in the United States,* ed. Cathy Davidson and Linda Wagner-Martin. New York: Oxford University Press.

———. 1995. "The Other's Other: Chicana Identity and Its Textual Expressions." In *Encountering the Other(s): Studies in Literature, History and Culture,* ed. Gisela Brinker-Gabler. Albany: State University of New York Press.

V. Latina and Latin American *Testimonio*/Oral History/Life Stories (selected primary texts and criticism)

Alvarez, Celia. 1988. "El Hilo Que Nos Une — The Thread That Binds Us: Becoming a Puerto Rican Woman." *Oral History Review* 16, no. 2: 29–40.

Barrios de Chungara, Domitila. 1978. *Let Me Speak: Testimony of Domitila, a Woman of the Bolivian Mines.* New York: Monthly Review Press.

Behar, Ruth. 1993. *Translated Woman: Crossing the Border with Esperanza's Story.* Boston: Beacon Press.

———. 1996. *The Vulnerable Observer: Anthropology That Breaks Your Heart.* Boston: Beacon Press.

Benjamin, Medea, ed. 1987. *Don't Be Afraid, Gringo: A Honduras Woman Speaks from the Heart. The Story of Elvia Alvarado.* San Francisco: Institute for Food and Development Policy.

Benmayor, Rina, Ana Juarbe, Celia Alvarez, and Blanca Vázquez. 1987. *Stories To Live By: Continuity and Change in Three Generations of Puerto Rican Women.* New York: Centro de Estudios Puertorriqueños. Revised version in *The Oral History Review* 16, no. 2 (1988).

Benmayor, Rina, Rosa Torruellas, and Ana Juarbe. 1992. *Responses to Poverty: Identity, Community, and Cultural Citizenship.* New York: Centro de Estudios Puertorriqueños.

———. 1997. "Claiming Cultural Citizenship in East Harlem: 'Si esto puede ayudar a la comunidad mía.'" In *Latino Cultural Citizenship: Claiming Identity, Space, and Rights,* ed. William V. Flores and Rina Benmayor. Boston: Beacon Press.

Benmayor, Rina, and Andor Skotnes, eds. 1994. *Migration and Identity: International Yearbook of Oral History and Life Stories.* Vol. 3. London: Oxford University Press.

Beverly, John. 1988. "The Margin and the Center: On *Testimonio* (Testimonial Narrative)." In *Life/Lines: Theorizing Women's Autobiography,* ed. Bella Brodzki and Celeste Schenck. Ithaca, N.Y.: Cornell University Press.

Burgos-Debray, Elisabeth, ed. 1984. *I, Rigoberta Menchú: An Indian Woman in Guatemala.* London: Verso.

Buss, Fran Leeper, ed. 1993. *Forged Under the Sun/Forjado bajo el sol: The Life of María Elena Lucas.* Ann Arbor: University of Michigan Press.

Cocco de Filippis, Daisy. 1989. "Entre dominicanos: Una lectura de 'Las cuatro niñas.'" *Centro* 2, no. 7: 90–95.

Craft, Linda J. 1997. *Novels of Testimony and Resistance from Central America.* Gainesville: University Press of Florida.

Crespo, Elizabeth. 1994. "Puerto Rican Women: Migration and Changes in Gender Roles." In *Migration and Identity: International Yearbook of Oral History and Life Stories,* vol. 3, ed. Rina Benmayor and Andor Skotnes. London: Oxford University Press.

Davis, Marilyn P. 1990. *Mexican Voices/American Dreams: An Oral History of Mexican Immigration to the United States.* New York: Henry Holt.

de Jesus, Carolina Maria. 1962. *Child of the Dark: The Diary of Carolina Maria de Jesus,* trans. David St. Clair. New York: Dutton.

Gugelberger, Georg, ed. 1996. *The Real Thing: Testimonial Discourse and Latin America.* Durham, N.C.: Duke University Press.

Gugelberger, Georg, and Michael Kearney. 1991. "Voices for the Voiceless: Testimonial Literature in Latin America." *Latin American Perspectives* 18, no. 3: 3–14.

Hardy-Fanta, Carol. 1993. *Latina Politics, Latino Politics.* Philadelphia: Temple University Press.

Harlow, Barbara. 1987. *Resistance Literature.* New York: Methuen.

Hernández Avila, Inés. 1992. "Tejana Intonations/Nez Perce Heartbeat: Notes on Identity and Culture." *Auto/Biography Studies* 7, no. 2: 292–306.

Herzog, Kristin. 1993. *Finding Their Voice: Peruvian Women's Testimonies of War.* Valley Forge, Penn.: Trinity Press International.

Heyck, Denis Lynn Daly. 1990. *Life Stories of the Nicaraguan Revolution.* New York: Routledge.

Kiddle, Mary Ellen. 1985. "The *Novela Testimonial* in Contemporary Mexican Literature." *Confluencia* 1, no. 1: 82–89.

Kuppers, Gaby, ed. 1992. *Compañeras: Voices from the Latin American Women's Movement.* Nottingham, UK: Russell Press.

Latin American Perspectives. 1991. Special issue of *Voices of the Voiceless* 18, no. 4.

Lomas, Clara. 1994. "In Search of an Autobiography: On Mapping Women's Intellectual History of the Borderlands." Introduction to *The Rebel,* by Leonor Villegas de Magnón, ed. Clara Lomas. Houston: Arte Público Press.

——. Forthcoming. "La búsqueda de una autobiografía: Hacia la cartografía de la historia intelectual de las mujeres de la frontera." Introduction to the Spanish edition of *La Rebelde,* by Leonor Villegas de Magnón. Mexico City: Instituto Nacional de Antropología e Historia.

Ortega, Eliana, and Nancy Saporta Sternbach. 1989. "At the Threshold of the Unnamed: Latina Literary Discourse in the Eighties." In *Breaking Boundaries: Latina Writing and*

Critical Readings, ed. Asunción Horno-Delgado et al. Amherst: University of Massachusetts Press.

Padilla, Genaro M. 1993. *My History, Not Yours: The Formation of Mexican American Autobiography.* Madison: University of Wisconsin Press.

Partnoy, Alicia. 1986. *The Little School: Tales of Disappearance and Survival in Argentina.* San Francisco: Cleis Press.

Patai, Daphne. 1993. *Brazilian Women Speak: Contemporary Life Stories.* 3d ed. New Brunswick, N.J.: Rutgers University Press.

Peterman, Jean P. 1996. *Telling Their Stories: Puerto Rican Women and Abortion.* Boulder, Colo.: Westview Press.

Preciado Martin, Patricia. 1992. *Songs My Mother Sang to Me: An Oral History of Mexican American Women.* Tucson: University of Arizona Press.

Poniatowska, Elena. 1992. "Gender, Genre, and Authority: *Hasta no verte Jesús mío.*" In *Politics, Gender, and the Mexican Novel, 1968–1988,* ed. Cynthia Steele. Austin: University of Texas Press.

Randall, Margaret, ed. 1994. *Sandino's Daughters Revisited.* New Brunswick, N.J.: Rutgers University Press.

——. 1995. *Our Voices, Our Lives: Stories of Women from Central America and the Caribbean.* Monroe, Maine: Common Courage Press.

Rivero, Eliana. 1987. "Acerca del género testimonio: Textos, narradores y artefactos." *Hispamérica* 46–48: 41–56.

——. 1991. "Testimonial Literature and Conversations as Literary Discourse: Cuba and Nicaragua." *Latin American Perspectives* 18, no. 3: 69–79.

Salazar, Claudia. 1991. "A Third World Woman's Text: Between the Politics of Criticism and Cultural Politics." In *Women's Words: The Feminist Practice of Oral History,* ed. Sherna Berger Gluck and Daphne Patai. New York: Routledge.

Sánchez, Rosaura. 1995. *Telling Identities: The Californio Testimonios.* Minneapolis: University of Minnesota Press.

Sommer, Doris. 1988. "'Not Just a Personal Story': Women's Testimonios and the Plural Self." In *Life/Lines: Theorizing Women's Autobiography,* ed. Bella Brodzki and Celeste Schenck. Ithaca, N.Y.: Cornell University Press.

Stephen, Lynn, ed. 1994. *Hear My Testimony: Maria Teresa Tula, Human Rights Activist of El Salvador.* Boston: South End Press.

Torruellas, Rosa M., Rina Benmayor, Anneris Goris, and Ana Juarbe. 1991. *Affirming Cultural Citizenship in the Puerto Rican Community: Critical Literacy and the El Barrio Popular Education Program.* New York: Centro de Estudios Puertorriqueños. Also in *Literacy as Praxis: Culture, Language, and Pedagogy,* ed. Catherine E. Walsh. Norwood, N.J.: Ablex, 1991.

Valdés, Alisa L. 1995. "Ruminations of a Feminist Aerobics Instructor." In *Voices from the Next Feminist Generation,* ed. Barbara Findlen. Seattle, Wash.: Seal Press.

Westerman, William. 1994. "Central American Refugee Testimonies and Performed Life Histories in the Sanctuary Movement." In *Migration and Identity: International Yearbook of Oral History and Life Stories,* vol. 3, ed. R. Benmayor and A. Skotnes. London: Oxford University Press.

Williams, Gareth. 1993. "Translation and Mourning: The Cultural Challenge of Latin American Testimonial Autobiography." *Latin America Library Review* 21, no. 41: 79–99.

Yúdice, George. 1992. "Testimonio y concientización." *Revista de Crítica Literaria* 18, no. 36: 207–27.

VI. Feminist and/or "Native" Ethnography
and Autobiography (critical studies)

Alvarez, Celia. 1991. "Code-Switching in Narrative Performance: Social, Structural and Pragmatic Function in the Puerto Rican Speech Community of East Harlem." In *Sociolinguistics of the Spanish-Speaking World: Iberia, Latin America, United States,* ed. Carol Klee and Luis A. Ramon-García. Tempe, Ariz.: Bilingual Press/Editorial Bilingüe.

Aguilar, John L. 1988. "Insider Research: An Ethnography of a Debate." In *Anthropologists at Home in North America: Methods and Issues in the Study of One's Own Society,* ed. Donald A. Messerschmidt. New York: Cambridge University Press.

Behar, Ruth, and Deborah A. Gordon, eds. 1995. *Women Writing Culture.* Berkeley: University of California Press.

Burawoy, Michael, et al. 1991. *Ethnography Unbound: Power and Resistance in the Modern Metropolis.* Berkeley: University of California Press.

Cannon, Lynn Weber, Elizabeth Higginbotham, and Marianne L. A. Leung. 1988. "Race and Class Bias in Qualitative Research on Women." *Gender and Society* 2, no. 4: 449–62.

di Leonardo, Micaela, ed. 1991. *Gender at the Crossroads of Knowledge: Feminist Anthropology in the Postmodern Era.* Berkeley: University of California Press.

———. 1998. *Exotics at Home: Anthropologies, Others, American Modernity.* Chicago: University of Chicago Press.

Etter Lewis, Gwendolyn. 1993. *My Soul Is My Own: Oral Narratives of African American Women in the Professions.* New York: Routledge.

Flores, William V., and Rina Benmayor, eds. 1997. *Latino Cultural Citizenship: Claiming Identity, Space, and Rights.* Boston: Beacon Press.

Fonow, Mary Margaret, and Judith A. Cook. 1991. *Beyond Methodology: Feminist Scholarship as Lived Research.* Bloomington: Indiana University Press.

Frankenberg, Ruth. 1993. *White Women, Race Matters: The Social Construction of Whiteness.* Minneapolis: University of Minnesota Press.

Gilmore, Leigh. 1994. *Autobiographics: A Feminist Theory of Women's Self-Representation.* Ithaca, N.Y.: Cornell University Press.

Gluck, Sherna Berger, and Daphne Patai. 1991. *Women's Words: The Feminist Practice of Oral History.* New York: Routledge.

Golde, Peggy, ed. 1986. *Women in the Field: Anthropological Experiences.* 2d ed. Berkeley: University of California.

Grewal, Inderpal. 1994. "Autobiographical Subjects and Diasporic Locations: Meatless Days and Borderlands." In *Scattered Hegemonies: Postmodernity and Transnational Feminist Practices,* ed. Inderpal Grewal and Caren Kaplan. Minneapolis: University of Minnesota Press.

Hoffman, Lenore, and Margo Culley, eds. 1985. *Women's Personal Narratives: Essays in Criticism and Pedagogy.* New York: Modern Language Association.

Jack, Dana, and Judith Wittner. 1990. "Beginning Where We Are: Feminist Methodology in Oral History." In *Feminist Research Methods: Exemplary Readings in the Social Sciences,* ed. Joyce McCarl Nielsen. Boulder, Colo.: Westview Press.

Klein, Renate Duelli. 1983. "How to Do What We Want to Do: Thoughts about Feminist Methodology." In *Theories of Women's Studies,* ed. Gloria Bowles and Renate Duelli Klien. London: Routledge and Kegan Paul.

Kreiger, Susan. 1987. "Beyond 'Subjectivity': The Use of the Self in Social Science." *Qualitative Sociology* 8, no. 4: 309–24.

Lancaster, Roger N. 1997. "Guto's Performance: Notes on the Transvestism of Everyday Life."

In *The Gender/Sexuality Reader: Culture, History, Political Economy,* ed. Roger N. Lancaster and Micaela di Leonardo. New York: Routledge.

Lewin, Ellen, and William L. Leap. 1996. *Out in the Field: Reflections of Lesbian and Gay Anthropologists.* Urbana: University of Illinois Press.

Limón, José E. 1981. "The Folk Performance of 'Chicano' and the Cultural Limits of Political Ideology." In *"And Other Neighborly Names," Social Process and Cultural Image in Texas Folklore,* ed. Richard Bauman and Roger D. Abrahams. Austin: University of Texas Press.

———. 1994. *Dancing with the Devil: Society and Cultural Poetics in Mexican American South Texas.* Madison: University of Wisconsin Press.

Oakley, Ann. 1982. "Interviewing Women: A Contradiction in Terms." In *Doing Feminist Research,* ed. Helen Roberts. London: Routledge.

Oboler, Suzanne. 1995. *Ethnic Labels, Latino Lives: Identity and the Politics of (Re)Presentation in the United States.* Minneapolis: University of Minnesota Press.

Okely, Judith, and Helen Callaway, eds. 1992. *Anthropology and Autobiography.* London: Routledge.

Paredes, Américo. 1977. "On Ethnographic Work among Minority Groups: A Folklorist's Perspective." *The New Scholar* 6, no. 1/2: 1–32. Reprinted in *Folklore and Culture on the Texas-Mexican Border,* ed. Richard Bauman. Austin: Center for Mexican American Studies, University of Texas, 1993.

Passerini, Luisa. 1989. "Women's Personal Narratives: Myths, Experiences, and Emotions." In *Interpreting Women's Lives: Feminist Theory and Personal Narratives,* ed. Personal Narratives Group. Bloomington: Indiana University Press.

———. 1990. "Mythbiography in Oral History." In *The Myths We Live By,* ed. Ralph Samuel and Paul Thompson. London: Routledge.

Personal Narratives Group. 1989. *Interpreting Women's Lives: Feminist Theory and Personal Narratives.* Bloomington: Indiana University Press.

Reinharz, Shulamith. 1983. "Experiential Analysis: A Contribution to Feminist Research." In *Theories of Women's Studies,* ed. Gloria Bowles and Renate Duelli Klien. London: Routledge and Kegan Paul.

———. 1992. *Feminist Methods in Social Research.* New York: Oxford University Press.

Riessman, Catherine Kohler. 1987. "When Gender Is Not Enough: Women Interviewing Women." *Gender and Society* 1, no. 2: 172–207.

Roberts, Helen, ed. 1981. *Doing Feminist Research.* London: Routledge and Kegan Paul.

Romano, Octavio I. 1968. "The Anthropology and Sociology of the Mexican American." *El Grito* 2: 13–26.

Rosaldo, Renato. 1989. *Culture and Truth: The Remaking of Social Analysis.* Boston: Beacon Press.

Russel y Rodríguez, Mónica. 1998. "Confronting Anthropology's Silencing Praxis: Speaking of/from a Chicana Consciousness." *Qualitative Inquiry* 4, no. 1: 15–40.

Stacey, Judith. 1988. "Can There Be a Feminist Ethnography?" *Women's Studies International Forum* 11, no. 1: 21–27.

Smith, Sidonie, and Julia Watson, eds. 1992. *De/Colonizing the Subject: The Politics of Gender in Women's Autobiography.* Minneapolis: University of Minnesota Press.

Thorne, Barrie. 1979. "Political Activist as Participant Observer: Conflicts of Commitment in a Study of the Draft Resistance Movement of the 1960s." *Symbolic Interaction* 2, no. 1: 73–88.

Wax, Rosalie H. 1979. "Gender and Age in Fieldwork and Fieldwork Education: No Good Thing Is Done by Any Man Alone." *Social Problems* 26, no. 5: 509–22.

Weston, Kath. 1991. *Families We Choose: Lesbians, Gays, Kinship*. New York: Columbia University Press.

Zavella, Patricia. 1993. "Feminist Insider Dilemmas: Constructing Identity with 'Chicana' Informants." "Feminist Ethnography," special issue of *Frontiers* 13, no. 3: 53–76.

——. 2000. "Engendering Transnationalism in Food Processing: Peripheral Vision on Both Sides of the U.S.-Mexico Border." In *Las nuevas fronteras del siglo XXI: Dimensiones culturales, políticas y socioeconómicas de las relaciones México-Estados Unidos* (New Frontiers in the Twenty-First Century: Cultural, Political, and Socioeconomic Dimensions of US-Mexico Relations), ed. Norma Klahn, Alejandro Álvarez Béjar, Federico Manchón, and Pedro Castillo. *La Jornada Ediciones: Centro de Investigaciones Colección: La democracia en México*.

Zinn, Maxine B. 1979. "Field Research in Minority Communities: Ethical, Methodological and Political Observations by an Insider." *Social Problems* 27, no. 2: 209–19.

VII. Latina Feminisms and Latina Studies

Acevedo, Luz del Alba. 1983. "The Role of Women in Puerto Rican Society." *Women of Color* (summer).

——. 1987. "Política de industrialización y cambios en el empleo femenino en Puerto Rico: 1947–1982." *Homines, Social Science Journal of the Inter-American University of Puerto Rico* 10, no. 2.

——. 1990. "Industrialization and Employment: Changes in the Patterns of Women's Work in Puerto Rico." *World Development* 28, no. 2.

——. 1992. "Industrialization and Employment: Changes in the Patterns of Women's Work in Post-War Puerto Rico." In *Expanding the Boundaries of Women's History: Essays on Women in the Third World*, ed. Cheryl Johnson-Odim and Margaret Strobel. Bloomington: Indiana University Press.

——. 1993. "Género, trabajo asalariado y desarrollo industrial en Puerto Rico: la división sexual del trabajo en la manufactura." In *Género y trabajo: la industria de la aguja en Puerto Rico y el Caribe*, ed. María del Carmen Baerga. San Juan: Editorial de la Universidad de Puerto Rico.

——. 1997. "Género y trabajo en Puerto Rico: desafíos para una política laboral." *Boletín de Economía, Unidad de Investigaciones Económicas* 2, no. 3.

——. 1999. "Género y trabajo en Puerto Rico: desafíos para una politica laboral." In *Futuro Económico de Puerto Rico*, comp. Francisco Martínez. San Juan: Editorial de la Universidad de Puerto Rico.

Alvarez, Celia. 1996. "The Multiple and Transformatory Identities of Puerto Rican Women in the U.S.: Reconstructing the Discourse on National Identity." In *Unrelated Kin: Race and Gender in Women's Personal Narratives*, ed. Gwendolyn Etter-Lewis and Michele Foster. New York: Routledge.

——. Forthcoming. *Intersecting Lives: Puerto Rican Women as Community Intellectuals*. Philadelphia: Temple University Press.

Anzaldúa, Gloria, ed. 1990. *Making Face, Making Soul: Haciendo Caras*. San Francisco: Aunt Lute.

Arredondo, Gabriela, Aída Hurtado, Norma Klahn, Olga Nájera Ramírez, and Patricia Zavella, eds. (Forthcoming). *Chicana Feminisms: Disruption and Dialogue*. Durham, N.C.: Duke University Press.

Cantú, Norma E. 1996. "Virgen de Guadalupe: Symbol of Faith and Devotion." In *Familia, Fe y Fiestas/Family, Faith and Fiestas: Mexican American Celebrations of the Holiday Season.* Fresno, Calif.: ArteAmericas and Fresno Arts Council.

Castillo, Ana, ed. 1996. *Goddess of the Americas: Writings on the Virgin of Guadalupe.* New York: Riverhead Books.

Córdova, Teresa et al., eds. 1993. *Chicana Voices: Intersections of Class, Race, and Gender.* Albuquerque: University of New Mexico Press.

de la Torre, Adela, and Beatriz M. Pesquera, eds. 1993. *Building with Our Hands: New Directions in Chicana Studies.* Berkeley: University of California Press.

Delgado, Linda. 1995. "Arroz con Pollo vs. Slim-Fast." In *Women: Images and Realities: A Multicultural Anthology,* ed. Amy Kesselman, Lily D. McNair, and Nancy Schniedewind. Mountain View, Calif.: Mayfield Publishing Company.

García, Alma M. 1997. *Chicana Feminist Thought: Basic Historical Writings.* New York: Routledge.

Hernández-Avila, Inés. 1992. "Testimonio de Memoria: For all the mujeres de movimiento que saben de estas cosas." *New Chicana/Chicano Writing,* ed. Charles M. Tatum. Tucson: University of Arizona Press.

——. 1997. "Open Letter to Chicanas: On the Power and Politics of Origin." In *Reinventing the Enemy's Language: Contemporary Native Women's Writings of North America,* ed. Joy Harjo and Gloria Bird. New York: Norton.

Lamphere, Louise, Patricia Zavella, and Felipe Gonzáles, with Peter B. Evans. 1993. *Sunbelt Working Mothers: Reconciling Family and Factory.* Ithaca, N.Y.: Cornell University Press.

Lomas, Clara. 1986. "Reproductive Freedom: The Voice of Women in Margarita Cota-Cárdenas's 'A una madre de nuestros tiempos'/Libertad de no procrear: La voz de la mujer en 'A una madre de nuestros tiempos' de Margarita Cota-Cárdenas." In *Chicana Voices: Intersections of Class, Race, and Gender,* ed. Teresa Córdova et al. Austin: Center for Mexican American Studies, University of Texas.

Lugones, María C. 1995. "Sisterhood and Friendship as Feminist Models." In *Feminism and Community,* ed. Penny A. Weiss and Marilyn Friedman. Philadelphia: Temple University Press.

Mujeres Activas en Letras y Cambio Social Editorial Board. 1993. *Chicana Critical Issues.* Berkeley, Calif.: Third Woman Press.

Romero, Mary, Pierrette Hondagneu-Sotelo, and Vilma Ortiz, eds. 1997. *Challenging Fronteras: Structuring Latina and Latino Lives in the U.S.* New York: Routledge.

Ruíz, Vicki. 1987. *Cannery Women, Cannery Lives: Mexican Women, Unionization, and the California Food Processing Industry, 1930–1950.* Albuquerque: University of New Mexico Press.

Trujillo, Carla. 1995. "Chicana Lesbians: Fear and Loathing in the Chicano Community." In *Women: Images and Realities: A Multicultural Anthology,* ed. Amy Kesselman, Lily D. McNair, and Nancy Schniedewind. Mountain View, Calif.: Mayfield Publishing Company.

Zavella, Patricia. 1987. *Women's Work and Chicano Families: Cannery Workers of the Santa Clara Valley.* Ithaca, N.Y.: Cornell University Press.

——. 1988. "The Politics of Race and Gender: Organizing Chicana Cannery Workers in Northern California." In *Women and the Politics of Empowerment: Perspectives from the Workplace and the Community,* ed. Ann Bookman and Sandra Morgen. Philadelphia: Temple University Press.

——. 1989. "The Problematic Relationship of Feminism and Chicana Studies." *Women's Studies* 17: 25–36.

——. 1991. "Mujeres in Factories: Race and Class Perspectives on Women, Work and Family."

In *Gender at the Crossroads of Knowledge: Feminist Anthropology in the Postmodern Era*, ed. Micaela di Leonardo. Berkeley: University of California Press.

——. 1994. "Reflections on Diversity among Chicanas." In *Race*, ed. Steven Gregory and Roger Sanjek. New Brunswick, N.J.: Rutgers University Press.

——. 1996. "Living on the Edge: Everyday Lives of Poor Chicano/*Mexicano* Families." In *Mapping Multiculturalism*, ed. Avery Gordon and Christopher Newfield. Minneapolis: University of Minnesota Press.

——. 1997. " 'Playing with Fire': The Gendered Construction of Chicana/Mexicana Sexuality." In *The Gender/Sexuality Reader: Culture, History, Political Economy*, ed. Roger N. Lancaster and Micaela di Leonardo. New York: Routledge.

——. 1997. " 'The Tables Are Turned': Immigration, Poverty, and Social Conflict in California Communities." In *Immigrants Out!: The New Nativism and the Anti-Immigrant Impulse in the United States*, ed. Juan Perea. New York: New York University Press.

——. 2000. "Engendering transnationalism: in Food Processing: Peripheral Vision on Both Sides of the U.S.-Mexico Border." In "Latinos in the U.S.: The Politics of Racial Identity," special issue of *Latin American Perspectives*. Reprinted in *Las Nuevas Fronteras del Siglo XXI: Dimensiones Culturales, Políticas y Socioeconómicas de las Relaciones México-Estados Unidos*, ed. Norma Klahn, Alejandro Álvarez Béjar, Federico Manchon, and Pedro Castillo, 2000.

——. (Forthcoming.) "Talk'n Sex: Chicanas and Mexicanas Theorize about Silences and Sexual Pleasures." In *Chicana Feminisms: Disruptions in Dialogue*, ed. Gabriela Arredondo, Aída Hurtado, Norma Klahn, Olga Nájera Ramírez, and Patricia Zavella. Durham, N.C.: Duke University Press.

Zavella, Patricia, and Louise Lamphere. 1997. "Women's Resistance in the Sunbelt: Anglos and Hispanas Respond to Managerial Control." In *Women and Work: Exploring Race, Ethnicity, and Class*, ed. Elizabeth Higginbotham and Mary Romero. Beverly Hills, Calif.: Sage Publications.

VIII. Other Feminists and Women of Color Studies

Acevedo, Luz del Alba. 1995. "Feminist Inroads in the Study of Women and Development." In *Women in the Latin American Development Process*, ed. Edna Acosta-Belén and Christine Bose. Philadelphia: Temple University Press.

Anderson, Margaret, and Patricia Hill Collins, eds. 1992. *Race, Class and Gender: An Anthology*. Belmont, Calif.: Wadsworth.

Bannerji, Himani, ed. 1993. *Returning the Gaze: Essays on Racism, Feminism and Politics*. Toronto: Sister Vision.

Baca Zinn, Maxine, and Bonnie Thornton Dill, eds. 1994. *Women of Color in U.S. Society*. Philadelphia: Temple University Press.

Cocco De Filippis, Daisy. 1998. "The Politics of Literature: Dominican Women and the Suffrage Movement; Case Study: Delia Weber." In *Winds of Change: The Transforming Voices of Caribbean Women Writers and Scholars*, ed. Adele Newson. New York: Peter Lang.

Collins, Patricia Hill. 1992. *Black Feminist Thought*. New York: Routlege.

Cyrus, Virginia. 1993. *Experiencing Race, Class, and Gender in the United States*. Mountain View, Calif.: Mayfield Publishing Company.

Davis, Angela. 1981. *Women, Race and Class*. New York: Random House.

Dill, Bonnie Thornton. 1983. "Race, Class, and Gender: Prospects for an All-Inclusive Sisterhood." *Feminist Studies* 9, no. 1: 131–50.

Dubois, Ellen, and Vicki Ruíz. 1990. *Unequal Sisters: A Multi-Cultural Reader in U.S. Women's History*. New York: Routledge.

Gould, Janice. 1995. "American Indian Women's Poetry: Strategies of Rage and Hope." *Signs* 20, no. 4: 797–817.

Green, Rayna. 1984. *That's What She Said: Contemporary Fiction and Poetry by Native American Women*. Bloomington: Indiana University Press.

Harjo, Joy, and Gloria Bird, eds. 1997. *Reinventing the Enemy's Language: Contemporary Native Women's Writing of North America*. New York: Norton.

Hernández Avila, Inés. 1996. "Mediations of the Spirit: Native American Religious Traditions and the Ethics of Representation." "To Hear the Eagles Cry: Contemporary Themes in Native American Spirituality," ed. Lee Irwin, special issue of *American Indian Quarterly* 20, nos. 3–4: 329–52.

Higgenbotham, Elizabeth and Mary Romero, eds. 1997. *Exploring Race, Ethnicity, and Class*. New York: Sage Publications.

hooks, bell. 1984. *Feminist Theory: From Margin to Center*. New York: South End Press.

——. 1997. "Sisterhood: Political Solidarity Between Women." In *Dangerous Liaisons: Gender, Nation, and Postcolonial Perspectives*, ed. Ann McClintock, Aamir Mufti, and Ella Shohat. Minneapolis: University of Minnesota Press.

Hurtado, Aída. 1989. "Relating to Privilege: Seduction and Rejection in the Subordination of White Women and Women of Color." *Signs* 14: 1–23.

——. 1996. *The Color of Privilege: Three Blasphemies on Race and Feminism*. Ann Arbor: University of Michigan Press.

King, Deborah. 1988. "Multiple Jeopardy, Multiple Consciousness: The Context of a Black Feminist Ideology." *Signs* 14, no. 1: 42–72.

Madison, Soyini D., ed. 1994. *The Woman That I Am: The Literature and Culture of Contemporary Women of Color*. New York: St. Martin's Press.

Min-ha, Trinh T. 1989. *Woman, Native, Other: Writing Post-Coloniality and Feminism*. Bloomington: Indiana University Press.

Mohanty, Chandra Talpade, Ann Russo, and Lourdes Torres, ed. 1991. *Third World Women and the Politics of Feminism*. Bloomington: Indiana University Press.

Perreault, Jeanne, and Sylvia Vance, eds. 1990. *Writing the Circle: Native Women of Western Canada*. Norman: University of Oklahoma Press.

Romero, Mary, and Abigail Steward, eds. 1999. *Women's Untold Stories: Breaking Silence, Talking Back, Voicing Complexity*. New York: Routledge.

Rothenberg, Paula S. 1992. *Race, Class, and Gender in the United States: An Integrated Study*. New York: St. Martin's Press.

Spivak, Gayatri. 1989. "In a Word: Interview." *Differences* 1, no. 2: 128–56.

Walters, Anna Lee. 1992. *Talking Indian: Reflections on Writing and Survival*. Ithaca, N.Y.: Firebrand Books.

Wilkinson, Doris, Maxine Baca Zinn, and E. Ngan-Ling Chow, eds. 1992. Special issue of *Gender and Society* 6, no. 3.

IX. Latinas and Women in the Academy

Aisenberg, Nadya, and Mona Harrington. 1988. *Women of Academe: Outsiders in the Sacred Grove*. Amherst: University of Massachusetts Press.

Bannerjji, Himani, Linda Carty, Kari Dehi, Susan Heald, and Kate McKenna. 1992. *Unsettling Relations: The University as a Site of Feminist Struggles*. Boston: South End Press.

Cuádraz, Gloria H. 1996. "Experiences of Multiple Marginality: A Case Study of Chicana 'Scholarship Women.'" In *Racial and Ethnic Diversity in Higher Education,* ed. Caroline Turner, M. García, A. Nora, and L. Rendón. Needham Heights, Mass.: Simon and Schuster.

——. 1997. "Chicana/o Generations and the Horatio Alger Myth." *Thought and Action* 13, no. 1: 103–20.

——. 1999. "Stories of Access and 'Luck': Chicana/os, Higher Education, and the Politics of Incorporation." *Latino Studies Journal* 10, no. 1: 110–23.

——. Forthcoming. *A Fluke of History?: Chicanas/os in the Era of Affirmative Action in Higher Education.* Philadelphia: Temple University Press.

Cuádraz, Gloria H., and Jennifer L. Pierce. 1994. "From Scholarship Girls to Scholarship Women: Surviving the Contradictions of Race and Class in Academe." Special issue of *Explorations in Ethnic Studies* 17, no. 1: 21–44.

Fiol-Matta, Liza. 1988. "English Composition." *Gender-Balancing the Curriculum: A Handbook for the Community Colleges,* ed. Sue Rosenberg Zalk. New York: Center for the Study of Women and Society/Graduate Center (CUNY).

——. 1991. Introduction. In *Mainstreaming Minority Women's Studies Program.* New York: National Council for Research on Women.

——. 1993. "Litmus Tests for Curriculum Transformation." *Women's Studies Quarterly* (fall/winter): 161–63.

——. 1996a. "The Community College in the U.S.: A Profile of Innovation and Change." *Women's Studies Quarterly* (fall/winter): 3–15.

——. 1996b. "Teaching in (Puerto Rican) Tongues: A Report from the Space In-Between." *Women's Studies Quarterly* (fall/winter): 69–76.

Fiol-Matta, Liza, and Mariam K. Chamberlain, eds. 1994. *Women of Color and the Multicultural Curriculum: Transforming the College Classroom.* New York: The Feminist Press at the City University of New York.

Fiol-Matta, Liza, and Myrna Goldenberg, eds. 1996. *Curriculum Transformation in Community Colleges: Focus on Introductory Courses.* Special issue of *Women's Studies Quarterly* (fall/winter).

James, Joy and Ruth Farmer. 1993. *Spirit, Space, and Survival: African American Women in (White) Academe.* New York: Routledge.

Orlans, Kathryn P., and Ruth A. Wallace. 1993. *Gender and the Academic Experience.* Amherst: University of Massachusetts Press.

Rossi, Alice S., and Ann Calderwood. 1973. *Academic Women on the Move* (New York: Russell Sage Foundation.

Tockarczyck, Michelle M., and Elizabeth A. Fay, eds. 1993. *Working-Class Women in the Academy: Laborers in the Knowledge Factory.* Amherst: University of Massachusetts Press.

Women's Studies Quarterly. 1990. Special Issue on Curriculum Transformation. 2 vols. New York: The Feminist Press.

About the Authors

LUZ DEL ALBA ACEVEDO was born in Santurce, Puerto Rico. She holds a Ph.D. in Political Science from the University of Illinois at Chicago. She was Assistant Professor of Women's Studies and Latin American and Caribbean Studies at SUNY Albany. Currently she is Associate Professor in the Department of Political Science at the University of Puerto Rico, Río Piedras, where she teaches methodology and courses on gender and political power. Her research on gender, work, industrialization, and development in Puerto Rico is published in *Futuro Económico de Puerto Rico*, Francisco Martínez (compilador); *Women in the Latin American Development Process*, ed. Edna Acosta-Belén and Christine Bose; *Género y trabajo: La industria de la aguja en Puerto Rico y el Caribe*, ed. María del Carmen Baerga; *Expanding the Boundaries of Women's History, Essays on Women in the Third World*, ed. Cheryl Johnson and Margaret Strobel; and in the journals *Boletín de Economía; Unidad de Investigaciones Económicas; World Development; Homines: Social Science Journal of the Inter-American University of Puerto Rico*. Currently she is researching the political economy of gender relations in Puerto Rico with a grant from the National Science Foundation. She is also one of three editors of the Puerto Rican Studies Series of Temple University Press.

NORMA ALARCÓN is Professor of Ethnic and Chican@/Latin@ Studies, Women's Studies, and Spanish and Portuguese at the University of California, Berkeley. She is the author of *Ninfomania: The Poetics of Difference in the Work of Rosario Castellanos*, and the forthcoming book *T(r)opology of Hunger: The Inscription of Chicanas* (Duke University Press). She is co-editor of *Between Woman and Nation* (Duke) and Publisher of Third Woman Press since 1979.

CELIA ALVAREZ was tenured as Associate Professor of Women's Studies at Arizona State University West, serving on the faculty from 1992 to 1999. She received her Ph.D. in Linguistics from the University of Pennsylvania in 1988 and was Assistant Professor of Bilingual/ Bicultural Education at Teachers College, Columbia University until 1992. Since 1973 she has been affiliated with the Centro de Estudios Puertorriqueños at Hunter College, where she contributed to the research projects of the Language Policy and Oral History Task Forces. Her publications include "Code-Switching in Narrative Performance: A Puerto Rican Speech Community in New York," in *English Across Cultures: Cultures Across English*, ed. Ofelia García and Ricardo Otheguy; "*El Hilo Que Nos Une:* Becoming a Puerto Rican Woman," in *Stories to Live By: Continuity and Change in Three Generations of Puerto Rican Women*, ed. Rina Benmayor et al.; and "Multiple and Transformatory Identities of Puerto Rican Women in the United States: Reconstructing the Discourse on National Identity," in G. Etter-Lewis and M. Foster, *Unrelated Kin: Race and Gender in Women's Personal Narratives.* As an activist-scholar she served the International Cross-Cultural Black Women's Studies Institute from 1987 to 1995. She continues to participate in numerous national and international forums on cross-cultural and comparative dialogues among women. Her forthcoming book, *Intersecting Lives: Puerto Rican Women as Community Intellectuals,* will be published by Temple University Press.

RUTH BEHAR was born in Havana, Cuba, and has resided in the United States since 1962. She is currently Professor of Anthropology at the University of Michigan in Ann Arbor. The recipient of many prestigious fellowships, including the MacArthur Fellows Award in 1988 and a John Simon Guggenheim Fellowship in 1995, she has traveled to Spain, Mexico, and Cuba and written on a range of cultural issues as a poet, essayist, editor, and ethnographer. She is the author of *The Presence of the Past in a Spanish Village: Santa María del Monte* (Princeton University Press); *Translated Woman: Crossing the Border with Esperanza's Story* (Beacon Press); and *The Vulnerable Observer: Anthropology That Breaks Your Heart* (Beacon Press). She is the editor of *Bridges to Cuba* (University of California Press). Her poems have appeared in literary journals and anthologies, both in the United States and Cuba. She is currently at work on a book about her Jewish-Cuban family and her re-encounter with the Afro-Cuban woman, still living on the island, who was her caretaker as a child.

RINA BENMAYOR is founding faculty and Professor of Oral history, Literature, and Latina/o Studies at California State University Monterey Bay, where for the first five years she chaired the university's integrated humanities department. From 1982 to 1995 she was Research Director of the Culture and Oral History Task Forces at the Centro de Estudios Puertorriqueños, Hunter College. Born in New York, from third through sixth grades she lived in Mexico City with her family. She earned her Ph.D. from the University of California, Berkeley, in Romance Languages and Literatures and has authored *Romances judeo-españoles de Oriente* (Madrid: Gredos); coauthored and coedited *Migration and Identity: International Yearbook of Oral History and Life Stories,* vol. 3 (Oxford); *Stories to Live By: Three Generations of Puerto Rican Women* and *Responses to Poverty among Puerto Rican Women* (Centro de Estudios Puertorriqueños); and *Latino Cultural Citizenship* (Beacon Press). She has also written on multiple identity in Latina literature, on the Cuban *nueva trova,* and on new digital technologies and pedagogy in the oral history classroom. She has produced radio documentaries (*Nosotras trabajamos en la costura*), translated lyrics for Cuban music releases in the United States, and subtitled documentary films on Cuban music (*Roots of Rhythm with Harry Belafonte*). Currently she is producing life stories in digital formats and writing oral history books on Puerto Rican *pioneras* and on first-generation college students.

NORMA E. CANTÚ is a daughter of the borderlands. She received her B.S. and her M.S. from Texas A&I University in Laredo and Kingsville, respectively. She earned her Ph.D. in English from the University of Nebraska, Lincoln, and is Professor of English at University of Texas at San Antonio. In 1998–99 she served as Acting Director for the Center for Chicano Studies at the University of California at Santa Barbara. Her scholarly interests include Chicana literature and folklore and Borderlands Studies. She has published extensively in these areas as well as publishing poetry and fiction. Her forthcoming book from the Texas A&M University Press is a study of the Matachines de la Santa Cruz, a religious dance tradition in Laredo. Her novel, *Canícula: Snapshots of a Girlhood en la frontera,* received the Premio Aztlán in 1996. She is completing a second novel, *Hair Matters.*

DAISY COCCO DE FILIPPIS is a native of the Dominican Republic who has lived in New York City for the past thirty-seven years. Like many immigrants, she studied at the City University of New York, where she received her B.A. summa cum laude from Queens College (Spanish and English literatures) and her Ph.D. from the University Center and Graduate School in Hispanic Literatures. She is presently Professor of Spanish and Chair of the Department of Foreign Languages, ESL and Humanities at York College (CUNY), where she has taught Spanish language, Hispanic, and Latino literatures and humanities since 1978. She has spent the better part of two decades promoting and disseminating the study of Dominican, Caribbean, and Latino literatures in the United States. She has published extensively and points with particular pride to her groundbreaking anthologies of Dominican women authors and of Dominican authors in the United States. She has been married to Nunzio De Filippis for the past thirty-three years, and they have raised three wonderful sons: Joseph Nicholas, Nunzio Andrew, and James Louis. Their home has been a welcoming meeting place for Caribbean, Latina/o, and Latin American writers. For the past five years the monthly meetings of "La Tertulia de Escritoras Dominicanas en los Estados Unidos" has been a valued addition to the busy De Filippis home.

GLORIA HOLGUÍN CUÁDRAZ is originally from the agricultural borderlands of the Imperial Valley, California. She is Associate Professor of American Studies at Arizona State University West, where she currently directs the Ethnic Studies Program. She received her doctorate in Sociology from the University of California at Berkeley. Her areas of interest include the sociological and interdisciplinary study of education (with an emphasis on graduate education); Chicana/o studies; autobiography; race, class, and gender studies; and qualitative methodologies. Her journal publications include "Stories of Access and 'Luck': Chicana/os, Higher Education, and the Politics of Incorporation" (*Latino Studies Journal*, 1999); "The Chicana/o Generations and the Horatio Alger Myth," in *Thought and Action: NEA Higher Education Journal*, 1997; "Experiences of Multiple Marginality: A Case Study of Chicana Scholarship Women," in *Racial/Ethnic Diversity in Higher Education*, 1996; and a 1994 co-authored article about her own scholarship trajectory, "From Scholarship Girls to Scholarship Women: Surviving the Contradictions of Race and Class in Academe," in *Explorations in Ethnic Studies*. Her forthcoming book from Temple University Press is titled *A Fluke of History? The Making of a Chicana/o Political Generation in the Era of Affirmative Action*. She was one of seven faculty members featured in the 1997 video *Shattering the Silences: Minorities Break into the Ivory Tower*.

LIZA FIOL-MATTA is Associate Professor of Women's Studies at New Jersey City University, where she directs the Women's and Gender Studies Program. She received her Ph.D. in Critical Literary and Cultural Studies from the Graduate College of The Union Institute in Cincinnati, Ohio. She is the coeditor of *Women of Color and the Multicultural Curriculum: Transforming the College Classroom* (Feminist Press, 1994), which was named 1995 Outstanding Book on the Subject of Human Rights in North America by the Gustavus Myers Center for the Study of Human Rights in North America. She is a member of the Program Administration and Development Advisory Council of the National Women's Studies Association and has served on the Executive Council of the Puerto Rican Studies Association, of which she was a founding member. Besides her professional affiliations and academic research interests, Fiol-Matta is also a poet. Her work has appeared in several journals in the United States and Puerto Rico, including *Callaloo, Diálogo,* and *The Peace Review*. She is currently working on two book projects: the first explores feminist and gendered notions of nationality and nationalism in the writing of Latinas in the United States, and the other is a book for teachers based on her

About the Authors   375

article "Litmus Tests for Curriculum Transformation" (*Women's Studies Quarterly*), which is widely used in faculty development workshops around the country.

YVETTE GISELLE FLORES-ORTIZ is Associate Professor in Chicana/Chicano Studies at the University of California, Davis, where she developed the family and community mental health emphasis for the Chicano Studies major. A practicing clinical psychologist, she has published extensively on feminist psychology, Latino mental health, family injustice, HIV/AIDS prevention, and identity formation. With a Fogarty Fellowship, she is investigating family violence among urban couples in Mexico City. She also received a Fulbright in 1994 to teach in Panama, her country of origin, where she consulted with women's community-based organizations and trained family therapists to treat intrafamily abuse. Currently she is researching the psychological sequelae of family violence among Latino college students and the formation of gender and sexual identities among Latina adolescents. Her academic publications include "The Role of Cultural and Gender Values in Substance Use Patterns among Latina Secondary and University Students: Implications for AIDS Prevention," in *International Journal of Addictions;* "Chicanas at Midlife," in J. Adleman and G. Enguidanos, eds., *Racism in the Lives of Women;* "Voices from the Couch: The Co-Construction of a Chicana Psychology," in *Living Chicana Theory,* ed. Carla Trujillo; "The Broken Covenant: Incest in Latino Families," in *Voces: A Journal of Chicana/Latina Studies;* "Fostering Accountability: A Reconstructive Dialogue with a Couple with a History of Violence," in T. Nelson and T. Trepper, eds., *101 More Interventions in Family Therapy* (2d ed.); "*Migración, Identidad y Violencia*/Migration, Identity and Violence," in M. Mock, L. Hill, and D. Tucker, eds., *Breaking Barriers: Diversity in Clinical Practice.*

INÉS HERNÁNDEZ-AVILA is Tejana and Nimipu (Nez Perce), of Chief Joseph's band, enrolled with the Colville Confederated Tribes. She is a poet, a cultural worker, and an Associate Professor in the Department of Native American Studies at the University of California, Davis, a program distinguished by its hemispheric perspective in relation to the study of Native peoples and Native intelligence of the Americas. Her research interests include contemporary Native American women's literature; the contemporary hemispheric movement of writers in indigenous languages; Native American religious traditions; early twentieth-century Chicana literature; Native American and Chicana feminisms; issues in Native American and Chicana/Chicano cultural studies; the retrieval of her own Nez Perce family/tribal history. She has published widely, including in *Reinventing the Enemy's Language: Contemporary Native Women's Writings of North America,* ed. Joy Harjo and Gloria Bird. Her forthcoming works include *Native American Women's Studies: Critical/Creative Representations* (edited volume); *Entre Guadalupe y Malinche: Tejanas in Literature and Art,* coedited with Norma Cantú; *Dancing Earth Songs: Poetry;* and *Notes from the Homeland: Essays on Identity, Culture, and Community.*

AURORA LEVINS-MORALES was born in the mountains of Puerto Rico and migrated to Chicago at the age of thirteen. She writes essays, fiction, and poetry. Her early work appeared in *This Bridge Called My Back: Writings by Radical Women of Color; Cuentos: Stories by Latinas* (Kitchen Table) and in many other anthologies. She is the coauthor, with Rosario Morales, of *Getting Home Alive* (Firebrand) and is a frequent contributor to *Bridges: A Journal for Jewish Feminists and Our Friends.* Her most recent works are *Remedios: Stories of Earth and Iron from the History of Puertorriqueñas* (Beacon Press) and *Medicine Stories: History, Culture, and the Politics of Integrity* (South End Press). She has a doctorate in Women's Studies and History from The Union Institute and works at the Oakland Museum of California with the Latino History Project, training Latino youth to collect community history. She is a founding member of the California Puerto Rican Historical Society, for which she created an exhibit, and is working on several community-based history projects. She is currently writing a series of historical mysteries set in the early twentieth-century Puerto Rican labor movement.

CLARA A. LOMAS is Associate Professor of Spanish at the Colorado College, where she teaches Spanish language, Latina/o literature in the United States, Chicana/o literature, and contemporary Latin American literature as well as courses in Southwest Studies, Women Studies, and American Ethnic Studies. She received her Ph.D. from the University of California, San Diego. Currently she is directing the *Annotated Periodical Literature Project*, a subproject of the national *Recovering the U.S. Hispanic Literary Heritage Project*. She has published in *Women's Studies International Forum* (London); *Dictionary of Literary Biography*; *FEM: Revista feminista* (Mexico); *La Palabra*; and *Revista Chicano-Riqueña*; and has contributed chapters to *Multi-Ethnic Literature of the United States*; *Longman Anthology of World Literature by Women, 1895–1975*; *Estudios Chicanos and the Politics of Community*; *Chicana Voices: Intersections of Class, Race, and Gender*; *Cultures D'Amérique Latine Aux Etats-Unis: Confrontations et Métissages*; and *Between La Virgen de Guadalupe and La Malinche*. She coedited *Chicano Politics after the 80s* with John García and Julia Curry Rodríguez and edited the autobiography of Leonor Villegas de Magnón and *The Rebel* (Arte Público Press and Instituto Nacional de Antropología e Historia, Mexico City). She is currently writing a book on women's intellectual production in the Mexican borderlands at the turn of the century and compiling an anthology titled *Latina Narratives and Identities, 1860–1960*.

IRIS O. LÓPEZ was born and raised in Brooklyn, New York. She is Associate Professor at City College of New York and directed the Women's Studies and Latin American and Caribbean Studies Programs. She received her Ph.D. from Columbia University in Cultural Anthropology. As a Visiting Professor at the University of California at Los Angeles in the Anthropology Department, she was affiliated with the Chicano/a Studies Program. She also did a postdoctorate at the University of Hawaii at Manoa. She has been the recipient of fellowships and grants from the Ford Foundation, National Institute of Mental Health, and National Science Foundation. Currently she is conducting a longitudinal ethnographic study on Puerto Ricans in Hawaii. She has written about ethnic identity among Puerto Ricans in Hawaii and has been guest editor of an issue of the *Boletín* of the Center for Puerto Rican Studies dedicated to this topic. Her community and academic work has focused on migration, globalization, and reproductive rights and she has published numerous articles on sterilization and Puerto Rican women. The title of her forthcoming book is *Sterile Choices: The Medicalization of Puerto Rican Women's Reproduction*.

MIRTHA N. QUINTANALES was born in Havana, Cuba, and immigrated to the United States in 1962, at the age of thirteen. She received a Ph.D. in Anthropology from Ohio State University. She teaches in the Latin American, Caribbean, and Latino Studies Program at New Jersey City University, where she was Program Coordinator for ten years. She is currently involved in several projects in religious studies, literature, and literary translations. She has publications or translations in *Women of Cuba*, by Inger Holt-Seeland; *This Bridge Called My Back: Writings by Radical Women of Color*, ed. Cherríe Moraga and Gloria Anzaldúa; *Sinister Wisdom*; *Test-Tube Women. What Future for Women* by Rita Arditti et al.; *IKON*, second series; *Off Our Backs*; *The Black Scholar*; Jersey City State College *Women on Campus*; *Source* (American Translators Association); *Bridges to Cuba. Puentes a Cuba*, ed. Ruth Behar; *Tertuliando. Hanging Out. Dominicanas and Amiga(o)s. Dominican Women and Friends*, ed. Daisy Cocco De Filippis; *Ballads for a Dream (Baladas para un Sueño)*, ed. Nancy Morejón (forthcoming).

ELIANA RIVERO was born in Cuba and immigrated to the United States in 1961. She is Professor of Spanish and Adjunct Professor in Latin American and Women's Studies at the University of Arizona, Tucson. She has written about the experience of U.S. Latinas/Latinos and has published many essays on the topic, among them "Hispanic Literature in the United States: Self Image and Conflict" (*Revista Chicano-Riqueña*); "(Re)Writing Sugarcane Memories: Cuban Americans and Literature" (*The Americas Review*), and "Fronterisleña, Border-Islander" (*Bridges to Cuba*, ed. Ruth Behar). She is coeditor, with Tey Diana Rebolledo, of the best-selling *Infinite Divisions: An Anthology of Chicana Literature* (University of Arizona Press). She is also coeditor, with Margarita Cota Cárdenas, of a collection of Latina poets, *Siete Poetas* (Scorpio Press), funded by National Endowment for the Arts. She has authored two other books on Hispanic literature and more than fifty articles and essays. Her poetry has been included in *Floricanto Sí! An Anthology of U.S. Latina Poetry* (Penguin); *Daughters of the Fifth Sun: An Anthology of U.S. Latina Writers* (Putnam); *Veinte años de literatura cubanoamericana* (Bilingual Press); *Nosotras: Latina Literature Today* (Bilingual Press); *Woman of Her Word: Hispanic Women Speak* (Arte Público); and other collections. During the academic year 2000–2001 she served as Phi Beta Kappa Visiting Scholar, lecturing on the Latino/a experience across the United States.

CARIDAD SOUZA is a Research Associate at the Center for Puerto Rican Studies at Hunter College, CUNY. Her research and teaching interests include racialized gender and sexuality, women in poverty, urban ethnography, and adolescent pregnancy.

PATRICIA ZAVELLA received her Ph.D. in Anthropology from the University of California, Berkeley. She is currently Professor of Latin American and Latino Studies and the Director of the Chicano/Latino Research Center at the University of California, Santa Cruz. Her research interests include Chicana/o Studies, especially regarding poverty; regional labor markets in the Southwest; the relationship between women's wage labor and changes in family life; Mexican transnational migration; sexuality, social networks, and social change. Her work combines history and feminist ethnography, placing the experiences of individuals, particularly women and small-scale social organizations (families, kin and social networks, community-based organizations), into a larger structural context. Among her publications are "Engendering Transnationalism in Food Processing: Peripheral Vision on Both Sides of the U.S.-Mexico Border," in *Las Nuevas Fronteras del Siglo XXI: Dimensiones Culturales, Políticas y Socioeconómicas de los Relaciones México-Estados Unidos*, ed. Norma Klahn, et al. (La Jornada Ediciones; Centro de Investigaciones Colleción: la democracia en Mexico, 2000). "'Playing with Fire': The Gendered Construction of Chicana/Mexicana Sexuality," in *The Gender/Sexuality Reader: Culture, History, Political Economy*, ed. Roger N. Lancaster and Micaela di Leonardo (Routledge); "Reflections on Diversity Among Chicanas," in *Race*, ed. Steven Gregory and Roger Sanjek (Rutgers); *Women's Work and Chicano Families: Cannery Workers of the Santa Clara Valley* (Cornell University Press). She is the proud parent of two children, Laura Chávez and Anthony Gonzáles.

Library of Congress Cataloging-in-Publication Data
Telling to live : Latina feminist testimonios / the Latina feminist group,
Luz del Alba Acevedo . . . [et al.].
    p. cm. — (Latin America otherwise)
    ISBN 0-8223-2755-4 (cloth : alk. paper)
    ISBN 0-8223-2765-1 (pbk. : alk. paper)
    1. Hispanic American women — Social conditions — Anecdotes. 2. Hispanic American women — Biography — Anecdotes. 3. Feminists — United States — Biography — Anecdotes. 4. United States — Ethnic relations — Anecdotes. 5. Sex discrimination against women — United States — Anecdotes. I. Acevedo, Luz del Alba. II. Series.
E184.S75 T45 2001   305.48'868073 — dc21   2001023934